A Generation Abandoned

Why "Whatever" Is Not Enough

Peter D. Beau

D0931998

Hamilton Books

An Imprint of
Rowman & Littlefield
Lanham • Boulder • New York • Toronto • Plymouth, UK

For Families

Contents

Foreword   vii

Introduction   1

1   Are We Really Alone?   9
2   The Packrat Factor   33
3   "Nevertheless, It Moves"   59
4   A "Tiny Whispering Sound"   79
5   The Missing Piece   101
6   Word Games and Mind Traps   119
7   The Family Hearth   137
8   Toward a Human Ecology   165
9   Darwin or Darwin-ism   199
10   Oppenheimer and the Fireball   221
11   The Light of Fifty Thousand Suns   245

Bibliography   263

Foreword

Everyone agrees that the contemporary culture and its customs, practices, and habits have changed greatly especially since the mid-twentieth century, though there is disagreement about whether many of these changes have been more beneficial or harmful or even inherently evil. This dispute has become so sharp that it has generated a "culture war" about whether many of these recent practices should continue or be seriously questioned.

Some commentators on both sides of the divide consider the culture war over. They suggest, for example, that the Millennial Generation has simply put these things behind us. The new definition of marriage and family life, egg-donor and sperm-bank businesses, surrogate motherhood, genetic manipulation, and abortion are now routine and legally sanctioned. Cited in the book is Anthony Esolen, a prominent cultural critic at Providence College, who more recently writes that he has:

> . . . come to see that the winning side of the so-called culture wars has no interest in rational or equable conversation about the neuralgic issues of our time. I use the word interest advisedly. They have nothing to gain by it . . . The aim was never rational coherence, or even a concern for the common good. The aim was power: to get what they wanted, to keep it, and to crush those who would question their right to it ("Speak Truth to Power," *The Catholic Thing*, December 29, 2016).

A Generation Abandoned does not directly engage in the culture wars at either the ivory-tower or purely polemical levels. Rather, it confirms George Santayana's contention that "Those who cannot remember the past are condemned to repeat it." The book is offered first to millennials and other youth, but also to those who are curious, still searching for the possibility that the modern and deeply felt sense of abandonment is not preordained for their own lives. They ask how should I understand my very self and identity as a unique person and valuable member of my community and the larger society? Is there more to life than continuously adapting to ever changing popular culture made mandatory by laws and the courts. Such questions may seem irrelevant, but not to those who still suspect that their life may involve more than "going along to get along."

For these readers the author's account traces the development of modernity and its devolution in recent times due to cultural forgetfulness and denial of the universal and inborn "natural law" by social scientists from a range of academic disciplines, technocrats, judges, and the media, where too often "image prevails over argument."

As we discover with the author, the so-called freedom of "Modern family disintegration is actually a throwback to fallen forms of 'family' in the past." In scanning the history of "family structure in various cultures, we find that the monogamous nuclear family was a late development. In ancient Egypt children were killed as a religious sacrifice; in ancient Greece homosexuality and infanticide was practiced; in ancient Israel polygamy was permitted but not adultery; in ancient Rome marriage was monogamous but divorce and remarriage was permitted as well as concubinage, abortion, and infanticide; and in ancient Germany captives could be forced to marry. But, in the Middle Ages abortion and infanticide were not permitted and marriage became a public and even a graced act of exchanging vows between a man and woman of monogamous union, and oriented toward children and to last until the death of a spouse.

Thus, over a period of centuries it was discerned that such families are the foundation of a stable and flourishing society. And, stable and monogamous marriages generated the strongest families. Now, the culture is not evolving, but devolving.

A second cultural critic cited in the book, G. K. Chesterton, writing a generation before the disruptive 1960s and 1970s, also noted that marriage as a public act was already devolving into more of a private arrangement:

> It is quite right that there should be pomp and popular rejoicing at a wedding; I do not in the least agree with those who would have it a purely private and personal thing like a proposal or engagement. If a man is not proud of getting married, what is he proud of, and why in the name of nonsense is he getting married at all? But in the normal way all this merry-making is subordinate to the marriage: because it is in honour of the marriage. People came there to be married and not to be merry; and they are merry because they did. . . . But in the snobbish society wedding the serious purpose is entirely lost sight of, and nothing remains but frivolity. . . . When once they lose sight of the old suggestion that it is all about something, they naturally fall into blank pauses of wondering what it is all about ("The New War on Christmas," 1925, cited in *Gilbert*, 20:2).

What Chesterton observed was that as marriages were becoming less stable, families were less unified, and consequently both the individuals and society as a whole were becoming more conflicted and fragmented.

Modernity's fascination with the pursuit of new possibilities often entails a forgetfulness of even very natural consequences. The rapid industrialization and advancements in technology during the nineteenth and early twentieth centuries that improved the lives of countless people in countless ways simultaneously undermined them in others.

In the last half century have the harmful effects of the industrial era have begun to be addressed and corrected in a significant way. Advancements made by genetic scientists and engineers to create new species of plants and animals offer great benefits but also may entail certain risks, as yet unknown, to those who consume them. Similarly, advancements in genetic science to correct certain genetic defects in humans could also be used to create "designer babies" and creatures with genetic structures that are only partly human. All scientists are fascinated and inspired by the frontiers of new discovery. In the book we visit with J. Robert Oppenheimer and a group of nuclear scientists eager to know if nuclear fission can be unlocked by man. But this quest for what can be done cannot address the moral question of what ought or ought not to be done with our inventions.

At the front end of the most recent wave of scientific discovery, and only three years after the first International Exhibition of Industry (in London), the Englishman John Henry Newman, another thinker cited in the book, understood that each science considered separately is a distinct activity that can advance knowledge of only a particular kind. Even then he maintained that no significant field of inquiry should be excluded (theology, for example):

> I have said that all branches of knowledge are connected together. . . . [The] Sciences, into which our knowledge may be said to be cast, have multiplied bearings one on another, and an internal sympathy, and admit, or rather demand, comparison and adjustment. They complete, correct, balance each other. . . . [T]o give undue prominence to one is to be unjust to another; to neglect or supersede these is to divert those from their proper object. It is to unsettle the boundary lines between science and science, to disturb their action, to destroy the harmony which binds them together. . . . There is no science but tells a different tale, when viewed as a portion of a whole, from what it is likely to suggest when taken by itself, without the safeguard, as I may call it, of others. . . . (*The Idea of a University*, 1854).

The method of each science is an excellent means to discover the actual causes and effects of things and events that have happened and may yet happen, but no science by itself can state definitively what actions ought to be done.

Specialized knowledge now progresses geometrically while the relationship among disciplines regresses at the same pace. Fragmentation blurs and even violates the distinctions between physics and metaphysics, science and aesthetics, and political and moral action. This confusion has dissolved understanding and consensus about the human person and what the common good is, or even if there is a common good.

The unique contribution of this book to a possibly renewed discourse of any cultural depth is threefold. First, it is substantive but accessible to the reader on the street as well as academics. Philosophical insight is artfully summarized where needed, but the tale is told mostly through a very apt and even entertaining variety of anecdotes, quotes, historical overviews and viewpoints. Some narratives are personal and yet related to the momentous events of the twentieth century—the construction of the first atomic bombs, and eyewitness participation in the recovery of the first lunar astronauts in the Pacific. Second, the presentation is symphonic, like a Tom Clancy novel. Ground-level accounts and broad cultural themes are woven into a moving and engaging fabric. Separate chapters line up in a logical sequence, but can almost be read separately, for the reader who is more inclined to sample the work over time rather than read the book cover to cover. And third, the book provides focus. Unlike much culture war literature, the entry point for this work is the political and cultural "perfect storm" that erupted in the 1960s and 1970s. Surrounding this focus is a remarkable and coherent synthesis of material from a wide range of sources, all supportive of the central thesis that detached from our inborn moral underpinnings society tends toward dissipation. In many ways such is the unfortunate inheritance of our younger generations.

The author appeals to a wide audience, but is particularly sympathetic to the Millennial Generation growing up in a world where the last remnants of the natural law seemed to be lost or shouted down. Members of this generation sometimes are willing to confide that beneath it all they feel a profound sense of abandonment. Their common refrain in so many settings is simply "whatever." The response of this book is neatly summarized in the title: *A Generation Abandoned: Why "Whatever" Is Not Enough.*

Andrew Tadie
Seattle, Washington

Introduction

Eppur si muove: "Nevertheless, it moves." These are the words that Galileo Galilei (1564-1642) might have whispered at the end of his trial for teaching that the earth moves around the sun. Is there possibly a connection between the evidence of Galileo's sixteenth-century telescope and the scientific evidence of our twentieth-century's modern ultrasound? The first enables us to search an overhead solar system and universe beyond an earth that moves. The ultrasound reveals a world and universe within that today is too often denied and that also moves. Galileo's critics declined to look through the telescope, and the modern establishment shields an abortion client from the ultrasound imagery of her unborn child.

In our self-flattering scientific age, it seems that the shoe now is on the other foot (Chapter 3). The shotgun marriage between science and the inevitability of "progress" is not entirely convincing. Even scientific evidence is filtered. What is missing here, and what else is it that prevents us from even noticing the absence? And what's happening to the family because of what's missing?

The eleven chapters in this book are proposed as an evocative and sometimes entertaining crash course for young adults and for many others. As a response to the culture wars, the symbolic number for bankruptcy—the final "Chapter 11"—is a fitting coincidence. The future insolvency of Social Security is not the only kind of bankruptcy. The side stories and visits with many interesting people carry a message and hopefully are fun to read as well as sobering. The material beckons to a very wide audience who might still be curious about our culture wars. Chapter One begins simply enough with a misdialed telephone call from a troubled young girl who has just discovered that she bears a crisis pregnancy. Our tale ends with a father, who has participated in some of the worst deceptions of the twentieth century, taking a walk under the stars with his young son in a Maryland orchard.

Between beginning and end there is offered what is hoped to be a wide-ranging feast. We visit with the mouthpieces of modern-day deceptions and the deterioration of popular culture and elitist culture. There is also the "the silent scream" of (aborted) victims of our very mundane throwaway habits. Our own inner voice, the "tiny whispering sound" of well-informed conscience also scrambles for our attention. The emergence of complex evil in human affairs is revealed through the very simple initiating experiences of small children and adolescents. And the fine art of adult rationalization merits another full chapter.

In all of this, what becomes of the human person and the family? The history of the family is presented in a sort of photo album of narrative snapshots, from primitive society to the present, with surprises along the way. One big surprise is that much of what we flatter ourselves as being "modern" looks more like a throwback into the primitive darkness. And given our genuine appreciation of the natural ecology, we will unpack what has been proposed as the "human ecology"—both similar and different—the fulfilling density of human relationships that awaits us if we ever outgrow our narcissist individualism and abusive collectivism.

Given all of these considerations, meaningful questions are commonly derailed today by two default propositions. These are evolution-ism and the anonymity imposed by the concentrated Big Bang origin of the physical universe. Millennials often point to these quick answers. Our investigation offers some second thoughts as we visit with Charles Darwin (as apart from Darwin-ists), J. Robert Oppenheimer (inventor of the atomic bomb) and Stephen Hawking.

Prodding the actual preparation of this book is an incoherent event in a hospital maternity ward. At the heart of each family only a mother can fully know the depths of the "aha moment" when she first holds her new baby. And there is the later part of this "aha" moment when that baby first shows a bonding sign with his or her first smile of recognition of the mother. The awesome sense and fact of mutual *belonging* is bigger than either the child or the mother or even both together.

With this heartfelt moment before us, let's consider now the event calling for a book of this scope and nature. This event followed the very premature birth of twins. They are so much alike and yet so individually unrepeatable and totally unique. Living for several weeks in the neonatal intensive care unit (NICU) with her twins, the attentive new mother was urged by the staff to take a break. On the way to the cafeteria she overheard these words, "maybe I'll have an abortion. . . ." The alternative reality of this incoherent moment is stunning. By comparison the fragile twin babies were so exquisitely alive and beautiful, at only twenty-nine weeks, and the mother was totally devoted to each of them. Other babies at the same age are not so lucky or respected.

Not long ago your author heard a televised interview with a young woman who, with some professional help, had unlocked an emotional tension of several years. It came out that she remembered—and could describe—a traumatic event in her very earliest existence. The memory was spatial, not visual or verbal. Together with the psychologist she approached her mother with this question: "Did I have a twin?" After so many years, the mother admitted that, yes, there was a twin. The young woman had a pre-natal, spatial and emotional "memory" of her twin, her companion in the womb, being pulled away from her in what her mother revealed was a half-completed abortion.

Like the single twin, what is it that has been taken from us, and what have *we* not been told about the past and present? Today we cannot help but take note of the dumbing down of our common sensibilities by countless distractions like the gaming industry, unrelieved celebrity self adulation and the talking-head media. Musical content is displaced by gyrations and amplified electronic blasts. Political correctness deletes and invents truths. The subliminal suggestion, code language, and the redefinition of words cause an evolutionary mutation of how we understand and define who we are. School administrators usurp the primary parental space and responsibility for information on human sexuality, and then market technical data often bleached of moral content. To do otherwise violates the "neutrality" in which the administrative state and its educational bureaucracy now operates.

Still, the "tiny whispering sound" of natural moral law, and of conscience and objective truth, leave us wondering (Chapters 1 and 4). This inkling toward real natural law is interior and not imposed, and yet has been progressively neglected and denied in recent centuries. We sense that we are sociable by our very nature and not radically individualistic, that the names of real things (like child, or marriage, or family) are not simply arbitrary labels to be applied like counterfeit clothing labels, and that the act of human reasoning runs deeper than facile rationalization or a dismissive "whatever." The natural moral law—not endowed by the state—is our personal assurance we are not to be violated.

More than a "law", natural moral law in itself is neither antiquarian Classical nor any early-modern corruption of the Classical. Natural law, finally (or originally), is our *inborn* self-respect, especially as this instinctive worth is shared with others. It is innate, it is our very selves, and is as fitted to each of us as flying is to birds and singing is to even a "sparrow that is sold for two farthings." That is to say, the natural law is not simply an external school dragged from some shelf.

We appeal here to an original and fitting insight from a work by G.K. Chesterton. He writes about a fully human predisposition:

> . . . the primary feeling that this world is strange and yet attractive [....]
> Whatever the reason, it seemed and still seems to me that our attitude towards
> life can better be expressed in terms of a kind of military loyalty than in terms
> of criticism and approval [....] It is a matter of primary loyalty; [the world] is
> the fortress of our family, with the flag flying on the turret (*Orthodoxy*, 1925).

This primary loyalty—more than a feeling—is our wings of flight; this song of loyalty is the natural law written into our hearts from before languages were invented, as a divine assurance and therefore as a sure beacon or commandment.

One battleground struggle between natural law and modern-day myths sometimes is affirmed by peaceful sidewalk witnesses for human life outside of abortion clinics. Opposite these is a strange (and estranging) coalition of the abortion industry and the civil courts. The witnesses hang their hope on a song and a prayer, *and* overwhelming scientifically-based information of the beating heart and real life of the unborn child. The bargaining chip on the table is as much the unsuspecting young mother-to-be as it is her unborn and unnamed child.

There is also the conscience, the interior echo of truth from the "tiny whispering sound" noticed in history more as a revelation than a mere concept (1 Kings 19:12). Our interior self tells us when we are wrong in our external words or actions toward others, and even wrong to our own deepest selves. All of us are challenged to listen anew to this tiny whispering sound from the deepest secret places of the heart. It assures us that we are not estranged, that we belong to one another, that we are responsible to one another, that we are governed by something more than pleasure and pain, and that we might be drawn to a living God other than ourselves and who is not simply a mental construct.

The tiny whispering sound sometimes speaks to us in the tiny heartbeat of an eighteen-day old unborn child. The conscience is not the discounting and possibly frightened voice overheard (above) in the hospital hallway: "I think I'll have an abortion." Instead, the voice in the hallway, overheard by the mother of premature twins, echoes the Big Lie (Chapters 2 and 3). Once we realize that we are being conned by the Big Lie dream world, we are free to clearly face deeper "choices." Along with a dose of sound judgment—yes, sometimes being judgmental is the right thing to do. In a noisy world our conscience still "gets it" about what is right and what is not (Chapter 5).

The capacity to turn one way rather than the other should not be suffocated by habitual negligence, or any cult of being non-judgmental, or any spectrum of random okay-ness. Falsehood in word or action or neglect (not of persons themselves) invites and demands judgment, something deeper than our free-form "decisions" to simply choose one way rather than the other, or neither.

Any reader of mystery stories might remember that moment when a homicide is suddenly solved by a single piece of evidence, something that was missing. Let's say a clever detective realizes that the victim's dog didn't bark on the night of the crime. He concludes that the assailant must have been known by the victim and by his watchdog. In this famous case the writer, Arthur Conan Doyle, presents us with a "dog that did not bark." There was ". . . the curious incident of the dog in the nighttime. . . . The dog did nothing in the nighttime. . . . That was the curious incident," remarked Sherlock Holmes in his great "aha" moment as a detective in "Silver Blaze" (*The Memoirs of Sherlock Holmes*, 1894). And so, the assailant is identified by something that was missing, by what did *not* happen.

This book proposes a similar mystery story about "a missing piece" (Chapters 4 and 5). The informed conscience is our own personal watchdog. Missing too often is the admission that we are creatures, not God. This instinctive sense of belonging is not always missing and has not always been anesthetized away from our culture. To not belong is not neutral; it is to be abandoned. So, what has happened to the voice of belonging, our inner compass echoed in conscience? We might still sense its absence, but don't know why. Our missing repose has been hijacked and substituted with a counterfeit. The "Big Lie" seeps into the vacuum (again, Chapter 2).

We are assured biblically that in the long run all can be well. We are urged to suspect and believe that there is justice in or above any world pretended by us or by others: "Eye has not seen, ear has not heard, nor has it so much as dawned on man what God has prepared for those who love him" (1 Corinthians 2:9). Should at least some of this higher truth be present even here and now? Or am I just an expendable accident within a larger cosmic lottery? Should I settle for being part of the lie? Why not go with the flow by carving out a niche for myself—and then rationalizing the rough edge? There is no interior conscience, only guidelines that can bend in whatever wind blows.

Do we really have to submit to this isolation, the artificial and lonely independence and the disinformation pedaled by modernity today? In a better definition of modernity, Pope St. John Paul II wrote that "if by modernity we mean a convergence of conditions that permit a human being to express better his or her own maturity, spiritual, moral, and cultural, then the Church [sees] itself as the 'soul' of modernity."[1] But this is not the modernity we find before us. Modernity is often the notion that the human mystery a branch of the natural sciences and, therefore, that natural science is the answer to all human questions.

The latest twist of post-modernity might be the notion that truth is whatever bubble or "context" I happen to be living in or fashion for myself. Identity politics (self "profiling") and the juggling of nothing more than special interests are big ticket examples. For our purposes, identity politics is understood as group tribalism so exaggerated that appeals to universal human nature and even to the act of "reasoning" are branded as "Eurocentric" and "racist" bigotry. The banner cause of womens' rights to real respect and undiluted admiration—championed through chivalry once upon a time—deserves better than this. Instead, at a protest and sit-in at a Jesuit campus, Plato and Aristotle were demeaned as "dead white dudes." Special interest antibigotry erupts as reverse sexism and reverse racism. Authentic masculinity and femininity devolve into sexism, and sexual identity is airbrushed into gender theory.

How this substitution of falsity for reality became so total in just a few decades, compared to what endures through the millennia, is a strange and fascinating story that needs to be told. The me generation didn't get where it is on its own steam. Many in the Millennial Generation—and equally in the older generation—are the frog in hot water. We have failed to notice. This moral climate change is due largely to the drumbeat repetition of the Big Lie (Chapter 2). In the following pages we will put some faces on the Big Lie and on the alternative. One face is possibly the misused portrait of Charles Darwin. His research into natural connections is thought by Darwin-ists to replace the need or relevance of human moral judgments (Chapter 9). If self-organizing evolution is the wrap-around meaning of all things, all we need do is just check the wind sock and work to "move things along." The twentieth-century nuclear physicist J. Robert Oppenheimer hesitated at this mindset once it is amplified by morally ambivalent modern technology. He noticed a moral dilemma on a massively global scale and likely affecting unborn future generations (Chapter 10).

How are personal responsibility and the relentless march of anonymous history to be lined up on the same page? As if this connection matters. We will hear some wisdom from various others, especially the prolific English writer, G. K. Chesterton (already cited above). Another such writer did a remarkable and very modern piece of self-reflection as far back in the fourth century. Literature specialists tell us that nothing like St. Augustine's introspective autobiography (*The Confessions*, a prayer of thanksgiving more than an autobiography) appeared again for a thousand years until the character development of William Shakespeare.

Augustine (b. A.D. 372) fathered and then came to love and admire an illegitimate son. The twentieth-century Catholic pacifist and founder of the Catholic Worker Movement, Dorothy Day, also had a shady beginning. Several years before giving birth to her daughter, Tamar, she aborted an earlier child. She writes about her experience: "Even the most hardened, the most irreverent, is awed by the stupendous fact of creation. No matter how cynically or casually the worldly may treat the birth of a child, it remains spiritually and physically a tremendous event."[2]

To be young today is sometimes like surviving a late-term abortion, by finding oneself both alive and a victim to a cultural and spiritual lobotomy. Many millennials confide a deep-seated feeling of having been abandoned. What kind of communication is possible between generations so divided as we are today? What caused this? Even the older generation, including your author, remembers what it is to feel isolated and cast adrift with a disrupted confidence in a personal future, e.g., in the 1960s the Selective Service (military draft) was still very active. But the difference between then and now is that there was still a sense of normalcy and cultural inheritance. "Whatever" was not even part of our vocabulary.

From our subtitle: "Whatever" is not enough. We will investigate three recurring themes, not as an authoritative lecture, but as the reflections of one drawn from the audience. Perhaps no one will be convinced, but the goal is more modest, that a few readers at least might say: "Oh, I never thought of things quite that way before." Here then are the three themes tying these things together. *First,* what is missing today in the air we breathe? *Second,* what grand deception has slipped into the vacuum? And *third,* how is this two-step hijacking undermining our lives and families today? The familiar quip is that if we cannot define our terms then hyphenate them, and no one will think to ask. In this case, "value-neutral" is neither a value nor neutral. Let us now explore the value-neutral endgame hovering over especially the Millennial Generation.

NOTES

1. St. John Paul II, "General Audience Homily of November 24, 1999," quoted in Tracey Rowland, *Ratzinger's Faith: The Theology of Pope Benedict XVI* (New York: Oxford University Press, 2008), 152. Your author draws particularly from Heinrich A. Rommen, *The Natural Law: A Study in Legal and Social History and Philosophy* (Indianapolis: Liberty Fund, 1936/1998).

2. Stanley Vishnewski, comp., *Dorothy Day: Meditations* (Newman Press, 1970), 26; cited in Johann Christoph Arnold, *Their Name is Today: Reclaiming Childhood in a Hostile World* (New York: Plough Publishing House, 2014), 145.

Chapter One

Are We Really Alone?

"There is only one suffering: to be alone." In the decades immediately before the social revolutions of the 1960s (of which more later), the philosopher and playwright, Gabriel Marcel, penned our opening words on our "only one suffering."[1] But are we ever really "alone?" The conversation below is a true event that took place in December of 2013. The bell rings on a landline telephone hanging on the wall. But the one called is not home to pick it up. A troubled and unrehearsed monologue enters onto the recorder, the voice of an anonymous caller: "This is really important to me, and I want you to be the first to know . . . please call me back." More followed: "I just found out that I'm pregnant. Please call me as soon as you get this call." The caller spoke as to her boyfriend but had punched my number by mistake. This was a wake-up call. What was I going to do?

A CONVERSATION

The unknown caller's number had been recorded. I worried if there was no return call to the young girl, would she conclude that she was abandoned, betrayed, and doubly alone? What was the story behind this caller? It's not hard to imagine the caller's emotional box canyon. Most likely she is suddenly unable to see the future even a few days ahead. But regardless of the situation, might the new mother make room in her own heart for the natural wonder and fulfillment of becoming a mother? The Christian view is that there is a future and that it calls us forward and even upward, that we do belong, and that no matter what, the future is capable of being graced. Every day we are at a crossroads, a tipping point, and tipping points are always open to grace.

I dialed the number and returned the call . . . and listened. The voice, it turns out, was that of a seventeen-year old girl, a junior enrolled in a nearby high school. No names were asked or given. Friendly interest and anonymity seemed to help. Was she living with her parents? "Sort of" came the response. Missing already, and for whatever reason, is the confident sanctuary of the family. What was she considering? The so-called "planned parenthood" network routinely channels such a complex situation toward a simple "technical" fix, the mythical silver bullet. For ninety-four percent of their cases the fix is an abortion (Planned Parenthood annual reports).

I referred to the "baby" she was now carrying. Two months along, she guessed, so if the question had come up I might have mentioned that the child's heart beat and even brain activity were already in play and detectable. I asked if she was interested in another choice—it's all about a real "choice" is it not?—and gave her the number and address of a pregnancy aid center not far from her high school. People donating time there could stand with her in the months ahead, and show that she was not abandoned. Even in today's world we are never completely alone. This does not mean that suddenly all things will be solved and easy, but a truly empowered and principled decision at this tipping point can lead to another, and another. There is a better path and a higher road.

The phone call came just a few weeks before Christmas. We will never know what decision was made by this young and frightened teen for or against her child. My hope is that she carried to term and found one of many families waiting to adopt her baby. We can hope she has not become one of those lost in the crowd, another emotionally wounded teen, or that she is not a single mom and probably in need of help, probably with a rich uncle— Uncle Sam and government welfare—as her only path. And where is the guy in all this? In a culture of government entitlements, surely there is also a social entitlement for him to just sample the goods and move on. And there is plenty of precedent for this—in primitive times the males routinely raided nearby tribes on missions to capture sexual partners. The only thing new under the sun is the motel room.

We know what the numbers are. But, what do those numbers mean? And what are the personal facts behind the numbers? And what are the missing pieces that have put this society and countless individual lives into a moral freefall? First, young and unmarried women account for eighty-five percent of all abortions. Nearly half of these become "revolving door" clients who have had at least one previous abortion. Today some seventy percent of all abortions are performed on women in their twenties or even younger. In 1980 teens accounted for thirty percent of all abortions, but his ratio does seem to have improved of late. Surveys detect a growing proportion of pro-lifers among the informed young. Since 1991 the annual number of teenage births has gone down by well over half according to the National Center for Health

Statistics (2015).[2] The Center for Disease Control reported that one in five sexually active teens have used the morning-after pill (up from one in twelve in ten years). This poison pill can be bought without a prescription.

How entrenched is our bored, disconnected and morally rudderless "hookup" culture? Many abortion clinic walk-ins are young people who looked for a cure to loneliness in the wrong place, bogus companionship however fleeting in a world gone sideways. Before the car ride and drop off, the real driver also might be damaged self-esteem, or a deep-seated rejection or abandonment. Or maybe nothing more than the heavily marketed pleasure principle. It feels good, and Freudians and Darwinists say that I'm really not much different than a pleasure-seeking amoeba. The hormones are in the driver's seat, or rather the back seat. Have the young never really been shown which way is up, or even that there is an "up"? Who failed to simply show them—with the kind of clarity that is genuine gentleness and respect, and sometimes tough love? When is the feeling of abandonment itself a cop out? Sometimes, is the sense of abandonment really a lack of personal coping skills—skills for coping with the reality that the world is not our footstool, and that living in an imperfect world involves dealing with rejection or even with personal failure? Trophies for mere attendance do not teach this.

Or, instead, abandonment can be the lack of a social and cultural grounding that we all deserve. How many of the young especially have been deceived by the Big Lie of sexual "readiness," prodded by relentless promiscuity from the entertainment industry? Theoretically, actions still have consequences, but nothing that can't be managed from four-to-eight at a local clinic, including Saturdays. Life-and-death abortion becomes simply an exit strategy—the nuclear option. In our coping-challenged culture many college students demand that the campus classroom should be an intellectual "safe place"—something like safe sex—where "politically incorrect" ideas are detected and aborted. Shouting and office sit-ins are becoming routine, with orchestrated protests sometimes oriented at commencement day platforms. If seedy gas stations feature coin-operated condom dispensers, then surely tuition-supported classrooms should be equally supplied, with cerebral condoms.

The genuine safe place in this imperfect world is a very special kind of friendship. This is the trust and permanence of one person solidly married to another. But why in the world would anyone want a "relationship" with a real future? Another original safe place used to be the womb of the expectant mother, but it's defenders are now silenced. Today the fact of pregnancy itself is made into a threat to the mother's safe space, even though the private "I" is already "we." The selfie is not individual, but plural. The bigger picture socially gets us into a lot of numbers. So patience is needed for a few more paragraphs before we move on.

Prior to the 1960s the overall illegitimacy rate in the United States was in the low single digits. After the 1960s and so-called sexual revolution, Senator Daniel Patrick Moynihan, in his book-length *Moynihan Report* (1965), published by the Department of Labor, told us the changing story. He wrote:

> [F]rom the wild Irish slums of the 19th-century Eastern seaboard, to the riot-torn suburbs of Los Angeles, there is one unmistakable lesson in American history: a community that allows large numbers of young men to grow up in broken families, dominated by women, never acquiring any stable relationship to male authority, never acquiring any set of rational expectations about the future—that community asks for and gets chaos. Crime, violence, unrest, disorder . . . are not only to be expected, they are very near to inevitable.

New brain research links stunted brain development in children to poverty. But have we noticed that reduced family incomes usually come with broken and other single-parent families? Even in the 1960s single parent families were the major explanation of family poverty in Black communities. Even then, at the front of the sexual revolution, the Black illegitimacy rate was already forty percent, a figure that today is now matched by the Caucasian majority. So, what was the answer? Was it nothing more than the big platter of government-funded social welfare programs—part of President Johnson's Great Society catalogue?

Today, among Blacks the illegitimacy rate has climbed to seventy percent. By the early 1980s it was reported that by age nineteen, eight of every ten males of all races and seven of every ten females in the United States have "had sex"; four of every ten of those teenagers had had at least one pregnancy. Again, by that general period nearly one-third of all abortions each year were procured by teenagers, and the number was still some four hundred thousand out of 1.5 million annually in the early 1990s. The sexual revolution and its signature Woodstock orgy of the late 1960s are not the cause of family meltdown, but serve at least as an apt symbol and license for a cheap future.

Again, some of the numbers have eased since 1980, but a pattern of teen pregnancies becomes the norm and is passed on from one generation to the next. Eighty percent of girls who are mothers at age fifteen are the daughters of women who gave birth when they were teens. Most girls who have children before they are nineteen drop out of school. Sold as a solution to the crisis of illegitimacy, the contraceptive mentality has become a source of our larger social and family meltdown. Outlets for mass marketing of contraceptive fixes—sometimes enabled by our schools and bypassing parental involvement—serve as franchises for the pharmaceutical companies and for a malleable and willing public. In Oregon and California hormone contraceptives no longer even require a doctor's prescription.

These dispensaries are a kind of fifth-column presence serving the backup abortion industry. Four out of every five aborting women have used contraceptives.[3] Contraception and abortion are parts of just another blurred spectrum, and not really alternatives as we are coaxed to believe. The more radical abortion advocates paint unrestricted abortion as "part of the continuum of reproductive health care," and assert that it is this spectrum, rather than the unborn child, that is "under active assault."[4] The Centers for Disease Control (CDC) annual surveys up to 2014 find that the total number of abortions and the abortion rate are in decline (12.5 women of child-bearing age, compared to 25 in 1980, with technology as part of the reason). Still, some sixty percent of births outside of marriage are in homes with couples whose commitment is to cohabitation rather than the permanence of marriage. Between 2006 and 2014 the teen birthrate continued to drop but of the four million babies born in 2014 about a quarter million were born to mothers aged fifteen to nineteen (CDC, 2016). This group accounts for about twelve percent of all abortions. Pregnancy is a CDC "disease" and abortion is part of "reproductive services." Apart from the numbers, culturally this blight remains what Pope St. John Paul II accurately termed the "unspeakable crime" which he likened to "chemical warfare" against the unborn.

RUMINATING A BIT

Professional researchers on both sides of the abortion divide have run some numbers on abortion and its relationship to the mental health of the mothers. Here are some of their findings. A mother who has aborted has a sixty-five percent higher risk than others of clinical depression. She is three and a half times more likely to die from suicide, accidents or homicides in the following year. She is likely to have trouble bonding with and mothering later children, and is five times more likely to get into drug or alcohol abuse. She is nearly twice as likely to be hospitalized for psychiatric treatment and will have a higher death rate in future pregnancies and a sixty percent higher risk of miscarriage, and apparently is more likely to become a breast cancer victim.[5]

And yet, some of this is thrown into question by the more recent "Turnaway Study" from the University of California. The study reports that during the five years after an abortion there was no increase in depression, anxiety, low self-esteem or dissatisfaction with life. A bioethicist not part of the study finds "resilience" in these outcomes: "What's sort of a revelation," she finds, "is the ordinariness of it."[6] "Revelation" or rather a conclusion fitting to a state of denial? And, "ordinariness?" Not a single one of the billions of persons who have walked the face of earth should be cursed by us with ordinariness. Of all the atrocities against millions of Jews, Albert Speer as a lead operative explains, "I didn't hate them. I was indifferent to them" (*In-*

side the Third Reich, 1971). Perhaps somnambulism and prideful indifference is an everlasting whiff of the "original sin" committed from the beginning against one another.

The big picture for us today—a more real revelation—is that a large share
of an entire generation or two is now trapped—willingly or unwittingly—in
fast-lane ordinariness: sexual experimentation, comfort zone morality, and
the mislabeled quick fixes of misapplied technology. Our culture of broad
brush ordinariness is intergenerational sabotage—the denial of a common
heritage—forgetfulness of the universal natural law. In 1999 the respected
cultural critic and writer Francis Fukuyama summarized much of the previous half century. He pointed out the obvious:

> . . . the pill was supposed to give women more control over their reproductive
> lives; instead in the United States and other Western countries, its introduction
> was followed by an explosion of illegitimacy, divorce and single parent fami-
> lies . . . The fatherless household that subsequently emerged contributed to a
> host of other social ills, such as poverty, crime, poor educational achievement
> and drug use.[7]

In 1948 the defeated minority at the Anglican communion Lambeth Conference already told it like it is:

> It is, to say the least, suspicious that the age in which contraception has won its
> way is not one which has been conspicuously successful in managing its
> sexual life. Is it possible that, by claiming the right to manipulate his physical
> processes in this manner, man may, without knowing it, be stepping over the
> boundary between the world of Christian marriage and what one might call the
> world of Aphrodite, the world of sterile eroticism?[8]

Does the idea of a "boundary" sound discriminatory? Even today's popular culture understands the boundary between mastering video games and the
entire Internet becoming a virtual reality to be exploited by hackers. Even
George Bernard Shaw—an atheist and moderate socialist and supporter of
eugenics—disapproved of contraception as "mutual masturbation." To directly interrupt the dual purpose of human sexuality against either purpose—
either a shared unity, or openness to procreation of children—isn't this a
violation of nature and of the whole truth of the human person? Even the
Declaration of Independence speaks in the same phrase of "nature and nature's God" . . . to reject either one is to lose eventually the other as well.

Traditional and natural marriage is part humanity and part of history, but
also partly above history as coming fresh from "the beginning." Should we
moderns have a thing against old-hat "tradition"? Breathing normally is also
traditional, as is a normal heartbeat. Real marriage is a profoundly personal
decision and commitment of permanent self-giving—of one man and one

woman—exclusively to each other. Marriage is naturally inclined toward the formation of new and unique biographies—real babies in the eyes of the real parents, in real society, and before the Creator God of all reality. Animals and insects "propagate" facing the same direction, but human beings are uniquely designed to pro-create face to face. It is personally "face to face" that we are even destined to see our God in eternity.

By comparison, how often is adolescent and "sexually active" contraception the effect and the cause of routine and flat-earth boredom? In the long run constant entertainment, especially, generates boredom. Psychologists tell us that today our attention span is less than that of a goldfish, eight seconds. Boredom. In 1968 Pope Paul VI spoke to what was by then the very widespread embedding of the contraceptive technology and mindset into marriages. The contraceptive separation of sexual union from the transmission of life, he warned, would "lead to conjugal infidelity and the general lowering of morality." Three years after the writing from this pope Cardinal Wright in his "reflections" quoted a well-read Jesuit cleric:

> What fundamentally distinguishes 'perversion'—as homosexuality, lesbianism and bestiality—from the bisexual relationship is precisely its fundamental lack of relationship to the transmission of life and its consequent inevitable fact and sense of natural frustration. [9]

Can modern society simply fix things by presuming to validate free-floating immorality in all of its forms? But who listens to popes and priests anyway, or to parents or even the whisperings of inborn personal conscience—when we can just settle for "whatever"? After all, it was Cardinal Ratzinger, later Pope Benedict XVI, who was so insensitive as to notice that modern across-the-board equality is satisfied with nothing less that the new triumvirate of suicide plus abortion and euthanasia (not to be confused with a moral decision to forego so-called "aggressive medical treatment").

Let's ask a repentant abortionist what's going on. A very successful former abortion czar, Bernard Nathanson, disclosed that the original abortion agenda was very much about discrediting the Church. Nathanson revealed that the

> [. . .] anti-Catholic warp was a central strategy, a keystone of the abortion movement. . . . The more vigorously the church opposed, the stronger the appeal of the anti-Catholic line became to the liberal media, to the northeastern political establishment, to the leftist elements of the Protestant Church, and to Catholic intellectuals themselves. [10]

Then there followed a new generation of Catholic "intellectuals." These were nurtured on the obscurities of "seamless garment" rhetoric that is so often attached to the letterheads of busy chancery offices. The seamless garment label was a clumsy effort at what is now better framed as a "consistent ethic of life," more than the social gospel alone. Under the old label moral absolutes against abortion, for example, could be falsely balanced against varied strategies of political and economic advocacy. Today, if inorganic chemicals are bundled into the burger, this warrants legal surveillance and government edicts from on high, while a pass is still given to the bundling of an intrinsic evil like abortion into the mix of government social programs.

The bundling of misguided good intentions with direct evil is a slippery slide into the abyss. Perhaps hell is the end state of permanently accelerating free fall into zero, a sort of spiritual black hole. Here on earth morality is not denied, but just bracketed to the side as we wink at an ambiguous double life. At first, absolute evil is bartered against client groups and always urgent political goals. The corrupting Caiaphas Principle multiplies itself into the twenty-first century. As the high priest, Caiaphas, said of Christ, ". . . it is better for you that one man should die instead of the people, so that the whole nation may not perish" (John 11:50). Of such bartering, St. Paul reminds us that as morally consistent human beings we may never "do evil that good may come of it" (Romans 3.8).

BRANDING THE PROBLEM

In tiny baby steps do we detect a weak but modern version of Adolf Hitler's "final solution"? What was Hitler's final solution to the Jewish question and for the German nation? After the First World War, he asked, what it was that was holding Germany back from being great again? The Holocaust (Shoah) was his selected reset button. We all have probably heard the number, that some six million Jews were exterminated because they didn't fit into his plan for the blond and blue-eyed German people. The real number is more like eleven million if we include non-Jews. The less reported bigger number covers a lot of others branded as misfits—gypsies, Soviet war prisoners, the mentally and physically disabled, Poles, homosexuals, and political enemies like the communists . . . and not to be forgotten, thousands of Catholic priests and nuns. All of this was preceded by the distribution of eugenics and abortion propaganda for non-Aryans in the Eastern territories outside of Germany. All of this has been traced farther back to small-scale eugenics pioneered in the United States.[11] Germany transplanted eugenics into Europe from its seeds partly in the United States.

How was the German public maneuvered to democratically elect racist Hitler as German chancellor in 1933? That's another story, but mass reeducation—the brainwashing element (today's sensitivity training on steroids?)—is something to be soberly viewed in all democracies. Who would have guessed that another democracy of the cultural elite would sideline not only racism, but also the "family" and traditional "marriage"? Consider this—in a dissenting opinion to a 1986 case (*Bowers v. Hardwick*) Justice Blackman asserted the fallacy of limitless individual rights—at the expense of the family as a bonded unity—when he wrote that "we protect the family because it contributes so powerfully to the happiness of *individuals* not because of a preference for *stereotypical* households" (italics added). Individualism prevails over stereotypical family households?

Where the Soviet artwork of "social realism" depicted the dedicated female factory worker of the new socialist state in place of stereotyped women, Justice Blackman celebrated residential incubators of individualism within the new society. This individualistic way of thinking—collectivism in disguise—has only gained ground in recent years as the traditional family has been edged aside. Families are divided into cross-cutting market segments. Today mothers are even divided against fathers; the father has no right within a marriage to hear about a spouse's abortion intentions. Marriage is no longer a bonded unity in its own right; it has deteriorated into a "juxtaposition of solitudes" rather than offering a foundational "communion of persons."[12] With free all-day kindergarten at one end of the spectrum and multiversity high-tech job training at the other, where is this conveyor belt taking us?

Let's recall the phone call mentioned above and consider my own high school graduation. In her valedictorian address, a straight-A classmate proposed that "the reason individuals do anything at all is because they are alone." The atheist Jean Paul Sartre announced that "hell is other people," but isn't the inborn natural law our deepest inclination toward togetherness rather than simply making the best of aloneness? Marriage, the most common example, is the attraction to be exclusively valued and cared for by another, one who fully complements oneself, and vice versa. But the valedictory address was accurate in a way; our individualism is evidence of a deep rupture and then the sense of abandonment.

Yet, many celebrated thinkers of the past salute such loneliness. Take the seventeenth-century political philosopher, Thomas Hobbes, for example. Sobered by the devastation and desolation of the sixteenth-century English Civil Wars, in his *Leviathan* ("Or the Matter, Form and Power of a Commonwealth, Ecclesiastical and Civil," 1651), he made a famous remark. Before state power could forcefully protect people from each other, at its deepest end life was "solitary, poor, nasty, brutish, and short." In our acquired aloneness, we surrender whatever true freedom we have to the state, he says, in order to survive inevitable anarchy among other violently lonely people. In the absence of authentic human nature and of sound religion, self preservation through state compulsion becomes the default religion.

Are Hobbes and the rest of his ilk right? Is the "solitary" thing the most basic ground floor of our souls (if we have souls)? In the 1990s a former

archbishop in Seattle often made a point of speaking about such things to young adults. He began by asking what is the loneliest place in the entire world? And after some guesses, his response would be "the main hallway of high schools during the crowded noon lunch break." Apart from the scattered pockets of noisy chatter there's a larger and gnawing loneliness for all of those on the outside of the cliques, all of those left out by "the popular kids." In their chatter the superficially popular kids, too, often manifest the same deeper loneliness.

In the human person is there something more primary than such solitude? Over thirty years after the valedictory address mentioned above, I found exactly the right words:

> . . . yes, religion is in fact that which man does in his solitude; but it is also that in which the human person discovers his essential companionship. Such companionship is, then, more original to us than our solitude...Therefore, *before solitude* there is companionship, a companionship that embraces my solitude. Because of this, solitude is no longer true solitude, but a cry calling back that hidden companionship (italics added). [13]

It is this most foundational level of *belonging* that protects us from gnawing loneliness. It's not about constructing an egghead theory of "natural law." The natural law is about peeling back the layers to discover what is actually within us from "the beginning." Our hidden companionship is what makes all of us a "we" even before we invent language enabling us to clearly think it and to speak it, or in our fallen-ness to deny it.

Let's peek back at Hitler's moment with the demoralized German nation following the First World War and the punitive Versailles treaty, and his toxic politics of we versus they in his "final solution." The extermination of the Jews was signaled in his book *Mein Kampf* (*My Plan*, 1925), almost ten years before he was elected to power. This was a full fifteen years before he triggered the Second World War by invading Poland. Even with his corrupt and calculating mind, one of the more pivotal statements in his *Mein Kampf* is this: "Anyone who thinks he can arrive at a religious reformation by the detour of a [superficial] political organization only shows that he has no glimmer of knowledge of the development of religious ideas or dogmas and their ecclesiastical consequences." [14] This line comes in a typically radical chapter subsection headed as "the 'away-from-Rome' movement." So why is Hitler sometimes painted as, you know, still a Catholic?

Hitler's general preoccupation was the failure of the pan-German movement in multicultural Austria to resolve political tensions between its diverse populations and his own agenda. He championed the German nation and this nation's political future in a politically complicated Europe. Parliamentary approaches are a trap, he thought, because they muddle things. They are ineffective because they force the common people to deal with more than one political adversary at a time. Hitler's counterfeit religion, his cult of National Socialism, is a made-to-order fabrication rooted in nothing more complicated than blood line and mythology, combined (some say) with post-Reformation individualism. This formula is a useful and visceral substitute for the more real communal solidarity and companionship which it destroys. A less fickle educational system would remind us that five hundred years before Christ, Aristotle warned that democracy is unique as a political form because it can degenerate into its opposite and worst enemy.

THE GEOMETRY OF INSANITY

The reduction of parliament to a forum for but one idea, as Hitler would have it, is a view that itself fits one definition of insanity. G. K. Chesterton helps us out with this. Author of countless novels, columns, poems, articles, serious pieces and even the popular and televised *Father Brown* mysteries, in 1924, only one year before Hitler's *Mein Kampf* was published he wrote:

> The madman's explanation of a thing is always complete, and often in a purely rational sense satisfactory . . . his mind moves in a perfect but narrow circle. A small circle is quite as infinite as a large circle; but, though it is quite as infinite, it is not so large . . . the most unmistakable mark of madness is this combination between a logical completeness and a spiritual contraction. [15]

Hundreds of schools across the country are pledged to never mispronounce students' names, because to fail in this would be nothing less than "micro-aggression." But to deprive the young of names altogether—through earlier abortion in the womb—this is a mandatory civil right. This is not to say that the mother's decision is anything less than complex, confusing, and excruciating. It is to say that the political mentality of "choice" is a slogan smacking of pseudo-religion. Another "narrow circle" would be the science of global natural ecology if this ever *replaces* such other questions as eternity and immortality, or even the "human ecology" (which we will visit in Chapter 8).

Hitler's insight into other belief systems, exploitive as it was, might actually explain a strange event near the end of the Second World War. Was he the only one not surprised by Stalin's action, however cynical, when the German armies had advanced to within a few miles of Leningrad and Moscow? From the Siberian labor camps Stalin retrieved the exiled patriarch and other prelates of the Russian Orthodox Church. The window-dressing Church was intended to energize the morale of a nearly beaten Russian nation. The news commentator and Christian convert Malcolm Muggeridge stresses that Stalin chose this decoration as opposed to marketing his less engaging Marxist end game of state-sponsored atheism and Socialism. [16]

Some are reminded of some White House prayer breakfasts and especially the cozy relationship again today between the post-Cold War Russian government and the Russian church.

Looking to the Middle East today, the sects internal to Islam—each nearly a different religion—are also wired into a global political chessboard. Today it falls to our secularist and unraveling Western civic culture to presume to work these things out. (Secular comes from *saecula,* meaning the world or the current age.) With the East-West Cold War mostly obsolete, now comes a dual threat to the human person, the threats of jihadist interpretations of Islam and plus radicalized secularism. What's in a word? On this side of the Atlantic secularity might mean tolerance, but secularism is hardened into an ideology and an agenda. As often as not, it is now an open door for reverse discrimination and the suppression of religious institutions broader and deeper than the subjective and isolated individual.

Broadly assaulted is the Christian thing, but before this is disdain for the innate natural law worthy of respect in everyone and by everyone. The little-understood Catholic Social Teaching (CST) is little more than this universal natural law written on Church letterhead. The CST seeks to leaven—but not replace—the social and political realm, as well as economics and first of all the culture. CST is not a "third way" midway between conservatism and liberalism, but instead is the *negation* of all such divisive ideology. It is not one ideology among many. It is the pre-condition of credible trust before the air has been sucked out of the room. It makes problem-solving at least possible.

The CST—essentially the natural law—begins at the beginning, with the very nature of the body-soul human person. The CST is a principled affirmation of each concrete human being, not any idea about the person, but the real person. The fully human person *is* the core principle. Each of us has a right to real flourishing, and is truly free and responsible to simply feed the really poor, and to not hanker after each other's wives. On paper the CST is seen in the biblical Acts of the Apostles and, over the centuries, it has been resuscitated and distilled, largely in response to the most recent ideological and global upheavals of the nineteenth and twentieth centuries. In terms of only its charitable works, today Caritas Internationalis is a federation of one hundred sixty-five national-level Catholic charities active in two hundred countries and territories worldwide.

Turning to civil society, the CST respects the distinct (but not divorced) domains of Church, society and state. Again, its core principle is the intrinsic and *transcendent* dignity of each human person, and therefore our mutual respect for the whole person and each and every person without exception. This is more than political "diversity". The counterfeit is the intolerant tolerance of today's Silicon Valley diversity, the political mythology of the procrustean-bed equality (one-size-fits all. (Don't know what that is? Check it out on Google.) The concrete human person is not a class, or a race, or a skill set, or an interest group, or a political identity, or least of all a digit within the collective state itself. The awkward reality proposed by the CST is that each irreducible human person has an eternal destiny, nothing less, and therefore has the "tiny whispering sound" as his compass and inner orientation.

And yet, the religion of state-supervised Secular Humanism receives a smug nod from our civic culture, while the CST and any public act of Christian human witness from outside the bubble of modernity is branded as "extremist." Secular Humanism holds that there is only one kind of humanism, and then commits to just moving things along—to stay on "the right side of history." In the shadow of neighborliness (a good thing) we are to be equally distant and patronizing toward religions and religious questions (a good thing?). Just as individuals have the civic right to vote or not vote, or on Sunday morning to either pray or watch football or to sleep in, or during the "holiday season" to light candles or instead to get lit up, or "whatever."

This is the flat earth of Secular Humanism. Can dogmatically tolerant moderns simply step back from what we know to be a conveyor belt of inevitable consumer boredom? The rhetorical "arc of history" too easily air brushes away the real "arc of relations." The arc of relations *does not exclude or reject* the vertical Ark of the Covenant and the Law of love preached in the complete Sermon on the Mount. Instead of drifting along in current events, aren't we also always at the headwater as "in the beginning?" Isn't our call to newness and the "new life" our opening into the mystery of a Creation? While this mystery might be ignored, it must not be denied.

The spent rationalism of the modern age is a false "equality." Such equality tolerates everything except a principled affirmation of what is, a principled dissent. As a religion, Secular Humanism holds that today's societal turmoil is still due to "religious" residues rather than its own formlessness. It holds that the radicalized terrorist can be eradicated through better management—more correct dosages of economics, politics and secular nation building. Admonitions to just get along in our modern way ring hollow especially to the victims of nihilistic terrorism in the Middle East. Over the very, very long path of human history is it only our secularist mindset which deserves our attention?

CODE LANGUAGE AND THE NATURAL LAW

Let's go biblical here for a moment. In the Bible the words of a transcendent God—a God above the world—are "inspired" in the listener (not "dictated" in Arabic as is believed of the *Qur'an* under Islam). The deeper meaning is more true because not only literal, rather than less true. In its moral, allegorical and salvation story telling the Bible speaks a language at least as valid as

that of computer software code-writers. Something interesting happens especially when we take biblical allegories in pairs. In the tower of Babel, a
confused human-only effort to reach the heavens, we find a futile world view
built literally from the ground up (Genesis 11:19). How very modern! That's
one historical allegory.

But another biblical allegory gives us the clue that our connection to a
realm beyond our imagination is available (to finite minds) only as a "revelation" from the top down. Jacob's humble vision is not of an ascending Tower
of Babel, but of a stairway *extending down* from a realm above. The stairway
"rested on the ground, with its top reaching to the heavens" (Genesis 28:12).
Does a truth that is higher, rather than only larger, come only as a gift from
above? Is there wisdom from above our politics and even above our imagina-
tions? What, really, do we know about the mystery of the human person?
What might we know? In this generation of bumper-sticker unconsciousness,
many are content to edit onto the fish symbol of Christ the lettering for
"Darwin" and a set of salamander legs at the foot of the stairway. Evolution
is God. (We will visit with Darwin in Chapter 9).

In the broadest scriptural pairing, the Old Testament prefigures the New
Testament, just as the New Testament abundantly fulfills prophetic expectations recorded in the Old Testament. This is what happens when eternity
enters into time as the Incarnation, the central event of Christianity and
human history. By what failing do we conceive of eternity as endless and
even boring duration, rather than as the uninterrupted epiphany of a timeless
present?

Our visual imagination can help us be receptive to the truth of eternity as
the timeless present. We might try to see a white chess board with black
squares as simply the opposite, as a black chessboard with white squares. We
might then believe that the Incarnation—the proposed *fact* of Christ—is not
only his life and teachings over a period of some thirty-three years—but first
the unfathomable mystery of the divine taking our human nature into himself. From the New Testament we also learn that human time then enters into
eternity—the historical fact of Christ's physical resurrection at Easter.

By what self-inflicted darkness do we imagine a God who is so ham-
strung that it is beyond his reach to enter into and transform his own curious-
ly fractured creation? Such a reality would involve an Encounter greater than
any competing mere idea, and would evidence a human dimension vastly
exceeding any "civil rights" conferred by any human agency or state apparatus. We have real obligations as well as real rights, and both are inalienable
from "the beginning." These rights are ours not by any later social contract
but by a prior and *origin*-al entitlement that is divine. Before anything else,
these rights are innate and *define* our shared and already-existing human
nature as persons. This grounding as creatures more than as self-made arti-

facts is the universal natural law. The *Declaration of Independence* offers at least a fading hint:

> We hold these truths to be self-evident, that all men are created equal, that they are endowed by their Creator with certain unalienable Rights, that among these are life, liberty and the pursuit of happiness."[17]

When our justice system pretends to uphold the Constitution while detaching it from the touchstone of a Creator and natural law as explicitly noted in the cornerstone *Declaration*—another "wall of separation"?—it opens the door to ever-expanding abuses of power. Human nature, which is equally shared by every man and woman, is not one seemingly arbitrary orientation among others. Human nature includes a well-grounded inclination toward what is complementary, an orientation toward the distinctly other, because toward the infinitely Other. The disorientation today is that society no longer wants to recognize such reciprocity. Society wallows too much as the homogenous popular culture to be readily enforced by the hammer of the state.

Rather than settling for orientations and social fluidity, might the key be better-formed "consciences" open to the genuine good and human flourishing? The meaning of natural law can be blurred around the edges, but what concerns us throughout these chapters is the possibility that the natural law is more than simply another optional mindset. Is the natural law imprinted directly and equally into each human person as what it is simply to be a human "person"? Is it the stable North Star, unmoved by myths old or new or by the tabloid constellations of idolized and clueless Hollywood stars? Once we see that we have been conned—and in Chapter 2 we will explore the Big Lie—the inner giant comes fully awake. We can't fully live except at a higher level.

It is no accident that following the swamp of the Holocaust, the German constitution (the *Basic Law*, 1949) starts at "the beginning" with this: "Human dignity is inviolable. To respect and protect it is the obligation of all state authorities" (Article 1[1]). Unlike what many suppose, the natural law is the opposite of a closed mind, or a mind inattentive to real history. The German constitution arose from the ashes of recent history, literally the ashes of Hitler's death camps. The natural law is our *inborn* openness to each other and to the one, the true, the good, and the beautiful. G. K. Chesterton remarked on his atheist friend H. G. Wells: "I think he thought that the object of opening the mind is simply opening the mind. Whereas I am incurably convinced that the object of opening the mind, as of opening the mouth, is to shut it again on something solid." The quest for truth is not catch and release; the innate and universal—as in truly non-exclusive—natural law *is* something solid.

How the solid and always new truth is echoed in the conscience in an always aging world is not complicated. A dash of reverence should come naturally—as part of the natural law. In addition to the well-known Golden Rule we also have the silver rule: "First do no harm"..."*primum non nocere.*" Until recently, this has been the unquestioned starting point and creed of the medical profession and of jurisprudence. But radical secularism erases this standard from medical school curricula. On the altar of modernity the secularist state would finally sacrifice the child, marriage, and the family itself. It would sideline the family *because* the family is the foundation to the human person and *because* the family as an institution—rather than a statistical detail—precedes even the existence of the state. In truth, it is the continuously malleable apparatus of the state that is an artifact or construct of fickle history. From beginning to end, the full human person is always more than any artifact, whether a sharpened archaic stone ax or a dull modern bureaucracy honed by electronic gadgetry.

Another dangerous reversal of history today is the lost understanding of personal "freedom of religion." The human person, by his very nature (and not by abstract theology alone), has a right to religious freedom, both personally and institutionally. Religious freedom, now endangered, includes not only individuals but their institutions serving the public: morally grounded adoption services, schools at all levels, and consistently ethical hospitals. These are to be eradicated and redefined as freedom of one-day-a-week "worship." This politically correct stunt would turn religion into just another private association like the local garden society or the Rotary, or the newspaper editors' guild, all monitored by the administrative state.[18]

AN ALLEGORY

On the religious mystery of good and [or] evil in the world, Herman Melville (1819-91) wrote a famous novel that ran deeper than its cover story of whaling (*Moby Dick*, 1851). Melville's fictional piece is said to be the world's greatest sea novel. It is *both* an action story about wooden ships setting out from New Bedford in the exciting and dangerous days of whaling *and,* at a deeper level, a powerful allegory about good and evil. It even has a biblical tone right from the start with the opening line: "Call me Ishmael." Ishmael was the illegitimate son sired by Abraham (around 1800 B. C.) before his sterile and aged wife, Sarah, gave him Isaac.

The White Whale is usually understood as the untamed forces of nature and destiny, even incarnate evil. Captain Ahab is a whaler out to settle an old score for an earlier encounter when the whale sliced off his leg. But is this the real truth? Why is the whale white, and why is Captain Ahab (whose name is an Old Testament symbol of evil) dressed in black? The British author William Somerset Maugham reviewed the book and many mainline critiques before he turned everything right side up. He proposes the alternative that the White Whale is the elevating symbol of Good while its pursuer and avenger, Ahab, is really the symbol of Evil. Maugham's sidesteps even Melville's own explanation that the whale is "all evil, visibly personified" and writes instead:

> Why should the White Whale not represent goodness *rather than* evil? Splendid in beauty, vast in size, great in strength, he swims the seas in freedom. Captain Ahab with his insane pride is pitiless, harsh, cruel and revengeful; he is Evil; and when the final encounter comes and Ahab with his crew of 'mongrel renegades, castaways and cannibals' are destroyed, and the White Whale, imperturbable, justice having been done, goes his mysterious way, evil has been vanquished and good at last has triumphed (italics added). [19]

While Melville was deeply into symbolism, he himself admitted in a letter, before it was pointed out to him by his lifelong friend Nathaniel Hawthorne, that he didn't see any allegorical meaning in what he had written. He thought of his most famous novel as simply a richly woven action story. Whatever the symbolic allegory of this novel, we are moved to consider the ease with which men like Ahab turn things upside down. Even we do this, by sometimes projecting our own darkness upon a God (the White Whale) whom we then choose to reject. As with the whale and Ahab we can no longer tell the difference between good and evil. The take home lesson for us is that truth is where we find it as in the natural law, and not where we sometimes presuppose it to be. Good and evil are binary, not a spectrum entirely stripped of these bookends.

Everyone enjoyed the later Hollywood box office hit, *Pirates of the Caribbean*. Did we notice the possible hidden meaning in the code of conduct applied by pirates to themselves? For them the "Pirates Code" was provisional; it could be bent and broken as needed because it was only, what, a flexible "guideline." Consider instead the stable prohibitions—the flip side of love for God and neighbor—in the Ten Commandments which are reliable and absolute. One is not to murder (or euthanize); one is not to destroy another's reputation (as in political campaigns!); one is not to steal; one is not to fornicate or possess another's wife (either in fact or even in fantasy). Such things cause us to no longer trust ourselves and then to not trust God. In step with the inborn natural law, the fully human orientation is not an imagined freedom *from* restraint, but the liberating freedom *for* the truth.

About our vocation to consistent integrity, what was the reminder given by the recent Pope St. John Paul II regarding provisional, on-again-off-again morality?

[. . .] this kind of behavior is in no case compatible with the goodness of the will of the acting person, with his vocation to life with God and to communion with his neighbor. It is prohibited—to everyone in every case—to violate these precepts [more than guidelines]. They oblige everyone, regardless of cost, never to offend in anyone, beginning with oneself, the personal dignity common to all. . . .[20]

Who is the real Ahab today? And who is the White Whale—certainly not the free-wheeling popular culture. Surely not self-absorbed television celebrities. At the beginning of Melville's novel Father Mapple's sermon reveals us to ourselves in all times: "If we obey God, we must disobey ourselves; and it is in this disobeying ourselves, wherein the hardness of obeying God consists."

A corrupt turning point in American civic life and toward radical individualism, happened when the United States Supreme Court issued its split ruling (5 to 4) on the case of *Roe v. Wade* (January 22, 1973)—the least restrictive abortion law in the world except for Communist countries. This ruling asserted the constitutional right to abortion, and it wiped the slate clean of legal restrictions in dozens of states. Never mind that the plaintiff (Norma McCorvey) seeking a legal abortion later admitted to not having been raped, but was propped up into "Jane Doe" in the class action lawsuit. She later became a prominent pro-life advocate until her death in 2017.

In this contradiction between natural law (things as they truly *are* in themselves) and positive law (things the courts might *say* they are), the court offered a contorted logic that invites direct quotation. The court claimed that it chose to not "speculate" as to the moment when a unique, genetic human life is a person distinct from the mother. The court announced from on high:

We need not resolve the difficult question when life begins when those trained in the respective disciplines of medicine, philosophy, and theology, are unable to arrive at a consensus. The judiciary at this point in the development of man's knowledge, is not in a position to *speculate* as to the answer (*Roe v. Wade*, italics added).

The serpentine nature of lying cannot excel this example—the rationalization that government must not intrude into private decisions combined with the removal of all barriers to the worst form of intrusive child abuse one can imagine. To justify this fantasy as a refusal to "speculate" is worse than irony. The revolutionary mentality so evident here is to substitute speculation and abstract slogans at the expense of the real and the concrete. Abstract slogans win; the particular pre-born child loses. Sanctimonious posturing at the highest level sidesteps a real heartbeat in favor of imaginary social harmony and advancement. By this court speculation society is pushed into the confusion of a permanent culture war. Are we not maneuvered away from solid realities to be lived, defended, and passed along in an erratic world? All state-level deliberations and statutes are swept away. As a mandatory path haven't we been handed a speculative dream world that signals the progressive erosion of both human rights and universal civil rights?

Radical secularism speculates a breakthrough into ultimately a New World Order in one collectivist form or another, a sort of jigsaw puzzle not of real rights but rather mutually adjusted and shifting interests. A new patchwork of extreme localism and nationalism beckons from the opposite direction. But what if the root of our political problems is deeper than both trends, having something to do with natural law and even theology? What if the root of our political problems is connected finally to the truth of what we *ought* to know about God and Man? The time-tested reality of human history is that things do not move automatically forward by human pronouncement, but often go sideways or backwards.

How is it, we ask, that our hometown neighbors become "radicalized" as terrorists? Instinctive animal nature is better than this; but with speculative free will our distinctly human nature is more volatile. We used to have as an unquestioned norm the responsible harmony between a mature man and a woman in a permanent marriage, oriented toward mutual growth and the creation and formation of children. Children in the womb were safer. Even here we now we have the risk of the floor falling out and of freefall descent far beneath the animal kingdom where species naturally pair as male and female, and in some cases for life (not the birds and the bees, but some birds for example).

As a first principle, to directly affirm (not simply speculate) the reality of each newly created and novel human life—this is reality oriented. To assume a spectrum instead, resulting in denial and rejection is a kind of shared suicide inflicted on the "other." Above the Supreme Court's facile indecision about speculation is the first principle of common sense and medicine—again the Silver Rule, "first do no harm" (*primum non nocere.*) In its neutral and non-judgmental judgmentalism the Supreme Court actually did far worse than speculate. The armed hunter does not shoot if he is unsure of his target in the bush.

The losers in *Roe v. Wade* are some sixty million aborted children in the years since the 1973 ruling, not to mention their misled and very often remorseful mothers. This "enlightened" outcome is one hundred times the number killed in the American Civil War to end political neutrality toward the slavery of the then four million Blacks. In that case, against two centuries of momentum, it was still possible to walk things back, so to speak. Can we do this again? Against this record, the leading pro-abortion presidential candidate in 2016 insisted, "We have come too far to have that [*Roe v. Wade*] turned back now." Again, the false mental imagery is one of turning the clock back rather than setting it right.

In such intellectual paralysis the judiciary turns away from the very real pre-born children, rendering these unnamed children as non-existent in reality as well as in mind. This disruption is euphemistically smoothed over as a "termination of pregnancy." In a total contradiction, the terms abortion and maternity care are rolled under the single heading of "reproductive health services," and a collage of regulatory minutia. The court's ruling even flies in the face of known science in the twentieth- and twenty-first centuries. As an absolute death sentence to tens of millions it is a far cry—many times over—from the comfortable years of house arrest assigned by earlier and equally unscientific minds to Galileo in the seventeenth century.

The *Roe v. Wade* decision was an exercise in judicial fiction. We now live in a fictional world. After a few years the foot draggers of the universal natural law and of conscience were supposed to fall in line with the "right side of history," but they didn't. The evil was not to be waved aside and smiled away. On street corners they continue to give witness to our modern day "slaughter of the innocents" (Matthew 2:16-18). We affirm the natural law not only through religion but first through the elementary use of reason. First, some so-called scientists overreach to reduce reason to the weights and measures of empirical truth. And then second, the court goes much farther so as to deny the empirical fact of unborn children every bit as real as ourselves, and third, the court finally resorts to double-speak to ratify its stream of consciousness.

The Old Testament codified our inborn natural law in the Commandments while the New Testament deepens this law with the summary commandment to love our Creator and ourselves, and one another as ourselves as He has loved us (e.g., John 3:11-13 and 4:7-21). We are reminded that those who think that mind games are the sum total of reality, and who deny the reality of sinfulness are "the liars" (1 John 1:6-10, 4:20-21). In the court's *Roe v. Wade* edict the first principle of medicine and of human morality—"first, do no harm"—is stuffed into the incineration bag along with the unborn. The clinic removes the unseen; the stressed mother amputates herself from her own maternity; and frequently the father first splits from the mother. Even before love, where is any basic justice in all of this?

The companion case to *Roe v. Wade* was *Doe v. Bolton* (1973). *Bolton* decisively extended this see-no-evil license into the ninth month of a human life. The United States Supreme Court effectively replaced modern science with the incantations of alchemists from yesteryear. By court edict, a child is redefined as not a child and, therefore, not worthy of protection until s/he comes into contact with air! And even then this so-called cluster of "non-viable" tissue is not safe. In 2015 a Colorado woman was assaulted and her eight-month old child carved from her belly. While the mother survived the baby did not, yet the criminal charge was not homicide. The loophole is that the autopsy showed "no medical or physical evidence the baby ever took a breath outside her mother."[21] The evidence and rationale, disputed by those actually present, is that the baby failed to survive even an instant apart from the mother and, therefore, was not a human person.

In olden times, before modern science, there were only four elements, water, fire, earth and air. By the modern court pronouncement from on high we have come full circle. The innocent child in the womb is redefined as earth (nonviable tissue), measured by his or her contact with air, and tossed into the fire (a medical incinerator). The throwback modern mindset supports even late-term abortions into the ninth month.

Yes, in honesty, all of us sometimes cut corners in one way or another, but this cut is often decapitation. Surviving children of late-term abortions have been passively left to die on the table. No legal consequences for this active neglect, and yet a mother is given a twenty year prison sentence for actively killing her birthed (but "unwanted") newborn child. Had she sought a late-term abortion a week earlier, this "health care service" would have been legally protected and publicly funded. Hospitals that refuse to participate in the abortion culture are threatened with severe penalties.

The seventeenth-century (so-called) Enlightenment political philosopher Thomas Hobbes (noted above) got it exactly right when he said that life is "solitary, poor, nasty, brutish, and short." For the unborn child this is especially true. What an evil irony it is when the state becomes the agent for such an unspeakable crime. Hobbes' Leviathan state compels universal participation through the fine print of health policies and taxation. If every "right" is also a right to be subsidized, then even gun owner in town should demand a place in line. For himself, the last words from Hobbes were these: "It's my turn, to take a leap into the darkness."

HELPING HANDS

Why do we so often follow the path of the Big Lie? Young women have good reason to feel alone in our dismembered and anonymous "society." As the child is physically dis-membered rather than re-membered, so too is society as a whole, and so too is its foundation in families. But the young—if they are alert and willing—always still have a fresh chance to see through the web of carefully tended deceptions. The bottom line is pretty simple: how many of the upcoming generation are as naïve and fickle or predatory as was today's morality-challenged generation when it was young? For starters, instead of Woodstock, why not take a look at a short poem by Robert Frost: "The Road Not Taken"? For the young unwed and pregnant woman today "the road not taken" is the truly free choice to recognize and then affirm continued life for her inner child. Hers is the radical freedom to not deny birth to another human being.

In this kind of decision we are never alone. Very personal help is available in every city. Throughout the world there are those who invite us to at least hesitate before crossing the threshold of any "abortuary" (abortion/ mortuary). A scan through the phone book or on the Internet can also locate locally the better path. One example from Manhattan and now present in numerous cities here and abroad is the Helpers of God's Precious Infants.[22] The Helpers—whistle blowers?—fall back on no signs, no noise, no blocking of doorways. Instead of attorneys there is simply a personal presence and a prayer, some information otherwise withheld about gestation, and a real choice with a helping hand—uncomplicated acts of real justice and kindness, even a personal God who is infinite mercy and truth and who is really present to us, rather than not. When we decide in this way to be "personally present in our gift",[23] rather than anything less, what place is there for self-appointed managers of mere programs? And what is it about some programs that they overlook the adoption option, or then make adoptions so costly?

The founder of the Helpers, Monsignor Phillip Reilly, saw the futility in the early 1990s of winning any time soon over an entrenched and see-no-evil legal establishment. He simply began to meet daily with young girls on the streets. He was there to offer an alternative—a real choice. Over the years, from his own personal presence—and he is far from alone—he has guided tens of thousands of thankful girls onto the better road too often not taken. We see hospitals and fire stations signed to accept newborn children, no questions asked. There is no need to panic and dump the child into the nearest dumpster as is sometimes reported on the evening news.

Here, then, is another instance where words matter. The birth mother does not "surrender" her child. By accepting a helping hand she *affirms* this child and assures a more promising future. She turns away from the calculations of "planned un-parenthood" and acts responsibly. She rises above the parroted criticism coming partly from those who have not yet stood up to the Big Lie by which they themselves have been victimized.

As a restoration of culture, this face-to-face presence should not be overlooked. Personal encounter exposes the fallacy of depersonalization that infected the medical world of the 1970s. Human patients, like hubcaps on the automobile assembly line, became anonymous "health service consumers" and private doctors became "health service providers." It seems that when we privatize and consume human sexuality (the apple at the center of the Garden?), then all things are affected, even medicine. And if one orients toward random sexual experimentation, why would one believe in anything other than a random universe finally devoid of intrinsic purpose?

As for the abortion industry, how might the total humanity of each and every unborn child and each and every mother be seen, respected, and restored? In every instance, each has a pulse and a face. Today the battleground for reality is no longer academic or military or political; the battleground is politicized sex, marriage, and the family. Trapped on the wrong side of a rupture between generations, young adults are abandoned and handed a seasoned mess of pottage—the loneliness of cheap self-esteem and appetite satisfaction, confused sex with abortion as a routine exit strategy, language manipulation, an entitlement culture combined with government bullying of any who dare affirm a deeper vision of ourselves and of others. The victimized Millennial Generation is much like its predecessor, but now no longer with even the memory of a lost reality—an entire generation abandoned.

NOTES

1. "Le Coeur des Autres" (a play: The Heart of Others), Paris: 1921.
2. William A. Donohue, *Catalyst*, January-February 2015.
3. Janet Smith, "Pope Paul as Prophet," *Catholic World Report*, July 1993.
4. NARAL Pro-Choice Washington, Letter to the *Seattle Times*, June 20, 2015.
5. Citations are listed by Liz Saurez, republished in the *Population Research Institute Review*, March/April 2008.
6. M. Antonia Biggs, Turnaway Study, in the *Journal of American Medical Association Psychiatry*, December 14, 2016; the commenter is Katie Watson, Northwestern University Feinberg School of Medicine; reported by Pam Belluck, *New York Times*, December 15, 2016.
7. Francis Fukuyama, Syndicated newspaper column: "Pill may bring unexpected changes to Japan", June 13, 1999. Fukuyama is the author of *The Great Disruption: Human Nature and the Reconstruction of the Social Order.*
8. Cited in Wright, "Reflections on the Third Anniversary of a Controverted Encyclical," St. Louis: Central Bureau Press, 1971.
9. Ibid.
10. Bernard Nathanson, *The Abortion Papers: Inside the Abortion Mentality* (New York: Frederick Fell Publishers, 1983), 196.
11. See, for example, the DVD by John Mychalzyk (Director), *In the Shadow of the Reich: Nazi Medicine*. 1997. In the United States of the 1920s twenty-three states sanctioned eugenic sterilizations.
12. Donald DeMarco, "How the U.S. Supreme Court is Waging War on Marriage, *National Catholic Register*, April 18, 2004.
13. Luigi Giussani, *The Religious Sense* (San Francisco: Ignatius Press, 1990), 75. The Russian novelist Dostoevski, in his *Crime and Punishment*, speaks of a "subterranean solitude" that is deeper than sin, and of a still deeper fellowship.
14. Adolph Hitler, *Mein Kampf* (Boston: Houghton Mifflin Co., 1943), 114.
15. G. K. Chesterton, *Orthodoxy* (Garden City, New York: 1959), 19-20.
16. Malcolm Muggeridge, *The End of Christendom* (Grand Rapids, MI: William B. Eerdmans, 1980), 15.
17. Sources of political thought in the colonies are more complex than is popularly believed. Sylvester J. McNamara proposes that the philosophy and wording of *Declaration of Independence* derives as much from the writings of the Jesuit Robert Cardinal Bellarmine (1542-1621) as from the more credited and late seventeenth-century British John Locke (*American Democracy and Catholic Doctrine* [Brooklyn: International Catholic Truth Society, n.d., c. 1920], 106-122, esp. 155). John Locke appears in the dissenting opinion to the *Obergefell v. Hodges* majority ruling for gay marriage (Chapter 8), for the constitutional defense of traditional marriage, parental moral authority and limited government, but Locke unlike Bellarmine also tended to equate natural law and rights with relatively shallow self-interest.

McNamara points to the exact wording of Jefferson's five principles in the preamble of the *Declaration*: sovereignty, equality, divine and Natural Law, the right to select magistrates, and the right to change the form of government. McNamara draws from Filmer's *Patriarcha* (a compendium of Bellarmine's philosophy), Jefferson's copy of which remains in the Library of Congress. The more rationalistic term "self-evident" (truths) was an edit supplied by Benjamin Franklin, replacing Jefferson's original "sacred and undeniable" (Paul Johnson, *A History of the American People* [New York: Harper Perennial, 1999], 155). If McNamara et al are correct then the American constitutional project is accountable to deeper origins than the individualism of modern liberalism.

18. Under German National Socialism, and in an order from Herr Kerrl, the Gestapo Minister of Ecclesiastical Affairs (December 1937) made this ruling: "It is my firm conviction that the Church must confine itself to the purely religious sphere. Apart from the actual church building and its sacristy, we can only regard as necessary an adjoining room for weddings, baptisms, etc. and a hall for Bible-classes, Passiontide devotions, etc. . . . Building enterprises which overstep these limits are a violent intrusion of the Church into the secular domain, and this cannot be tolerated" (Quoted in *The Persecution of the Catholic Church in the Third Reich: Facts and Documents Translated from the German* [Fort Collins, Colorado: Robert A. McCaffrey Publishing, n.d./1941], 199).

The longer-term Nazi strategy was to discredit (or kill) Catholic/Christian leaders and to re-indoctrinate the memberships with a new faith—Germany's Third Reich (rare and original documents of the International Military Tribunal at Nuremberg made available in 2002, and researched by the Cornell and Rutgers University School(s) of Law, originally posted at www.lawandreligion.com; reported through the media by Edward Colmore, *Knight Ridder Newspaper* (Jan. 12, 2002). A somewhat analogous and current version of this tactic is noted in Chapter 7, fn. 20.

19. Herman Melville, W. Somerset Maugham (editor and introduction), *Moby Dick or the White Whale* (Philadelphia: John C. Winston Co. 1949), xxvi.

20. Pope St. John Paul II, *Veritatis Splendor* (*The Splendor of the Truth*), n. 52, 1993.

21. Sadie Gurman, "Woman Charged Under New Law in Womb Attack," Associated Press, March 28, 2015.

22. Monsignor Philip J. Reilly, Helpers of God's Precious Infants, Monastery of the Precious Blood, 5300 Fort Hamilton Parkway, Brooklyn, New York, 11219. Other help lines are: www.PregnancyCenters.org (1-800-395-4357 [HELP]), and National Life Center (1-800-848-5683 [LOVE]).

23. Pope Benedict XVI, *God is Love*, 2005, n. 34.

Chapter Two

The Packrat Factor

What does it mean to routinely deny each other a name? What does it mean to extinguish the unnamed and most vulnerable in society? What does it mean to not really notice what are we being told? Is the cover story a sort of modern day lie to each other—the Packrat Factor? In the forest ecology of the Rocky Mountain area we find a large bushy-tailed rodent termed a "pack-rat" (*Neotoma cinerea*). Equipped with a big mouth he hoards his findings, often replacing one thing another with whatever—bait and switch. In human society, is there another Packrat Factor? Is there a Big Lie where we deny an inconvenient truth and replace it with something else more palatable?

A PURELY MUNICIPAL IDEA

Is the Big Lie the inability to see the forest for the trees? Or dare we be so *un-modern* as to wonder, possibly, whether behind the Big Lie is something else, "the Father of Lies" (John 8:44)? The Father of Lies, the Con Artist, is legion, a forest of untruths unnoticed and unquestioned. As a mindset, was one cornerstone in the United States cobbled into place by the United States Supreme Court? In the 1973 *Roe v. Wade* decision the Court legalizing abortion on demand. It was not always so. Or can the cornerstone of the Big Lie be located farther back in nineteenth-century academia? In the *Harvard Law Review* (1895) Associate Justice Oliver Wendell Holmes Jr. had already set the tone for relativistic legal invention when he wrote: ". . . I often doubt whether it would not be a gain if every word of moral significance could be banished from the law altogether. . . ." Earlier, he had written: "I think that the sacredness of human life is a *purely municipal idea* of no validity outside the jurisdiction" (italics added).[1]

Laws devoid of morality—this fiction displaces the natural law we all possess as our inborn openness toward the good and the true. Still partly free of brainwashing, we might recall John Adams, a graduate from Harvard (1740) and under George Washington our first Vice President. He said: "Our Constitution was made only for a moral and religious people. It is wholly inadequate to the government of any other." Of these others, the tellers of lies, are they really deliberate "liars"? Or perhaps are they only human inchworms beyond their depth? As we discovered in the previous chapter, with the *Roe v. Wade* a marriage of footnote scavengers and suspended morality erased local laws in most of the states by the stroke of a single pen. The balancing game was more interested in being consistent with past rulings than in being right. We would rather bow to tea leaves and the entrails of goats than notice the dismembered body parts of aborted children.

The regal and almost bishop-like robes of our court jesters grow threadbare. An old fashioned and possibly still relevant adage holds that "when you pull off the miter (the bishop's head gear), the head comes with it." In our irreligion we also have lost our heads. Which is to say, when we erase all fixed truths whatever is left of human reasoning also risks losing direction. G. K. Chesterton in his *Heretics* said it this way: "take away the supernatural and what remains is the unnatural." And as Martin Luther phrased it, reason (by itself) becomes a wax nose that can be pulled in any direction. The only legitimate question now seems to be legalistic precedents and expediency for how to "move things along." The more ideological Soviet leaders had a more blunt word for their inevitable unfolding of history: "the correlation of forces" (Nikita Khrushchev, Premiere 1958-64).

In future decades, or maybe a hundred years and in a new human springtime, historians will be less enthralled with modernity and its long-dead inner circles of choristers. Much of modernity will be seen as a period piece to be grouped together with other cultic enthusiasms, like those of pre-Christian Druids, or the fourth-century Manichaeans who hated nature, or the twelfth-century Albigensians who repudiated much including (traditional) marriage, and who believed in aborting oneself by starvation. The dark site of modernity even resurrects memories of the non-European Aztecs. Prior to Cortez, who brought his own brutalities to Mexico, the Aztecs each year had performed literally tens of thousands of open-heart human sacrifices on long lines of living victims.

Even before *Roe v. Wade*, a 1965 case (*Griswold v. Connecticut*) placed society on the slippery slope with its contraceptive thinking. This ruling made contraception legally available to married couples, and in 1972 *Eisenstadt v. Baird* extended this availability to unmarried individuals. In the secular domain, the message was indiscriminate market access—free sex in a free market. Sex and babies were disconnected by legal edict. You can have one without the other. Justice William O. Douglas offered an inventive perspective on individualism with his instruction that the specific guarantees of the *Bill of Rights* have elastic "penumbras" which are "formed by emanations from those guarantees that help give them life and substance."

Penumbra individualism: paraphrasing *Animal Farm*, all penumbras are equal, but some penumbras are more equal than others. The easily inflated penumbra of "right to privacy" (planted by Justice Brandeis in a much earlier Prohibition case) flourishes under the dim lighting of a magic show. The "penumbra" doctrine also reminds one of the mystified Winston Churchill who a few decades earlier said something equally obscure about a problematic wartime ally, the Soviet Union. During a radio broadcast in October 1939, the month after Germany triggered World War II, he said: "Russia is a riddle wrapped in a mystery inside an enigma" (unoriginal wording lifted from the agnostic David Hume who in his *Essays* wrote of God as, "a riddle, an enigma, an inextricable mystery"). Why so mystified about fact-strewn history? For centuries the history of Russia had been one of "defensive" expansion in all directions, toward the Mediterranean and all the way to the Pacific Ocean a full ten time zones east of Moscow. After having conceded Eastern Europe to the enigmatic Russia and Communism he remarked, "I could have prevented this war!" And later on his own deathbed, "What a fool I have been!"

Instead of a foolish enigma, Churchill could have joined our court jesters and said penumbra. Finally, the domestic and foreign culture of death is veiled in fog and then conjured to look like truth. After the 1973 abortion oracle, in 1992, the U.S. Supreme Court upped the ante in *Casey v. Planned Parenthood*: "At the heart of liberty, is the right to define one's own concept of existence, of meaning and of the mystery of life." This borders on plagiarism or lip syncing: "your eyes will be opened, and you will be like God" (Genesis 3:5). Objective truth is replaced by the court with opinions, impressions, orientations, all spawning the wraparound cult of "whatever."

Carefully consider this—the court announces that for all practical purposes all orientations toward the real are equally true, or equally untrue. All except one. The only position rendered not legitimate is to question the court edict. We now can decide that you as an unborn child are not real. We are free to edit you out of existence. Is this not the biblical "knowledge of good and evil" (Genesis 2:17) by which we replace the binary with a vague spectrum and pretend to be the authors of a substitute for truth—to be God?

As possible hyperbole, the words on liberty in the *Casey* decision are surely lifted from the philosophy of Jean Jacques Rousseau. He was the eighteenth-century Swiss born philosopher who, as a youth, enjoyed the dizzy feeling that came with mountain climbing. Do we detect the eighteenth-century equivalent to drugs? Rousseau announced that "it is therefore essential, if the General Will is to express itself, that there should be no partial society within the State, and that each citizen should think only his own thoughts." To solve this riddle of arbitrary concepts for the individual versus society, in his *Social Contract* (1762) he then said that "whoever refuses to obey the General Will shall be compelled to do so by the whole body. This means nothing less than that we will be forced to be free. . . ." Connect the dots: if civil government is redefined as the public *will* rather than justice, then personal self-government, too, is not guided by reason but rather by personal self-will. . . . The unborn generation is one of Rousseau's disenfranchised partial societies: the mother decides "I think I'll get an abortion."

John Locke, a widely credited mind behind our *Declaration of Independence*, held more directly to some sense of objective natural law. But he saw this law more as a bundle of external goods to be protected than as a still deeper and interior compass common to human nature. In charge with us today are the sophomoric legal interns, the footnote scavengers and the down-loaders of term papers from the Internet and convenient deductions from prior case law.[2] The *Casey* wording is worse than any random private opinion or "subjectivism." The "right to define one's own concept of existence" gives license to rationalize any fiction, or narrative, or identity politics. It generalized and goes far beyond the false logic of abortion.

This is the path to incoherence between cultures and a "tyranny of relativism" and "globalization of indifference" (Pope Benedict XVI). These compact terms simply point to our inability to seek the truth of the real beyond our self-made bubble universes. Under very recent Supreme Court edicts of Secular Humanism—the supreme bubble—are we now at the point where those of any non-Establishment religion will be "forced to be free"? The only response might be biblical, "Your commands are all true; help me when lies oppress me" (Psalm 119:86).

LESS THAN A FULL DECK

With such cap and gown legal props from the courts, is there any wonder that our fading twilight of distracting affluence ends up in a morality of absolute "freedom," where whatever has become the law of the land? The unborn child's continued existence depends upon my individualized consent and how I freely choose to define—or un-define—persons other than myself. The courts find that mothers are free to impose their decisions however difficult on the most vulnerable.

Those who dare to defend the tiny whispering sound of the heart, and the whiteness of snow and the blueness of the sky, and the reality of the unborn child, have been arrested from the public streets as "racketeers." Believers, those who question society's mandated belief in political correctness, become the plaything of legal bullies in a sandbox courtroom. Why not limit personal freedom under Rousseau's General Will; why not exterminate the undeveloped "fetus/child"; why not market fetal body parts to the makers and marketers of cosmetics and soft drinks; why not primitive cannibalism made stylish or tasty; why not Hitler's culture of the "final solution" where the skins of human victims were fashioned into stylish lampshades for the elect.

Recall with me a university class in the middle of the 1960s and 70s. This was a graduate course in political science and how things work in "underdeveloped" countries. In south Asia—India, Pakistan, Sri Lanka, and Bangladesh, for example—the public pulse was already measured not by the ballot box but by the size of open air protests. Our own devolving political institutions have shown every sign of dragging the nation into the idiom of these lands. Well beyond the Civil Rights movement, now every grievance *against* something requires a photo-op street blockage. Disruption of commuter traffic seems a favorite version of our constitutional right (rite!) to freedom of speech.

Positive demonstrations *for* the basic right of our most vulnerable children to simply live are not disruptive or destructive. Anarchists and paid demonstrators stay away. After decades the annual pro-life marches (on the January date of *Roe v. Wade*) at the national and state capitol buildings continue unabated. Under the new media politics of selective outrage these massive demonstrations are either too routine or too countercultural to attract more than token prime-time coverage. Similar protests affirming the family and resisting other anti-family policies have occurred overseas, in Hungary and Croatia, and not only in regions recently freed from Soviet domination. In the Western Europe of 2013 some two million signed an initiative to protest European Union funding of technologies that either destroy "extra" embryos or market them to willing consumers. In France in 2014 the *Manif Pour Tous* (Demonstration for All) drew a million to the streets of Paris and Lyon, including large numbers of the young generation, to resist state parliamentary rejection of "marriage" as understood between one man and one woman. In an early 2015 demonstration a nineteen year old Parisian female student explained: "The government is trying to create a new type of family, which is not natural. We are very against surrogacy and the marketing of women in this way."

In 2014 the new Pope Francis backed the Slovakian bishops in their proposal for a referendum in defense of the traditional family in their country. In 2015 he also warned Filipinos of "ideological colonization" of the family, whenever acceptance of foreign economic aid comes with the blackmail pressure to impose abortion as the law of the land. Pope Francis has strongly confronted so-called "gender theory"—the stumbled upon fiction that the body-soul unity of each man and each woman dissolves into a spectrum or amalgam involving optional sexual accessories from A to Z, or rather

LGBTQ. Gender theory is the myth that while persons may be biologically male or female, they have a willful "right" to identify themselves as male, female, both or neither. After all, if an unborn child or even marriage can be redefined into oblivion, why not something so inconsequential as sexuality? What is the meaning of equality if we cannot be at least equal to artificial transformer toys?

Without exception, everyone deserves respect and barring a felony merits civil rights. But by what twist do we brand defense of traditional marriage as a "hate crime," as against today's LGBTQ tiny demographic minorities? Visiting in Washington D.C., Cardinal Robert Sarah from West Africa re-marked: "This is not an ideological war between competing ideas. . . . This is about defending ourselves, children and future generations from the wicked and even demonic idolatry that says children do not need mothers and fathers. It denies human nature and wants to cut off an entire generation from God."

As the sixteenth-century Thomas More said at his trial for an alleged crime against the king of England, "I do none harm, I say none harm, I think none harm. And if this be not enough to keep a man alive, in good faith I long not to live. . . ."[3] In an irrational world we might expect accusers from college safe-spaces to profile More's crime or Sarah's above remark (or this book!) as hate crimes. In our arguably demonic society we abandoned simple truths some time ago. In the century following More's martyrdom, the phi-losopher, Rene Descartes (1596-1650), sought the certainty of truth in the logic of mathematics. The cosmos and the human body are machines to be dissected by mathematics. We can say that he invented to original "wall of separation" when he quarantined the human soul as a side plate "ghost in the machine." The earlier Francis Bacon (1561-1626), who like More was also a Lord Chancellor of England, gave his support to the experimental method, but is criticized for saying he wanted to put nature "on the rack" to reveal her secrets for our control.

Some trace this dissolving of the thought back to one William of Ockham (1300-1349) who held that broad words (universals) are only convenient fictions ("nominalism" which derives from *nomen* or word), and that only individual "things" really exist. Today those who hold that everything is just clouds of stardust have done little more than add some mathematics to ideas blowing around seven centuries ago. Today some rejoice that we are made of the same stuff as the stars, and then dissolve the meaning of "stars" and "we," the reality of real substances and then, logically, any hope for a moral natural law. In our throwaway culture we routinely toss stuff out, especially our own history. We discount whatever is not the self. Is our cultural amnesia a form of group suicide—collective pain relief in what we fear is a meaning-less universe?

In advance of such a hollowed universe of random fictions, the twentieth-century architect le Corbusier already prided himself in redefining and redesigning the family hearth. The home was really a geometric shape with working parts, a "machine to live in," hardly a home for treasured knick-knacks and heirlooms or even children.[4] And now, assaulting what is inside the home, the radical secularists redefine even marriage itself. Each human body is only an individualistic unisex jacket randomly burdened with arbitrary plumbing accessories, like a digital device with one too many disposable apps. And now, accessory children can be added, or not, depending on whether they are preferred over puppies or maybe cats or cars.[5]

Natural children can even be replaced by genetically altered designer models. Playing with meaningless words, designer jeans lead to designer genes! Language can be flexible, but redefinition hasn't worked that well. A grade-letter C is not really an A performance (grade inflation); a trophy for "attendance" is not really an adolescent achievement, and a Nazi gas chamber is not really a "group shower facility." We enter a world of vocabulary demolition derby. Even the terms "dignity," "partner" and "marriage" get rear-ended.

A PULSE CHECK

In our unfolding scientific era, the seamless package of contraception, abortion and now open range gender theory all become the thin edge of a much larger wedge setting interest group politics against the scientific evidence itself. Part of the Big Lie is the false claim that at twenty weeks of age the unborn, whatever they are, feel no independent pain. As the Marxist Lenin once said of facts that contradict his theory, then "too bad for the facts." In early 1984 our newly re-elected President Ronald Reagan already felt the need to remark publicly that "[W]hen the lives of the unborn are snuffed out, they often feel pain—pain that is long and agonizing" (Washington D.C. convention of religious broadcasters). The prepackaged reaction of the American College of Obstetricians and Gynecologists was unscientific denial: "We are unaware of any evidence of any kind that would substantiate a claim of pain is perceived by the fetus."[6]

Two weeks later the medical profession, in the *Washington Times*, retracted its voodoo science and politically-correct un-awareness. But, today any state-level legislation to restrict abortions after the twentieth week still faces a stiff headwind. Harvested paralegal footnotes prevail over dismembered human footprints. Speaking to this moment, long ago it was asked, "Can judges who do evil be your friends? They do injustice under cover of law; they attack the life of the just and condemn innocent blood" (Psalm 94: 20-24).

The fetal child, now routinely excluded by our "concept of existence" and now deprived of perhaps a personal name, still exists. From the moment of conception our brothers and sisters have forty-six chromosomes and sixty thousand genes and over three billion base pairs of genetic code—all distinct from the mother. The child begins to pump its own blood at eighteen days and with a blood type often different from the mother's. At forty-two days the skeleton is complete and reflexes are present. The child demonstrates brain action before the end of the second month of gestation.

It is science that shows us this—with the technology of the EEG or electroencephalogram. Between the eighth and tenth week we find measurable activity in the thalamus area or pain center of the brain. At ten weeks the child sucks its thumb and has a heart rate of one-hundred twenty beats per minute. In 1969, astronaut Neil Armstrong wore and artificial-womb lunar space suit and tallied up a pulse of one-hundred fifty six (!) while navigating the first landing on the lunar surface. In this seemingly remote situation (also out of sight, out of mind?) his high count was still human: "one small step for man, one giant leap for mankind." As another small step for humanity, the still-in-the-womb child shows swallowing action by day seventy-seven, or the eleventh week. By this time a bright light placed on the mother's abdomen stimulates the child within to shield his eyes. Loud music has the same effect on tiny hand movements to cover the baby's ears. By the nineteenth week rapid eye movements (REM)—indications of waking, sleeping and dreaming—have been recorded.[7] Again, here is a human life totally *distinct* from the mother—a new person with potential, not simply a potential person.

The good news is that about a dozen states now at least prohibit abortions after twenty weeks, based on the fact that unborn children of this age do feel pain. The general federal threshold allowing state restrictions has been the arbitrary "age of viability" outside of the mother, or twenty-four weeks. Invasive action to abort the child elevates the tiny heartbeat of one-hundred twenty to two-hundred beats per minute when the menacing instruments of a suction abortion are introduced. The first evidence of this startling (and startled!) moment on a ten-week old child was an ultrasound film back in 1984 shown by New York physician Dr. Bernard Nathanson. Nathanson (author of *The Abortion Papers: Inside the Abortion Mentality,* 1983 and abortion czar in New York City) later held himself personally responsible for some sixty thousand "procedures." His image of the endangered child is the tiny whispering image documented as the "silent scream" in a movie and book of this title (American Portrait Films, 1995).

This evidence would not have escaped the keen interest of the nineteenth-century Charles Darwin who wrote of himself that the only talent he had was "an unusual power of noticing things which easily escape attention, and of observing them carefully." And where the fifth century B.C. Socrates taught that "the unexamined life is not worth living," the barbarian side of modernity asserts that the non-recognized life is not permitted to live.

In the ultrasound, the child of the silent scream recoiled to escape the execution of being drawn and quartered—reenacting the worst excesses of the Reign of Terror (1891-93) in revolutionary France. Eventually the forceps are inserted to remove the body parts. If the pregnancy is far enough along, the procedure requires first crushing the skull which is too large to remove intact. Suction curettage is the method described. Another method is called dilation and evacuation and requires an initial stage of multiple stab wounds.

After the fourteenth week the favored option involves injection of a highly concentrated saline solution into the amniotic sac. Forty-eight hours after this scalding death—which might take two hours—the child is expelled. For late-term abortions the method of choice (isn't abortion about choice?) is the injection of prostaglandin chemicals. These chemicals constrict the child's blood vessels and damage the heart function. Unless something goes "wrong," this induces a stillborn birth. Otherwise the live birth is either neglected on a table or, in some cases the partially born child was executed with scissor punctures to the skull during the birthing process. Despite a 2007 U.S. Supreme Court ruling, upholding Congressional action, an estimated eleven thousand late-term abortions are still performed each year.

MESSAGE MANAGEMENT

The language de jour for ending another human life thrives on euphemisms, slogans and cliches. Of the unborn—the stock phrases are "non-viable tissue" and "termination of pregnancy." Hospitals that provide maternity care are required to also provide abortions as part of the bundle of "reproductive services." In 2008 such bundling of bad financial debts with the good (the "derivatives" crisis) contaminated much of the banking system and eventually led to a global economic meltdown. Where billions of dollars are involved damage control and corrective actions are demanded, but not where the lives of millions of unborn children are involved.

The terms "safe sex", the "right to choose" and "sexually active" are the path not chosen by other apparently backward adolescents who see the better sense of self-mastery and growing maturity. But for those into the real-time readiness thing, the reality of fornication becomes "cohabitation" and sodomy is brightly "gay" (a pirated term that used to mean happiness, for anybody). We market the delete-key "morning after pill" which often works as a very early stage abortifacient. In the economy we replace former bulky computer parts with very tiny computer chips; in the medical world the morning after pill down-sizes the Auschwitz crematorium into the private medicine cabinet.

Ever advancing medical evidence threatens this primitive and legally imposed mental map that denies the existence of pre-born human life. The modern vocabulary becomes absurd. With politically correct euphemisms we steal the meaning of words, as we do at the retail counter with counterfeit clothing labels. The Big Lie is the United States Supreme Court allowing states to unreasonably force all pharmacists to supply morning after pills as a service, while at the same time all hospitals are reasonably not required to offer such services as neurosurgery or Magnetic Resonance Imagery (MRI) diagnostic capabilities.

What is the long-term price for accepting what is in fact a "culture of death"? What is the permanent and irreversible price to the unborn themselves? As part of the expanding Big Lie, what is the price of messaging, even in preschool years, a novel gender theory which sexualizes children at such a young and innocent age? Coupled with esteem management, we now induce identity insecurity with all of its psychological damage. We victimize the young at exactly the time in their lives when growing up normally already involves some loss of meaning and confidence or identity. Hit them while they're down and call this the freedom of the General Will.

Parental permission is needed to pierce a child's ears, or for tattoos, or for a single aspirin—but not to end the life of a child in a teen's womb. In the United States, fully one-third of pregnancies are aborted. By comparison, in the fourteenth century one-third of the population of Europe was swept away by a plague of a different sort. The doors of homes were thrown open each morning as the dead were collected and carted off to bon fires. What did one say to the surviving and traumatized children of that generation? Teach them a song—not unlike the mindless lyrics of many of today's pop and rap celebrity singers and the scripted reassurances of school therapists: "Ring around the rosie/a pocket full of posies/ashes, ashes/we all fall down." Yesterday, convert into a song the splotches of the plague, the flowers tearfully offered for the dead, the bonfire for the corpses, and the airborne ashes of the cremated. Soften and routinize the disaster by teaching the children to sing together. Desensitize and indoctrinate them with sexualized readings.

Today, as we define our "own concept of existence" and kill a third of the future generation, we also erase from memory all past generations. History is bunk, said the assembly-line Henry Ford. Today the therapy of the Big Lie calls for continuous denial and moving on. We "all fall down" into a penumbra of distractions supplied by the lucrative toys and gaming industry. The *Brave New World* (Aldous Huxley) is the supremacy of public manipulation driven by a steady dose of virtual reality, war game fantasies, transformer toys, mega-disaster reruns and, in general, the non-committed "reset" mentality. Spouses are replaceable parts and unborn children are often fully out of mind and out of luck. There is no need for stable depth perception and real attention if attention spans are reduced to near zero. At the cultural level, even in the 1950s twice as much was spent on advertising as on public school education.

Several years ago the media carried the story of a four-year old boy who had found is father's pistol and had shot and killed his little friend. "Don't worry, mommy," he explained, "Billy will come back again tomorrow to play." In our mind-numbed culture in an unhinged world random school shootings are now routine, abortions are routine, and "tragedies" of all kinds are a daily occurrence. All of this is reported 24/7 by always perky and smiley-button media talking heads as they chirp out one abomination after another like Bingo numbers. It's all about cosmetic news and prime time ratings. There will be other stories tomorrow to help us forget those of today.

A PARALLEL UNIVERSE

The most insidious messaging is subliminal suggestion. In the earliest years make sure that pre-school classes are the norm, and introduce such children's books as *Heather has two Mommies* (1989 and again after twenty years, in 2009) or *Jennifer has two Daddies*, or *Daddy's Roommate*, or *Billie has two Daddies*. Dozens of like books and others normalizing societal disintegration are out there now for children, some for ages three and up. Not to be out of date, little ones now are groomed toward the transgender sex-identity crisis in the picture book *I Am Jazz*. Might we call this indoctrination agenda NAMBLA-Lite? Gay and lesbian organizations now denounce the nearly defunct and pedophile North American Man/Boy Love Association (NAMBLA), but not so much all else that can be found under the covers of such books.

We can be assured that officially certified surrogate-parent teachers will march lockstep with the market-dominant publishers. The task is only technical, to indoctrinate our children on every detail of what a sex-fixated society and what bad people have in store for unwary children, and how to defend themselves. What else is there? Do our well-intention authority figures even suspect that they are often dealing with two coiled problems—predatory assaults on children *plus* state-sponsored early-age sexualization? How much is the first addressed by worsening the second? In protecting against predators have these clumsy social engineers from the education union never heard of imprinting? (Or, maybe they have. . . .)

We can be sure that at least some things will be censored. Too bad that it's Dr. Seuss whose childrens' stories remind us of the obvious, "A person is a person, no matter how small." Have we noticed how kiddy-book recruiting mimics the pitch made to adolescents in the 1990s by Big Tobacco? Or the similar method today of the marijuana industry as it markets laced candy? The dark side of modernity is a plague gone viral. This includes a crop of young and captive audiences to the textbook cartels. The abortion culture is only part of this much broader trend line.

During testimony at a public legislative hearing in Washington State in 2012, your author witnessed a key speaker in favor of a proposed gay "marriage" bill. Here was a quite handsome young man in white shirt and tie whose parents divorced when he was twelve. Having been shaped by his father's absence (another missing piece), he had recently met his father for whom he discovered that he now had a deep attachment. He testified that he would like to find an older man like his father to intimately share the rest of his life. The bobble heads of legislators nodded in compassionate sympathy.

Betrayed with poor nurturing, the young man is stuck in a zone where he chooses to live in a physically intimate relationship with a same-sex father figure. He would do this rather than be a father himself in a real marriage between a man and a woman. And he wants validation under state law. His being deprived of real nurturing *is* the problem, and yet we are tutored that as the solution this pattern should be (and is now) legalized—and imposed on all of society as the new worldview. Only moments before in the crowded front of the chamber two sympathetic male staffers, also in white shirts and ties, embraced each other with prolonged excitement, each chortling aloud without blushing, "I have 'straight' love. . . ."

Bracketing the public hearing later was a key legislator's brief stare-down of his colleagues, as he also faced the prime-time news camera. His surely scripted and postured message was that he and his partner demanded legal and public validation as a (redefined) marriage because of its "intimacy." Then came a pregnant pause. Is there nothing original here? In the social anonymity of the 1960s it was *private* intimacy that was the poster-child justification for cohabitation. Under the new dispensation only mandatory *public* endorsement and compliance will do. As a concession to reality, real marriage is to remain as an antique-store option on the "tolerant" spectrum. To advance this cause our state legislator had taken full advantage of his position as chair of the senate budget committee. Challenged by later initiative, and against an opposition too little and too late, the "civil rights" mantra stuck and the movement won the popular vote. Only then did the novelty pass muster in an inevitable wash of other states. Such is the arc of history.

A left-of-center media poll (CNN/ORC International) in 2015 reported a shifting tide among American citizens, with about sixty percent now thinking that gay "marriage" is accurately branded as a signature "civil rights" issue. Because individuals as persons are due protection against discrimination, we are instructed that the homosexual lifestyle—a behavior—is a constitutional right on a par with the personal integrity of religion or national origin. No politicized cause will be left behind. If virtually anything can be rolled into civil rights, then instead of the keen-sighted bald eagle, perhaps the national emblem should be the tumble bug. The solid morality against pre-marital sex has long been gagged as an oddity and maneuvered into exile by the popular culture, and is now rendered incomprehensible by the redefinition of "marriage."

As for public opinion polls in general . . . do most of us really have well-formed opinions on everything that is polled on a daily basis? Or instead of opinions have we reverted mostly to impressions? Lest we forget, governance by "pollsters" came into use in the mid-twentieth century precisely because the term sounded so much like hucksters. One is reminded of a species of fish in the ocean caves on the West Coast of Mexico. These fish have also evolved backwards. In the total dark they have no eyes at all. They just move things along by nosing around in the flow of events and bumping into whatever they need. Like the modern world, their only absolute is absolute darkness. "And if the light in you is darkness, how great will the darkness be" (Matthew 6:23).

The only operative principle is pragmatism—"what works and what doesn't work as we move forward." Forward? In 2012 a young woman in the Seattle area donned the veil and "married" a landmark brick building that had captured her affection. What further need is there for proof—as with the spectrum definition of marriage, the only difference between a woman and a man is the plumbing, and even this can be remodeled like any kitchen or bathroom.

Public impressions often go no deeper than slogans and name recognition. At the same time as the 2015 media poll of shifting views on gay "marriage," a scientific survey by the American Council of Trustees and Alumni (ACTA) found that eighty percent of college graduates do not even know when Abraham Lincoln lived. Just one dead white dude among so many! Nearly the same percentage (72 percent, civil rights advocates one and all) do not know the meaning of Lincoln's Emancipation Proclamation. More than a third of those surveyed did not even know with accuracy when the Civil War took place. Someday in a society more enlightened than our own, our exchange of study for leisure might be compared to the seventh-century destruction of the irreplaceable library of Alexandria. Of this disaster it is written that the burned scrolls and timbers were sufficient to heat the water in the four thousand baths in the city and that the fuel was enough for a full six months.[8]

The picture today is not complicated. We live in real time. In countless small steps backward we have brainwashed ourselves of the past and the future, and in this have abandoned and betrayed our own children. We erase our own history and then go neutral or worse on vital moral questions where history might give us a clue. Today everything and everybody is trapped in amnesiac real time, a "culture of the temporary." Perspective and commitment—as in the permanence of marriage and family—are out the window.

Too often real time means instant gratification, limited human memory and discernment, and even less of a sense of the future as a goal. The world of real-time has removed any sense of real commitment from the world. The only permanent "commitment" left intact is probably a life term in prison without parole.

Many members of the abandoned and even victimized Millennial Generation no longer suspect that marriage is more basic and precedes the existence of Nintendo or of government-awarded entitlements (now including generic marriage licenses). Parents betray their children and children betray their parents. The young and all of us no longer understand or appreciate why a florist, a human being no different than ourselves, will risk a punitive fine and loss of livelihood to avoid providing bouquets for a gay marriage. In Coliseum days Christians were martyred because they refused to toss a pinch of ash toward the pagan deities or a shrine of the Emperor. How else to ensure the unity of public consensus and divine favor? Today the litmus test is a flower petal.

The penalty for conscientious objection is forced conformity to the popular culture, elitist courtroom edicts, orchestrated show trials in the clannish media, and deconstruction of the constitutional First Amendment freedom of religion. Church-state relations are as intricate and volatile now as ever. Especially since a superficial and national religion of Secular Humanism is now established by the United States Supreme Court, e.g., from *Roe v. Wade* to *Obergefell v. Hodges* (of which more in Chapter 8). The First Amendment restrains Congress from establishing a national religion, but the Founding Fathers never guessed at the need to restrain the other two branches of government.

Does anyone even remember from recent history what a "show trial" is? In communist-overrun countries dissidents were falsely charged, falsely tried, and falsely condemned—all publicly staged—not to serve justice but to instruct the captive audience masses. Disruptions today are now to be shunted aside as homophobia. In the long run, the standoff is not even about religious liberty so much as it is about the universal natural law evident down through the ages. A sad sign of our times, is it not, that realism about human nature finds its last defenders only our battered religious institutions? One might search history in vain to find another topic so insistent on the right to privacy to justify the gay lifestyle, and yet that is so demanding of absolute public validation and endorsement. Dissent—or affirmation of natural law— is "homophobia." Likewise, when a Catholic priest at the altar (!) in Normandy is beheaded by a radical Islamist during a religious liturgy, where is the outrage from Western civilization? Is there a Western civilization? Muffled short-term reporting at best, confined to page three and even wondering whether this is only a hate crime, or maybe a civil crime instead of international terrorism by a radical Islamic sect. In a phobia-phobic world, do the mainstream media dare being labeled as Islamophobic?

Closer to home, again, to ensure that nobody who still matters is offended, on marriage licenses the masculine husband and feminine wife are now branded generically as Spouse A and Spouse B. This, even as homosexual (sic male) partners arbitrarily refer to each other as either "husband" or "wife." Conjugal unity is redefined as two males pretending that one of them is female. Mother and father are replaced with "parents." The scholar and writer, Anthony Esolen from Providence College (and demonized as a bigot), says it all. Speaking of our mental abuse especially of the young, he says:

> These are the people who should be first in our minds, these boys and girls. The world we've given them is worse than squalid. It is mad. The boy knows nothing about soldiering, but a lot about sodomy—more than his grandfather knew even after his turn of duty in the world war. The girl knows nothing about ovens or looms or pianos or poetry, but plenty about diaphragms, spermacides, and condoms. The boy and girl yawn at old-fashioned fornication, laugh at the Bible, and blush to admit that they blush over anything.[9]

How many addictions are really symptoms of failed experiences in true "belonging" as in real families? Why do an increasing number of the young and others "choose" to bunker down in mutually incoherent bubble worlds? The hanging-out subculture points its members to the school therapists and health professionals who then regiment them toward after-school abortion clinics conveniently co-located near shopping malls. The cultural center of our world is the shopping mall! The young are coaxed into buying this or that, they learn to download term papers from the Internet, in a culture modeled by inside trader scandals and worse, and they can also choose in a few minutes after school to download their "pregnancies" into bed pans. The Big Lie is that truth is whatever seems to work or the moment.

DISSECTING THE BIG LIE

Let's take a closer look at the Big Lie. The Big Lie has created health departments to groom students through explicit questionnaires on a full range of sexual activity, still claiming that "without that [sic] data, we are not sure" what issues to address. Not sure about the issues and not sure about anything else either.

The Big Lie is a Presidential Commission for the Study of Bioethical Issues reconstituted in 2010 to no longer to ask whether something *ought* or *ought not* to be done, but only *how* it can be done most efficiently. It is a commission that in 2015 concluded that national quarantine policies against the global threat of Ebola should be based on science,[10] but then remains silent on abortion policies and the scientific evidence of elementary embryology and the ultrasound.

The Big Lie detects no difference between marriage parity and a parody of marriage, between marriage and mirage, between a real human right and a manufactured legal rite. It sounds the same. The Big Lie condones the non-recognition of Christian student groups on our college campuses while rubber stamping even duplicative radical groups.

The Big Lie is the double standard of demonizing (with some just cause) the roughly top one percent on the economic system while, at the same time, championing the LGBTQ lifestyle and demonizing and bullying as "homophobes" a different ninety-nine percent or so who represent the historic and natural understanding of marriage.

The legal profession and the Federal Government would reduce the First Amendment right to freedom of religion (and broader defense of the natural law) in the public square to a once-hour-a-week "freedom of worship" in church building ghettos. The federal *Religious Freedom Restoration Act* (RFRA, 1993), with parallel legislation in twenty states, is immediately met with interstate business boycotts, aka establishment blackmail. Recent history shows us that the difference between freedom of religion and freedom of worship is cousin to the difference between democracy and a police state.

The Big Lie is a cult of seeming "tolerance" that prohibits discrimination against its pet issues, but then mandates reverse discrimination against reasoned and religiously-defended moral codes. The President Obama Administration (2008-16) decreed that every school district in the land must open all bathroom doors to transgender students or else risk the loss of all federal funds (*New York Times*, May 13, 2016).

And states that might decline to march lockstep on open transgender access to any bathroom might find themselves at risk of losing federal tax support for everything from education to highways (*New York Times*, April 2, 2016). Street level bullying is prosecuted but politically accepted if federally mandated. If this kind of blackmail works with foreign aid then why not on the home front? A "no fly" zone is proposed for Iraq, but on the home front is removed from the girls' bathroom.

Meanwhile, the Big Lie abortion industry is illustrated by the former director of a particular Texas abortion clinic. She confided (in 2009) to the public that her end game was to become a millionaire. This repentant confession came after opening an unused Bible, and after an admitted thirty-five thousand abortions performed on teenage girls in her clinic. The scam: a predator is given privileged access to infiltrate schools with the message of sexual "readiness," and a business card. Promiscuous teens then were furnished with deliberately low-dose contraceptives. A second and third and fifth return visit placed the financial goal within reach.[11]

Apart from the possibly well-intended and clueless minions in the abortion clinics, at the top of the abortion industry is big money. No one makes money in the pro-life movement. The big money is in contraceptives and abortions. In 2010 a director of a clinic in Houston finally viewed an ultrasound abortion and only then comprehended the Planned Parenthood agenda when it proposed a new facility for late-term abortions up to twenty-four weeks. The price to play jumps to three or four thousand dollars a head compared to early-term abortions. [12]

In 2015 corporate America formally positioned itself in favor of gay "marriage" as well. As broadly reported and rewarded in the media, AT&T and Verizon, Dow Chemical, Bank of America, General Electric, Coca-Cola and Pepsi, Google, Apple, Facebook and Microsoft, and the San Francisco Giants, were among nearly four hundred agenda-assimilated corporations and business organizations that weighed in. Together they spontaneously filed their own legal argument asserting a constitutional right to the oxymoron same sex "marriage." The reason: stock market numbers might benefit marginally from spending patterns! By this capitulation to the homosexual narrative the business world has given an entirely new meaning to the term: bottom line.

As for the corporate Profit Motive, the current annual drain on national spending—absent more homosexual households—is "an estimated cost to the Gross National Product of over one billion dollars per year." Earlier in the year corporate bottom-liners reported that a year-long dip of just one cent per gallon of gasoline at the pump also tallies up to the same amount, a billion dollars of freed-up alternative spending. Add this amount to the real-time credit card debt of a whopping seven-hundred billion dollars. Multiplied thirty-fold, the sought-after new market niche (one billion dollars) is only one percent of the annual federal budget. At seventeen trillion dollars, not counting unfunded liabilities of ten times this amount, the national debt is twenty-thousand times as great.

Let's take this line of thinking a step further. For a corporate America and others committed to redefining the natural and Christian understanding of the human person, sex and traditional "marriage," why not deal equally with the Islamic forty-day pilgrimage event at Mecca (the *hajj*)? Why not institute a forty-day NASCAR race and, of course, label this novelty as part of a redefined and more inclusive *hajj*? Or, to better assimilate Judaism into Secular Humanism, why not market a seven-barreled Roman Candle for the national Fourth of July celebration? Society must be moved further away from anything even remotely Roman (as in Catholic). The last residues of discrimination will not be done away with until the civil courts mutilate the definition of seven-branched Jewish menorah. Peddled as "civil rights," the market value of these diversity reforms would certainly exceed a billion dollars a year for GNP, particularly in spin-off litigation against dissenting "bigots."

In the political arena, the Big Lie is the words of New York Governor Mario Cuomo who in his private conscience—and following the lead of the earlier and evasive President Jack Kennedy—could not see the difference between the universal natural law and any defense that might be offered by one church or another or by reason alone. To defend this truth about humanity, he argued (in 1984), would be to impose his Church's morality on all of society and would constitute a sectarian "Catholic theocracy." And yet in truth, "the Church is in no way the author or the arbiter of this [moral] norm . . . [she] proposes it to all people of good will. . . ."[13]

The entire multitude of decked-out and double-life politicians of today does not measure up well against the reasoned conviction of a single sixteenth-century martyr to self-serving state power, Thomas More. To the get-along-go-along majority, he proposed this: "I believe, when statesmen forsake their own private conscience for the sake of their public duties ...they lead their country by a short route to chaos."

Following the first Cuomo, the next-generation Governor Andrew Cuomo, a fully retailored modern-day theocrat of Secular Humanism, dropped the other shoe when he announced in 2014 that those who oppose abortion and gay "marriage" (that is, affirm life and man-and-woman marriage) "are not welcome in New York." More recently (2016), it is reported that the New York City Commissioner on Human Rights declared no less than thirty-one kinds of sexual identity. He ("he") wants the use of the "non-binary" spectrum "zie" in place of "he" and "she," and threatens heavy fines for not following the new script. How very sophisticated . . . are we now to suppose that the basic moral distinction between right and wrong, between good and evil, is also just a "binary" mindset and nothing more?

At the international level hospitality is sometimes less putty-like than in New York. The LGBTQ advocates were still welcome at the 2014 Moscow Olympics, but they were not allowed to hijack the non-political event into a factional and politicized platform. Likewise in 2016 was the Chinese response to the openly homosexual and aggressive mayor of Seattle. He embarked on an international business and "cultural" mission to the Far East, partly to market gay "marriage." China exercised its right to not officially honor his "husband" who then opted out of the trip "due to a personal matter." Said the mayor: "One of the biggest statements we could have made was Michael being treated as a First Gentleman, something that we made clear to the Chinese government had to happen."[14] As a fitting contribution to real cultural dialogue—more than any imperial and predictable statement—a Chinese emperor once was asked what he would do to save his country. His answer: "I will restore the meaning of words."

The battle over words is more than semantic. It's more than what's in *Webster's Dictionary*. It's about those who would rearrange the external world of others because internally they won't arrange themselves. The Big

Lie can be a six-digit legal penalty every time an outsider to Secular Humanism at a bakery refuses extortion, every time she declines private business
services for a parody of marriage. If Planned Parenthood (about five hundred
million dollars each year) can market human body parts as economically
useful "tissue," then why should cake dough and frosting be treated any
differently?

The Big Lie is the partnership of Socialism and the science of early brain
development used to replace family time with expanded public education for
pre-school children. And at the university level, rather than fostering mature
debate as with a mix including "conservative" commencement speakers, the
university culture redefines itself as a "safe zone" free of such challenge. All
the better to extend high-priced day care centers into the late adolescent
years. No wonder the "occupy" movement becomes the chosen method of
discourse. Occupy Wall Street, occupy the university administration building, occupy main street during rush hour, but do not presume to occupy the
womb of your own mother.

Conservative values need not be stereotyped as an ideology allergic to
thought or as the enemy of long-term global stewardship. It was President
Theodore Roosevelt (a Republican) who is known in American history as the
corporation "trust-buster" and the founder of the ecologically-attuned National Park System. Today how might we instill a less intolerant tolerance
and greater diversity of thought at more of our campus collectives?

The Big Lie is the more established sequestering of the elderly into age-
specific barracks alongside the potted plants. They become as invisible as
pre-born children and some of the elderly are the unwitting victims of the
same veterinary ethics. The ethics of the contraceptive spay-neuter clinic is
marketed to teens and then later in life euthanasia shows us through another
door of legalized, self-administered physician-assisted suicide (PAS). In
Washington State, Oregon, Vermont, Montana, California and parts of Europe a quick exit is already offered. PAS is legalized only as a very curious
statutory exemption from standard homicide laws. [15]

That PAS resorts to such an exemption is a fascinating admission. But
after all, how can we submit the unborn to our "choice" if we are not willing
to make the same choice for ourselves? What could be more equal than this?
But already in Europe involuntary euthanasia is routinely documented, especially in Belgium and the Netherlands. What was unthinkable only a few
years ago is becoming routine. Lurking in the wings are legal attacks against
conscience clauses respectful of principled non-participation in abortion, euthanasia, transvestite operations and whatever—a fearful threat to both the
general public and especially medical professionals.

The Big Lie was a "community organizer" President in the White House
deciding in 2013 not to attend the 150th Anniversary celebration of President
Abraham Lincoln's *Gettysburg Address*. Is it because this address traces our

national origin back to a Creator and certain inalienable rights ("four score and seven years ago" points to 1776), rather than to a government apparatus and a Constitution (1787) academically decapitated from this real origin? Or is it because ninety-nine percent of the casualties in a war ultimately for Emancipation were white? Something else? Whatever.

The Big Lie is also his appointed United States Attorney General refusing to defend the *Defense of Marriage Act* (passed in 1996) and then signaling his state counterparts that they were equally free to skip their obligation to defend dozens of voted state-level protections of traditional marriage. A legal regime that does not speculate about pre-born children need not trouble itself with something so trivial as marriage.

The Big Lie is the United States Supreme Court (*United States v. Windsor*) in 2013 gutting the *Defense of Marriage Act* passed by Congress. Swing vote Justice Anthony Kennedy pedaled his own heterophobic hate speech when he pronounced in the majority ruling that the historical and natural status of traditional marriage is actually rooted in "homophobia." Parroting the get-along-go-along consensus emanating from Wall Street boardrooms, the people and their Congress are reminded that they are to be tutored and herded, but not heard.

On main street America the site of the Stonewall gay bar incident of the late 1960s now is elevated to the rank of a national monument (2016), while a decade ago a front yard monument to the Ten Commandments was ordered taken down at an Alabama courthouse. The Big Lie is the tale that there is no pattern here, that there is no trend line of removal and substitution. An apt monument: "stonewalling."

The Big Lie is nongovernmental organizations (NGOs) and United Nations committees (not the Assembly) seeking to override sovereign countries by mandating non-binding "guidance" by UN bureaucrats for abortion as an international "right" to "eradicate social barriers in terms of norms and beliefs" about homosexuality; to impose immoral "sex education;" to offer sexual health services to minors; to nullify conscientious objection protections for health care providers and insurers, and so on.[16]

The Big Lie is a former President of the United States actually acting out the Big Lie with hands-on experience, so to speak, with an intern right there in the Oval Office of the White House. You just can't trust people who live in public housing. The denial under oath appealed to the sophisticated perjury that "(I)t all depends on what the meaning of 'is' is." Another falsehood moment not wasted. The Big Lie says to our youth that desire is what is, and that what is, is right.

At about this time, by Christmas of 1997, I was long-employed by an intergovernmental agency. A passing remark was made in the hallway—in the main lobby might a menorah be displayed in addition to the decorated tree? A simple "yes" was above the pay grade of the "management team."

Instead came much hand wringing and then the oracle that to avoid offending anyone the lobby tree must not happen. So then, "might a token poinsettia, at least, be retained on the lobby coffee table?" Another closed door session for a management team beyond its depth . . . a generic white poinsettia would be okay, but not a red one which bespeaks too much of religious content. Another scene patterned after George Orwell's *Animal Farm*: "white poinsettia good, red poinsettia bad." In this contrived outpost of politically correctness, the most offended was our Jewish friend and colleague: "I intended none of this!"

There was the risk that "a member of the visiting public might be offended!" But by now nothing less than the managerial image was also at stake. Another layer of deception: the notion that managing people is the same thing as managing issues. Thus it came to pass that the office lobby was marked not unlike the way territories in the wilds are marked. Finally a generic "holiday wreath" rather than a watered bush. This tale of strained neutrality in the faces of a captive audience would be comical were it not a microcosm of our heralded social evolution. The microcosm was made complete with staff permission to display red and green in their isolated and standardized cubicles.

Social evolution is the Big Lie. Fresh from the university and at the front of a standing-room-only bus yours truly stepped up to offer his seat to a Black lady. She smiled and accepted. Near the same time the same was done for a younger white lady, and she rebelled and cursed loudly enough to be heard in the back seats. Mine was seen as condescending gesture against equality. A few decades later (2016) a Black celebrity athlete speaking at a mostly-Black high school (again in Seattle) urged students to expect husbands to defend wives from harassment. He is heckled by a member of the audience who then walks out for implying that women can't stand up for themselves. The speaker, a survivor of a near fatal brainstem injury, is left twisting and turning by brainstem social evolution: "I didn't *feel comfortable* staying," she said.

THE SLIPPERY SLOPE

The Big Lie is legion in its very, very human omissions, disguises, audacity and discourtesies of all stripes. The deliberate goal of some is to deconstruct reality, to force society politically and legally to live in their self-validating bubble. Such is the delusion of a self-appointed vanguard elite. To tally up the list as has been begun here is to risk branding as racist, a xenophobe, a homophobe, a sexist male Caucasian bigot, and as a likely target for yet another round of predatory litigation. *In our upside-down world where there is no truth, to affirm even the idea of truth is to offer oneself to the most litigious subculture in the history of the world.* The theory of social evolution is the full employment act for a glut of law school graduates lusting after a corner office with windows.

The first steps in this novel direction of free-form morality came early. First, it was child-proofed free love, then no-fault divorce, then the late 60s open range sexual revolution, and then the *Roe v. Wade* court endorsement of abortion on demand in 1973. The evolved redefinition of reality was already far advanced long before advocates of gay marriage ever seized the "bully" pulpit. The LGBTQ demographics are more a symptom of moral free fall than the problem.[17]

To have settled for "civil unions" rather than "marriage" could have achieved to goal of civil recognition without igniting what is now a permanent political, social and cultural crisis. The voting public (and the Church) was even reassured in statements to the press that the campaign to recognize civil unions was not a half-way house to demanding gay "marriage." But such recognition was never the end game, so this assurance, too, was a lie. The public now is told that extending marriage recognition to gay couples "will not deprive anyone of any rights." This probably is accurate, because freedom of religion is targeted to be de-legitimized as a right by the courts.

In Canada, where gay "marriage" was federally mandated in 2005, after ten years the legal persecution of "homophobia" is epidemic. Not to be outdone, in 2016 the U.S. Commission on Civil Rights issued a report concluding that antidiscrimination laws should have greater weight than religious freedom which should be framed as threat to civil rights. In releasing the document, the chairman of the commission, Martin Castro, branded religious freedom as "code words for discrimination, intolerance, racism, sexism, homophobia, Islamophobia, Christian supremacy, or any form of intolerance."[18] In this composite cliché do we see a mindset of multiform infection, something like the mutant and variable strains of HIV (human immunodeficiency virus)?

The Big Lie is also the 2002 sex scandal—those victimized in past decades by some of the Catholic priesthood and by the negligence of some higher-ups. (Over ninety-six percent of past priests were *not* implicated.) Payouts have mounted into the billions of dollars, but widespread sexual abuse in the medical profession and public schools remains mysteriously underreported.[19] No deep pockets? Even the energetic atheist Richard Dawkins identified the media feeding frenzy as "unfair," and it had only begun (*The God Delusion*, 2006).

But then there's the role of artful branding in the 2002 sex scandal. Even years after the broad and independent research was commissioned, an important and publicly released finding of *The John Jay Report* (John Jay College of Criminal Justice, 2003) goes unnoticed. It shows that most (seventy-eight percent) of the priest abuses involved young men eleven years old and above, rather than very young children. Yet, the headline from a media, with its own cultural agenda, is still "pedophilia" rather than something else more fitting of an older age group.

A thin, silver lining in the Church sex-abuse scandal might be that as overdue as it was for correction, it hit the headlines in 2002 rather than, say, 2015. It is the secular Establishment that now grooms society toward moral blandness—a unisex fantasy where even the natural vocation of real "marriage" is rinsed away. For this broader "social evolution" we can look to get-along-go-along corporate board rooms and social engineering in public agencies and even abuse of the military as social experiment (gagging of Christian chaplains, and mandatory transgender training), and courtroom edicts. Some day it won't be only conspiracy theorists who detect a movement's three-pronged strategy to redefine traditional morality as a mandatory civil right. A fringe lifestyle has infiltrated and neutered our public institutions and private institutions, but after much damage it finds itself still not in command of a third institution, the Church. In 2015 a global synod of bishops spoke with uncharacteristic candor to the issue of "gay marriage": "there are absolutely no grounds for considering homosexual unions to be in any way similar or even remotely analogous to God's plan for marriage."[20]

Even common sense demands a voice here—real marriage is *binary* between males and females (a binary unity), something like real business with double-entry bookkeeping, or evolution as a joining of internal genetics with external factors, or research and real science as the meeting of what we know with what we don't know, and yes, philosophy and theology as the fit between always-finite human minds with the infinite. The Revelation is that the infinite has a name and a face and a place in human history.

Asked for reasons behind any battered hope we might have for the future—or why "whatever" is not enough—we are to be "ever ready to reply, but [to] speak gently and respectfully" (1 Peter 3:15-16). Again, when we still listen one-on-one, we often hear that the root of widespread malaise and anger is the gut feeling from the millennials as a generation is that they have been—abandoned. Abandonment is an incubator for all distractions, desperation, narcissism, and addictions. Historically, primitive societies appeased such cosmic fears by tossing young virgins into volcanoes, and today we seem to do much the same. Today modern therapeutic society as a whole backs away from the Creator-God and into the hollow Crater of Secular Humanism.

At the 2015 World Meeting on Families held in Philadelphia the depth of this crater was surveyed by David Warren, pastor of the Saddleback Church:

> In today's society, materialism is idolized, immorality is glamorized, truth is minimized, sin is normalized, divorce is rationalized, and abortion is legalized. In TV and movies, crime is legitimized, drug use is minimized, comedy is

vulgarized, and sex is trivialized. In movies, the Bible is fictionalized, churches are satirized, God is marginalized, and Christians are demonized. The elderly are dehumanized, the sick are euthanized, the poor are victimized, the mentally ill are ostracized, immigrants are stigmatized, and children are tranquilized. In families around the world, our manners are uncivilized, speech is vulgarized, faith is secularized, and everything is commercialized.

The war waged by Secular Humanism on the unborn, on traditional marriage, and on the family is the Big Lie. The Big Lie is the archaic "war on women" alive and well, but simply in a new form tailored to modern folklore and technology. Weighing the spiritual collapse of the West, in our own day Solzhenitsyn remarked in a New York City speech in 1975: "We are approaching a major turning point in world history, in the history of civilization. . . . It is a juncture at which settled concepts suddenly become hazy, lose their precise contours, at which our familiar and commonly used words lose their meaning, become empty shells. . . ."[21]

And, appearing before a judge finally for a felony sentencing, a young millennial was asked: "Didn't anyone ever teach you right from wrong?" His wide-eyed answer: "no."

NOTES

1. Mark de Wolfe, ed., *The Pollock-Holmes Letters*, 1874-1932 (Cambridge, England: Cambridge University Press, 1942), Vol. 2, p. 36.

2. Under the Administrative State, as of 2010 forward, such compulsions include: withdrawal of federal funds from the U.S. Bishops anti-human trafficking program because contraception is not included; the Health and Human services requirement for faith-based entities to provide for abortion, contraceptives and sterilization; businesses forced to participate in gay "marriages;" adoption entities forced to close their doors or not placing children in same sex partnerships; and and forced public participation through the tax system (see for example, "The Secularist Assault on America's Moral Consensus," *Catalyst* (Catholic League, May 2016).

3. Robert Bolt, *A Man for All Seasons* (New York: Vintage Books, 1962), 93.

4. For a critical analysis of the architectural International Style, see E. Michael Jones, *Living Machines: Bauhaus Architecture as Sexual Ideology* (San Francisco: Ignatius Press, 1995), and Tom Wolfe, *From Bauhaus to Our House* (New York: Farrar Straus Giroux, 1981).

5. To advance this agenda, even the American Psychological Association (Committee on Lesbian, Gay and Bisexual Concerns, LBG Committee) has fallen in line be discounting and excluding scientific research that might weaken the propped-up consensus that the children of lesbian or gay parents suffer no emotional damage. On this culture of harm denial, see D. Paul Sullins, "Truth and Anti-truth: Faith, Reason, and Rhetoric in the Public Square," *Catholic Social Science Review* (Society of Catholic Social Scientists, 2016), 207-217.

6. *New York Times*, January 31, 1984. Thirty years later, in November 2014, the Quinnipiac University Poll found that sixty percent of registered voters would support a law such as the Pain Capable Unborn Child Protection Act prohibiting abortion after twenty weeks, while only thirty-three percent opposed such legislation.

7. These and the following accounts are based on Patrick Kaler, C.SS.R., *The Silent Screams: Abortion and Fetal Pain* (Liguori Publications, 1984).

8. Daniel Haskel, *Chronological View of the World*, (New York: J. H. Colton, 1846), 91.

9. Anthony Esolen, "Suffer the Children," *Touchstone* (Chicago: Fellowship of St. James, March/April 2015), 3-4.

10. Lauran Neergaard, "Quarantine decisions should be based on science, ethics panel says," Associated Press, Feb. 27, 2015.

11. Carol Everett, "Highlights" television interview, May 8, 2009. Additional stories by a different and former Texas abortion clinic worker are recounted in Abby Johnson, *The Walls are Talking* (San Francisco: Ignatius, 2016).

12. Abby Johnson, *Unplanned,* (Tyndale House Publishers, 2010).

13. Pope St. John Paul II, *Veritatis Splendor* (*the Splendor of the Truth,* n. 95), 1993, citing *Familiaris Consortio* (*The Community of the Family*, n. 33), 1981; and for Catholics he asserts that "*the right of the faithful* to receive Catholic doctrine in its purity and integrity must always be respected" (n. 133, italics in the original).

14. Daniel Beekman, *Seattle Times*, May 7, 2016, Section B.

15. Multiculturalists might begin to notice that Islamic folk literature also consists of liberal appeals to exceptions. In fixed his attention on a Coptic slave girl and even on the wife of his adopted son, Mohammed discovered exceptions for himself from other entries in the *Qur'an*. We might begin to ask, in their contempt for the natural law, how are Western elites any different?

16. The embedded United Nations anti-family agenda is monitored by the Center for Family and Human Rights (C-Fam), 1730 Rhode Island Ave. NW, Suite 212, Washington D.C. 20036, www.c-fam.org.

17. Here the term "demographics" is plural because the composite LGBT "community" is a political invention. Theoretically, the included "transgender" (T) demographic is different. It may be the one person in ten thousand of the total societal population actually affected by a pre-birth abnormality. Some propose that a real transexual affliction might be due to a mismatch between fetal physical sexuality and obstructed later chemical development in the brain (British Broadcasting Corporation [BBC], Part 2, "Your First Nine Months," July 2016). In such cases would the desire to feel "comfortable" in bathroom access rise to the level of a constitutional right canceling the rights of the affected other 99.99 percent of the population? The broadened term "transgender" is itself a political construction to include those with only a psychological orientation toward surgical mutilation.

18. "Peaceful Coexistence: Reconciling Nondiscrimination Principles with Civil Liberties," Sept. 17, 2016; reported by Joan Desmond, "Claim: Religious Freedom Threatens Civil Rights," *National Catholic Register*, Oct. 2, 2016.

19. The *Associated Press* documented 2,570 cases of *reported* sexual misconduct in schools in only a five-year period, between 2001 and 2005, with students being two-thirds of the victims (Martha Irwine and Robert Tanner, October 21, 7007). In a review of all fifty states, the *Atlanta Journal-Constitution* reported 2,400 doctors sanctioned for abusing patients, but with half retaining their licenses ("License to Betray," July 6, 2016). Both cited and linked in Carl E. Olson, "More Sex Abuse Scandals", *Catholic World Report*, July 10, 2016.

20. Synod of Bishops, "The Vocation and Mission of the Family in the Church and in the Contemporary World," (Vatican City, October 2015), n. 76.

21. Aleksandr Solzhenitsyn, *Warning to the West* (New York: Farrar, Straus and Giroux, 1976), 79.

Chapter Three

"Nevertheless, It Moves"

As the cardinal invited to Rome in 2012 to launch the Year of Faith, American Cardinal Donald Wuerl summarized our Big Lie dumped in the laps of the Millennial Generation—confusion or not even being told right from wrong (or sometimes not listening . . .). He said: "It is as if a tsunami of secular influence has swept across the cultural landscape, taking with it such societal markers as marriage, family, the concept of the common good and objective right and wrong." As a fresh revolution this abandonment falls in line with other radical revolutions in history.

The quest for a radical version of "equality" is often a camouflage for uprisings against something so basic as fatherhood and, ultimately, the very idea of a providential God. The revolution in France and then the Reign of Terror (1791-93) beheaded an imperfect past and then genuflected before "liberty, equality—and fraternity."

Clan fraternity replaces the bond of paternity. Breathes there anyone who still thinks that the woman-priest movement in the Church is about equality rather than removal of the "priesthood" altogether? Such was unwittingly confided by one nun to the press already in the 1970s. Another nun still valued her pastor—because "he affirmed my okay-ness." The only equality offered by the Big Lie is the damage done equally to fatherhood, motherhood and childhood. Social evolution: instead of the apostolic Church we are to await a therapeutic mutual admiration society.

Where George Washington is the "father of our country," the French Robespierre was a ringleader of the Terror. The Terror shortened the king by a head, and Robespierre wanted to do the same thing to church steeples because they violated the radical equality of a flat-earth skyline. Over two centuries earlier, Johann von Leyden mandated the same in Germany's Muenster, site of his wife-swapping utopia of the early Reformation. He

enforced polygamy and took sixteen wives of his own. The identical decapitation of church crosses is underway across Communist China today (*New
York Times*, May 23, 2016) as natural fatherhood is replaced across the globe
by paternalistic state as the go-to-guy. In the West "equality" mocks fatherhood in television sitcoms and commercials and idealizes the progressive
feminization of popular culture. Where identity politics is the new idol,
fatherless boys question their own identity.

FATHERHOOD ON TRIAL: THE PERFECT STORM

The Big Lie is the habit of thinking in terms of new and old and left and
right, rather than true and false. Too often this sleight-of-hand blurs the truth
radically and politically in order to redefine its meaning. The Big Lie used to
be known more accurately as sin—sin being not merely this or that transgres-
sion, but the death of the good of the soul and "the misuse of power given to
us by God to do good" (St. Basil the Great). The twentieth century Russian
cultural critic and political dissident, Aleksandr Solzhenitsyn who spent
many years freezing and starving in a Siberian prison camp, put it this way:

> Men have forgotten God . . . the line dividing good and evil cuts through the
> heart of every human being. . . . The concepts of good and evil have been
> ridiculed for several centuries; banished from common use, they have been
> replaced by political or class considerations of short-lived value. It has become
> embarrassing to appeal to eternal concepts, embarrassing to state that evil
> makes its home in the individual human heart before it enters the political
> system.[1]

Robespierre was a key mover and shaper of the French Revolution before
it got totally out of hand and turned on him as well. His inadequate sense of
fatherhood was probably shaped by his own out-of-wedlock birth. He was
abandoned by his own father. The influential philosopher, Jean Jacques
Rousseau, trumpeted political equality while also abandoning his own illegitimate children to orphanages. Today the psychologist Paul Vitz researches
such nihilists or atheists as Friedrich Nietzsche and our modern evolutionary
biologist and atheist Richard Dawkins. He finds that in neither case "do we
find a strong, beloved father with a close relationship with his son or daughter." Even the atheist Sigmund Freud said that psychoanalysis "daily demonstrates to us how youthful persons lose their religious belief as soon as the
authority of the father breaks down."[2] Authority as in authorship, not blind
power. The new twist today is that this outcome has become a poorly disguised agenda.

The Big Lie leads up to population collapse in many parts of the Western
world. Legitimate and urgent concern for the natural ecology has eclipsed the

same kind of attention to the more urgent and important "human ecology" (see Chapter 8). The human ecology differs in both degree and kind from any natural ecology. But they connect and the comparison is still helpful. The human ecology is less shaped by instinct than by the unity of the human person. The whole human being is capable of acting for higher purposes, sometimes seemingly against his instincts. That is to say, by mastering his instincts, even if deformed by habits accumulated over eons. Self mastery means such virtues as innocence, simplicity, gentleness and harmony as well as courage. We are capable of restraint and monogamy even during periods of backsliding such as our own.

Where the end game of the gay "marriage" movement is to eradicate marriage and families as archaic institutions, it is this movement and others of the same ilk that are the smoke of the past. The authentic human ecology begins with the *transcendent* dignity of the human person, the fully human person in relation with others as first in the family, and then in solidarity as within society and between generations. Our true orientation is an inner compass that does not exclude the past or the future, or our present calling to secure the common good.

To not educate for the purpose of our authentic common good is the Big Lie. The unmasking of the Big Lie has not yet been entirely eliminated from required reading lists in public schools. There's the book about pigs. We have already bumped into this piece, Orwell's *Animal Farm* (1945). The original title included the phrase *A Fairy Tale*, but this it was not. It's a satire on total state control, or totalitarianism. A clique of farm animal pigs learns human language and then trashes the nature of things by simply changing the meanings of words. As in the worst of modern totalitarian experiments, the word-merchants are the lunatics who end up running the asylum.

The 60s gave us the perfect storm of at least three recent crises at the same time: the adolescent-tantrum sexual revolution, a legitimate ecology of "spaceship earth" degraded often to the level of a cult, and fears of both demographic and nuclear Armageddon. Not to mention the long loss of faith over centuries, the related trauma of two world wars in a single generation, and then the torching of American cities from Los Angeles to Washington, D.C., the overdue Civil Rights movement, and widespread Vietnam anti-war protests. Wrap-around attitudes on the minds of millennials, and against the religious spark, are the blanketing dogmas of evolution and the self-suffi-cient, Big Bang universe. (We visit with Charles Darwin and Stephen Hawking and their discoveries in hopefully refreshing and encouraging ways in our final three chapters.)

The inflection point in American politics—when the culture war rede-fined party politics—came in 1980 when a major political party endorsed in its platform strong support for feminism and the principle of abortion on demand, no recognition of the pre-born child and only token attention to families, and specific support for homosexuals as a legitimate minority "comparable to members of religious organizations, ethnic, or national groups."

Slightly earlier than Orwell's *Animal Farm* (above) is the equally fictional *Kinsey Report* (1948, 1953), a report that pretended to be a statistically valid survey of sexual practices in the West, and then promoted mainstream casualness and pornography under the cover of scientific respectability. The report was later revealed to be based on non-scientific research of a very *non-random* survey, including willing prison inmates with a disproportionate share of abnormal personalities.[3] Another widely read book at the time was Margaret Mead's *Coming of Age in Samoa* (1928) that also was used by social radicals to validate promiscuity. Mead claimed to have discovered unrestricted sexual license on Samoa, and only much too late was this thesis disproved by another anthropologist, Derek Freeman, in his *Margaret Mead and Samoa: The Making and Unmaking of an Anthropological Myth* (1983).

As a clue into the Big Lie, it seems that Mead's fantasy was projected from her own life. She was married and divorced three times, had several other affairs, and was bisexual as were the fictional run-of-the-mill Samoans in her constructed account.[4] Freeman, her later critic who was with the Australian National University for forty years, demonstrates that the Samoans were devoted polytheists and that they valued virginity very highly. In his *Mere Christianity* (1943) C. S. Lewis has a word for pre-marital sex: "monstrosity." He writes "The monstrosity of sexual intercourse outside marriage is that those who indulge in it are trying to isolate one kind of union (the sexual) from all the other kinds of union which were intended to go along with it and make up the total union."

The remainder of the perfect storm in the 1960s included a wakeup call for global ecology from Rachel Carson's *Silent Spring*, Barry Commoner's *Closing Circle* in the early 1970s, and a the less perceptive Malthusian worldview from Paul Ehrlich in his *Population Bomb*. More ominous than human numbers to spaceship earth is our much more rapidly expanding Western ecological footprint. The specter is raised: is modernity's *per capita trend line* of resource use sustainable on a global scale if the undeveloped world is uplifted to Western "standards"? But what about human creativity and enterprise as expanding any theoretically fixed "carrying capacity"? Who knows? In any event, Ehrlich's global population scenario is disproved by rising health standards and urbanization. Then comes the calculated de-meaning of motherhood, as in forced and sex-selective abortions. China is the familiar poster child for this abuse, but in the United States it is worse than irony to signal young girls that they have value and every right to pursue their dreams, even as they are coaxed to demand abortion as a "right" and to tolerate sex-selection as an abortion option.

The first Earth Day took place in 1970. The 1960s also gave us a disruption and abdication of much formal mainstream education. Secular and religious schools no longer clearly proclaim the inborn natural law and this fully human (not only Christian) vision as having a rightful place in the civic forum. Instead each human person is framed more as a drag on resources. The narrative is more about an accidental cosmos complicated by accidental human parasites that have to think more about fouling the nest. But human numbers have been published more visibly than data on individual (per capita) consumption or on corrupt and economically suppressive political regimes.

The end state to such postured moral neutrality is a throwback, and *not* progress toward a liberated and responsible future. Instead, a regression into unquestioned coarseness and state totalitarianism. The "heart" of radical secularism is a transplant over the long term to replace indulgent agrarian fertility cults with an equally indulgent high-tech infertility cult. A widely respected historian of culture concludes that anti-religious sexual hedonism is actually camouflaged pseudo-religious behavior. "Movements of complete sexual freedom," writes Mircea Eliade, reflect a misguided nostalgia for a "paradisal state before the Fall, when sin did not yet exist and there was no conflict between the pleasures of the flesh and conscience."[5]

It is a very false modernity that actually sets the clock back. This unwinding was already seen and well-expressed by a seventeenth-century university educator (Joachim Campe):

> All our German universities, even the best, greatly need a reform of morals . . .
> Even the best are abysses in which a horde of young people are irretrievably
> losing their innocence, health and future happiness, and from which emerge
> creatures destroyed in body and soul, more a burden than a help to society . . .[6]

This could have been written yesterday or today. Today only one German Catholic in eight sees God as personal rather than abstract and irrelevant; the rest genuflect before an impersonal and primordial fate of some sort, perhaps the inevitability of evolution. Betrayed by the popular culture and the Establishment elite, the bewildered and despairing parents of sexually active eighth-graders are sometimes heard to say, finally, "I just want my daughter to be popular."

The perfect storm of the mid-twentieth century has upended things. Here's a way of looking at the big picture. The science series NOVA includes a piece on giant cruise ship accidents. The narrative pauses midway with a very simplified schematic cross section of such a ship when it is stable. The diagram is very much in error. It shows the center of gravity as a point directly *above* a second point, the center of buoyancy of the hull. This authoritative solution is upside down. A good storm—let's call it the perfect storm—will flip the center of gravity toward the bottom of the sea while the center of buoyancy seeks the surface. Such an event victimized a large naval ship during the Second World War. With its fuel tank ballast empty it was found after a typhoon floating keel up and with no survivors. Modern society is a crowded cruise ship built around the NOVA diagram and flipped by the perfect storm. Like this, our entire fixation on unquestioned modernity is at best an editing error.

Modern-day paganism is even worse than any throwback to pre-modern times. The end-game is even broader than gay "marriage" versus religious freedom. Each such collapse becomes cause for more of the same. The end game is a total *rejection* of human buoyancy in the universal natural law, and a deeper rejection of its Christian validation. To frame the current moment accurately as deconstruction, the choice is between the fully human (and therefore Christian) vision and a radically secularist mirage. Close up, the hookup culture still resembles pre-Christian religion, but it is actually the pagan temple prostitutes stripped of the archaic temple cover-up.

Groomed at first by television scripts to accept pornography and the gay culture, next on the agenda may be permissible and routine incest. (Already we notice such a television plot which by the time these lines are published will probably be a popular rerun.) We should understand that even very primitive cultures had elaborate customs to prevent and punish incest. Today we debunk the fertility gods of yesterday, but fail to notice that such reverence also protected against the sexual randomness that we enable and even promote under the cover of so-called modernity.

The Big Lie is a kind of dance in small steps into unbounded sexual fantasy. If dividing sex from even the possibility of babies is fine, then why not literally sever pregnant mothers from their maternity? And if this is okay, then why not sex-selective abortions and transvestite sex selection? Why not same-sex "marriage" or designer babies from the Petri dish? Simply discard the undesirable or redundant extras like so many unneeded walk-on athletes. Why not polygamy or incest or any other random biological grouping? What practical need is there of mothers or fathers and the outdated notion of what United States Supreme Court Justice Blackman disdained as the "stereotypical" family? The Big Lie is not the blatant denial of the truth. Rather it is the clever bracketing aside of the truth and even common sense into first neglect and then total irrelevance.

On the full range of moral issues, we may allow the truth to be believed and taught, but in actions of our choosing we tolerantly set it aside. We put the truth on hold, and then forget it. We legislate a new truth from the bench. This self-deceiving double-speak is accurately exposed in the Bible as the indifferent "knowledge of good *and* evil." "Thus did I lose you (God)," laments St. Augustine of his own early and divided life, "because you disdain to be possessed together with a lie."[7] In short, the Big Lie is believing what we do, *rather than* doing what we believe. Even before the Christians, we have an expression of this universal and common sense knowledge, attributed to Julius Caesar: *"Homines simper quod volunt credunt*—that which men will they always believe."[8] Moreover, we actually become what we do. We grow in that direction. The darkness is not a matter of misinformation, but finally a corruption of the will, then actions, and then the depths of the very self.

The Big Lie is the assumption that society as a whole can retain the civic virtues when detached from the morality of natural law. This is Lewis Carroll's *Alice in Wonderland* (1865) fantasy, to retain the grin of the Cheshire cat even after the cat has disappeared! To this oddity, Alice replied that she has often seen a cat without a grin but never a grin without a cat. The theory is that the universe just keeps rolling along like the Mississippi, but has no origin. In Harriet Beecher Stowe's *Uncle Tom's Cabin* (1852) the little orphaned slave child, Topsy, is asked who made you? And with the insight matching some modern day cosmologists and radical evolutionists he responds: "Nobody as I knows. . . . I 'spect I (just) grow'd."

SPLITTING THE DIFFERENCE?

The biggest lie of all is the lie within the lie. This is the lie that we tell to ourselves while rationalizing the deepest betrayal of all—betrayal of ourselves. It is not a simple matter to choose evil . . . rather, we first set aside the good (the natural law) such that the desired evil in a diversity of forms then looks like the good.[9] In abortion we kill the child, and as in all other mortal sins we simultaneously kill our own souls. All people are motivated by one love or another, and all of us want our selected love to also be the truth. This, again, from the timeless St. Augustine: "They hate the truth for the sake of that very thing which they have loved instead of the truth. . . . [They] do not wish to be deceived but wish to deceive, they love it [the truth] when it shows itself to them, and they hate it when it shows them to themselves."[10]

Is the real truth ever obsolete? With a baby brought to him by two women both claiming to be the mother, did Solomon simplify his eight-to-four job by splitting the difference—by threatening to cut the child in half (1 Kings 3:16-27)? No, of course not, he acted according to his innate rational intelligence. One was the mother; the other was not. Under the principle of non-contradiction it *is self-evident* that two precisely and genuinely contradictory propositions *cannot* both be true. *One or the other is false.* This is the non-demonstrable first principle, the start point, of universal human intelligence and reasoning. (The alternative proposition of "dual truth" is one part of lyrical Islamic thought that was rejected by the thirteenth-century Christian thinker, St. Thomas Aquinas; the spectrum mentality of modern secularism merits the same intelligent scrutiny.) Solomon's wisdom did not pretend any false in-clusiveness or any facile spectrum, but rather he prayed: "Give me an under-standing heart to judge your people and distinguish right from wrong" (1 Kings 3:9).

With the universality of natural law, even Mark Twain's Jim understood what was self-evident in the dispute set before Solomon: "De' spute warn't 'bout a half a chile, de 'spute was 'bout a whole chile; en de man dat think he kin settle a 'spute bout a whole chile wid a half a chile, doan' know enough to come in out'n de rain" (*The Adventures of Huckleberry Finn*, 1884). Even with the "n" word deleted throughout, one wonders if Twain's masterpiece would ever be restored to school bookshelves, given its violation here of today's political correctness and facile rationalizations.

With the young in mind, let us consider a display of recent political history at the Seattle Museum of History and Industry. On the second floor one finds an enlarged press release for the State of Washington in 1970 when it became the first state to approve abortion by popular vote (the dominance of Referendum 20 over the "Voice for the Unborn"). For balance, and imme-diately to the right, is a second display. This one reports that in 1994 the Seattle firm Advanced Technology Life (ATL) became the manufacturer of ultrasound developed at the University of Washington. The text reports that this invention has "saved countless lives," and an ultrasound image (sono-gram) of a child in the womb is depicted. Junior high school students breeze past the first display but pause at the second before hurrying along without perceiving the contradiction, "That's cool, really neat." It's just a matter of choice. Of such as these junior high school students, Winston Churchill got it right: "'Men occasionally stumble over the truth, but most of them pick themselves up and hurry off as if nothing ever happened." Rather than a mere technical detail, the ultrasound as a scientific reality puts the lie to our cultu-ral blank check for abortion and whatever else the cat drags in.

To be unaware of real contradictions or to negotiate with genuine evil is already to have lost. Does a fireman negotiate with the fire? Rootless and sophisticated ambivalence is the Big Lie. In today's world to consent to a "dialogue" is sometimes an unwitting step toward a clever and unconditional surrender. When the air we breathe is sucked out of the room—when the truth is missing—smoke seeps in through every crack in the walls.

Technology being morally ambivalent, are we now to be made in the image and likeness of our own technology? How are we to uphold universal human moral reality in the public square, assuming there still is a true *public square*? How are we to do this when this message comes only from cornered and slandered religious institutions and a few scientists and philosophers? The pastoral Pope St. John XXIII, convener of the Catholic Church's much misrepresented Second Vatican Council (1962-1965), had this to say:

We are concerned with the danger of the growing power of error and evil, studied, organized and full of menace. We see the vulnerability of poor human nature disconcerted by the iridescent brilliance of modern life, and every day exposed to the temptation of compromise—I repeat this word—compromise between the spirit and matter.[11]

An evangelist and other writers can help us a bit more with these questions about compromise. From St. Matthew we discover that we are called to be both "wise as serpents and innocent as doves" (Matthew 10:16). Simplicity and street smart prudence are never to be separated. In an imperfect world we are to maneuver, but without manipulating. We are not to cross dress into the image and likeness of practical deceit.

The Evangelist underlines singleness of heart: "But let your word 'yes' be 'yes,' and your 'no' be 'no.' Anything more than this is from the evil one" (Matthew 5:37). Where Solomon said "yes" to higher truth; we too often say both yes and no, or maybe just whatever. The disputed child is indivisible. True marriage is also like this. At its core (as we say, from "the beginning") it is a calling to become one with a chosen member of the opposite sex to whom one decides "I do" rather than "no" or any middle ground.

FREEDOM OF CHOICE AND THE CHOICE OF FREEDOM

What is the difference between "freedom" and a false and yet exhilarating freefall? St. Augustine warns us that real freedom "cannot be reduced to a sense of choice: it is (instead) freedom to act fully . . ." and to resist what he termed *"fantastica fornicatio"*—the prostitution of the mind to its own fantasies, e.g., gender theory. The lie is biggest when it insinuates itself into our very selves, when we lie to ourselves and "choose" to believe nothing. This cult of random choice is a camouflage for a deeper abyss of forgetfulness over what is missing. This experience is what the Prussian military strategist Karl von Clausewitz (1780-1831) called the "drop of poison". We give in so many times that when we finally catch on, we are incapable of choosing to resist.

In his youth St. Augustine hopped a fence with friends and stole some pears from a neighbor's tree. The evil was not in taking pears so much as in the very act of stealing and in the yielding to the group mentality. As he reveals: "we took great loads of fruit from it, not for our own eating, but rather to throw it to the pigs . . . we did this to do what pleased us for the reason that it was forbidden."[12]

The Church is among those who remind us of this self trickery. It defends the natural law as our innate and deeply personal—and too often assaulted— inclination toward the good, our universal inclination, not any merely individualistic interest or tendencies. The universal natural law is not true because a supposedly sectarian Church teaches it; the Church teaches the natural law because it is true. It is *not* the imposition of a "Catholic theocracy" as former governor Cuomo would have us believe (Chapter 2).

The natural law is our "pre-religious" openness and receptivity to reality. To follow natural law one need not be a Christian (or a Jew or a Muslim). In the words of a Church spokesman: "the Church navigates in a pre-religious space." This means that "it can enter into dialogue with any interlocutor who is open to rational debate. In such a realm as this, "the prerequisites can be created for announcing and accepting the Gospel. . . . The only thing left for them (Catholics) is the strength of argumentation, of reason."[13] The appeal to memory and human reasoning cannot ultimately be dismissed as a particularly religious oddity. That "memory is the treasury and guardian of all things" comes to us from Cicero, a pre-Christian Roman statesman executed by the power brokers of his own time.

Without memory or future we stew in boredom. Is even the mystery of good and evil lost in modern amnesia and boredom? Why are we blind to the sacred and to the fulfillment found in fidelity to even the littlest of things? The novelty of the present moment is that it is only a moment. We live in a disconnected bubble. Our denial is the Big Lie. But before the collapse into boredom and deceit, is it possible that God actually talks to people? Can we remember? Is the forgotten Christian encounter essentially an inoculation against denial? G. K. Chesterton proposes a really revolutionary picture in the memory and testimony of eyewitnesses. Of the Gospel and these witnesses he writes:

> Those runners [messengers of the Gospel] gather impetus as they run. Ages afterwards they still speak as if something had just happened. They have not lost the speed and momentum of messengers; they have hardly lost, as it were, the wild eyes of witnesses. . . . We might sometimes fancy that the Church grows younger as the world grows old.[14]

Especially when moral dilemmas crowd us, the routine of a moral universe, with good friends and good habits, keep us young spiritually, even as the world grows old. To outgrow denial is to remain open to the world of good moral *judgments*—not self-gratifying "decisions." To not be judgmental in this sense is to sink into animal instincts. Fidelity to little things alerts us again to the tiny whispering sound which sometimes is the heartbeat of an unborn child.

Habits not so good are absorbed from the world around us. These lure and hold us in the mindless cult of "whatever." So many of the young girls who suddenly find themselves visiting abortion clinics are victimized in one way or another. Satisfied for a moment possibly, but in no way fulfilled. Are they escaping from boredom, lured by the tantalizing anesthetic of "readiness"?

Sometimes it's surely the deep human need to be valued, by someone, somewhere—for even a moment and at whatever cost. Or maybe it's all very simple. Maybe we do stuff "because, like, it feels good"? Is the pleasure principle the highest meaning of our lives? Even single-cell amoebas in the nearest mud puddle do this much, but is this really enough for us? Then comes the "crisis pregnancy," and then the compounding betrayal and self-betrayal of "termination."

Again, all of us are hard hearted and cut corners in one way or another. And rarely is the situation as excruciating as this. And even in the cases of consent rather than sexual assault, it is not that sexual sins are the worst on the list. Intellectual sins in high places are probably greater—like the deceit of detaching human rights from corresponding responsibilities. But sexual sin (lust) probably ranks first in Genesis—in a meaningful way more than a bedtime story after all—precisely because it opens the door to all the other capital sins listed: pride, avarice, anger, gluttony and that kind of sloth that includes mental laziness. The garden becomes a desert because now missing is the willingness to "to be" in the original way, to live in and for the other where: ". . . a man leaves his father and mother and clings to his wife, and the two of them become one body" (Genesis 2:23).

Isolation in the world is ever relentless and serpentine, a deceit always tangled with the surviving good. Disguised like Druids in white robes, the clinical enablers teach "readiness" instead of a greater interpersonal presence—maturity. Instead of teaching shared morality or even self-respect, there's the world of front-page finance and the calculating mentality of immediate benefits. We are lured into moments of something at least intimate if not truly personal, in a world that is not. Do we look for happiness too much in all the wrong places?

Is mad-boundless love honestly possible if still missing from him or her is the unrestrained rejoicing and commitment of "I Do"? Fleeting intimacy absent the public promise is a stolen treasure. Even worse, fool's gold; or maybe the buried damage of a young victim of someone else experimenting? Movie sex idol Mae West found a few words for the short-term frolic: "I used to be Snow White, but a drifted." And as for the same old wakeup call the next morning—the only thing really new under the sun is still the Christian thing, our sure protection from deserved despair. Despair, from whatever cause, does not lie in doubting that God is still unconditional love; but rather it's the fear that this cannot possibly be true *for me*.

Despair and the reflex of self-assertion are the incubator for teen abortions. Still, "Rachel is weeping for her children; she refuses to be comforted for her children, because they are no more" (Jeremiah 31:15). These lines contain the grief that came with Herod's massacre of the innocent children two years old or younger (Matthew 2: 17-18). *Dejas vu.* The dark side of modernity entices the young to kill those even younger than themselves. But before she decides to fix her situation does she sense for an instant that as a pregnant woman she is on the shared threshold of a mystery bigger than herself?

Betrayal of the child, and of the self-disclosing Thou, are inseparable from what is also a self-betrayal. The lies against Ultimate Reality come in many forms and layers. From the Old Testament we have these mysterious words, "Your commands are all true; then help me when lies oppress me" (Psalm 119). God is more than putty to be shaped by our private decisions. He is not a spigot to be turned on and off. He is not even a consistent human intuition or feeling waiting to be evolved forward as our personal histories move along. In the self-donating Christ of intelligent and unconditional love—who is one with the Father—the piled up lies of yesterday and of today are exposed forever: "A new command I give you: Love one another, as I have loved you" (John 13:34).[15] Might we suppose the God also and first, takes things personally?

The emotional life of the mother is almost as permanently disfigured as the physical life of the aborted child. She knows that a "pregnancy" today really cannot be walked back to yesterday after a one-hour visit to an anonymous and (probably) antiseptic abortion clinic. Healing comes with recognizing the truth. Women of Silent no More have "been there and done that." These women give courageous witness against the mistake that once upon a time deceived and claimed ownership over them. By inviting us to help one another in tough times, like this, the infinite and equally merciful Divinity is eager to touch his thumb on the scale for our happiness and salvation. Might this be what that moment of unconditional self-donation on the Cross—and the Resurrection—are all about? We can stop midstream and say yes to new life.

And if we fall, are we given a second chance? What does a recent pope have to say to each of our unhappy mothers lured and anesthetized into the counterfeit solace and self-betrayal of an abortion clinic? St. John Paul II (Pope, 1978—2005) wrote this:

> I would now like to say a special word to women who have had an abortion. The Church is aware of the many factors which may have influenced your decision, and she does not doubt that in many cases it was a painful and even shattering decision. The wound in your heart may not yet be healed. . . . The Father of mercies is ready to give you his forgiveness and his peace. . . . You will come to understand that nothing is definitively lost and you will also be able to ask forgiveness from your child, who is now living in the Lord.[16]

The biggest of the Big Lies is the assumption that we fall outside of the loving glance of the living and infinitely loving God. In a fully human universe that is spiritual and redemptive—more than evolutionary and backsliding—our past bridges are never completely burned. The first letter of St.

John the Evangelist turns things on their head for us: "Love then consists in this: not that we have loved God, but that he *first loved us* and sent his Son as expiation for our sins" (1 John 4:10, italics added). At the crucifixion it was barely an eye-to-eye glance and a total spiritual u-turn, in barely the twinkling of an eye, that enabled Christ to announce to the repentant criminal: "I assure you, this day you will be with me in paradise" (Luke 23:42).

Another helping hand is the one-on-one Project Rachel,[17] always ready to help an unexpected mother or a shattered ex-mother finally hoping again for her deepest self-worth to be restored. We discover that God is bigger than ourselves and even bigger than our irreversible transgressions. One Project member was a vibrant white-haired priest of sixty-five. But what could an old, white male priest with a deep Irish brogue possibly say that would help a post-abortion teenage girl?

"Those poor darlings," he said of them. From the heart he truly cared for each one. There are also those under age girls (sexual assault crimes which business-as-usual Planned Parenthood consistently refuses to report). Sometimes this priest was the only genuine "father"—the only figure of both authority (as in author-ship) and consuming gentleness—that these girls had ever known. Above us all and the rest of creation is another Father with a reconciliation that is total, unconditional, and larger than all our sins and foolishness combined. We are never alone. This is the meaning of Redemption in history but also above and larger than history.

THE GHOST OF GALILEO

The student of history detects a direct parallel between the United States Supreme Court's sweeping ruling favoring of abortion (*Roe v. Wade*, 1973) and another ruling by another high office back in the seventeenth century. Back then it was Church officials who refused to weigh the evidence supplied by the new science and Galileo. Galileo (1564-1642) was a believing Catholic and in his own words regarding the Bible, was of the same mind as the other thinkers in the Church. He wrote that "Scripture cannot err, but its interpreters can."

The earlier Ptolemaic school of astronomy harmonized with Scripture as it was understood at the time by its interpreters. Now with his new telescope, Galileo perched himself on the shoulders of Copernicus who decades earlier already had proposed that the earth revolved around the sun. Copernicus was a Catholic priest who freely said his piece and later died a full twenty years before Galileo was even a twinkle in his father's eye. And even earlier, in the fifteenth century, Leonardo da Vinci already had written that "the sun does not move." So, Galileo's telescope contribution was not totally original, but with it he was (nearly) able to prove this hypothesis which was so at odds with a different mental map based on a different train of thought and only the unaided eye.

Galileo's new evidence was sunspots on the moving surface of the sun, moons like ours that circled around the planet Jupiter, and craters on the lunar surface showing clearly that the moon was solid. Scientifically conclusive experimental proof of Galileo's solar system really did not come until 1838 when Bessel showed that stars fixed in the sky were not fixed. Against a more distant backdrop, the nearby stars were displaced when viewed from the earth as it orbited once each year around the sun. The parallax displacement of distant stars was revealed by our slightly changing angle of vision as the earth orbited from one position to another six months later (separated by nearly two hundred million miles). Things are not always what they seem. This is as true for us today as it ever was.

Now let's revisit the 1973 United States Supreme Court in its own postured caution relative to the science of embryology and common sense. The Court claimed to be studiously free of speculation, but in fact it did speculate. It speculated against an unseen universe—the life of the unborn human being—in effect imposing on these children the court's own dismissal of their now self-evident lives. As with a pre-scientific solar system, things are not always what they seem. Why are there two heartbeats in the mother instead of only one? Prior to the unjust decree against Galileo, Cardinal Bellarmine, as the Church watchdog over Galileo, had written in 1615 that

> if the orbiting of the Earth around the sun were ever to be demonstrated to be certain, then theologians . . . would have to review biblical passages apparently opposed to Copernican theories so as to avoid asserting the error of opinions proven to be true. [18]

Where is there today a court in the entire country open minded enough to say the same thing about the passages in the 1973 *Roe v. Wade* ruling? Galileo's findings about the solar system endangered entire schools of status quo scientific thought that coalesced against him, and yet, it was Bellarmine, the theologian and critic, who earlier at least left some wiggle room. Where is the wiggle room let for a pre-born child?

In our seemingly scientific age, might we see another parallel here with Einstein's initial rejection of an expanding universe (which implies an origin rather than a steady state universe), compared to his early mathematics supporting the General Theory of Relativity (1917)? In 1922 the Russian mathematician Alexander Friedmann flagged and published a math error in the Theory falsely supporting Einstein's steady-state universe. The astronomer Vesto Slipher had discovered receding galaxies—galaxies moving away from each other—as early as 1913 and reported his findings in 1914 to the American Astronomical Society. (In the audience was Edwin Hubble, after whom the more recent Hubble Telescope.) Receding galaxies point backward to a common start point, a beginning. Einstein tried to prove Slipher wrong and called his work "suspicious," but then in 1923 graciously retracted his own "error in calculation."[19] Even today, the fate of the universe turns on an error in calculation. As for the seemingly radical newness of Einstein's modern scientific thought, we have this from the philosopher Leibniz (1646-1716), from three centuries past: "I have said more than once that I hold space to be something merely relative, as time is."

In addition to such continuity, it seems that in human affairs there also operates an equal and constant human factor of resistance, every bit as constant as the speed of light in physics. In a small way, at least, Bellarmine and even Einstein have this frailty in common with each other and with the rest of us. As an aside, Galileo's final years of house arrest seem trivial by comparison to the sentence imposed on the unborn by those who discount modern optics in the ultrasound. As a further aside, unlike his Catholic colleague Galileo, the Lutheran Johannes Kepler was actually excommunicated from his church.

SCIENCE DROPS THE OTHER SHOE

The legacy of Galileo is not only that the moon is made of solid stuff and that the earth revolves around the sun. All of society was changed by the greater knowledge that a mathematical approach to nature could unlock many of her powers. All of enchanted nature also could be domesticated to rational purposes and wants. In the years after Galileo and even the Renaissance, the new Enlightenment idea of a rational universe could be progressively set in place by human effort. All kinds of good outcomes and worldly conveniences could be extracted. Later still, the new age of machines and inventions, and mechanical spindles and steam engines were a mixed blessing. These contraptions would move beyond and temporarily disenfranchise an entire mass of society organized around hand skills and trade and craft guilds.

In response to the screams of the so-called "working class," in 1812 England a law was passed imposing the death penalty for anyone who destroyed a machine. In 1848 the upshot of the new manufacturing routines initially broke into social revolutions across Europe. Many of our American immigrant ancestors sailed across the Atlantic in mid century. The new routines and the new economics brought about such mass unemployment and exploitation that Karl Marx would redefine all of recorded human history from an atheistic perspective. His belief was that human history consisted only of physical matter passing through stages of evolution ("dialectical materialism"). His belief (a belief that he insisted was scientific) was that the most complex stuff (us) was hardwired into inevitable conflict between the owners of machines and money and those who were enslaved to dig the coal and move the levers.[20] The new sense of economic alienation undermined any deeper understanding of human society and deeper alienation, or of a God who nevertheless is involved in both the cosmos and human lives.

Today the dark side of this mechanized worldview has spun off pharmaceutical inventions and chemicals capable of erasing the possible inconvenience of the unborn child. The death sentence is inflicted directly by the machine. Usually in medical questions, at least, the general routine is to double-check things by seeking a second opinion. As a very broad second opinion, is there a role for moral discernment here? As a second opinion to be heard, is the unborn child permitted a voice or at least a silent scream?

In *Roe v. Wade* the United States Supreme Court painted itself into a corner. The Court and its public chorus recoil at the prospect of ever reconsidering a second opinion against the ruling that victimizes the unborn child. After all, how do you take back the sixty million abortions that have been performed legally since 1973? The default position of modernity is that we must always move forward, not "backward." History is a ratchet. Here's the real logic: we're in too deep to change our story now. Better to indoctrinate the upcoming generation, the millennials, to established conventions. While marginal adjustments in the law at the state level are increasingly successful, these or any reversal are tenaciously resisted. In reality, the scientific evidence has advanced so much even since 1973 that the court ruling is clearly a remnant of the pre-scientific Stone Age.

Centuries ago when the Galileo trial was all done, the legend is that he cut through it all with the famous remark we have already mentioned, "*eppur se muove*"—"nevertheless, it moves." How much like this pithy remark are the real and wrenching ultrasound images of a moving and real child undergoing abortion? Not actually recorded in the official court transcript, Galileo's remark might have been captured by the court recorder only as a tiny whispering sound from his nearly closed lips immediately after his trial was adjourned. The moons of Jupiter were safe as concepts if they remained "hypothetical." And equally so today, the euphemistic label "non-viable tissue" attempts to keep the unborn child hypothetical and innocuous to a distracted and controlling society.

Before the social revolutions of 1848, the 1812 English death penalty for destroying machines held social unrest in check. This tactic is repeated today. We have a death penalty against another kind of outcry that also refuses to remain silent: the ultrasound and "The Silent Scream." Nevertheless, it moves! Today in an age the prides itself in the science of Galileo, the shoe is on the other foot. The arrogance and deception are stifling. To the unsuspecting young the evidence of ultrasound is presented as only a decorative afterthought in a local museum: "that's cool, really neat" say the glancing young visitors in a fog of spiritual darkness and moral incomprehension. "We do not err because the truth is difficult to see," said Aleksandr Solzhenitsyn, "it is visible at a glance. We err because it is more comfortable."

Ultrasound technology and fiber optics—like the "aha" moment seen through Galileo's telescope—show undeniable reality. Each "pregnancy" is a new universe and a distinct human life, more than an incremental data point in some flat-earth mythology. Where Galileo saw mountains on the moon, modern science shows us fingerprints on the pre-born baby. On the table before us is scientific evidence of an entirely new world, a life fully distinct from its mother with its own DNA and blood type. The ultrasound imagery is permitted, but any step at the state level to require showing this information to mothers is legally and routinely obstructed. No sense upending the apple cart yesterday with Galileo's telescope or today with our modern ultrasound and fiber optics. Of his evidence, Galileo was told he "must neither hold, defend, nor teach that opinion [the motion of the earth around the sun] in any way whatsoever." This seventeenth-century muzzling sounds so modern when defenders of the reality of the unborn child are subject to prosecution as racketeers.

Yesterday's political correctness denied the real moons of Jupiter and what they really meant; today's political correctness denies the evidence of real living persons essentially the same as ourselves, and what this means. The immense hollow feeling cuts deeper and deeper. In its *Roe v. Wade* ruling the court in effect instituted a science-free-zone within which it simply announced from on high that "the word person used in the Fourteenth Amendment does not apply to the unborn." Not mere "tissue," but a tissue of lies—the Big Lie.

With each advance in embryology the marketability of this myth, like any other myth, becomes more preposterous. Of course the "world of Aphrodite, the world of sterile eroticism" (1948 Lambeth Conference, minority report) thrives like any other fungus in this shady culture. In its ruling the Supreme Court enables in advance each new abortion. The assumption in 1973 was that within a few years those who affirm each human life would fall in line with the new legal fiction. As with slavery, the routine of the passing years would surely deaden all consciences. But now, again, after nearly half a century it is clear that this has not come to be. What was unimaginable in the mid-twentieth century is now a nation deeply and permanently divided in a culture war deeper than any politics.

With a lie so big in the world, why do we not see it? John Ruskin gives us a clue even as he writes about truth in art and architecture. Regarding falsehood, he writes:

It is not calumny nor treachery that does the largest sum of mischief in the world; they are continually crushed, and are felt only in being conquered. But it is the glistening and softly spoken lie; the amiable fallacy; the patriotic lie of the historian, the provident lie of the politician, the zealous lie of the partisan, the merciful lie of the friend, and the careless lie of each man to himself, that cast that black mystery over humanity. . . .[21]

NOTES

1. Aleksandr Solzhenitsyn, "Men have forgotten God," acceptance address for the 1983 Templeton Prize for Progress in Religion, *National Review*, July 22, 1983.

2. Paul Vitz, *Faith of our Fathers* (San Francisco: Ignatius Press, 1999).

3. Judith Reisman and Edward Eichel, *Kinsey, Sex and Fraud: the Indoctrination of People* (Huntington House Publishers, 1990). The Kinsey findings are based on eighteen thousand "sex histories," all of whom were self-selected volunteers and a quarter to half of whom were prison inmates, and 1,400 of whom were sex offenders, apparently even including nine sex offenders who engaged in direct experimentation on children aged two months to fifteen years. Prostitutes and cohabiting females were classified as married, leading to the claim that a quarter of married women committed adultery. Janice Shaw adds further that Kinsey "was promiscuously bisexual, sado-masochistic, and a decadent voyeur who enjoyed filming his wife having sex with his staff" (see Janice Shaw Crouse, "Kinsey's Kids," at www.nationalreview.com/comment/crouse200311140923.asp).

4. Ben Wiker (Franciscan University of Steubenville, Ohio), "Anthropology Afoul of the Facts," *National Catholic Register*, May 19, 2002.

5. Mircea Eliade, *The Sacred and the Profane: The Nature of Religion* (Orlando, FL: Harcourt Brace Jovanovich, 1959), 207.

6. Joachim Heinrich Campe (1746-1818), cited in an editorial footnote to Joseph De Maistre, *On God and Society* (Chicago: Henry Regnery Co., 1959), 52-33, fn. 34.

7. St. Augustine, *The Confessions*, Book 10, Chapter 41.

8. Cited in Thomas Dubay, S.M., *Authenticity: A Biblical Theology of Discernment* (San Francisco: Ignatius, 1997), 237.

9. For a scholarly treatment of how individuals construct a fantasy world within which self-justification in then (falsely) validated, I am indebted to Kirk Kanzelberger, *The Mystical Daydream: Fictive Being and the Motive of Evil* (doctoral dissertation, Fordham University, 2011).

10. St. Augustine, *The Confessions*, Book 10, Chapter 23.

11. John XXIII, John P. Donnelly (ed.), *Prayers and Devotions from Pope John XXIII* (Garden City, NY: Image, 1969), 192-93.

12. St. Augustine, *The Confessions of St. Augustine* (Garden City, New York: Image, 1960), Book 2, Chapter 5, Section 9.

13. Walter Cardinal Brandmuller, President Emeritus of the Pontifical Committee for Historical Sciences, "Europe, in its Crisis, Needs a Catholic Revolution," Address in Nursia, Italy on October 25 on the 50th Anniversary of the proclamation of St. Benedict as Patron Saint of Europe, *Inside the Vatican* (Rome: December 2014), 23-25.

14. G.K. Chesterton, *The Everlasting Man* (Garden City, New York: Image Books, 1925/1955), 268.

15. Pope St. Pius X's defense of reason (*Oath Against Modernism*) in 1910 still has something to teach us: "...faith is not a blind sentiment of religion welling up from the depths of the subconscious under the impulse of the heart and the motion of a will trained to morality; but faith is a genuine assent of the intellect to truth received by hearing from an external source" [i.e., the gospel witnesses].

16. St. John Paul II, *Evangelium Vitae* (*The Gospel of Life*), n. 99, 1995.

17. Contacts are Rachael's Vineyard (1-877-HOPE-4-ME [467-3463]) and National Helpline for Abortion Recovery (1-866-482-LIFE [5433]).

18. Letter of response to the Provincial of the Carmelite Order (April 12, 1615) in Giorgio de Santillana, *The Crime of Galileo* (Chicago: University of Chicago Press, 1955), 98-100. The concluding paragraph of the letter remains committed to the still visual experience that the

earth is motionless. Bellarmine erred in his superficial attention to the writings of the earlier Copernicus. He read only the Introduction of 1543 which describes the heliocentric view as "purely a mathematical supposition . . . with no bearing on the reality of the heavens." This Introduction was written by "Osiander, a Lutheran pastor who was trying in this way to make it [Copernicus] acceptable to fundamentalist prejudice" (101).

19. Robert Jastrow, *God and the Astronomers* (New York: W.W. Norton and Co., 1978), 23-29.

20. The saying is that the materialist Karl Marx turned the earlier Friedrich Hegel on his head. Hegel, also German, was a pantheist—one who believes that God and the universe are synonyms—but maintained that his works were still consistent with Christianity. He held that consciousness and the unlimited *idea* of rational freedom drive history forward (George Wilhelm Friedrich Hegel, *The Philosophy of History*, lectures of 1830-31).

21. John Ruskin, "The Lamp of Truth," *The Seven Lamps of Architecture*, 1849.

Chapter Four

A "Tiny Whispering Sound"

When we discover the Big Lie we see that it is a parallel universe where good and evil switch places. The truth is left unsaid and the noisy Big Lie helps us to forget that anything is missing. Even scientific evidence is eclipsed by political correctness, whether we box up the telescope or, in our day, put a shroud over the ultrasound as well as the aborted child. This isn't just about bad information. It's about bad will. We are being used, and there is something biblical about allowing ourselves to be used: "Therefore God has given them up . . . they who exchanged the truth of God for a lie, and worshiped and served the creature rather than the Creator who is blessed forever, amen" (Romans 1:24-25).

WHAT REALLY COUNTS?

The Big Lie is the rationalization—the craftiness—that comes before, during, and after the willing participation in evil. We have a better chance of noticing the truth when we see not only *with* the eyes, but *through* the eyes (the poet William Blake). We are more than light-sensitive stuff in a blind universe. In the first case we are simply receptors to light waves. We see only quantity and mechanics; in the latter and spiritual case we see substance, things as they really are, and even inexplicable beauty. We too often miss the point of Adam being given the power and the freedom to *name* the astonishing mystery of each living beasts and bird (Genesis 2:19-20), rather than to only mechanically count them.

The fatal flaw of modernity is that it knows more and more about measurement and numbers, but less and less about names and substance. Naming is an act of creative discovery, particularly the naming of one's spouse as the exclusive and permanent selection of a particular woman or man. Marriage is not just another randomly numbered motel room or a time-share condo with routinely updated occupants. Random numbers come after the Fall, or more accurately, numbering at the expense of knowing and naming . . . possibly *is* the Fall. With our souls' falling out, so to speak, counting becomes estrangement and boredom, what C. S. Lewis calls our "horror of the same old thing."

The genius of the Hebrew culture is that while names mattered, numbers were also sacred. More than arithmetic numbers, their symbolic numbers supply a manner of poetically and concisely speaking the truth about real things that also are not nameless. From the beginning poets have also reminded us that absolutely none of the cosmos is dull or prosaic or reducible to mere words or arithmetic numbers alone.

Special numbers can also give us those iconic moments in time that have unlimited shelf life even across generations. It is no mystery that the wonder of symbolic numbers is planted throughout the Bible. And yet even the chosen people of the Old Testament eventually flattened and multiplied the Ten Commandments into numbered observances intricately monitored by the Scribes and Pharisees. But we do the same, even more so, finally by inventing sets of "positive laws" ever more remote from morality and finally in opposition to the affirmations of natural law and the corresponding prohibitions of the Ten Commandments.

The pages of *Federal Register* regulations are beyond counting, almost as infinite as the stars in the sky. Annual numerical and public confessions are extracted via the minutely detailed workings of the Internal Revenue Service (IRS). By comparison, the Hebrew laws of the Scribes and the Pharisees were really quite simple. Instead of thousands of pages, more or less a few hundred, they were divided into exactly 613 parts, each of meticulous importance, but not 612 or 614 or any other higher count. Why is this? This particular figure is the sum of two numbers important to the Israelites. The first denotes things above the earth. It is the 365 days on the permanent solar calendar. And the second is what was understood to be the number of parts to the less permanent or mortal human body (248).

Today we insist that two plus two equals exactly four and no other. Perhaps the Hebrews knew with equal clarity that 365 plus 248 equals exactly 613 legal prescriptions of the Old Testament. Need we wonder for long whether the close knit between heaven and earth was expressed in the sum 613? The connection between the cosmic and the earth is commonly symbolized in other primitive cultures. But beyond the mythical, for the Hebrews (and for us) there is something more. Throughout the entire Old Testament the chosen people await a messiah in history. Christians testify to this prophesied encounter with the historical mystery of Christ.

The big surprise—the Revelation—is that Christ is not simply another lad from down the dirt road with improved table manners. He is not simply another individual planted somewhere in history; instead the Trinitarian Oneness takes on our *universal* human nature. It is not that Christ is an individual, but instead that He takes up into Himself each and all of our personalities without exception. The Incarnation is concrete, not merely another cerebral idea. Translation for philosophy majors: by isolating faith entirely from the mind or even from reason, Immanuel Kant opened the door to those like Darwin who later dismiss faith as no more than an idea serving private emotion or feeling. As the intellectual godfather to modern rationalism, Kant also dispensed with "religion" as a touchstone for the higher values, but at this very point he still appealed to "common sense." Shouldn't common sense—not only freedom of religion—also serve as some kind of restraint on courtroom rationalizations?

Pertinent to values in politics, the novelist André Gide gives us a hint. Deeper than identity politics, a bit of each of us is really in all of us: "There is nobody more English than Shakespeare and no one more universal; none more Italian than Dante and no one more universal; none more French than Racine and no one more universal."[1] There is something about early Jewish symbolism—not faith as such—that already understands mystery of real pluralism within real unity, and that one searches for in vain in post-Enlightenment science, hyper-rationalism, and especially legislation from the bench.

The scientific method is inductive. It works from assemblies of selected natural facts. Symbolic numbers and even verbal logic are different. Science replaces myth, but for our always finite minds symbolism still has its place. Symbolism provides at least a handhold on common sense (and the innate natural law). A very rough analogy is suggested by Albert Einstein himself, who commented that his own manner of thought was in fact visual rather than verbal. Post-mortem evidence suggests that the intuitive and analytical lobes of his brain were connected physiologically to each other (the normal "Sylvian fissure" of separation in his brain was unusually joined.) He seemed to do alright blending rigorous science with an intuitive and visual mentality!

Now let's go back to the religion thing and Christian witness. The mystery of the Incarnation—the mystery of the person of Christ is that our human nature is drawn to participate in His divine nature. And we thought that only politics was radical. St. Bernard says in a sermon: "When God reveals his humanity, his goodness cannot possibly remain hidden." For scientific minds this encounter and our possible conversion do not show up at all through the telescope or a microscope. And, unlike the symbolism of primitive religions, Christians respond reasonably to a real and precisely dated event—the *Logos*—within human history. Myths are not grounded in reason in this way; they are imagined and always come before and outside of history. Christian witness to this Encounter is then articulated as best we can by reasoned concepts first explored by the Greeks (such as Aristotle and Plato). It is from them that we receive the notions of the one, the true, the good, and the beautiful. We have been prompted by Providence to better encounter the

Gospel question posed to each of us, "Who do *you* say that I am?" (Mark 8:30).

In the first encounter with an angel who spoke to them about the risen Christ following the absolute novelty of the resurrection, the women were anything but saccharin. They were "amazed" (Luke 16:5) or even "afraid" (Matthew 28:5), or yet again "terrified" (Luke 24:5) or as others translate the moment, "astonished" or "alarmed". Why so terrified, when confronted face to face with something that very suddenly is no longer missing from our view, that is, with the Ultimate Reality? Is the resurrection simply hyperbole, or given the testimony of witnesses, is it a profound wake-up call from across the centuries?

We *should* be thunderstruck, even today, to discover that the root fact of the entire universe is not structured chaos, but rather a higher and deeper being, the Spiritual Being who by his nature is eternal and who is intentional and active love clear through. Possibly anticipated, then, in the Old Testament symbolic number 613 is this mystery of this living God, but at the same time the suddenly deepened mystery of ourselves as receptive human persons.

The body and soul unity of the whole "person" does not fully collapse into an elusive modern-day "missing link" lurking in the shadows from the ground up. Instead the unity of each person is revealed as a bonding between the material *and* the distinctly spiritual. Our link is with a calling from the top down. The human person exceeds his bundle of lower instincts and entire physical nature. In a homily the early bishop Saint Peter Chrysologus said it this way: "The Spirit brings forth as men belonging to heaven those whose earthly ancestry brought them forth as men belonging to the earth, and in a condition of wretchedness; he gives them the likeness of their Creator."

But modern-day bone diggers no longer suspect the possible sacredness of creation and especially of themselves and their own inquiring souls. Instead the human spirit now is redefined as a function of chemistry and complex biology. Again, the Hebrews, the people chosen or the Chosen People, saw things quite differently. And, again, it is in light of the astonishing Resurrection that Christians read all of their Hebrew Old Testament. The Old Testament prefigures, anticipates, and is later illumined by the singular and non-replicable encounter with Christ. Based on repetitions, the scientific method is inadequate to this Encounter.

More than a passing episode, Christ is the permanent center of any history that is fully human. He is the center of each personal history. In the singular and divine moment of the Cross and Resurrection, together, is concentrated the elevation of humanity. It is no small thing to be a human being, even if dismissed as a statistical and seemingly abandoned blip in the twenty-first century. A sad tale it is that so many millennials just walk away from all this. Of those raised Catholic, half leave religion by age twenty-three. Of these, seventy percent just drift away, and two-thirds never having really heard the "good news" (the Gospel) say they just stopped believing (PEW research, "Faith in Flux" survey of 2009). Intrusive substitute mindsets are evolutionism and modern cosmology. (Therefore, in Chapters 9 and 11 we will visit with Darwin and Stephen Hawking.)

The Encounter with the singular Resurrection comes with the singular evidence of Christ's miracles and then the emptiness of His hollow burial tomb.[2] That which is missing in this hollowness sends ripples in all directions, even in the form of earlier Old Testament prophecies. After the earthquake and fire, the prophet Elijah then attended instead to a "tiny whispering sound" at the mouth of another hollow cave:

> . . . the Lord was not in the wind. After the wind there was an earthquake—but the Lord was not in the earthquake. After the earthquake there was fire—but the Lord was not in the fire. After the fire there was a *tiny whispering sound* (1 Kings 19:12, italics added).

And centuries later, one week before the total self-donation at the crucifixion, Elijah is seen atop a mountain conversing with a radiant Christ at the moment of the nearly blinding Transfiguration of Christ. In this moment is heard a distinct voice: "This is my beloved Son. Listen to him" (Mark 9:7). We can listen to him partly in that "tiny whispering sound" of conscience which is his echo within each of us. To listen in this silence is to be free for a second or two from the organized noise of modernity: the empty winds of media and celebrity talking heads. It is to be free from courtroom *fatwas* indifferent or even hostile to realities larger than our cult of individualism—such as the unborn child, marriage and family.

PAINTING BY THE NUMBERS

Today in place of symbolic numbers such as the Hebrew 613, our mathematical mindset and instrumentation have opened up an entirely new and expanding universe of science and physics. Science replaces myth. But should the natural sciences crowd the college catalogue so much that metaphysics—part of the range of human inquiry that is neither myth nor natural science—is reduced to near zero? A naïve and very uncomprehending Soviet cosmonaut sophomorically reported that in space he saw no angels. How does an educated person make such a peculiar statement? Are we really living in a God-free zone where the difference between spiritual good and evil are replaced by, say, the physical laws of nature, atoms and light waves? Is reality really confined to what we see only *with* the physical eyes and not through the eyes?

Can symbolic language be totally replaced by light meters and software code-writing? We should dread the day when the meanings of body or soul are bartered against each other, and when other contrived zero-sum tradeoffs are subcontracted to technical code-writers. Such apples-and-oranges comparisons are not to be reduced to a technical exercise. For these matters the supposedly modern politics of the middle ground is actually a return to primitive thought games. In so many pagan myths, imagined deities had relations with human beings such that their offspring split the difference as hybrids. Some of the offspring of Zeus (Zeus to the Greeks, and Jupiter to the Romans) were of this kind, half god and half mortal (not to be confused with the person and unity of Christ who is the fully human drawn into the fully divine).

The modern-day equivalent to pagan myths is television specials preaching a self-recreating cosmos as a blend of scientific data and the Hindu doctrine of an endless chain of existences (*samsara*). Some readers will recall the theological shading of Carl Sagan's *Cosmos* television series and book from the 1980s. As long before, today the modern mind looks for nothing higher that a hybrid being. Rather than a hybrid between earthly and divine things joined in the ancient creative imagination, today the hybrid is sought in the grunts and groans of a clueless pre-hominid "missing link." This Unlink comes from the slime of the earth (as in Genesis), but has no higher nature (unlike the rest of Genesis). It can never discover the presence of "Thou" equally beyond both the waterhole clan and our own trough-addicted collectives. The post-modern mindset wants to believe that we fell completely from low hanging branches, rather than that we lost our way in an altogether much richer Garden.

This is to say that today's circular argument is obvious. From the top, our modern age imagines itself liberated from error by our advances under only the scientific method. At the same time we dismiss all questions for which this method is irrelevant. Fossils never reveal that which does not fossilize. Clan burials fossilize, but graced togetherness does not fossilize. Spiritual evil does not fossilize. God is not stuff and does not fossilize. And without God, we humans really are little more than enlarged brains in meat suits barking this new dispensation back and forth. Limiting ourselves to physical evidence like fossils, even the most advanced science still remains stumped by the image on the Shroud of Turin. The Shroud is believed by many to be the burial shroud of the resurrected Christ—the *Logos*—the gratuitous and creative "reason" for and in all that is. This may or may not be the case, but honest science has failed to prove a fraud. The applied science includes everything from mass spectroscopy to the Sandia Laboratory VP-8 image analyzer used by the National Aeronautics and Space Administration (NASA) in planetary exploration.

Science declines to "speculate," but real scientists no longer decline to at least take a look. How unlike the less-than-scientific Supreme Court confronted with ultrasound evidence of the unborn child! Discovery of the "Thou" and the mystery of each other is tied up with the depth of human nature, not merely with human metabolism and burial artifacts. More than a missing link or leap in physical evolution, the spiritual core is a radiant leap in being, or the "ontological leap" as Pope St. John Paul II called it. This leap or discontinuity into the spirituality of the soul is not contained within nor ruled out by physical science. Holding that "the theory of evolution is more than hypothesis," he goes on to say that

The moment of transition to the spiritual cannot be the object of this kind of observation [meaning natural science], which nevertheless can discover at the experimental level a series of very valuable signs indicating what is specific to the human being. But the experience of metaphysical knowledge, of self-awareness and self-reflection, of moral conscience, freedom, or again of aesthetic and religious experience, fall within the competence of philosophical analysis and reflection, while theology brings out its ultimate meaning according to the Creator's plans.[3]

The missing piece proposed here is neither a mythical demi-god somewhere in imaginary star constellations, nor is it a dehumanized missing link perhaps still buried in the Omo Valley of southern Ethiopia or in Kenya. Instead, our ever greater, missing and silenced piece is planted both *within* ourselves *and* from outside ourselves. The missing link is in the very present and irreducible gap between humans as "persons," rather than as bundles of chemical elements worth less than five bucks each on the commodities market. Again, not to be confused with the physical laws of nature, the interior and universal natural law of the whole person involves an inner compass capable of lighting up the conscience.

Man is natural, but does not live by instincts alone. The fully human thing is sometimes to *not* follow our instincts, e.g., not to shack up in a motel room. This natural law is responsible human freedom. It reminds us what *not* to do in order to protect and even flourish in our nearly divine freedom. The natural law is also a positive thing, our unfolding path to real personal fulfillment, creativity, and true happiness as in the Sermon on the Mount. It is our fiery and heartfelt need to give our first loyalty to what is most real in ourselves and in others. Not to be diluted, the "don'ts" in the last six Commandments are the floor below which we may not fall without committing the rupture of "sin" against the reality of ourselves and of the God who speaks within.

THE WALL OF SEPARATION

So, what about man-made laws? Several years ago I was asked to speak to a small class of high school age students. After the session two of them approached me quite wide-eyed. They had experienced an "aha" moment and thanked me for what seemed no more than a passing remark. "Thank you for showing us," they said, "that what is legal is not always moral." "Aha", the downside of too rigorous a "wall of separation" between Church (or even natural morality) and state. We hear the endless drumbeat over "civil rights," but little about civil "wrongs." The old Jim Crow laws are familiar enough, but what now of the color blind but size-discriminatory United States Supreme Court's ruling under *Roe v. Wade*?

When is a branded "civil right" a counterfeit label and a violation of real law? Less gullible than ourselves today, in 1831 the abolitionist William Lloyd Garrison got these things right in just one sentence: "That which is not just is not law." Shouldn't a legality of majority-rule be held accountable to a higher standard than itself? While many products of positive law have only a minor bearing on morality or immorality, others do directly violate real persons—the universal natural law. They violate the inherent nature and transcendent dignity of the human person and of the common good. Less than a biblical prophecy, in 1835 the most acclaimed analyst of American culture, Alexis de Tocqueville, forecasted the dangerous future of our democracy:

> By whatever political laws men are governed in the ages of equality, it may be foreseen that faith in public opinion will become for them a species of religion, and the majority its ministering prophet. [4]

Is the divorce of morality from legality, and specifically the doctrinal "wall of separation between church and state," a legal fiction that has invited a new "species of religion?" Is this how best to understand the elite and what is in fact the establishment of Secular Humanism as the national religion? Is this how best to understand the two related realms of morality and civil law, when this absolutist choice of words ("wall of separation") appears in two Supreme Court decisions: *Everson v. Board of Education* (1947), and *McCollum v. Board of Education* (1948). The "wall of separation" is not found in the Constitution (1787), but rather is taken from a *private* letter by Thomas Jefferson written to a group of Baptists in Connecticut in 1802.

The Father of our Country, George Washington said something much less easily twisted in his *public* Prayer for the United State of America. He began with this: "Almighty God; we make our earnest prayer that Thou wilt keep the United States in Thy holy protection." He then prays that we imitate

Christ; otherwise we "can never hope to be a happy nation."[5] Today are we a happy nation? Jefferson himself had this to say:

> And can the liberties of a nation be thought secure when we have removed their only firm basis, a conviction in the minds of the people that these liberties are of the gift of God? That they are not to be violated but with His wrath? Indeed I tremble for my country when I reflect that God is just; that His justice cannot sleep forever."[6]

Many different schools of thought over the past few centuries have explored the details of inborn natural law as it applies to cases. Yes, our understanding of cases needs to be continually unpacked, but our conscience is the echo of permanent truths that are not invented, because they come to us ultimately from God. The artist Georges Braques said it simply, "truth exists, only falsehood has to be invented" (*Thoughts on Art*). In the politics of church and state a *legal* wall of separation—with possibly a few windows!—is one thing, but in the culture wars where is the *rational* wall of separation between discrimination and runaway reverse discrimination?

Compared to our culture of postured neutrality, the natural law is not just another brick that an older generation or dominant white bigots want to stuff into our backpacks. The natural law is more like a cure for such burdens and the boredom of not thinking. The natural law is our innermost core. It is our inner sense of the rightness of some things and the wrongness of others. It is not alien to our human nature. When Moses delivered the Ten Commandments, even back then he added: "This command which I enjoin on you today is not too mysterious and remote for you. No, it is something very near to you, already in your mouths and in your hearts; you have only to carry it out" (Deuteronomy 30:11, 14).

In the New Testament St. Paul also shows to us some of this primal truth: "When the Gentiles who have no law do by nature what the Law prescribes, these having no law are a law unto themselves. They show the work of the Law *written in their hearts*" (Romans 2:14-15, italics added). Only seeming to strain at gnats, in A.D. 325 the Church fathers met in councils to clarify the depth of the truth "written in our hearts." Is the Christ, whose echo is heard within, fully equal to the Father above, and is He *not* created? Yes, He is uncreated and of the same substance as the Father, and affected likewise is the universal natural law of who *we* really are. A few decades later, in A.D. 381 the Church clarified our historical and enduring Encounter with Christ by defining that this Christ in history is of two natures. Our human nature is lifted into the divine with the one "person" who is also one with the Father. As complete human beings we already are more than we can ever fully know in this life.

Again, by the natural law we do not mean only those other physical laws of nature. The laws of nature discovered by science give us only regularities of physical cause and effect. The famous inverse square law of gravity, discovered by Isaac Newton, is a law of nature and not the moral natural law. Likewise, at the atomic and cosmic levels we have the measured and statistics-based methods of modern Quantum Mechanics and the General Theory of Relativity, but these do not erase that which cannot be measured.

Natural law is of a different sort. Inside our heads the mind is always more than brain chemistry. While natural law is knit with divine law, it firstly can be known by the gift of unaided human reason. Such is the nature and capacity of open human intelligence as distinguished from closed rationalization. We should be allowed to talk about universal natural law without being charged with imposing "religion" on each other. The flourishing and even the survival of the human community depend upon it. Under the natural law we understand the difference between what we *can* do and what we *ought* to do. Never accused of being a religious voice, even Albert Einstein spoke against bracket creep, whether by the churches or by scientists. Science has to do with means of achieving ends; its method is not geared to define values and ends. He wrote:

> This is where the struggle of the Church against the doctrines of Galileo and Darwin belongs. On the other hand, representatives of science have often made an attempt to arrive at fundamental judgments with respect to values and ends on the basis of scientific method, and in this way have set themselves in opposition to religion. These conflicts have all sprung from fatal errors. [7]

Considering the outcome of abortions, the scientist makes a very good choice of words when he says "fatal errors." The real "creationist" in modern arguments is the one who sees the universe as only a projection of his own creative preferences. He is the one who believes that there is nothing in wo/man to be discover, only a world to be constructed. So-called rights are simply to be asserted, and so-called "creative" decisions are to be calculated based on cost and benefit analysis. Solzhenitsyn, survivor of years in the Gulag, saw through these mathematics: "We have lost the clarity of spirit which was ours when the concepts of Good and Evil had yet to become a subject of ridicule, shoved aside by the principle of fifty-fifty." [8]

WHAT ABOUT HISTORICAL EXCEPTIONS?

But skeptics then demand an explanation about the universality of natural law: what about the cannibals or about the head hunters in New Guinea in the southwest corner of the Pacific? Where then was the natural law, that tiny whispering sound of conscience? Oh yes, in New Guinea it gets even worse.

New mothers were even forced to feed their first child to the pigs and then in their place to suckle the sow's piglets. (We recall how during his conversion St. Augustine lamented tossing nothing more than stolen pears to the pigs.) Such was the extraction required by the dark forces of pagan customary religion. The big surprise is that in this, history actually repeats itself. This is the Big Lie (Chapter 2): today, mothers are induced to sacrifice a child here and there in order to hold onto a needed job in the consumer market. The answer to our skeptic is that the customary modernity he imposes is in fact a throwback.

Early Rome and Greece also exposed to the elements those children deemed (as we still say today) "unwanted." Other more primitive habits also challenge our intuitive sense of an innate natural law. In tribal Arabia female babies were often buried alive in the sand dunes for any number of calculated reasons—too many girls, too little water and food. As in New Guinea the Arab mothers also stuck together to share and even participate in each others' trauma. As also today, customary abuses of the natural law (ourselves) were normalized through socialization as in political groupings and now the social media. We recall the descent of abortion into "ordinariness" (Chapter 1).

But in Arabia, and notwithstanding all of the *Qur'an*'s internal contradictions that today lend themselves to terrorism, the seventh-century Mohammed was the first Arabian leader to reject female live burials (*Qur'an* verses 6:141, 152; 16:60-1; 17:31; and 81:3). Probably from the hadith is added this remark delivered to a guilty father: "Sons and daughters are both gifts of God, the Prophet reminded him. Both are equally gifts, and so they should always be treated equally."

The Christian gospels are not alloyed with moral contradictions. Instead, the commandments are transformed into the Sermon on the Mount. How utterly un-modern! The violence of Christians in history cannot be denied, but such events are a violation of both reason and their faith or religion. Even outside of canonical scripture, a recorded second-century Christian teaching, the *Didache*, already includes this specific natural law prohibition: "Do not murder a child by abortion or kill a newborn infant." In this matter of abortion, to the degree that modernity is estranged from Christianity, it is not an advance but instead is a throwback, if not all the way back to the Stone Age then at least in that general direction.

In so many ways we are living today in an uprooted world more and more like the final days of the Roman Empire as it, too, self destructed. A small bright spot challenging this anachronism is the positive defense made by a growing number for the rights of (preborn) human life. As on our sidewalks today, in imperial Rome small groups of Christians huddled in back chambers of the Coliseum. Hidden here they encouraged and prayed for martyrs as they passed in view into the arena to entertain and stupefy the jaded public of an earlier era. The witnesses to the truth will always be here. Like the sunrise, to be alive is perhaps an incredible gift rather than an accident, and if a gift then there is a Giver.

The answer to decadence as it masquerades as progress is to be steadfast in the sense of rightness and human purpose. In defense of this natural law G. K. Chesterton was attuned to more than he may have known when he said, "There is one way to stand up straight but a thousand ways to fall." To follow the natural law is to stand up straight against a legion of historical alternatives or exceptions. Moral neutrality today discounts too much the force of a kind of gravity in human affairs.

Continuing our inquiry into the more recent past, what about the widely varied norms among the Indian tribes in North America? Maybe here's an exception or two to the above patterns of false starts and repeated relapse. For ten years a tribal leader in the Rocky Mountains sought out the Jesuit missionary Pierre-Jean De Smet. This Flat-Head Indian chief was estimated to be at least eighty years of age. He knew of the Black Robes (Jesuit missionaries) and wanted to be baptized. For ten years he sought De Smet and finally had him brought back across the Great Plains from St. Louis. At the Rocky Mountain encampment, and as a condition for baptism, De Smet encouraged contrition by the chief for any past "offenses he might have committed against his Maker." This noble chief who De Smet describes as comparable in bearing to any Western aristocrat from the courts of Europe, gave this reply:

> No doubt, I have done many things that have offended the Great Spirit—but it was unknowingly; I never in my life did anything which I knew to be evil; from my childhood it has been my constant endeavor to avoid sin, and I never did a second time any action, when I was told that it was wrong. [9]

Natural law awaits conversion, as we kneel at the feet of Giver of divine and natural law and the life of the spirit. In another instance De Smet encountered an old Sioux who still wore a copper cross De Smet had given him twenty-six years earlier. The Sioux convert explained:

> When I was younger, I loved whisky to madness, and at every chance I would get drunk and commit excesses. It is now twenty-six snows since my last turbulent orgy. . . . Since then I have often had opportunities. . . . Every time the cross has come to my help. I would take it between my hands, imploring the Great Spirit to give me strength, and your words, Black-robe, would come to my mind. Ever since we first met, I have renounced drink, and have never tasted a drop. [10]

In 1868 De Smet ignored threats of death and, unarmed, entered the notorious Sitting Bull's camp. He was sent by the Great White Father in Washington to arrange a truce as he had done many times before. A revealing scene, this, that the leaders in Washington regularly had to turn to a Jesuit priest for someone enough trusted to do their bidding. It was violation of De Smet's treaty by the Whites that led to Custer's defeat at the Battle of the Little Big Horn in 1876. So much of history is a sad tale, but perhaps natural law keeps popping up as something always more enduring than any mere artifact or passing event of this chaotic history. Natural law has to do with the permanent nature of the human person, with the very truth of ourselves and what we sense from within about what is good and true.

Migration trails and smoke signals have been replaced by highways and electronics. Our new neighborhoods are non-territorial, and such accessibility can sometimes compensate for some of the anonymity that it creates in the modern world. To reach De Smet in St. Louis today one would not have to send runners on foot across the Great Plains. We should think of the disabled who, because of the Internet, are in touch with many others like themselves, and truly know that they are not alone. But as with so much else in technology, there are pluses and minuses. Even our new long-distance relationships like Facebook are virtual realities always at the mercy of the delete key or of hacking.

So many technological gadgets are often forces of vulnerability and of dispersal. These forces either erode ordinary relationships or, even worse, cause us to puddle into clans, generational tribes (millennials) or networked special interest groups. Sociologists call our electronic and atomized new loneliness *anomie,* or lost-ness. Listed in two-thirds of divorce filings are Facebook indiscretions and revisionist marital history as contributing to family breakups. Spouses talk less to each other than to others ready-at-hand whom they might never have met. The next time the reader is on public transit, notice how many family secrets are loudly announced by cell phone addicts in the presence of an unwilling and captive audience.

CONSCIENCE AND OPINION

Does conscience still matter more than our real-time electronic culture? Is it part of the Big Lie to redefine or morph what is meant even by "conscience"? Dissenters from the natural law and the notion of objective moral truth or moral absolutes sometimes point to nineteenth-century John Henry Cardinal Newman. They cast Newman as giving the upper hand to "private conscience" as the trump card in making applying moral principles to real world complexities. But the misquoted Newman actually understood conscience not as the court of last resort, but as a free and "dutiful obedience" in concrete cases. The exercise of conscience is both objective and personal, but let's let Newman speak for himself. A well-formed conscience might still be in error, but firstly,

[C]onscience has rights *because* it has duties; but in this age, with a large portion of the public, it is the very right and freedom of conscience *to dispense with* conscience, to ignore a Lawgiver and Judge, to be independent of unseen obligations.... Conscience is a stern monitor, but in this century it has been superseded by a *counterfeit* which the eighteen centuries prior had never heard of, and could not have mistaken for it if they had. It is the right of self-will (italics added).[11]

The conscience is obedience to the "tiny whispering sound" that echoes within each and all of us. Each of us is "alone with God whose voice echoes in his depths . . . [conscience is] a judgment of reason by which the human person recognizes the moral quality of a concrete act."[12] Conscience rises above license or false complexity or self-will. As our personal invitation and duty to "obedience" (from the Latin *ob odere*, the humility to listen deeply), conscience is not a putting down but a lifting up. Absolute prohibitions reflect absolute affirmations. The *transcendent* dignity of each human person is prior to any social contract, majority rule, social media messaging, or private balancing acts. The existing and living and pre-born child has—and even is—the right to not be abruptly un-chosen and violated, abandoned and extinguished.

Writing at the same time that Newman converted to Catholicism, the broad essayist, cultural critic and Anglican, John Ruskin (1819-1900), gives us more literary access to a nearly forgotten world ruled by reason rather than rationalization:

The enthusiast would reply that by Liberty he meant the Law of Liberty. Then why use the single and misunderstood word? If by liberty you mean chastisement of the passions, discipline of the intellect, subjection of the will; if you mean the fear of inflicting, the shame of committing, a wrong; if you mean respect for all who are in authority, and consideration for all who are in dependence; veneration for the good, mercy to the evil, sympathy with the weak; if you mean watchfulness over all thoughts, temperance in all pleasures, and perseverance in all toils; if you mean, in a word, that Service which is defined in the liturgy of the English church to be perfect Freedom, *why do you name this by the same word* by which the luxurious mean license, and the reckless mean change; by which the rogue means rapine, and the fool, equality; by which the proud mean anarchy, and the malignant mean violence (italics added)?[13]

Today Newman is regarded as the father of the Second Vatican Council (1962-5), the first worldwide convocation of bishops (some twenty-five hundred of them) since the First Vatican Council convened in Newman's time nearly a century earlier. Those who would use Newman to change the nature and teachings of Christianity to conform to new circumstances and to accommodate secular colonization misread Newman. Newman addressed the nature of ideas which might appear to alter through time: ". . . old principles reappear under new forms. . . . [An idea] changes with them [controversies] *in order to remain the same.* In a higher world it is otherwise, but here below to live is to change, and to be perfect is to have changed often. . . . The refutation and remedy of errors cannot precede their rise" (italics added).[14]

With regard to conscience the Second Vatican Council itself is misquoted by those averse to careful reading. "The Council's *Declaration on Religious Freedom* does not base the right to the free exercise of religion on 'freedom of conscience'. . . . Religious freedom, in turn, which men demand as necessary to fulfill their duty to worship God, has to do with *immunity from coercion* in civil society" [italics added].[15] But without the natural moral law, the West too quickly has dismissed the duty to discern objective truth from falsehood. It too often has replaced objective morality with the middle case of good intentions. Can we see that in its most extreme form this self-deceit—about the will of God—eventually gives us the suicide bombers of domestic terrorists and of radicalized Islam?

Do references to the Bible deaden some of our readers' capacity for curiosity and alertness about right and wrong? It is among the non-biblical and ancient Greeks—the civilization that pushed unaided human reasoning to its natural limits—that we find Plato telling much the same truths. Let's recall Elijah at the mouth of the cave (above). In a similar vein, in his *Republic*, Plato famously speaks of a tribe that lives totally in caves but facing the back wall. To these cave dwellers of all times and places, reality is taken to be our own shadows cast on the back wall of our contemporary echo chamber. And then one day, in our narcissist culture at large, we turn around to notice that the origin of our faint light is a fire and, further out, the sun at the mouth of the cave. The "aha" moment is the discovery of truth, the moral good, and the challenge to grow by daily reaching toward a stable truth that is ultimately outside of ourselves. There is something absolute, enduring and always new here, as is also found in the words of St. Paul: "It is not licit to do evil that good might come of it" (Romans 3.8).

A "NEW" WAY OF SEEING

The echo discovered within ourselves is the natural law, the true way of being at home with ourselves. Hearing the natural law is like turning from carved totems to surround-sound music. Fr. Savaterra (1648-1717), the Apostle to California, went off to meet the most resistant indigenous tribes, with no weapons of his own except a lute and the ability to play and to sing "I believe in thee, O my God. . . ." To the astonishment of many, the tribe gathered and simply . . . listened. We too should turn from the noise of modernity and simply listen to the music. Imagine the most sublime choir at its best, and by comparison the Big Lie comes across like the barking of hyenas in the bush.

The epiphany of the entire Western and human moment rose up in silence and contemplation, lifted by sacred Gregorian Chant performed in mountain top monasteries beyond the reach of every disorder. To be authentically "Western" is to be open to such a universal; it is not narrowly Eurocentric simply because of geography. This clarity waits to be rediscovered, even in the West. At the cosmic scale, Hildegard of Bingen, a thirteenth-century mystic and Doctor of the Church, comments on the difference between the localized body and the universal spirit, "the word stands for the body, but the symphony stands for the spirit. . . . All of creation is a symphony of the Holy Spirit which is joy and jubilation." [16]

Compared to this "aha" moment of spirited inspiration, trying to capture God and his creation in *only* mass-produced books or even mathematical equations is akin to swinging at the fresh breeze with a butterfly net. Math at least is musical in a way, but the higher mystery of the universe is always a complete symphony, not a one-string violin. An expansive reading of Scripture might alert us to the profound musical meaning of Genesis and of the mystery of creation. On the *seventh* day (the music of symbolic and holy numbers) God rests in silence from the activity of his totally gratuitous Creation, the humanly incomprehensible fact of existence and the cosmos. [17] This resting is the *silence* behind the musical notes of starlight and birds singing: "God looked at everything he had made, and he found it very good" (Genesis 1:31). Very good, especially, is mankind. Silence is not simply a dull note in a sequence of notes. It is the awesome holiday behind such notes. And more than a work break, we too *are* a holiday of spirit and reason barely touched by a knotted cosmos of mere matter. We are the only thing created for its own sake, with the capacity to hear within ourselves His silence.

Why does anything *exist*, rather than nothing, as in no-thing? And even before this, what then is the nature of these things that exist? With "man" on board (and human nature as more than a bundle of stardust) all of creation is found not only to be, but to be good, and now very good. Such an in-your-face "creation" is the delight of a Poet, an Author and an Artist of all that is. This self-sufficient God exists in some real sense in all of His things. Otherwise this pallet in all of its parts remain at zero. (In answer to the mocking Oval Office riddle cited in Chapter 2, *this* is what the meaning of *is* is.) God shares the selfness of His very existence through a totally free labor of love. Christianity is the message that what is "very good" in the poem is invited home to meet the Poet as *Logos*.

This invitation toward a higher future preoccupied a growing but imperfect population for centuries. But after the so-called Dark Ages, Renaissance Europe turned its eyes back to the pre-Christian memories of Classical antiquity, the Greeks and the Romans. Like the postmodern mind today, the motivation of what followed as the Enlightenment was to frame the individual alone within worldly society alone. The new dispensation is uncomplicated by the near-impossible but gifted spiritual tension of the Christian vision. As this vision of the Dark Ages is totally abandoned man becomes the measure of all things, and to keep up to date even our history is rejected— abandoned. Keeping in step, today the charter of the modern European Union points to the Classical world but admits nothing of formative Christianity in Europe (or the world) over the past two millennia. The modern revelation is that Reason is allergic to Revelation, and that in society we are all more or less holding hands on a flat-earth terrain, a real Dark Age.

Prior to the fifteenth-century Renaissance and then the Enlightenment, the language of art, for example, was particularly infused with Christian themes and symbolic content. These signs are evidence of an interior and yet continuously new, different and supernatural way of seeing. It was these "religious" themes that, to new thinkers at least, seemed to get in the way of greater engagement in the natural world. Writings of all sorts give evidence to this devolution. The trail is literally visible in the visual arts. In the history of art we read that sophisticated linear perspective with eye-level vanishing points in the earthbound distance are a new invention dating only from Renaissance Italy. The earliest breakthrough is a church fresco in Florence painted by the twenty-one year old Masaccio (1425). This wall painting depicts Mary and John in the foreground at the foot of the cross, but now standing against the visual depiction of a receding, Roman style vaulted-ceiling. The illusion of volumetric space is revolutionary. Art historians have spent a lot of time writing on this transition into Renaissance art and architectural design. But the most common detail is that all the craftsmen and artists are known by name. They sign their work. Medieval art is anonymous, as if giving glory to another and not as if positioning for the next patron and commission.

With the coming of the Renaissance and later scholarship, the earlier and medieval architecture was termed Gothic as an expression of contempt. With this term the earlier cathedrals of Europe, even the best of the past such as Notre Dame Cathedral in Paris, were thrown in with the migrating invaders (Goths) who for centuries had intruded westward from the plains of central Asia. Such was the cultural perspective or viewpoint. Yet, in medieval times the master builder of the communal cathedral stood inside when the final scaffolding was removed. He was buried alive on those few occasions when it didn't stand. In the entitlement world of today we have, instead, golden parachutes and plausible deniability, and future generations who are vulnerable the collapse of overdrawn economies or ecologies.

The post-Gothic style of linear perspective in architecture and painted illusions was seen with the eyes of the liberated and freestanding individual viewers, and not to the transcendent and timeless eyes of the living God. Medieval works had been more symbolic, although often more realistic than is commonly admitted. But distant figures and nearby figures of equal importance are the same size. Within this light there are no shadows. Here's the question: is this medieval way of seeing *through* the eyes really inferior? Or does a fully human understanding rest more than we admit on a dialogue between past and future insights and generations? An inchworm crawling over a Renaissance portrait and then the fallen face of a medieval icon would probably report that from his perspective there is no meaningful difference. Likewise for an inchworm stroll across the face of a modern-day smart phone.

And, however advanced technically, is the new way of rendering—with linear perspective from the viewer outward—really that new? Does this subjective vantage point invalidate a deeper silence and humility? On the question of newness even the cave paintings of Lascaux in the Dordogne Valley in southwestern France speak to us. We find the profile of a horse whose head is actually turned toward the viewer. This in itself is remarkable, stunning even, and strikingly modern. In addition to this frontal turning, the horse's head is disproportionately large. Is this apparent distortion deliberate and a foreshadowing of modern perspective? This "modern" innovation even has a name; it is called foreshortening. One of the wall paintings even bears the silhouette of a hand print . . . is this a (Renaissance-style) signature, but unaided by written language? The Lascaux cave paintings were done thirty thousand years before our time. Perspective, and even realism, also shows up surprisingly in the excavated ruins of pre-Renaissance Pompeii. Rather than being invented full blown from the head of Zeus, as the expression goes, did we Renaissance moderns mostly relearn and only then perfect perspective? But even here, the blessing is a mixed one. The technique of foreshortening, within the mind, distracts us with current events and dismisses the longer lessons of history. In the market place of ideas today, we ask, why teach history?

I cannot recall now the title or the exact date, but one of the "pre-modern" Gothic paintings depicts a multitude of human figures in a rather puzzling way. Not only are the distant figures and near figures all on the same picture plane up front, but we find superimposed on top of or even within a few large figures, a dense pattern of these additional figures. The primary figures include within themselves a sort of tapestry of additional smaller figures. What might this mean? Are these primary figures connected to future generations within themselves, or are they connected to past generations? Or both? Is this a medieval painting of time perspective? Is the "individual" seen in continuity, as part of an intergenerational family that transcends the modern fixation on divisive generation gaps? Is our being intergenerational one of the best ways to be part of something bigger than ourselves? Do the medieval artists see a time-defying solidarity while we moderns choose to record only real-time digital selfies? In a dinner gathering where imperfect politics had become the topic, a millennial protested that *"our generation* wants a president who is clear and moral." To which I asked, "How does this make yours any different from any other generation?" Then there came an uncomprehending silence. Just pass the mashed potatoes.

Taking these musings further, we might wonder whether the Israelite men, not counting women and children, really numbered "six hundred thousand" when Moses led them out of Egypt (Exodus 12:37). Is this a symbolic number too, or even better yet, does it also represent a sort of intergenerational way of seeing individual people at any given point in time? Does the large number include future generations from those walking in sandals in the moment of freedom from Egypt? Near-sighted modernity discounts everything—our currency for sure, but also the past and the future. We might do well to think of "creation" as the rejection of discounting and as the true valuing of all things.

Less precise than mathematics, are symbolic numbers still quite as true? Within fully human history, when is modern individualism more of a descent than an imaginary ascent of "moving forward"? In numerous biblical accounts we are invited not to look down, but to "look up." Take the seemingly minor detail of Gideon in the Old Testament book of Judges. Gideon is instructed to take into battle only those Israelites who drink water in a certain way, by looking up. What is this all about? The Lord says,

> There are still too many soldiers . . . You shall set to one side everyone who laps up the water as a dog does with its tongue; to the other, everyone who kneels down to drink. [Those who lapped up the water raised to their mouths by hand numbered three hundred....] By means of the three hundred who lapped up the water I will save you and will deliver Midian into your power (Judges 7:4-7).

This first group, small as it was, remained poised for action in a big world. Their eyes were still open and watchful of the common threat and the shared mission. Such watchful readiness is a far cry from the small-world Big Lie of "readiness" pandered today to sexually-active teens and even pre-teens.

Today what is it that we no longer hear or see from the mouth of the cave of Plato or Elijah? The biblical watchfulness is a readiness and attentiveness toward the real, toward oneself and others, and toward a God who is other than ourselves. Do we no longer hear the echo of that "tiny whispering sound?" In the academic world does the need for successful peer reviews too often discount any inkling toward what is beyond ourselves or beyond the cocoon of our particular research or research method? In so many academic citadels the scientific method and overspecialization are the message.

Professional courtesy and tunnel vision assure that the (traditional!) university is more and more of a flattened and fragmented multiversity. Residents of the various dialects, or disciplines as they are called, too often lose the zest for broad and fully human inquiry into the truth. In competition for administrative favor we become ever more interested in lining our nests. At the multiversity the overall administrators speak only the Esperanto language of budgets and alumni donations. The vision of politically correct multiculturalism looks a lot like administrative supervision.

The original wall of separation between church and state has taken its revenge even on academia where it took shape. In the catalogue of specialty courses, the universal and "tiny whispering sound" is the piece missing and no longer permitted. The big bucks and tenure tracks are in technocracy and social science. Research grants are jostled to guide the juggernaut of social evolution along its inevitable path. However, some of the churches still remember and wonder at the blinding-light experience of St. Paul on the Road to Damascus (Acts 9:4, 22:7, 26:14). Under the library Dewey decimal system things of faith are grouped with mythology. Case closed. But which is the more cursory, capitulation to the myth of social evolution toward equality in history, or a bent knee toward the One above history and yet echoing equally (!) within each of us? "Jesus Christ is the same yesterday, and today, and forever" (Hebrews 13:8). In a comment on our present moment in our tormented history, and still worthy of any faculty lounge, the Russian novelist, Dostoevsky, offers this assessment: "If there is no God, everything is permissible." Prior to the New Testament and such modernity, the Old Testament hints at the testimony of Hebrews (above): "The first man never finished comprehending wisdom, nor will the last succeed in fathoming her. For deeper than the sea are her thoughts; her counsels, than the great abyss" (Sirach 24:26,27).

NOTES

1. Cited in Jean Cardinal Danielou, *Prayer as a Political Problem* (New York: Sheed and Ward, 1967), 115.

2. For thorough answers to the critics of the bodily resurrection of Christ, see Carl E. Olson, *Did Jesus Really Rise from the Dead?* (San Francisco and Greenwood Village, CO: Ignatius Press and Augustine Institute, 2016).

3. Pope John Paul II, "Message on Evolution to the Pontifical Academy of Sciences," (October 23, 1996), nn. 4, 6.

4. Alexis de Tocqueville, *Democracy in America*, Vol. II, Bk. 1, Ch. II.

5. In his *public* Prayer for the United States of America, Washington said: "Almighty God; we make our earnest prayer that Thou wilt keep the United States in Thy holy protection; that Thou wilt incline the hearts of the citizens to cultivate a spirit of subordination and obedience to government. . . . And finally that Thou wilt most graciously be pleased to dispose to all to do justice, to love mercy, and to demean ourselves with that charity, humility and pacific temper of mind which were the characteristics of the Divine Author of our blessed religion, and without a humble imitation of whose example in these things we can never hope to be a happy nation. Grant our supplication, we beseech Thee, through Jesus Christ our Lord. Amen." (Marjorie Barrows, *One Thousand Beautiful Things* [Chicago: Peoples Book Club, Inc., 1947], 425).

Benjamin Franklin, another Freemason but more radical, sometimes expressed an either-or mindset, "The way to see by faith is to shut the eyes to reason."

6. From the fair copy of the drafts of the Kentucky Resolutions of 1798.—*The Writings of Thomas Jefferson*, Paul L. Ford (ed.), vol. 7, p. 305 (1896).

7. Albert Einstein, "Science and Religion" (1939), *Out of My Later Years* (New York: Philosophical Library, 1950), 25-26.

8. Aleksandr Solzhenitsyn, "We have ceased to see the Purpose," Liechtenstein, Sept. 14, 1993, in Edward Ericson and Daniel Mahoney (eds.), *The Solzhenitsyn Reader* (Wilmington, DE.: Intercollegiate Studies Institute, 2008), 591-601.

9. Pierre-Jean De Smet, "Origin, Progress, and Prospects of the Catholic Mission to the Rocky Mountains" (Fairfield, Washington: Ye Galleon Press, 1967, a reprint from a possibly unique original in the Oregon Province Archives dated 1843), 12 pages. Three centuries earlier, between 1531 and 1548 some *nine million* Indians in Mexico sought and received baptism. This astonishing record was in response to the apparition of the Mother of God, Our Lady of Guadalupe and now the Patroness of the Americas, to Juan Diego on Tepeyac hill outside of what is now Mexico City, on December 12, 1531. (This event and its influence coincide with the early Reformation in the Old World—and in Luther's Germany the brutal suppression of the Peasants' Revolt.) Brought to an abrupt end was the Aztec devil-god cult of human sacrifice that had claimed tens of thousands of victims each year. See Warren H. Carroll, *A History of Christendom: The Cleaving of Christendom* (Vol. 4), (Front Royal, VA: Christendom Press, 2000), 615-27.

10. Pierre-Jean de Smet, *Life, Letters and Travels of Father Pierre-Jean de Smet, SJ, 1801-1873*, Vol. 3 (Bibliolife.com: Washington State University, n.d.), 913.

11. From a Letter to the Duke of Norfolk," in Vincent Blehl, *The Essential Newman* (New York: Mentor Omega, 1963), 264-65. Newman once wrote: "there are but two alternatives, the way to Rome, and the way to Atheism: Anglicanism is the halfway house on the one side, and Liberalism is the halfway house on the other."

12. See the *Catechism of the Catholic Church*, 1994 (nn. 1776-1802).

13. John Ruskin, "The Lamp of Obedience," *The Seven Lamps of Architecture*, 1849.

14. *Essay on the Development of Christian Doctrine*, London: Longman, Green, 1885; extract in Vincent Blehl, The Essential Newman, New York: Mentor-Omega, 1963), 115-155.

15. Abbott, The Second Vatican Council's *Declaration on Religious Liberty*, fn. 1. Also, on the difference between unformed conscience and the voice of truth: "Conscience frequently errs from invincible ignorance without losing its dignity. The same cannot be said of a man who cares but little for truth and goodness, or of a conscience which by degrees grows practically sightless as a result of habitual sin" (Second Vatican Council, *Constitution on the Church in the Modern World*, n. 16).

16. From Hildegard von Bingen, *Scivias* (*Know the Ways*).

17. Regarding the "days" of creation, the early theologian St. Augustine said this: "The fact is that the world was made simultaneously with time . . . As for the 'days', it is difficult, perhaps impossible to think—let alone explain in words—what they mean" (St. Augustine, *The City of God*, Part 3, Book 6 (c. 213-226 A.D.).

Chapter Five

The Missing Piece

Against the backdrop of biblical Wisdom, how many times have we heard that something is merely "inappropriate?" Even actions that are downright evil are watered down under this catchall. In reality, some things are truly evil. Some things—and we do know what they are—betray the silence within and the reality of who we really are. Some things betray the tiny whispering sound of conscience—the echo of wisdom and truth. It's the Big Lie that mislabels these betrayals. What's wrong with this picture?

THE BIG PICTURE TORN

My first stark memory of an inappropriate action that was also evil started simply enough. In 1950 this author, a young boy of only six years, is Little Peter. Little Peter admired his older brother's drawings of sailing ships. His own romantic view of the sea would even carry over into his stint in the United States Navy in the late 1960s. At that earlier time his brother, older by three years, drew a marvelous study of the ocean floor, colored it, and made a gift of it to our younger budding artist. The composition is vividly recalled even today as including a sunken sailing ship to the left and a deep sea diver to the right at the bottom end of a breathing hose that extended to the top of the page. The blue undersea world reached in all directions far enough to also include a school of fish and a shark circling overhead.

The magic of this mysterious underwater world centered on a treasure chest on the ocean floor. It fit in to the composition like the North Star surrounded by its ring of constellations in the sky. And the treasure chest was sprung open to reveal pirates' jewels and coinage from distant places far beyond the edges of the drawing. Here were all of the almost inaccessible mysteries of the "deep calling on deep" (Psalm 42:7).

Little Peter treasured the gift of this drawing more than anything else. On the first day of such an epiphany he could not contain himself. So he arranged to share his best treasure with his best friend, Little David, from across the street. Such a very special disclosure with Little David had to be done in a very special place, in the enclosed shade under the front porch. Finally the moment arrived, and Little Peter retrieved the treasure carefully from his pocket and carefully unfolded it. Little David's eyes were so drawn into the picture and its world that he seized the treasure and in an instant tore it into small pieces before it could be rescued. With the fragments scattered, David ran home to hide himself, leaving Little Peter as shattered as the picture, and quite alone and deeply abandoned.

What happened between best of friends was not simply "inappropriate." The modern gurus of social adjustment know nothing of such ruptures in the lives of even little ones. Yes, now there was a certain equality; both were equally deprived of the gifted drawing. Finally Little Peter collected the fragments, all except one, and retreated back into the house. Missing was the sunken and now stolen treasure at the center of it all. All the rest was suddenly a meaningless cloud of disconnected details. Tape could never restore the big picture. The older brother stepped in and promised that in time he could draw a second picture every bit as good as the first, but this could never be more than a consolation prize, a substitute or counterfeit for the real.

The rest of this sad tale is that Little Peter settled for go-with-the-flow revenge. (With Dostoevsky, ". . . everything is permitted.") Now everything was broken. Little Peter and Little David were divided and had no one to play with. The facing front yards were doubly silent. Then, as dusk approached, a phone call was made—I do not know who spoke first—and friendship grew deeper that day, rather than being ruptured permanently. The great revelation was not the role of shallow appropriateness in daily events, but the poised precipice of either festering evil or of a total course change into reconciliation.

Less than ten years later, an older and somewhat wiser Peter was to learn again the hard lesson of the "missing piece." As an eighth grader and beyond his years in his own art work, Peter was asked to make for the school a very large window mural for the coming Christmas season. This work would measure fifteen feet on a side (five vertical side-by-side panels, each three feet wide and fifteen feet high). The display area was a two-storey bank of windows over the main entrance. The scrolls for this Christmas manger scene were a tough oat meal paper. The painted panels were saturated with linseed oil and dried to become translucent to the lights behind.

On a Monday afternoon the panels went up, but by the next morning the entire manger scene went missing, torn down. Another missing piece, this time much larger than before and centered on a manger with gold, frankincense and myrrh, rather than only pirates' gold. Someone had complained about a student's religious art work displayed in a public school, even as "In God we Trust" remains on public currency (another controversy and scandal to the young). This was in 1957. Why was I not totally surprised? Two years earlier, our sixth-grade public school teacher, widowed in 1944 by a Nazi torpedo in the North Atlantic, had been a model of faith, uncommon courage and morality in her manner of teaching. With her we began each class day by standing for the Pledge of Allegiance. This was followed by the Lord's Prayer. "The reason we are doing this," she announced, "is so that if they ever come down the hall to drag me away, you will at least know the reason why." The drift into radical secularization had already begun. Today—the Pledge is awkward in public schools . . . and the Lord's Prayer? Today, under the fictional constitutional "wall of separation," the wall separating grammar school bathrooms for boys and girls is demolished.

As the manger scene is expelled so too is the lighting from behind. In 1916 on the eve of the First World War, the British parliamentarian got it just about right: "The lamps are going out all over Europe and we shall not see them lit in our life-time." Today, the world is at our electronic fingertips, but the universe is unlit. What has such a spiritual exile done to our communal sense of what is truly real and what is not? In our schools we have the flat earth pragmatism of John Dewey (1859-1952) whose only truth is constant "social evolution" adjustment to whatever—based on the research methods and worldview transplanted from the natural sciences.

FALSE GODS

If the center doesn't hold, what takes its place? Nature abhors a vacuum. So, what more is there in the air that smells just a little bit like the Big Lie? Let us attend now to the parallel universe of entertainment celebrities . . . there's the constant buzz, the lights, the tabloids, the interviews, the grocery store pulp fiction, the second rate and soon forgotten movies, the pasty self-conferred awards, and always the money behind all the chatter. One leading narrative of such distracted heavy breathing is that of one man in particular attracted like a moth to this flame. The flame, in this case, was the widow of the legendary Elvis Presley.

Let's have a look. The military career of Priscilla Presley's adoptive father required a household move every few years. After being noticed by Elvis in Germany, at a very young age, and then her later divorce, Elvis passed away in 1977 at the early age of forty-two. Along came a well-tailored and self-admitted human mannequin. Knocking at the door was a male model for the exclusively priced designer clothes industry. He would later publish his tale with its steamy episodes, but as an introspective narrative it achieves other more noteworthy details.[1] At the beginning Michael

Edwards meets Priscilla as her invited guest to a socialite party, and one thing leads to another to where he becomes her live-in boyfriend for a period of six years.

Their time together is punctuated by a few mutual infidelities and other highs and lows, especially the frenzied and entirely predictable distractions of their respective and competing film careers. Escapes are made into one diversion or another, like their safari in Africa. Very early in the game Edwards discovers that cocaine makes it possible to shoot movie scenes day after day without sleep. Many such stars sign over their lives in this way to the fast-clipped movie industry and not all escape. Judy Garland, Marilyn Monroe and countless others, and maybe even the King himself (with excessive dependence on prescription drugs), all sputter out in the game of marketing their face and a talent, and often more. The troubled Monroe was molested when young, as she spent much of her youth in foster homes and an orphanage, all this before any dalliances with the high-society Kennedy clan.

In his book—really a public confession to show "how I had [later] changed to become a successful, independent man"—Edwards laments that good-looking people like himself are cheated in such a way that they never grow up, that there is always this thing that is missing. In the postscript he looks back on his hollow and lucrative modeling career: "I felt like a prehistoric man living in a cave, grabbing every woman in sight—not needing a brain." Prehistoric . . . cave . . . surely this admission from a trophy "relationship" validates our thesis that much of what passed for modernity is really a throwback. Such regression at the center of popular culture then becomes such a hollow affliction to a much wider generation of cheering and misled wannabes. Decades ago the Catholic novelist, Georges Bernanos, exposed the true face of moral relativism. Already in the late 1940s he wrote,

> The modern world will shortly no longer possess sufficient spiritual reserves to commit genuine evil. Already . . . we can witness a lethal slackening of men's conscience that is attacking not only their moral life, but also their very heart and mind, altering and decomposing even their imagination . . . The menacing crisis is one of infantilism.[2]

For the unreal world of unknown wannabes there are, of course, the compensating and ongoing distractions of party drugs, pain-numbing media games, corrupt television sitcoms, formless sex with its blurred boundaries and the inevitable "why not" and "whatever," the hookup culture of one-night flings. Reasonable boundaries are the difference between human society and a tub of interactive protoplasm. Add to this confusion the dysfunctional parents when they're even around, and broken families amidst a rising tide of economic uncertainty. Today the world of absentee fathers accounts for much confusion in vulnerable young men unsure about everything including their own sexual identity.[3]

The stories of other young people who do find ways to turn their overturned lives around give us more cause for hope. Many of these tell their own stories in writing, sometimes as part of alternative school programs. One short and readable volume is *You've Got it All Wrong* by students of Scriber Lake (alternative) High School just north of Seattle. This sanctuary is included on a broader Internet site for similar stories.[4] Students tell how they have outgrown physical and sexual abuse, broken homes, and their own mistakes with drugs and so on.

In Edwards' book length narrative of his years with Priscilla Presley, the most unguarded moment and a symbol of our times is his discovery that Priscilla is pregnant. "What about our careers," they ask. "Do we want to have a child? Are we ready?" So much for the ethics of "readiness" foisted onto a betrayed generation by our self-appointed opinion makers. Edwards speaks to himself about the conveyor belt decision toward an abortion. Of himself he writes, "It's against your morals," but then in the same breath finds that "I'd become confused."

Years earlier Priscilla had even briefly considered aborting her own Lisa who was born nine months after her marriage to Elvis. Once again here was a "situation," particularly for Edwards, always living in the shadow of Elvis, "The King." So, as he confides in his public confession, "I knew as a father it was my responsibility to stop the abortion," and then in the very next paragraph he picks up Priscilla, crushed, hiding behind dark glasses, coming out of the medical center/abortuary, "I regretted that I hadn't taken responsibility." A timeless reality—St. Augustine (as we have noted) also fathered an illegitimate son unwanted at the time, but quickly came to love and deeply respect him. His later writings recommend to young men that a child brings with it the sobering effect of responsibility. Augustine perceptively named his son Adeodatus—"gift of God."

Edwards writes that after the abortion, "We were depressed for months. We couldn't seem to get the enthusiasm together to do anything. A distance had opened between us like a chasm, and it kept widening." A few years later Edwards gets it right. And he at least was not a fortune hunter, an insincere motive that Priscilla always feared, but then this from Edwards: "Our perpetual, unremitting love life had been the devil's making. We'd become like two animals snared in a trap—snarling, eyes bulging and berserk, twitching and jerking. Our world was completely out of kilter."

He muses later that the child might have been the event that could have held them together, that then their liaison would have been not simply another distraction.

Here was a man who seemingly had everything, but yet something at the center was missing—what was it? "The big house, fine cars, tennis court, pool, people attending us around the clock—none of this could get you the moon. . . . Or even a little bit of serenity. That, I now realized, was what I wanted." Serenity . . . Are we possibly reminded here of St. Teresa of Calcutta? She also spoke of serenity: "The fruit of silence is prayer; the fruit of prayer is faith; the fruit of faith is love; and the fruit of love is service." How far is such an "orientation" from our organized noise, socialite high-fives, and whatever. . . .

Hollywood has trivialized family into a target for mockery and has reduced sex to a tell-all and show-all spectator sport. Celebrities do not literally immolate their own children—as did the Old Testament worshipers of Baal in Canaan and sometimes even the Israelites (the Chosen People) whenever they went native. Today celebrities often are content to deep-six real marriage, and on courtroom letterhead to mock the very idea of a "traditional family" (Justice Blackman's "stereotypical family"). Photo-op weddings are only snapshots of a spectrum of possibilities within a lifestyle of sedated boredom. The *a la carte* menu also includes alcoholism, drugs, multiple divorces, loneliness, depression, mental illness and now legalized marijuana. Like spiritual gluttony, the religion of on tap sex is also a formula for repetitive boredom. C. S. Lewis flags this similarity—what we see in temple prostitution old and new—the "momentary distraction [of simply possessing rather than desiring] . . . [the] deadly error, which appears on every level of life and is equally deadly on all, turning religion into a self-caressing luxury and love into auto-eroticism" (*Surprised by Joy*, 1955).

From Blaise Pascal, the nineteenth-century French philosopher and mathematician, we learn this about our compulsive distractedness: "the whole calamity of man comes from one single thing, that he cannot keep quiet in a room." Yes, the calamity of the lost silence of Genesis and of our own personal "tiny whispering sound." Michael Edwards helps us out with this. He admits of his life with Priscilla Presley: "Although Priscilla and I shared much love, we experienced very little mutual growth. Neither one of us was willing to spend time alone, to face that terrifying part of ourselves."

Of the one fleeting moment of serenity in his youth, Edwards recalls the quiet of a church, ". . . *Above the organ was a life-sized crucifix, and if I stared at Jesus long enough he came to life and smiled at me. I was filled with a warm feeling of love and understood the meaning of the words 'My cup runneth over.'*" Edwards recognized the missing piece and the missing peace in our lives. This piece—this peace—comes in something so simple as hearing, and hearing comes in the willingness to listen deeply to the One who is willing to "suffer with" us. The Christian would say that in a graced moment Edwards discovered the reality of unconditional love overflowing. He also discovered the sobriety of true love that is the permanent cure for boredom. We can catch a hint of our own in Scripture (especially 2 Corinthians 1:3-4, Philippians 4:7, and John 14:27).

But this all changed when Edwards' grandmother turned her attention to Christian Science and bullied the rest of the family to fall in line. Not long after, suffering from an accidental compound fracture and then refusing medical treatment, she died. "I saw grandma bleed to death and I lost my faith. . . . I blamed it all on religion." And why not, there are countless precedents. Nero blamed the conflagration of Rome—which he likely ignited—on followers of the Christian religion. The blame game is the broken trust that expels us from the Garden—to blame our own failings on others and finally on the Other.

HOLLYWOOD STUMBLES INTO THE DEEP END

In Edwards' early rejection of religion, we might see a bit of C. S. Lewis who also lost his faith early, at the age of nine, when his mother died of cancer. But, or course, Lewis' complete story is quite different and therefore is carefully excluded from many high school reading lists of modern education. His story of a faith regained is reflected in the movie *Shadowlands* (1993, starring Anthony Hopkins). Yes, even Hollywood does have many better moments. These possibly patronizing departures from the movie mainstream should be noticed and encouraged, and even can play a bit part of a more truly liberal education.

But such anomalies do not square with the prevalent religion of Secular Humanism. By definition this dominant cult has no room for the higher realities, no room for transcendence. Transcendence is the simple fact that the fully human horizon extends beyond the curvature of the earth. Transcendence is home to the missing piece. It is the only genuine "choice" that makes other choices truly real for us. We are to be "perfect, therefore, as [our] heavenly Father is perfect" (Matthew 5:48). This is the real choice—to get hooked on life and on life at the highest level, ultimately the "new life" proclaimed so clearly by St. Paul. Secular Humanism is the anti-religion of neutrality, and under this disguise has not only marginalized religion from the public square, but has become our court-established national religion—in violation of the United States Constitution (the First Amendment).

One of the recent Hollywood action movies that most young adults probably have seen is *The Hunger Games* (2012) based on the novel by Suzanne Collins. Did the reviewers get the right spin on the first movie? Or is something missing as with most reviews of *Moby Dick*? Possibly missing is an entire layer of messaging. Beneath the surface and from front to last the movie might serve as a brilliant allegory of another much discounted narrative. Here's a pitch for the popular *Hunger Games* movie as actually echoing a biblical story.

Following a history of self-inflicted catastrophe, a nuclear war, the surviving and impoverished population of District 12 is blocked from a forested abundance. The barricade is an electric fence. Is this the biblical account of wo/mankind's expulsion from the Garden of Eden guarded by a flaming sword (Genesis 3:23-4)? History is a severe and accurate teacher in this regard. It is when we expel the hand of God from our shoulder that we become abandoned. Is it merely a coincidence that the total number of districts (twelve) is also the number of the Old Testament tribes of Israel? Does the singling out of combatants echo how David was singled out to deal alone with Goliath in what otherwise would be general carnage between the Israelites and the Philistines? Paired teams are selected from each district to fight to the death until there is but one survivor.

The teenage heroine volunteers herself as a gladiator in place of her lottery-selected younger sister—whom she loves more than herself. Could this self-sacrifice be Christ's self donation for a fallen humanity, as witnessed in the Gospels? The gladiator games begin with a race to a house-sized cornucopia overflowing with various weapons of choice. Later, from the wired-in and ever watchful sky dome above the arena, there comes a voice of guidance to the heroine. She is to seek "the high ground, because water is life." A reference to baptismal waters? Soon a temporary coalition of gladiators commandeers the cornucopia as a base camp for squirreling away a great heap of wealth they have recovered and hoarded. (Thomas Hobbes' solution to the primordial battle of all against all.)

The stacked pyramid is surrounded by an unseen mine field whose destructive power marks the moral ambivalence of worldly wealth, especially when amplified by technological advance. At the top of the pyramid, however, is a bag of something ancient—apples. From "the beginning" the forbidden fruit at the center of Eden, the apple, symbolizes our hesitation toward either rapturous bonding and fulfillment or a lower appetite to possess all of creation. In Genesis the fall even includes our most intimate marital calling for bonding as co-creators—not mere owners—with God.

The heroine of the *Hunger Games* is more than a feminized William Tell. Skilled with a bow and arrow, with one shot she dislodges the seemingly casual bag of apples and they tumble down in all directions to detonate the entire surrounding minefield. Destroyed is all of the hoarded worldly wealth of the gladiator arena. Is this an echo of the "original sin" that dislodged our harmony with nature and within ourselves and with others, and even with the Giver? As the plot moves along, the endangered heroine finds survival and safety high up in a tree. So, is this sanctuary the Tree of Life (Genesis 2:9)?

But, then we find a danger nested in the same tree. Here is a surrogate for serpentine Evil coiled within the gift of Life (Genesis 3:1)—in this case it is a hive of killer wasps. Throughout the games we also find a wildly grinning voyeur and talk show host and interrogator. He plays to the massive audience in their remote and high-tech coliseum, much like the chief priest or Pilate did just prior to the conviction of the innocent Christ (e.g., Matthew 27:1-2).

The heroine freely decides to risk her life for her fellow gladiator from District 12. Again, is this a savior figure like Christ? "Greater love hath no man than this, that a man lay down his life for his friends" (John 15:13). The later decision by these two last surviving figures is to exercise the freedom of dying "together" rather than battling against each other for singular suprema-cy. Then, together, they eat grapes! Is this the wine consecrated and shared by Christ at the Last Supper, the mystery of self-sacrifice within a banquet of thanksgiving (Matthew 26:26-28, Mark 14:22-24, Luke 22:17-20 and John 6:48-65)? In the world are we invited to wonder at human nature as both our familiar selves and as openness to a "new life" in the Other from outside of ourselves?

Throughout the games the back stage puppet master (the well-cast Don Sutherland) recalls our diabolical Old Scratch—the "Father of Lies" (John 8:44). Near the end He makes a fateful exception to allow both surviving members from District 12 to live. And, then with stale predictability, this Father of Lies suddenly revokes this concession. All of the betrayals and deceptions of history, large and very small, are contained here in a single sentence! (For our purposes, this moment of betrayal is every part of the Big Lie in Chapter 2.)

Old Scratch finally takes his leave, but first he pauses for such a brief moment of reflection above his jungle game board, maybe half a second . . . a magnificent understatement! Only the half-awake viewer will miss it. It's like the mysterious break into silence of the nighttime crickets before they begin their serenade once more, as if nothing had happened. In that brief moment, what do we find? Rethinking his entire *Hunger Games* game, Old Scratch notices that by letting into the game responsible human freedom—if only for a moment—free will even to the point of self-sacrifice, the games will never, ever be the same again. Into fully human history there has entered cause for a hope. More than mere optimism, hope is the theological expecta-tion and willingness to be on the edge of the "already, but not yet." Hope and human freedom are nothing less than what Luigi Giussani identifies as our "capacity for God" (*The Religious Sense*). We can choose to believe and to say yes.

Old Scratch had instructed his minions to always keep the games moving along by giving "some hope, but not too much." Just move things along within the closed-loop arc of history, but now with responsible human free-dom, this tidy package is in question. In future games perhaps no one will follow the scripted descent into the survival of the fittest. Now with an example of self-forgetfulness and togetherness two by two, will the future gladiator pairs from all of the districts choose responsibility and self-mastery, and the expansiveness of self-donation to one another, and to others? Deeper than the common fight is companionship in true marriage and the ark of the common good.

Does the reader agree with this rendition of the *Hunger Games*? The question might be why our crop of movie reviewers seems so out of touch with so many parallels between a popular movie and the biblical narrative. Have they and their generation never even heard of Genesis and the Gospel? Do they simply want to evade the thought police in order to get published? Why is the living memory of millennia so totally missing? In polite society is the Christian vision so unknown because it might "make people feel uncomfortable?" Do the movie spin artists simply want to discount and mythologize revelation? The depth of the human mystery becomes a gaming industry computer app, ramped up to endanger movie land's real people. Rather than converting to the new and fully human life, we convert the universal human condition and our real hope into a consumer good.

In the real world arena of 2016, the reigning President of the United States in 2016 decreed to all local (?) school districts the "civil right" of transgender students to access to the restrooms of their choice: "the desire to accommodate others' discomfort cannot justify a policy that singles out and disadvantages a particular class of students." As if the most powerful figure in the global arena in history, a thousand times more powerful than Genghis Khan, has nothing more on his plate than whether the toilet seat is up or down. President Kennedy put a man on the moon, and a later president put a man in the girls' locker room.

In the days before the perfect storm of the 1960s the cultural critic Lewis Mumford (and a biographer of Herman Melville) wrote this about the despiritualization of society, in his monumental *The City in History* (1961): "Today, the degradation of the inner life is symbolized by the fact that the only place sacred from intrusion is the private toilet." In the politics of so-called gender ideology, how far we have fallen even from this. The culture war finally closes the loop: from "out of the closet" to the "water closet," and from Watergate to Makewater-gate. (Where are the word merchants when we need them?)

Those who do actually suffer from transgender *dysphoria* deserve respect equal to everyone else, no less and no more. But by what forced logic does this translate into a court-enforced license enabling men to forego the urinal and stand in line at the girls' locker room? Social engineering word games finally offer some comic relief: having suffered the redefinition of marriage, the peasants are tutored on the new etiquette of "minding our pees and queues"! Or, speaking of "P"s, we might say that the president prefers to prosecute peasant protest against prevarication on the previous privacy of the privy. It's all a joke, right?

A televised street interview (by television talk show host Jay Leno, no less) featured a college student and holder of a Master's degree in English from Harvard. Even aided with several hints of embarrassing directness, she was still unable to identify the author "Mark Twain". In all her advanced studies she had never heard of one of the most significant American writers and novels in our history, *The Adventures of Tom Sawyer* (1876). What has caused this empty crater in our schools and our culture, this amnesia in sophisticated cap and gown?

Together with high-brow Yale, powerful Harvard has a private endowment that pencils out to more the two million dollars per student. Go figure. Money talks and money gives access, but money still can't read. Considering our national budget deficits, money can't add or subtract either. For "the three Rs" young people might better consider enrolling in an affordable school close to home instead of becoming six-digit indentured servants to bank debts marketed as school loans. With such mounting debts (averaging thirty-five thousand dollars for undergraduates and twice that for graduate students) college students are just another targeted market segment. And the market price in this education industry rises to match the level of the loan pool. Is the university-banking complex teaching by its example the lucrative economic theory of "rent-seeking"?

Better economics is found in a free library card. The root meaning of education is more than getting our ticket punched at a high brow university. The term *educare* means to educe, or "to bring out" what is already a thirst within any inquiring student. This discounted orientation toward being informed is another part of the natural law of elementary self respect. Asked on the street whom the nation's capital was named after, the high school graduate did not know, but added "I can look it up on Google!" The flip side of digital learning is the flat-lining of memory and cumulative learning. Darwin's "descent of man" disguises a modern world of still-primitive opposable thumbs linked at once to large brains and neuron atrophy. Everyone is the center of his own universe—and this "universe" is no longer a universe but a digital cloud. Replacing the pious, medieval and anonymous *Cloud of Unknowing* we now have the data cloud, from which cometh forth even the Big Lie. The Big Lie is merely a subset of social-media "fake news." When Galileo removed the earth from the center of the solar system, the doctrine of human self-centeredness was quick to move in.

Institutional betrayal of the young student finally includes the replacement of self respect and respect for others with digital dexterity and the popular culture of esteem enhancement. Mark Bauerlein (author of *the Dumbest Generation: How the Digital Age Stupefies Young Americans and Jeopardizes our Future*, 2008) was asked by *Atlantic Magazine* to explain himself on his blunt writing. To which he responded, "Millennials in America today are the most socially conscious, hard-working, knowledgeable, skilled and savvy, globally aware, workforce-ready, and downright interesting generation in human history. Just ask them."

BUREAUCRACY IN A BUBBLE

Old Scratch in *The Hunger Games* recalls Screwtape in C. S. Lewis' *Screwtape Letters*. More on this writing in a future chapter, but for now it is enough to recall that Lewis's Devil, Screwtape, counsels his understudy in the art of backing men into various vices. Part of the tactic is to give false hopes to those on the verge of despair (again, "some hope, but not too much"). We mentioned above that C. S. Lewis' path differed from that of Michael Edwards. At the age of fifty-five and under the influence of converts G. K. Chesterton and J. R. R. Tolkien (who later wrote *Lord of the Rings*, 1954-55), Lewis discovered the authentic faith of Christianity. In reading two of Chesterton's leading works (*Orthodoxy*, 1908, and *The Everlasting Man*, 1925), Lewis discovered the "aha" moment of Christian faith. He tells of his conversion in his life story (*Surprised by Joy*, 1955) where he finds the fact—a real fact—that the scientific mindset of measurement is immeasurably heightened by the poetic imagination he had enjoyed in his youth. Unlike the yardstick or other more scientific forms of measurement, poetry points to things beyond ourselves and even beyond our imagination. There are many paths up Mount Fuji.

Surely we will always remember—we will remember, won't we?—the attack on the twin towers of the World Trade Center on the morning of September 11, 2001. This tragedy and murder of three thousand teaches us something about limited imagination. A new symbolic word is entered into the modern vocabulary, and this new word partly defines the new world in which the disrupted new generations are to live and make their home. The calendar date September 11, 2001, becomes the symbolic "9/11." With all of our technical sophistication why was this large scale, radical Islamic assassination of the West able to happen? Part of the answer shows up in the report of a special commission set up to dig out such answers. The 9/11 Commission found that modern bureaucratic man apparently lacks "imagination." We did not imagine and therefore could not prevent this dramatic and unthinkable targeting.

Even the massive human costs of utopian and deliberate "pogroms" (organized massacres) are enabled or deliberately carried out by functionaries who have lost the "faculty to imagine that which they know."[5] What we should know is not real because we choose not to imagine it. Most broadly, an education and training system stripped of the more imaginative liberal arts and its humanities is a generational lobotomy. What would our opposable-thumb and computer-literate graduate think if he also had a full-fisted grip of history? Would there be less a sense of abandonment? History and biography enable a stabilizing sense of orientation in times of turmoil, but even this term loses its meaning once it has been confiscated for more biological purposes.

No wonder even the reality of ultrasound science no longer opens our eyes to objective relationships beyond ourselves. In a computer-wired café your author fell into conversation with a young university professor. For a creative writing course her classroom of graduating college students was asked what they intended to do with their own lives. Did they have a purpose? All but one or two responded that they wanted to be "CEOs" (chief executive officers). "CEOs of what?" they were asked. Not even one had imagined an answer. Finally, the mentality of "span of control" is everywhere, in video games and education as well as politics. It's about lemmings on the move and all in the same direction, an entire lockstep universe of CEOs intent on moving things along.

One of the 9/11 Commission's final recommendations ventures into totally new territory: "Imagination is not a gift usually associated with bureaucracies ….It is therefore crucial to find a way of *routinizing*, even *bureaucratizing* the exercise of imagination" (italics added).[6] Routine imagination: like "gay marriage," another oxymoron. And, in addition to a lack of imagination is our erased institutional memory and sober realism. The Trade Center towers *already* had been hit before by the same terrorist group with a car bomb in 1993. The Founding Fathers fostered imagination by writing patent protections into the Constitution, and by respecting individual states as laboratories for problem solving. In the past century, especially, two world wars and then the initiatives of vending-machine government (aka the Great Society of the 1960s) seem to have centralized so much of the imagination into memorizing Beltway telephone numbers.

Sometimes new political appointees—and educators—are sure the world begins only when they arrive on the scene. We ambulate in "real time." We live in an artificial world of power relationships where computer accessible moment-to-moment data replace synthesis and the mental space for reflection. We discount and too often disdain the past as a guide and as an independent critic of the present. Span-of-control replaces the depth of institutional memory and, in higher education market-driven classes replace liberal-arts and humanities core requirements. The new (ever new) career path is computer code-writing. How can there be time for core courses when doctoral specialties drill into such politicized constructs as race, gender, identity, and social pressures and selective attention to current social events? At Stanford University in 2016 the students voted down a proposal to reinstate a core course requirement in Western Civilization. One might as well ask lemmings to question whether they like the direction things are headed and whether their world, in the long run, might not be comfortably flat after all.

Your author recalls sitting in on a large formal meeting of mostly local elected officials and private sector notables. The long-term task was to develop legislative ideas to retool public education to better serve the job markets of the future. In the mix of these educators and advocates was an attractively blond (of course) advertising consultant. When asked by others at the table how such a business was relevant to future education, she responded that she was an expert in "persuasive education." No one so much as blinked.

Also at the table was a representative from the largest computer software company in the world. He was asked how his firm regarded the corrosive effect that the video game industry could have on traditional non-Western cultures around the globe. "Oh, the characters in the games can be tailored to different races and can use culturally appropriate clothing and weapons." Color and culture options, but zero comprehension of the question and zero follow-up questions. Shoulder rubbing is the unwritten language of consensus building. Marketing and marketable technologies are truth. Finally in the twenty-first century, is this our answer to Pontius Pilate who infamously asked of Christ: "What is truth?"

VIVE LA DIFFERENCE?

Ours is becoming a featureless and unisex society. Any memory of the role of real women and real men in a more real world is also submerged in the business of the day. In a world where pets are valued more highly than children, why not neuter society as a whole? Masculinity is feminized, and femininity is masculinized. Superman and Superwoman are the social equivalent of superglue. Any feminine intuition and sense of relation and continuity, for example, is eclipsed by quarterly progress reports, possibly more colorful Powerpoint pie charts, and sometimes even more intense office politics. The journal *Psychiatric Services* searches almost-countless reasons why female military veterans suffer a suicide rate six times that of other women (for men the increase is *only* fifty percent).[7] Not on the list are the inherent, most obvious, and politically incorrect psychological and spiritual differences between women and men. Again, what is left out here in modern orthodoxy; what is missing?

Today why is it only the Church that has the conviction to seemingly drag its feet—to still consistently defend the mystery and fact of the human person and of human sexuality and the meaning of the family? The family is that place where authority and nurturing together have a unique role in child formation and in inoculating the young against so many deceptions of a fallen world. Today the leveling social agenda of the state, with its near monopoly on education, often marginalizes the family and any other competition with its efficient, value-neutral and problem-solving self. It services an ever more progressive agenda of "equality" that now prizes insipid sameness and resonance over differences and complementary. When we take time to look up do we notice that public education enables a unisex mass society as a family-free zone? Out of some kind of momentum we subsidize pre-school programs that replace the family breakfast table. In the broader society fatty fast foods on-the-run replace family dinners and conversation. No longer does it take a family to raise a child, nor even a village, but rather it takes a standardized federal government program administered from on high.

Finally marriage itself, between a man and a woman, is submerged in a featureless society linking androgynous "partners," presumably still in pairs rather than larger group communes. Sameness is a chessboard with no king or queen but only gender-neutral pawns of progressive social change. The sixty-four black or white game board squares now all shades of gray without edges. It's all about self-esteem. Everyone is awarded a trophy for just showing up.

With "gray" as yet another gender theory code word, one can only wonder whether Teddy Roosevelt will be totally edged out of public school text books. This former President still had the audacity to celebrate moral struggles above any version of "gray." He will be cut from the team not because he was an imperialist, but because he didn't bend to a therapeutic flat-earth ethic:

> Far better [he said] is it to dare mighty things, to win glorious triumphs, even though checkered by failure . . . than to rank with those poor spirits who neither enjoy nor suffer much, because they live in a gray twilight that knows not victory nor defeat.

Nearly a century ahead of his time, Roosevelt was talking about our flat-lined lifestyle of "whatever—no expectations and no regrets." Under some penumbra legal invention is acceptance of polygamy only a footnote away?

Islamic Shari'a law already has some legal standing in England, our former home of the Western *Magna Carta* of 1215 (and which was drafted mostly by Stephen Langton, a Catholic archbishop!). There is historical precedent for the case of men with multiple wives (polygyny: the common form of polygamy). How unequal that the opposite case of women with multiple husbands (polyandry) is historically unsupported and more hypothetical. (On such history, see Chapter 7). There's work to be done. Alert the courts! The absolute mythology of total church-state separation might be one thing, but now the traditional model of marriage as a "wall of separation" from a spectrum of other and random models is another. This wall must be eradicated.

When the juggernaut advance of liberty accepts polygamy, flat-earth equality will become in reality even more of a backsliding. An apt analogy might be drawn from physics. This is the concept of entropy, the tendency toward the eventual and total disintegration of matter and energy, form and structure, in the physical universe. Shortly after the Second World War, the cultural critic Richard Weaver said this about human communities:

. . . to have enough imagination to see into other lives and enough piety to realize that their existence is a part of beneficent creation is the very foundation of human community. There appear to be two types to whom this kind of charity is unthinkable: the barbarians, who would destroy what is different because it is different, and the neurotic, who always reaches out for control of others, probably because his own integration has been lost.[8]

In much of modernity these two perversions—barbarism and neurosis—converge. Much of modernity is both barbaric and neurotic. In the face of this intolerant tolerance of tradition the biggest lie is to remain silent about the truth of the human person. It is to replace the complementary distinction between a man and a woman with rhetoric about big tent "diversity." The seemingly unrelated lack of imagination even in our offices of national security—the 9/11 thing—is a remote symptom of deep cultural exhaustion and institutional somnambulism.

In healthy contrast, the suppressed natural law, especially as we are more fully understood through revelation, would have us celebrate the truth about the fully human person flourishing in community. The permanent truth of the human person remains the one detail of history that matters. The beauty of the natural law is our inborn openness toward the good, toward preservation of self and others, toward the particularity of true marriage and the raising of children, toward truth above any counterfeit, and toward the full life in society.[9]

What does it mean to get hooked on real life in the full? Our entire postmodern entertainment culture replaces achievement with attendance trophies; replaces morality with sensitivity training; and replaces personal maturity of graced courage with sexual readiness and backup abortions. We abolish fatherhood and motherhood. We euthanize the aged. We abolish marriage by redefining it. We raise a generation that gives no second thought to abolishing children of their own. What's missing from this picture?

The personal question might be: Who would really know if I were to question the momentum of the so-called "right side of history"? What if I were swim against group-think and this current? Soon to be martyred by the polygamist Henry VIII, the sixteenth-century family man, Thomas More, gives us an answer. In *A Man for All Seasons* he addresses the young Richard Rich who is content to troll for prominence in the flow of events in his day. More advises him to pursue teaching as a vocation, but Rich responds, "Who would know?" More's answer: "You . . . your friends, God. Not a bad public, that."[10]

NOTES

1. Michael Edwards, *Priscilla, Elvis and Me: In the Shadow of the King* (New York: St. Martin's Press, 1988).

2. Interview with *Samedi-Soir*, Nov. 8, 1947, cited in Hans Urs von Balthasar, *Bernanos: An Ecclesial Existence* (San Francisco: Ignatius, 1996), 457.

3. Resources of possible interest to those not interested in being defined or controlled by possible same-sex attraction include the Blackstone Films movie *The Third Way* (available on line at Vimeo.com/93079367), CourageRC.org; and CourageRC.org/ Encourage for families and friends of those experiencing same-sex attraction.

4. Marjie Bowker and Ingrid Ricks, eds., *You've Got it all Wrong* (Edmonds, WA: Scriber Lake High School, 2014), ISBN 978-0-9894381-0-0 (see also http://writetoright.org/).

5. Max Eastman, "Freedom and the Planned Economy" (1955), citation in William F. Buckley, Jr. (ed.) *American Conservative Thought in the Twentieth Century* (New York: Bobbs-Merrill Co., 1970), 203.

6. National Commission on Terrorist Attacks, *The 9/11 Commission Report* (New York: W.W. Norton and Co., 2004), 344. Max Weber, the early twentieth-century sociologist and author of *Bureaucracy*, laid out the blueprint for the "routinization of charisma."

7. Reported by Alan Zaremo, "Suicide rate of female veterans is 'staggering,' researchers say," *Los Angeles Times*, June 10, 2015.

8. Richard M. Weaver, *Ideas Have Consequences* (Chicago: University of Chicago Press, 1948), 175.

9. For example, see Servais Pinckaers, *Morality: The Catholic View* (South Bend, Indiana: St. Augustine's Press, 2001), 67-69, 71, and 97-109.

10. Robert Bolt, *A Man for All Seasons* (New York, Vintage, 1960), 6.

Chapter Six

Word Games and Mind Traps

Human imagination can be one portal toward what is beyond us. Intellect is another. Imagination can mislead but does double duty by also pulling inquiry ever forward toward new scientific theories and validations, and toward the transcendent. Ultimately our openness to the transcendent is "the missing piece" (the "serenity" abandoned by Michael Edwards, Chapter 5). In a void of our own making or foisted upon us, we resort to the comfort zone of holding hands in the dark at the back of Plato's cave, and we call this truth. Following the word-merchants nationalism replaces patriotism, identity politics replaces nationalism, tribalism replaces nationalism, selfies replace solidarity . . . and free sex replaces everything else. Whatever.

WHAT'S IN A WORD?

Let's revisit William of Occam (from Chapter 2). With his notion of nominalism we are to believe that universal meanings are linguistic fictions, that only individual things really exist. This book is not a "book." It stands only by itself in isolation. It is a book only because we call it a book. This notion is acidic; it destroys everything. Before we know it, we might assert that an unborn child is not a child until we call "it" a child. Why not just call it "nonviable tissue?" Or, in the lofty wisdom or *Roe v. Wade*, why speculate?

The Old Testament account in Genesis begins with open hearts, but also with the warning that to consort with evil is to have our eyes opened so as to think that we are God (if there is a God). The risk is one of seeing only with the eyes, and not *through the eyes of the heart* and with the physical eye sockets. The biblical account is at a loss for mere words and resorts to allegory. We read that "the Lord God . . . took one of his ribs . . . and made (it) into a woman" (Genesis 2:21, 22). The original Aramaic term for rib can

119

also mean "heart." Might this better wording incline us toward that "tiny whispering sound" of a deeper meaning and a deeper reality of the human person, alone and together?

It seems the Old Testament vocabulary-challenged writers, after all, might have been both in touch with the real as well as divinely inspired. And later amidst the seaport depravity of Corinth, St. Paul took another shot at the right words by letting transcendence lift us from the seemingly ordinary, by "describing spiritual realities in spiritual terms" (1 Corinthians 2:13). Because spiritual terms are no longer fashionable—and because so few transcendent references remain today—the modern cultural trend is also away from the unborn child. It is away from the commitment of traditional marriage and leads us backward toward a more provisional cohabitation. This seemingly private backsliding is a key part of the entire moral and cultural collapse of the West. *Modernity is not modern.* What is needed today is not folklore in new clothing. To be a true family today is to be countercultural. This novelty was unimaginable only fifty years ago.

Is it even possible that our shared human nature is infused with something more—the Christian revelation that we are to share, in a sense, in the transcendent divine nature? Such an extravagant invitation! It inspires nothing less than "alarm" in the first witnesses to the Resurrection. The women at the empty tomb were not starry eyed as depicted in so much pasty religious artwork. They were "terrified" (Luke 24:5). Why were these witnesses alarmed or even terrified? Better yet, why should we *not* be alarmed and shaken out of our modern-day stupor? What does it take to suspect, for just a moment that this most extraordinary possibility of redemption might actually be real? As C. S. Lewis explains, the resurrection is "a myth, but a myth that happens to be true."

This wording for this *encounter*, more than a mere idea, was crafted by a witnessing and pondering Church at some of its earliest global gatherings or councils. At Nicaea (A.D. 325) and Constantinople (A.D. 381) the important step of deepened clarity—on the stupendous irruption into history called the Incarnation—is expressed in the Creed that many still affirm in thoughtful recollection. If true, this gifted and eternal Presence means that, of all the religions which have ever been or ever will be, the Faith of Christians is the *only* religion that makes sense out of our undeniable human suffering. Emmanuel: God is with us. A God who gives us Himself—who literally gives his Word—is even greater than all of the human pain, stupidity and wickedness of our entire sojourn on this planet. The Incarnation and Trinitarian Christianity are not musty and antiquarian, instead Nicaea and Constantinople proclaim that Christ as both human and divine, fully both. The Encounter is the only thing really new—and forever new and beckoning—under the sun.

Is it really the divine nature of God to behold his creation to such an extent that he even *suffers with* us? While surely the transcendent God cannot suffer mortally as we do, still he has chosen to *suffer with and within* us, to transform every kind and degree of human suffering (and joy). "Incapable of suffering as God, he did not refuse to be a man capable of suffering."[1] In his divine nature Christ cannot suffer change, but in his human nature he does experience and change suffering. With Him, our universal human suffering might well be the unspoken proof of the dignity of a universal human nature.

And what of the divine nature? Is God to be humanly understood as infinite, uncompromising, and unconditional self-donation? With the Blessed Duns Scotus we even have a school of theology holding that our unconditional God would have made himself visible within His own creation—as the Incarnation—even if there had *not* been a Fall crying out for Redemption. It's primarily about His own goodness and the sharing of this goodness into His creation.

The simplicity and vulnerable smallness of the Bethlehem event—and then the added Scandal of the Cross—present "a stumbling block for the Jews and foolishness for the Greeks" (1 Corinthians 1:23) and especially to our side-trip, modern-day mindset.[2] But if the Redemption is not another graffiti slogan sprayed over a hellacious world; then . . . *it changes everything*. The Scandal of sacrificial love consumes the logic of any food chain, whether biological (Darwin) or political (Hobbes) or economic (Marx). But in times of cultural turmoil and decline like ours, we call ourselves modern even as we backslide into something even worse than the paganism of the late fourth-century Roman Empire. Disinterred today is the stale and cosmopolitan open-mindedness of a past long-gone. Like pagan Rome, even a cultural and communal kitchen blender of deities or "values" is not enough. But today things are worse in that we also reject what we have considered above.

Might we be called to a life of maturity, self-discipline and now grace in a truth that is not of our making? Such a truth is a great freedom and adventure, whatever our setting in history or our personal circumstances. We are all truly and already equal before this God who reveals the (Trinitarian) inner life of his very self, *and* then invites us in. There is no division in God since he is what he does and does what he is. "God is love" (1 John 4:8, 16). It is not so much that he has revealed the listed truths testified in the Creed mentioned above, but that He has directly and transparently revealed his very Self as love clear through. As St. Augustine put it in one of his sermons, not in a later Eurocentric world but in North Africa, [unlike the Big Lie] He "can neither deceive nor be deceived."

TAKING "IT" PERSONALLY

Let's take a deeper look at a very good stage play and movie that gets at this Ultimate Reality as it finds its way onto our stage and into our inner convictions: *A Man for All Seasons* (1958/1962).[3] We have already visited briefly with St. Thomas More. More was the secular chancellor of England and then a Catholic martyr of the early sixteenth century. The 1966 movie which starred the stage actor Paul Scofield in the lead role, earned six academy awards including Best Picture. Beheaded by King Henry VIII of England, More had refused to consent to words enabling the king's appetite for divorce and remarriage (sequential bigamy) beginning with Ann Boleyn.

The question was complicated further by the risk of a rekindled English civil war (recalling the very recent War of the Roses) in the absence of a blood-line family heir to the king. Another oddity was the Oath of Supremacy that tangled relations between this biological (national) dynasty and the spiritual family of the universal (transnational) Church. England was drifting into a separate Anglican church, a sort of ecclesiastical Galapagos Island.

In essence Thomas More's time was a lot like ours, or rather the modern world is not changed much. Is it any wonder that the Episcopalian communion in the United States now would jump to the front of the parade to approve formal gay "marriages?" (As of this writing, the Anglican communion has suspended this American faction from global participation.) When we are told that legal change is only about arbitrary social mores, we should think more about Thomas More. He believed that his personal safety lay in a country "planted thick with laws from coast to coast." He never suspecting that human law itself could become diabolical and lead to his execution for simply remaining silent rather than taking the Oath of Supremacy.

A remarkable side detail is that this brilliant play came from the hand of an agnostic (Robert Bolt). Some critics claim that the playwright scripted a compromised Thomas More around his own agnostic self. By this interpretation More simply stands up for his subjective self rather than for any objective truth with claims on his private conscience. So let's take a closer look. Perhaps More actually was standing up for the same kind of personal inner commitment to a higher truth (higher than majority law) that each of us makes whenever we begin together the Nicene Creed with the personal "I believe," or whenever we seal a real marriage ceremony with "I do." Worth more attention than can be given here is the way that "I do" creates a new reality (more than a mere idea or even an ideal), reminiscent of the ever present action of God as "I Am."

Let's see how this works in the play, this fit between objective truth—things as they really are—and our possible commitment. Listen to Bolt's More as he says ". . . but what matters to me is not whether it's true or not but that I *believe* it to be true, or rather not that I believe it, but that *I* believe it . . .

I trust I make myself obscure" (italics added). Before he was even pope, St. John Paul II wrote an academic piece where he approached this sort of thing (published as *The Acting Person*, 1979). The later-pope does not walk away from, but "brackets," objective truth so as to get at the same kind of well-grounded "personalism" that we really find in Thomas More. In personalism we establish ourselves less by intellectual demonstrations than by our authentic actions. Moral decisions and actions are how we *grow in the truth*. They are the path how virtue can become a pre-disposition and a personal habit deeper than instinct.

We can read the questionable line from Thomas More (". . . not that I believe it, but that *I* believe it . . .") as grounded in other remarks that Bolt also gives to More. In a confrontation with his friend, the Duke of Norfolk, the playwright has More saying that he cannot give in, and that this must be: "To me it has to be, for that's myself! Affection goes as deep in me as you think, but only God is love right through, Howard; and that's myself."[4] Norfolk finds this tenacity in the truth to be "disproportionate." Today the secularist would say "extremist" or, horrors, "inappropriate." Then we have this from More: "I will not give in because I oppose it—I do, not my pride, not my spleen, nor any other of my appetites but I do . . . I!"[5]

Today the secularist would ridicule More as a non-conformist out of step with the consensus, and on the wrong side of history. More's favorite daughter, Meg, suggests that her father might bracket the moment and just go with the flow and sign the oath while in his heart withholding consent. Are we reminded of politicians who are "personally opposed to abortion, but . . . ?" Of such a double life, More answers: "When a man takes an oath, Meg, he's holding his own self in his own hands. Like water. And if he opens his fingers then—he needn't hope to find it again." Meg begs that he has already done reasonably enough, but he responds: "Well . . . finally . . . it isn't a matter of reason; finally it's a matter of love."[6]

Meanwhile, the Duke of Norfolk is content to run with the pack for the sake of easy "fellowship." In the context of today's culture of abortion and euthanasia, Pope St. John Paul II identified a "grave and clear obligation to oppose [pro-abortion laws] by conscientious objection."[7] Pope Francis says the same when he exposes the more "'educated persecution' of Christians today, saying Christians are not only under threat by those trying to kill them, but also by those who want to limit their freedom and their right to conscientious objection. 'There's a persecution of which not much is being said.'" It's a persecution "cross-dressed as culture, cross-dressed as modernity, cross-dressed as progress."[8]

Do we sense the very layered lie of the world and of modernity as compared to the larger depth and simplicity of Genesis? Eve yields to the serpentine influences in the world, while the sin of Adam is the evasiveness to blame Eve and to go with a truncated togetherness here below that retreats from God (Genesis 3:6-13). St. Augustine confesses his own weakness before such cosmic self-isolation and compromise:

> . . . [I] rushed headlong upon these things of beauty [the world] which you have made. You were with me, but I was not with you. They kept me far from you, those fair things which, if they were not in you, would not exist at all.[9]

What about a tiny whispering sound of false conscience that might mislead us? What about a misled conscience? John Henry Cardinal Newman, the nineteenth-century convert from the now formally split Anglicanism, remarks on this possibility. Of such a presumably genuine person, he says ". . . still he must act according to that error while he is in it, because he in full sincerity thinks the error to be truth." Newman cites the very general statement of the thirteenth-century Cardinal Gousset: "He who acts against his conscience loses his soul."[10] Such is the integrity of the human person presuming that we are constantly seeking the real truth over error and disinformation. Absolute moral norms that prohibit intrinsically evil acts are binding without exceptions. With a well-formed conscience, Solomon did not decide to just split the difference and move on; he did not harm the baby, but restored it to his true mother.

While error has no rights, people do; still Newman explains that one is not to balance one's own private judgment against objective truth as simply opposite ends of a teeter-totter or spectrum, and then opt for one's opinion. Only if one is so totally misled as to fear loss of his soul—and we do have souls—is it defensible to follow an erroneous conscience.[11] It will be a heavy lift to argue before the living God why one has spent a lot of time just doing his own thing.

And for anyone laboring under such an erroneous conscience isn't there also an earlier accountability for possibly having drifted into habitual error?[12] Are the lunatic butchers of history still accountable, like Hitler for example? As an acquired predisposition, sloth is one of the worst kinds of sin. The great "why bother" and "whatever" just doesn't cut it. Because we are human, the responsibility to seek the truth is not just another casual throwaway. We are to seek this with our whole souls and hearts, minds, and strength (Mark 12:30). Doesn't the search for truth demand at least as much attention as we give to new social networks, or computer apps, or stomach abs? The recent Pope Benedict XVI comments on both Newman and Thomas More:

> Newman agrees with that other great British witness to conscience St. Thomas More, who did not in the least regard conscience as the expression of his subjective tenacity or of an eccentric heroism. He saw himself as one of those timorous martyrs who reach the point of obeying their conscience only after hesitation and much questioning, and this is an act of *obedience to that truth*

which must rank higher than every social authority and every kind of personal taste (italics added). [13]

We return to an earlier question. What's in a word? The words we choose to speak mattered to Newman and More. So, today, what does it mean when a doctor, a physical healer of the human person, is redefined as a "service provider;" or a patient becomes "service consumer;" or a child becomes "unwanted" and "non-viable tissue;" or explicit porn becomes "free speech" and even part of the sex-ed curriculum; or unwed mothers become "clients;" or a husband and wife become "spouse A and B;" or mother and father become generic and even same-sex "parents"; or freedom of "religion" becomes a narrowed freedom of "worship;" or the traditional family becomes "stereotypical;" or when homicide is parsed into "physician assisted suicide" (PAS)? What, if anything is in a word like "whatever"?

THE CHRISTMAS MESSAGE IN A BOTTLE

To follow the tiny whispering sound is our greatest human right and responsibility. It is part of the foundational right to go on living. We and the tiny heartbeat in the womb have a right to such a "culture of life." But the Big Lie would have us believe that it's all about clever courtroom rulings, the social media, a fatal "reset" button, personal taste and, for some, the money.

In December 1997 operators of an abortion clinic in Seattle thought it culturally instructive for the state's politicians to attend a December "Holiday Season" open house. The business location clung like moss in the afternoon shadow of the nearby Catholic cathedral. The featured display, in various stages of life, was the bottled and preserved fetal remains of aborted children. Merry Christmas! Modern glass bottles rather than a wooden crèche. Such was the Christmas message from a neighborhood franchise for the least regulated industry in America.

The original St. Nicholas was a real person from the fourth century. He distributed gifts as we still do today (but now as more of an offering to seasonal stock market reports). Additional legend holds that St. Nick resuscitated some children who had been murdered by an inn keeper and preserved in brine. With modernity, reality and legend switch places: brine in legendary yesteryear; formaldehyde today. And worse, an abortion technique of choice today is a fatal saline solution. Here we have the progress of sixteen centuries displayed in a jar. "The hour is coming for everyone who kills you to think that he is offering worship to God" (John 16:2). We no longer even recognize the faces of our blinded brothers and sisters staring back at us from inside the jar.

Here's another jarring Christmas story. It's about a child's innocent hope and, in a few thoughtless words, its loss. In my grade school years I witnessed and regrettably took part in a sad tale involving a small group of other nine-year olds. The four of us were standing on the school porch waiting for the end of the lunch time recess. Again, the Christmas holiday was fast approaching at the end of the week. Bright eyes were shining. We observed, too wisely it turned out, that one of our classmates in the fourth grade, from a family of very modest income, still believed in Santa Claus. I can still see him dressed in a clean and white long-sleeve shirt and dark slacks and sporting what we in those days called an inexpensive "bowl haircut." This was Little Carl.

Little Carl chirped, "but there is a Santa Claus!" We others were quicker than we intended to correct this error. Crestfallen, his eyes avoided ours in a world that was suddenly and irreversibly broken. Not only the symbol, but the reality and wonder of an abiding generosity—giftedness somewhere in a still-enchanted world—had been stolen away in nothing more than our few words. More than enchanted, His presence is everywhere and pervades all that is, "transforming all common things and yet itself unchanged" (C.S. Lewis, *Surprised by Joy*). So, what's in a word? Suddenly something critical was simply gone, missing. If his mother were to light a single white candle on the dinner table that night, we had just blown it out. Again, Little Carl came from one of the poorer families in a broadly middle-class town, poor enough that while their few Christmas presents were still wrapped in bright paper, it was in the recycled color-printed funnies section saved weeks in advance from the Sunday newspapers. No backpedaling words could undo the damage and the tears.

And at the age of nine we discovered that a technically accurate statement can also be a great falsehood, part of the Big Lie. By some kind of irony, the complete name of our betrayed friend was Carl Marks. As the denial to Christian hope, Karl Marx (with Friedrich Engels) as we all know, barely two generations earlier invented Godless, modern-day radical Socialism or Communism in his *Communist Manifesto* (1848). In place of hope as a theological virtue, he decided that the entire historical record was only a cruel game of economic competition governed by the rules of class warfare. He drew an analogy with Charles Darwin's biological evolution. (More on Darwin-*ism* below and in Chapter 9.)

Utopia was within reach, Marx insisted, if one could tap into the smoldering resentment of the working class only waiting to be organized. Vladimir Lenin activated this ideology by calling for a ruling elite (as with our own self-anointed "creative class"?) to move things along. The Russian dictator, Joseph Stalin, then gave this agenda a big push following the Russian Revolution of 1917 and the brutal murder of an ineffective czar and his entire family, plus the annihilation of countless Russians, seven million Ukrainians, and a total of sixty to seventy million. This starvation genocide by a modern dictator—known as "Genghis Khan with a telephone"—is little stressed in modern Western education. In China, Mao Tse-tung is credited with an equal number of casualties. By comparison, Hitler was a piker with only ten million exterminations (six million of these being Jews). All of this is statistics once one pretends to be part of a vanguard leading the way to the future. Unhinged from natural law and Christianity, the West itself has been Islamic in practice. The so-called ISIS (Islamic State of Iraq and Syria) claims that their violence is only a temporary interlude, to be no longer necessary once the new dispensation (Sharia) is firmly in place.

The Victims of Communism Memorial Foundation (2016 Annual Report) finds that only thirty-seven percent of millennials view Communism as "very unfavorable," and twenty-five percent have a favorable view of Lenin. At Stalin's death in 1953, his daughter, Swetlana Allilujewa, said this: "Father died terribly and difficult. God gives the righteous an easy death." As with the cult of Darwin-ism versus Charles Darwin, and specifically of Marxism, Marxism oversteps its figurehead. Karl Marx is said to have once rejected the extremism of his followers by asserting "I am no Marxist."[14]

THE LEGO BLOCK UNIVERSE

The ideas of Marxists and many others is that a social order must be fully constructed on the graves of those who stand in the way. Society is not spiritually grounded and grown. It is a mechanism of history. Such abstract social thinking ultimately finds its inspiration in the more abstract philosophical thinking of Rene Descartes. The speculating French priest, Descartes, was also the inventor of analytical geometry. His "method" of seeing reality begins by excluding our inner core and sense of belonging. We are outside observers like voyeur spectators in the Coliseum. As a start point, the accuracy of mathematics wins out over the depth of trust. His famous expression is *Cogito ergo sum*: "I think, therefore I am." By this he meant that the solitary reference point of doubting everything, even doubting his own existence, actually confirmed his existence. (Otherwise, how could he even doubt?) Descartes applied this step-by-step system of doubt to all of the things we normally just take more for granted, so to speak, the reality of the entire "universe." "To be, or not to be, that is the question" (Shakespeare's *Hamlet*). More than a question; it is the answer. It is binary. It is categorically one or the other; there is no imaginary spectrum. Likewise, the pre-born child either is or is not; the mother is not half pregnant.

Facing the fact of undeniable and even gratuitous being, theology begins on its knees. It proposes a great friendship with the Source of this stupendous reality that surrounds us. Anticipating Descartes' method of doubt by over a thousand years, St. Augustine responded to the God of "I am who AM" (Exodus 3:14). He writes, "It would be easier for me to doubt that I live than that there is no truth, which is 'clearly seen, being understood by the things that are made' (Romans 1:20)."[15] Marx recognized that anyone who admits this radical and dependency of man as a creature (our "contingency") has already admitted the existence of God. So, as an atheist, he imposed a restriction: "this question is forbidden to socialist man."[16]

What if there is a God? Out of the divine generosity of his nature—not by some kind of blind necessity—all that exists in some way comes into being. By his nature he does not need his creation or us, but we by our created nature—our contingency—need Him. To thus wonder about why there is anything at all is already to wonder about Marx's forbidden question. In the supposedly open society of Secular Humanism, how welcome in the public forum is this same very human question of contingency? For all of its claimed open mindedness, some versions of modernity begin by forbidding certain questions. The political romanticist, Jean Jacques Rousseau and his *Social Contract* nearly a century before Marx, would have deleted and replaced all existing social institutions. (In a letter to Rousseau, even the rationalist Voltaire wrote that "One feels like crawling on all fours after reading your work,' August 31, 1761.)

The nineteenth-century psychologist Sigmund Freud, another atheist, applied materialism at the personal level. And the biologist Charles Darwin gives us a moving organization chart with great explanatory power, slicing and dicing all of physical life into categories and subcategories, more or less fluid. Actually his ideas were first presented jointly to the Linnaean Society, together with the independent and less remembered researcher, Alfred Russell Wallace. Wallace later irritated Darwin by believing in an evolution that is in some way "guided." Looking much farther back, the new thinking of Darwin and Wallace was apparently anticipated 2,700 years earlier by the Chinese philosopher Tson Tse, who wrote:

> All organizations are originated from a single species. This single species had undergone many gradual and continuous changes, and then gave rise to all organisms of different forms. Such organisms were not differentiated immediately, but on the contrary, they acquired their differences through gradual change, generation after generation.[17]

Darwin's only partly original view differed from that of a contemporary, the non-scientist and historian, Jacob Burckhardt. His passion was the historical rather than the geologic record. He valued cultural institutions and it was he who crystallized the term "renaissance" (first used in 1855, fully two centuries after the fact), in *his Civilization of the Renaissance in Italy* (1860). Human history solidifies into a somewhat forced sequence of historical periods. Our identity as "persons"—from the beginning a universal concept—and now our shared human biography are on the move, and are made to be barely a branch of Darwin's evolutionary biology. Once named, the Renaissance period is a sort of picture frame for the following and more self-flattering Enlightenment.

Human reason alone is postured as the measure of all things. What then of the wraparound word, "evolution"? Do things exist at all, or is there only process? Darwin was not only a natural scientist but an overreaching social evolutionist. Living on the heels of Enlightenment optimism, and before the sobering evidence of the ruptured twentieth century, he believed that mankind was inevitably rising to ever greater heights. Darwin looked over this horizon less toward God than toward ever-ascending human perfectibility. The concept of evolution consumes all other concepts, including the concept of human nature.

> Believing as I do that man in the distant future will be a far more perfect creature than he now is, it is an intolerable thought that he and all other sentient beings are doomed to complete annihilation after such long-continued slow progress. [And he then added, that] to those who fully admit to the immortality of the human soul, the destruction of our world will not appear so dreadful.[18]

Once again, the universal solvent of evolution bumps up against the concept and nature of the personal soul, and the difference between this and the world, and between progress and immortality. Unlike Darwin-ism, Darwin the man at least seems to still pause at this threshold.

LIFE AMONG THE RUINS

Lacking all of modern science and fifteen hundred years of history, and our modern tendencies of evolutionism and utopianism, we find St. Augustine. In the early fifth century St. Augustine was freer to straddle the permanent chasm between what is only natural and what is fully human, and what is supernatural. On the one hand, he carefully noticed a fossil found on a beach at Utica, the molar tooth of a mammoth (he thought it human). Possibly anticipating a modern science beyond his reach, he writes: "The real proof, as I have said, is to be found in the frequent discoveries of ancient bones of immense size, and this proof will hold good in centuries far in the future, since such bones do not easily decay."[19] Augustine is credited with suggesting a partly naturalistic (scientific) layer of interpretation for Genesis, rather than only a scattering of special creations assumed by fundamentalists in his day and in ours (and opposed by Darwin). His speculation fits into a long series of philosophers and researchers up until the modern breakthroughs in evidence and theory.[20] But he also knows the truth of universal concepts within the human mind, more than the accumulated particulars or rock hounds and evolutionists.

The constructive tension between religious faith, with innate reason, and the natural sciences is permanent, more than a passing phase to be overtaken by an all-embracing evolution. This permanence of thought itself can be understood as seeing human reality in layers, architectonically, something like a building. Impermanence, then, is like seeing reality as simply part of a chronological chain of successive episodes, nothing more. Even the concept of "chain" is merely a linguistic convenience attached to what is ultimately meaningless. Up-to-date thinkers might say that if there's a Periodic Table of all the atomic elements, why shouldn't there be a Darwinian slicing and dicing and periodic division for all of human history into a spectrum or table of perhaps trending epochs? The latest evolution is to discount our own inheritance. Philosophy and theology are not on the table, so to speak, and history itself is incoherent, like the inability of one person to understand another. The tyranny of relativism is the core of the post-modern world.

We happen to live at just another arbitrary moment, when social science data seek to replace the nature of man and the echo of divine glory in ourselves. Even language and vocabulary must mutate. Modern word games become a mind trap, if there is a mind. The idea of eternity is a rogue, pre-rational desire, a projected mirage and nothing permanent. This side of the veil, being righteous before the God is replaced by being on "the right side of history." Being itself has no meaning. We are tutored that "inclusive" and "universal" mean the same thing. A garage sale and a flea market are *inclusive*, while genuine art at least has the possibility of speaking the *universal*. Either the Deity is only a projection from imagination, or else the living God truly exists. But this is a binary question, and such a risk of contradiction is ruled off limits. Still, the question remains, even if we don't have a word for God, might He have a Word for us?

In science we balance mathematical equations, with one side equal to the other. The punctuation is in the middle ($=$). The laws of thermodynamics are of this kind. On the other hand, we have other kinds of expressions that are not equalities but actually exceed themselves. Language is of this kind. A single sentence (including this one) is conceptually larger than the sum of the words placed before the punctuation at the end. The point is that the human person, in science and elsewhere, looks for the certainty of ever larger truths. And truth is larger than either our formulas or even our questioning. Our emeritus Pope Benedict XVI considers that more than one kind of proof serves this adventure:

> Christianity's claim to be true cannot correspond to the standard of certainty posed by modern science, because the form of verification here is of a quite different kind from the realm of testing by experiment—pledging one's life for

this—is of a quite different kind. The saints, who have undergone the experiment, can stand as guarantors of its truth, but the possibility of disregarding this strong evidence remains.[21]

The spiritual worldview is not so much disproved by the physical sciences and lab experiments—and the political ideologies that are annexed to the social sciences—as it is quietly *displaced* from our mental map. A new language of historical change substitutes new words for time-tested words, and for the concepts and realities that these foundational words represent. By such word games we presume to create and limit reality; we market disinformation; we bracket the truth and then set it aside altogether. Truth, like a euthanized patient, goes quietly in the night. What is a child; what is a marriage; what is a family? Committed to freedom of speech, we wallow for decades in selective headlines and double-speak—the Big Lie (Chapter 2), and finally find ourselves the open sea of social media "fake news."

Mark Twain quipped that "The difference between the almost right word and the right word is really a large matter—it's the difference between the lightning bug and the lightning." Friendship and deep caring for one another is one thing, and marriage is still another. Russian folk literature offers a similar proverb that will outlive the malignant dark side of modernity: "One word of truth outweighs the whole world." Secular Humanism correctly denounces ethnic cleansing, but then buys into ethics cleansing without a whimper. Secularity disdains the reverence of starving Hindus for roaming cattle, and then worships the fattest sacred cow of all, "political correctness." It delights in hybrid verbiage—if "free trade" benefits everybody, then why not "free sex"?

In the West the centuries-long collapse of the Roman Empire was due to multiple causes, but one kind of hybrid was surely at play. The Roman legions protecting the northern frontier were substituted with mercenary barbarians and their leaders. Such was the loss of clarity within an increasingly effeminate leadership (as with ancient Israel in its decline, 3 Kings 14:24). Attila, the "Scourge of God," king of the Huns, was raised and educated in Rome itself as a sort of foreign exchange hostage. Later he followed in the path of the more direct invader, Alaric the Goth, who a generation earlier was the first to sack Rome, in A.D. 410.

And if today the West as a whole really is in a similar internal collapse, then fourth-century St. Augustine still has a silver lining for us. In North Africa, when he heard of the sacking of Rome by Alaric, he preached in a sermon that "this is grievous news, but let us remember if it's happened, then God willed it; that men build cities and men destroy cities, that there's also the *City of God* and that's where we belong." We, too, have a greater belonging. Even on this side of the veil, the future is now global and will not be defined by the terminal narcissism of a Europe or of a United States in moral freefall—as in regard to the most basic and human understanding of marriage and the family. Long forgotten is the truth about all of the passions: ". . . for they are more easily mortified finally in those who love God, than satisfied even for a time, in those who love the world" (St. Augustine).[22]

Much like today, the Christians of the fourth and fifth centuries were scapegoated for the progressive collapse of the Empire (a most fitting word combination: progressive collapse). The Establishment of the day reasoned that because the pagan gods had been neglected for a full century, they now were displeased. In the early fifth century St. Augustine wrote his monumental *City of God* to expose the wooden and stone idols to the light of day and to shield the Christian scapegoats. In this defense, St. Augustine gives us the key to understanding the deepest currents of our equally troubled times. In the late Roman Empire the Christians were deplored for not fitting in with the old ways and honoring as God the emperor, and the deities of the clan hearths; today the Christian "deplorables" decline to knuckle under to the momentum of "social evolution" and its menagerie of special interest false gods. As with Augustine, even today the Church proposes the new life, it imposes nothing.

The self-evident decline of the post-Christian West today is partly driven by demographic suicide. This loss is due mostly to our rejection of personal ties to non-secular religion, and specifically our trashing of the Christian virtues. These values bind the present to the future as well as the past: "responsibility, sacrifice, altruism, and sanctity of long-term commitments"[23] including permanent ties of marriage between a man and woman. For Rome, then, in addition to economic disaster there were also underlying famine, moral decadence, effeminacy, and political corruption. But historians are beginning to date the decline of the Roman Empire mostly to widespread disease and depopulation beginning as early as the second century A.D. If this is the root cause for the flat-lining of Roman Civilization, then the barbarian invasion from the north and much later Islamic invasion from the east (into the surviving Byzantine half of the Empire) were more symptoms than causes of this decline.

Instead of plague and disease, other early writers point to a different explanation for the decline of both Greece and the Roman Empire. They cite the duties and pleasures of public life (much like today?):

> Late marriages and small families became the rule, and men satisfied their sexual instincts by homosexuality or by relations with slaves and prostitutes. This aversion to marriage and the deliberate restriction of the family by the practice of infanticide and abortion was undoubtedly the main cause of the decline of ancient Greece, as Polybius pointed out in the second century B.C. And the same factors were equally powerful in the society of the Empire. . . ."[24]

Today in the post-Christian West, are we again living among the ruins and entering a very similar death spiral? Is this for somewhat similar reasons? European fertility is far below the rate needed to maintain population (an average of 1.58 children in a woman's lifetime compared to a replacement level of 2.1 in a lifetime). Reasons for the demographic "plague" today are complex, but affluence and weakened morale are among them, and are aided by a contraceptive mentality and technologies. Our current generation finds itself at the front end of growing turbulence. Using even optimistic assumptions, United Nations demographers still predict that the European population will drop from 451 million in 2000 to 400 million by 2050, while Muslim North Africa and West Asia will double from 587 million in 2000 to 1.3 billion. The ground is shifting under what for centuries has been the demographic and cultural portrait of our world. And it is largely a fact that demography is destiny.

THE SOLITARY MUSHROOM

What is to be done in this historic moment that so much resembles the collapse of Rome in ancient times? Is the transcendent human person greater than any such collective history? Our history is well remembered by an unbroken line, two millennia of the Church and its popes dating from St. Peter. In our own time, and to mark the date of the collapse of state-sponsored atheism under the Soviet Union, in 1991 Pope St. John Paul II (pope from 1978 to 2005) proclaimed anew that, "Man receives from God his essential dignity and with it the capacity to transcend *every social order* so as to move toward truth and goodness" (italics added).[25]

Said differently, we are never "in too deep" to turn around and get it right. In a short poem on personal death he wrote: "In the moment of departure/ each is greater than history [!]/ although but a part. . . ."[26] By our very nature we are always free to rise above whatever unquestioned web of deceit has coiled itself around ourselves at one time and place or another. As with the triumph of the martyrs in a fading and accusing Roman Empire, even today our personal dignity transcends the Big Lie *du jour*.

But others ask, in our world of fingertip data and forceps "fixes," who needs the two-thousand years of memory found on dusty book shelves or in the institutional and sometimes charismatic Church? Who needs any kind of philosophy once they've displaced their interior compass with an opposable-thumb palm pilot and a driverless automobile? Twitter and Tweet messages of one hundred forty characters maximum, with "thoughts" devolving into single letters—giving so much attention to such images recalls Plato's cave-dwellers facing the shadows away from the light.

As Marshall McLuhan predicted in the 1960s, we have broken down boundaries together with renewed tribalism across the globe (*The Medium is the Message: An Inventory of Effects*, 1967). McLuhan also introduced the idea of the "global village" and even predicted the Internet thirty years before it was invented. Along the same lines, the cultural historian Lewis Mumford wrote that the radio, the automobile, and the camera did away with the impulse to sing, to walk, to see—and to remember. He said that technology becomes part of us as we are sucked into it. Is the human person inevitably diminished to despair even as he prides himself in his increased distraction and power?

To close our thoughts on secularist word games and mind traps, let us consider something as simple and plain as a single mushroom. On a side street in downtown Seattle not far from the iconic 550-foot high Space Needle rotating restaurant, your author noticed on the flat pavement a curious mound about the size of a half-flat basketball. What is this? I moved in to inspect my discovery. At the base of the mound was a horizontal crack. Poised inside this opening was a single mushroom pushing straight up, one millimeter at a time, lifting the center of the mound. One minute at a time a single mushroom was reshaping the city asphalt above.

Likewise, in a Soviet prison camp such a mushroom became an erect human being. To a camp guard this unbowed and irreducible person defended the twentieth-century novelist Boris Pasternak. (Pasternak's *Doctor Zhivago* was long forbidden in the Soviet utopian prison state.) In his greater freedom, the prisoner confronted his guard: "If the whole world were to be covered with asphalt, one day a crack would appear in the asphalt, and in that crack grass would grow."[27] In the fifth century Atilla, the "Scourge of God," boasted that grass would never grow again on the land trampled by his mounted hordes. That trampled land later flourished as Christendom.

Hold this thought—a single blade of grass or even a single mushroom—defies the pavement. The pavement does have cracks! Is the big picture supplied only by telescopes and microscopes and then a graffiti layer of Big Lies? In a world of explosive science, the nineteenth-century novelist Victor Hugo reopened the still bigger questions: "philosophy is the microscope of thought." As an earlier generation of pagans came to understand: "you can drive nature out with a pitchfork, but she keeps on coming back." The greatest delusion of all—shared by many millennials, but not all—is to think that the culture wars can be silenced permanently.

The twentieth-century thinker, Etienne Gilson, reminds us that eventually: "philosophy always buries its undertakers."[28] From another in the same generation, Kahlil Gibran, we discover this: "If there were only one star in the firmament . . . one flower in white bloom, and one tree arising from the plain; and if the snow should fall but once in every hundred years, then we would know the generosity of the Infinite" (a posthumous translation). The

Christian proposition is that the infinite is not measured in light years and that the generosity is seen in the one Incarnation of Christ. It is for this reason that the Reformation Era St. Francis de Sales still speaks of "little humble virtues which grow like flowers at the foot of the cross; helping the poor, visiting the sick, and *taking care of your family . . .*"[29]

NOTES

1. Letter from St. Leo the Great, *Liturgy of the Hours*, Vol. II [New York: Catholic Books Publishing, 1975], 1745-46

2. The irreducible and central difference between Christianity and Islam, too, is a monotheism of Triune Oneness as "love" contrasted with a distant monotheism of "compassion," a refrain repeated at the head of all (all but one) 114 chapters (*surahs*) in the *Qur'an*. God as "Father" is also absent.

3. Citations are from Robert Bolt, *A Man for All Seasons* (New York: Vintage, 1960. See also E. E. Reynolds, *St. Thomas More* (Garden City, New York: Image Books, 1958).

4. Ibid. 70.

5. Ibid. 71.

6. Ibid. 81.

7. *The Gospel of Life* (*Evangelium Vitae*), March 25, 1995, n. 73.

8. Ines San Martin, Homily at the papal residence in Santa Marta hotel, *Crux*, April 12, 2016.

9. St. Augustine, *The Confessions*, Book 10, Chapter 27.

10. Vincent Ferrer Blehl (ed.), *The Essential Newman* (New York: Mentor-Omega, 1963), 270.

11. Ibid.

12. Joseph Ratzinger, *Values in a Time of Upheaval* (New York: Crossroads Publishing, 2006), 81.

13. Ibid. 87.

14. Calvin Brown (general editor), *The Reader's Companion to World Literature* (New York: Mentor, 1956), 276.

15. St. Augustine, *The Confessions*, Book 7, Chapter 10.

16. Karl Marx, *Writings of the Young Marx on Philosophy and Society* (New York: Anchor Books, Doubleday and Company, Inc., 1967), 65; cited in Frederick D. Wilhelmson, *Citizen of Rome* (La Salle, Illinois: Sherwood Sugden & Co., 1980), 107.

17. Cited in Jawaharlal Nehru, *Glimpses of World History* (New York: John Day Co., 1942), 525-26.

18. Francis Darwin (ed.), *From the Life and Letters of Charles Darwin*, 1887.

19. St. Augustine, *The City of God*, Bk. XV, chapter 9. Augustine surmised that the mammoth tooth was that of a giant progenitor human.

20. Henry Fairfield Osborn, *From Greeks to Darwin* (New York: Charles Scribner's Sons, 1894/1929).

21. Joseph Cardinal Ratzinger (Pope Benedict XVI), *Truth and Tolerance: Christian Belief and World Religions* (San Francisco: Ignatius, 2003), 226.

22. St. Augustine, "Advice and Reproof for a Military Commander," in Henry Paolucci, *The Political Writings of St. Augustine* (Chicago: Henry Regnery Co., 1962), 284.

23. The Belgian demographer Ron Lesthaeghe, quoted by Allan Carlson, "As Goes Sweden: Neo-Pagan Family Policies Doom Any Recovery," *Touchstone* (Chicago: The Fellowship of St. James, March/April 2015), 26-32.

24. Polybius, paraphrased in Christopher Dawson, "The Patriarcal Family in History," *The Dynamics of World History* (New York: Mentor Omega Books, 1962), 163.

25. St. John Paul II, *Centesimus Annus* (*The One Hundredth Year*), 1991, n. 38.

26. John Paul II, Jerzy Peterkiewicz (trans.), *The Place Within* (New York: Random House, 1982), 122.

27. Cited in Whittaker Chambers, *Cold Friday* (New York: Random House, 1964), 324.

28. Etienne Gilson, *The Unity of Philosophical Experience* (New York: Charles Scribner's Sons, 1965), 306.

29. *Introduction to the Devout Life*, Part III, ch. 35 (emphasis added).

Chapter Seven

The Family Hearth

The new mental map of the postmodern and technological world is of single global household, a single spaceship earth consisting of a system of local and global ecologies. A leading transitional figure is Charles Darwin who still treasured his own family hearth as much as he did the natural sciences. J. Robert Oppenheimer is more of a godfather to modern applied technology and for many years, in his own words, he "had no understanding of the relation of man to his society." Before we visit with these shapers of the modern world (Chapters 9 and 10), let's pick up some earlier threads on the family in history, in shapes it took after or beneath "the beginning" where marriage is revealed as a truly full, mysterious and permanent union between one man and one woman.

THE EARLY FAMILY PHOTO ALBUM

Isn't it true that each of us normally exists within a biological family? In any event, aren't we more than mere accidents within a larger accident? On the other hand, why would a person want to read purpose into a dust storm universe of subatomic particles? A "person"? "Read"? "Universe"? The modern mind seems not so sure about all this, and in fact is quite intent to exterminate such "bigotry" in favor of random and transient combinations. As we have already discovered, the mindset that we label as liberated and "modern" is actually a throwback to much earlier times. The modern narrative gets it backwards—the so-called traditional family is actually the real family of a fully human and sustainable future; contemporary live-in novelties of whatever are a collapse into the past.

It is time to take a broader tour through the ancestral "family" photo album. When was it, exactly, that the public mind shifted to our one-course diet of entertainment celebrities or porno rap stars—these in place of a range of statesmen, inventors, military heroes, explorers and industrialists, thinkers and builders, writers and artists? Are these earlier and well-grounded figures simply too unacceptable to the preachers of ungrounded and endless change, immediate gratification, and dead-end narcissism? When did Nintendo and selfie friends replace the more fully human and common family photo album of history? Our microwave generation cannot understand patience, so how will they ever appreciate human history or even family history? Widespread interest in genealogy is surely a symptom of this broken continuity. One of the natural benefits of marriages oriented toward generating children is "generations." With generations we as individuals are less apt to feel abandoned in anonymous space and time.

The growing prevalence of individualism and single-parent families is thought to be a modern evolution on "the right side of history." But, truth to tell, this is not evolution but *devolution* (*Webster's Dictionary*: "retrograde evolution, degeneration"). It was in pre-modern times that the father of a new child often was not easily identified. There was no paper work and no DNA testing to make a case. In many societies the mother returned to her kin group with her child. Not exactly an isolated single mother, but a widespread female-based, "matriarchal" social structure. Respect the dedication of most single moms, for sure (and the single dads!), but we need not pretend this general arrangement is a new world.

For the following few pages your non-specialist author relies partly on a limited two works on the Semitic world (the Middle East) and more specifically, Arabia, another more global and preliminary (posthumous) source.[1] Other sources are Joseph McSorley and Walter Cardinal Brandmuller on Christian history, John Ferguson McLennan who deals with polygamy (a broad term), polygyny (the subset of multiple female partners), and polyandry (the subset of multiple male partners), and Jean Herbert on the cultures and history of Asia. McLennan focuses on the widespread practice of matriarchal families before the (exogenous) capture of females from distant clans, and before male preeminence and accountability became common and then universal.[2] (Think of the violent abductions today by Boko Haram terrorists in Nigeria.) In an included letter to Charles Darwin, dated February 3, 1874, McLennan differs with Darwin and proposes that monogamy generally came after a period of polyandry, and it is not explained by jealousy and a feeling of female property:

> As a system [polygamy, or polygyny] can have had less to do than any other with the history of marriage on the whole. . . . Polyandry [supported by *group opinion*], in my view, is an advance *from*, and contraction of promiscuity. It gives men *wives*. Till men have wives they may have tastes, but they have no obligations in matters of sex (italics in original).[3]

There is, then, according to McLennan's extensive and comparative re-search of human populations, a distinct and universal stage where primitive groups commit to wives and to marriage and to mutual obligations. This is as intended in our deeper selves as from "the beginning."

In his detailed review of primary sources for pre-western Asia, Jean Herbert finds that attitudes varied widely regarding virginity (and adultery and incest). But, "generally speaking," he concludes, "any breach of this rule [that a girl must remain a virgin until marriage] is thought extremely serious and may lead to heavy sanctions, either in Japan, China, India or Islam," sometimes including death or banishment. Incest is rare and adultery is almost unheard of among some groups in Ceylon and India, while homosexuality "seems to be extremely widespread throughout Asia [cultic examples given]." While the subordinate position of women has been nearly universal, this position changes with marriage. Unlike much of the West, the religious act (which is highly variable) and the physical aspect are separate, and in the case of child marriages the former aspect can continue separately for years. Family ties extend to the village, the tribe, caste, clan and religious community.[4] In the secular West marriage has progressively degenerated into an individual and civil event with little or no religious or communal dimensions, and is commonly preceded by premarital sex or replaced altogether by co-habitation.

Polygamy is a broad term referring to marriages involving either several wives or several husbands. Even a non-specialist reading into the history of early social groupings, in Asia and the rest of the world, will consistently give us common accounts of matriarchal families (involving several wives, or polygyny), for example, in the "days of ignorance" in Arabia meaning the period prior to Mohammed. (Polyandry refers to one wife with several husbands.) Some North America Indians practiced monogamy (one man and one woman) but many practiced polygamy and often were matriarchal. Across the globe extended families of several generations were most common, in contrast with today's Western nuclear families or unhappily broken "single parent" families.

As an ideology Secular Humanism's doctrinaire attachment to contraception adds another layer by also tracing back to third-century Manichaeism (St. Augustine's persuasion prior to his conversion). Manichaeism held that the entire material world is evil in origin and parallel to a separately created spiritual domain. The division was so total as as to warrant a veto against the unborn (an early version of "nonviable tissue"). Today sex selective abortion, also, is not so new. For example, it recalls Arabia in the earliest days of economic scarcity, and the practice of female infanticide because of too many mouths to feed. The bulk of the Semitic world is an exception to (Arabian) matriarchy in that the later family structure outside of Arabia was usually of the father's bloodline (patriarchal). It was his deity of the hearth, not the mother's totem, that oversaw the family show. The distinctive history of the Hebrews, the Chosen People, is especially patriarchal. Abraham, the father of faith, dates back to 1800 B.C. And the first several chapters of the first book of Chronicles in the Old Testament record the long genealogies of the patriarchs down from Abraham.

THE CLASSICAL WORLD

Apart from the Hebrew world, let's now dip very briefly into the later Roman and the barbarian marriage practices, and the still later influence of the Church on marriage as an exclusive, permanent, and monogamous institution.[5] The Greek world was different from both the world of the Romans and later barbarians in the West and the religiously unique world of the Hebrews in the east. Greek deities shared space with our exploration of human reasoning into the workings of the cosmos and the world of man. But, like the later Roman deities, the mythological figures from pre-history were believed to be active in our human history.

The Romans ruled for over a millennium beginning in about 753 B.C. This period lasted until the last emperor of the West was deposed in A.D. 476. The Eastern Roman Empire, or Byzantium, continued for another millennium until overrun by the Ottoman Turks (Islam) in A.D. 1453. To better control at least the demons of natural disaster, earthquakes, and famines the pagan Romans installed family and clan deities who could be appeased by routine offerings of one kind or another. The common view is that the earliest forms of polytheism like this eventually coalesced toward monotheism. But another prominent view is that all polytheism is really an opposite movement of deterioration from a more original and still undifferentiated monotheism. The biblical Tower of Babel perhaps symbolizes this understanding.

In the Roman Republic and the last days of the Empire one could live securely within the larger civil society of *Pax Romana* if one also burned incense before the emperor god who reigned above all the others. The most important of these others filled equal niches in the round Pantheon in Rome, first built in 27 B.C. (and rebuilt as we see it today, in the second century A.D.). The ancestral family hearth was okay as far as it went, but superimposed emperor worship held the clans together in a cosmopolitan city and across the far flung Empire. Pagan religion was not tied to any kind of innate morality, and members of families and society might do pretty much whatever they pleased, provided that stable public order was maintained. Food and circuses became useful distractions and imperial budget items, much like television and professionalized sports today.

Roman civil law clearly recognized marriage as a permanent relationship between one man and one woman with the intention of having children. As a lesser alternative Roman law also recognized the other relationship of concubinage in which the wife came from a lower social grade than her husband. As with barbarian law, concubinage was not regarded as "marriage" by another name. One could also divorce, but could have only one wife (or husband) or concubine at a time. Cohabitation with a concubine might be long term but was not permanent, and often was undertaken for calculated advantages (something like so-called contract marriages today). Perhaps one was waiting a long while for an expected inheritance or wanted the elders of an extended family to pass on so that, by marriage, one could be the head of one's own household. Or again, maybe it was a matter of differing social classes at a time when marriages between members of the upper and lower classes were prohibited.

Roman law differed in important respects from customary Germanic law. Germanic law intruded itself into the Empire under the succession of barbarian invasions or longer-term migrations from the north and east. Unlike Roman law, Germanic law did not require mutual consent between the parties, and did not prohibit forced marriages by abduction. While Roman marriages were monogamous, barbarian law—like Islamic law even today—permitted polygamy.

THE JUDEO-CHRISTIAN TRAJECTORY

Prior to the Roman law, and in contrast with it, the Jewish nation began at least a millennium before anything Roman. Israel was a nation when all other modern nation-states were still small clans huddled in mountain caves or around desert water holes. The Jewish faith recognized the gifted connection between the one true God and what goes on in each human heart. The insight and revelation to the Israelites was that there is but one God, that he maintained a Covenant with his mysteriously Chosen People, and that the morality of the Ten Commandments (the natural law) was literally a given. Adultery was anti-social as a violation of the covenant (Gen 20: 3-7) and a rupture from divine law (Exod 20:14). For Christians, too, adultery cuts us off from the life of God (1 Cor 6:9-11).[6]

Periodic lapses by the Jews into the polytheism of Canaan were a betrayal and regression from this gifted monotheism, rather than a possible prelude to an alternative and presumably evolving cosmopolitan unity. The Hebrew Scripture—the Old Testament—recounts this chronology of infidelities, new prophets and conversions. Infidelity toward the Hebrew law is commonly manifested through violation of biblical marriage laws. Prohibited marriages were contracted with the pagans and, predictably, the pagan practices then seeped into and compromised the higher Hebrew way of life. Idolatry and fornication are mentioned in the same breath. The stigma of the Samaritans, located between Israel and Judea, was partly that they had intermarried with the invading Assyrians.

Through forbidden intermarriage the surrounding Canaanite cult of Baal becomes, in effect, a fifth column movement.[7] This is not about communal prejudice or a failure of multiculturalism as some might be led to think today by our Establishment elite. The betrayal of the Covenant is the very reason for the prohibition in the first place. The wayward Hebrews, like the pagan worshipers of Baal, went so far as to surrender their own children to the sacrificial flames of the pagan deities. We see this in Jeremiah (32:35), Lamentations (2:20), Baruch (2:3), the Psalms (106:36-8) and elsewhere. Not a happy picture, especially for the victimized children, and a picture not unlike the abortion culture today.

Under Moses polygamy was tolerated in Hebrew society, but as Christ and the gospels teach us under the testament of the new life (the New Testament), divorce and remarriage was tolerated only "because of the hardness of your hearts" (Mark 10:5). Never mind the practical price to be paid for non-exclusive sex. For all of his wisdom, Solomon is also the polygamy poster child with his one thousand wives and concubines. The model of single-hearted wisdom eventually lapsed into idolatry; Solomon's offspring preyed on each other, and his unified kingdom inherited from King David splits apart shortly after his death.

In summary, while the Hebrew religion clung to the reality of one God and a universal morality (mingled with customary restrictions), the history of the Israelites becomes a story of repeated infidelities. But their infidelities happened then as now within an always larger reconciliation extended by a God who, though we might abandon Him, will never abandon us.

The Christian faith is in continuity with Judaism, but is more than a continuation. Christians testify that within global history is a unique trajectory of increasing participation by the divine. The Incarnation of the divine into recorded history occurs in Judea sometime around 4-6 B.C. precisely during the reign of Caesar Augustus, in the days of King Herod, and when Quirinius was governor of Syria (Matthew 2:1, Luke 2:1-2). This intersection of the divine with human history, Christians believe, is providentially timed by a God of infinite love and attention to detail, who is deeply interested in human affairs centered in part on human freedom bonded to responsibility. As often as not, other trajectories are ephemeral at best, chains of improbabilities which only look like evolutionary trends leading always upward, of course, to one's present vantage point of the past.

With the Incarnation of God into earthly history comes an entirely new understanding of both God and of the graced human person—each and all of us. And the precise entry point of Christianity into human history is well-situated to express itself through the exercise of human reasoning as explored by the Greek mind. Christian witnesses then reach out geographically on the expansive stage put in play by the highway engineers of the Roman Empire. At the risk of his life, St. Paul, the Apostle to the Gentiles, finds advantage in traveling to Rome as the nerve center of the Empire with its rich mingling of peoples and with its road system leading outward toward all horizons. For missionary St. Paul, one road leads to Rome and then all roads lead *from* Rome.

Under family civil law in the Roman Republic and then the entire Empire a sequence of multiple divorces and remarriages was not unknown. By Christian standards this is not marriage but serial polygamy. In continuity with Judaism, and unlike Roman law, Christianity maintains a bond between faith and morality. St. Irenaeus spells this connection out for us, "From the beginning, God had implanted in the heart of man the precepts of the natural law. Then he was content to remind him of them. This was the Decalogue."[8] The natural law is innate, not imposed. In the words of Christ himself, "Behold, the kingdom of God is within you" (Luke 17:21). Have we ever thought of the Ten Commandments as a simple reminder of the natural law already known (however vaguely) through the conscience, namely, the well-formed "tiny whispering sound" already echoing within ourselves?

Unlike the Greek poetics of hybrid beings half-god and half-man, Christ is radically near and something radically "other"—fully both, fully human and fully divine, "two natures in one Person" as we say however inadequately. We use Greek categories to proclaim Church teaching about this astonishing Encounter with the Infinite which tells us so much about our real selves as persons.[9] Throughout history it is the witnessed physical Resurrection that anchors our attention to this Encounter. The mystery of the Incarnation is totally unique and unexpected. Where science looks for abstract laws of replicable events, and where poetry celebrates the particular and the concrete, the "person" of Christ is uniquely the *concrete universal*—the Truth in person. Supernatural in origin, Christianity departs from the Roman mystery religions (e.g., Mithraism) and variants of natural religion in other parts of the world, i.e., Hinduism, Buddhism and Islam. The Christian revelation is not replicable in a science laboratory nor anywhere else on the stage of history. What is repeated is the testimony of witnesses, both alone and in groups, to seeing and speaking and eating with the resurrected Christ. (All of this is in contrast with the failure of those most intent on proving a fraud who never produced a dead body.)

The Christian take on the nature of the human person—and therefore of families of persons—is both grounded in human nature and uplifted by revelation. Before his late baptism, the fourth-century Saint Augustine, whom we have visited many times in these pages, lived with a concubine for thirteen years before questioning and dropping his adolescent appetites and flawed motives. The rest of his life, as a deepened thinker and active bishop, (he writes) was a struggle to forget what had come before. Young people today who might be breaking free from cohabitation or worse can take much encouragement from the track record of many who are now saints. (The applicable expression is that where sin has abounded, grace abounds even more.)

We are best shaped toward a graced future by well-grounded families. From the late second century we have an anonymous Letter to Diognetus regarding Christians: "They marry like all other men and they beget children; but they do not cast away their offspring. They have their meals in common, but not their wives." For reasons of social value and morality, and under the influence of leading saints (Ambrose, Augustine and Jerome) the Church went with Roman law rather than the German. Very broadly, the language and culture of Christianity are expressed in harmony with human reasoning, building on Greek and Roman ways of thinking rather than tribal myth. Over a period of centuries the Church introduced, as a teaching and as a requirement, that monogamous marriage between a man and a woman, by its nature, is in fact permanent and exclusive until the death of a spouse. The "I do" resolves in advance the tensions of apparent mitigating circumstances. In addition what would be explicitly defined as the sacramental dimension, the pastoral accompaniment of the Church was as witness to spousal accompaniment. Again, the biblical injunction is a reminder of the enduring natural law as part of divine law—"that what God has joined together, no human being must separate" (Mark 10:9).

The Church eventually enforced marriage outside of one's kinship group, partly as a practical guard against incest and the risk of genetic deformity. And the transformational explanation for marriage beyond the natural kinship group was to further the diffusion of the new Christian charity above any clan insularity of blood lines. In this feature Christianity is unlike the tribalism of Judaism. In the older system vengeance reprisals targeted outsiders and extended across generations, but with intermarriage this could no longer continue. Again, from the beginning and even in Celtic and German lands the Church held its members to indissolubility, and through the penalty of excommunication discouraged divorce. Remarriage following a separation was prohibited early on (Synod of Carthage, 407 A.D.), and marriage to the wife of a man still alive also merited excommunication (the Synod of Angers, 453 A.D.). Unlike Roman law the early Church recognized permanent concubinage across Roman class barriers as a real marriage because it included the commitment to lasting union.

Much later and in distant America, the confederation of Iroquois followed the policy of clan intermarriage for purely natural reasons. This confederation began in the sixteenth century under the prophet, Dekanawidah, and his more-than-legendary disciple and spokesman, Hiawatha (b. 1525). Lasting for three centuries, the Confederation was likely a deliberate construct from the very beginning and not an evolutionary outcome. The founders spread the original eight tribes among five new tribal groupings to ensure that the mingled (and matriarchal) family lines would halt old blood vengeance morality. Intertribal warfare was restrained by the new fact that opposing tribes now included members from one's own original tribe.

In later and central Europe the Austro-Hungarian Empire was but one monarchy that deployed its ethnic regiments broadly with the same political intent. The First World War dismembered this multinational empire and brought an end to this familial approach by equating "self-determination" with sovereign and separate statehoods. During the first decades of the Muslim world, in the seventh century, unity was based not on intertribal mixing but rather the overarching monotheism imposed by Islam and selectively borrowed from Judaism and Christianity. Following Mohammed's death (A.D. 632), the tribes did fracture for a few years but then were militarily suppressed and reunited. After that the shared benefits of expansion and plunder beyond Arabia served the same adhesive purpose and with extraordinary success in the following century and then beyond.

While divorce had been available ever since earlier Jewish law, in medieval Europe the Church prohibited this accommodation to the local culture. The Church also forbade the common practice of infanticide. It forbade the taking of concubines which came to be seen as not much different than prostitution. Further, in the Christian West the very nature of marriage was eventually recognized as a sacrament (Pope Lucius III and the Synod of Verona, 1184 A.D., and the Second Ecumenical Council of Lyon, 1274 A.D.)—"raised by Christ to a sign and means of salvation."[10] The spouses are channels of grace to one another in a graced and mutual presence that protects us and our children. Recognition of marriage as a sacrament of belonging is both biblical and very practical. It protects the wife and children from abandonment by the husband. Marriage is found by its nature to be a clear decision of self-donation "in His image and likeness." It is not a provisional ideal poised to be negotiated away in the drift of circumstance.

It is ignorance of history to dismiss the sacramental order as peculiarly "Eurocentric." The opposite is much more accurate. At its formation and later development Europe was Christocentric. This path is open to all cultures, not only to a pre-European Rome in decline and in collision with a Germanic periphery. Before there even was a Europe, we have the fifth-century St. Ambrose and his flock corralled into his cathedral church in Milan (later Italy), under the immediate threat of death. The state power insisted that Christ be melded into a pre-Christian collage of several equal deities, all within a resuscitated pagan system of "tolerant" civil religion.

Ambrose's refusal to allow Christianity to cohabit with pagan deities in a renewed pantheon is regarded as the first real institutional demonstration of freedom of religion and worship apart from state coercion. Exaggerated multiculturalism is nothing new. In his "no," Ambrose actually gave a bigger "yes" to a higher truth than the state. In the barricaded cathedral and by simply singing for days together to a higher God the bishop and his flock persevered successfully together. We might even be reminded of the singing done by the early eighteenth-century Fr. Savaterra in faraway California (Chapter 4). And for us today, part of this song is the meaning of real marriage and the natural family. From the late St. John Paul II we have this: "Each family is a beacon of light which must illumine the Church and the world for the end of this millennium [the twentieth century] and as long as the Lord allows this world to exist."[11]

A BROKEN RECORD

Everywhere, old habits die hard. Ireland is unique in Europe. Polygamy was widely practiced into the end of the seventh century, although forbidden by the Church. Such was the lingering of Old Testament practices with New Testament Christianity on the frontier. As a high-profile individual case even on the mainland, the early ninth-century Charlemagne (the Christian emperor) had five wives, two of whom he divorced, plus an additional five concubines, but possibly not at the same time. Pre-Christian marriage customs were mostly replaced only by the year 1000 A.D., give or take as much as a century depending on location. Marriage legislation was standardized in 1140 A.D. (the *Decretum Gratiani*), reaffirming the principle of unity and indissolubility.

We read that even at the Council of Trent in the sixteenth century, one of the socially ingrained problems especially in regions of the earlier Germanic invasions was still a pattern of secret and un-witnessed marriages. Another was open concubinage even among some members of the clergy.[12] Our most progressive ways today are not so unlike the primitive ways of those who came long before us. What we flatter ourselves with as modern and possibly liberating is really an anachronism, a backpedaling and a throwback. A footnote to the Reformation is Martin Luther's defense of the double marriage of Philip of Hesse. This, too, was a throwback argument—isolated but highly visible—based as it was on the pre-Christian practice of polygamy in the Old Testament.

Medieval Albigensianism or Catharism, which was centered in Spain and southern France, suddenly looks strangely modern. As a Manichaean sect it preached radical enlightenment and spiritual purity, not unlike some enlightened and utopian political elites today. Evil and the physical world were attributing to a second and equal god. As with many critics today, it was the Church that was painted as satanic in origin. The enlightened Cathars had no prohibitions against suicide, or contraception, or abortion. Wife swapping was mandatory. Trend-setting Hollywood is old hat. Disdain for the physical world led the Cathars to preach suicide by self-starvation. Few were so devout, but modern-day euthanasia is a rough equivalent.

We no longer need to ask of the modern-day establishment and its religion of Secular Humanism, is it modern or is it old fashioned? Even today's "no fault" divorce reintroduces an ancient abuse against wives and children, just as pre-Christian tendencies periodically blended the Hebrew religion with Canaanite paganism. Temporary cohabitation and trial marriages today remind us of Roman concubinage, only under a conveniently different label. This generation refers to live-in boyfriends and girlfriends as "partners." The new twist is that the modern vocabulary conjures up visions of temporary business partners. Modernity is as given over to trial marriages as it is to start-up companies that are shed after the five-year tax advantage (i.e., accelerated depreciation of investment costs).

The sexual revolution of the 1960s disconnected us from our natural, historical and then Christian heritage. We refuse to breathe the same air that sustained our ancestors without whom we are nothing. With the air sucked out of the room we imagine ourselves to be on the cusp of doing something new. We are divided between and within ourselves. We are amnesiac toward past wisdom, and the permanent fact of the family, and even the future. The timeline of our mental map does have key dates, but these are for the collective and secular state, and not the intergenerational family and especially not to authentic marriage as a prior institution, a pre-existing condition, so to speak. Under the new dispensation the "traditional" family is shattered and redefined by the courts as "stereotypical" on a stale spectrum of more random options. How dangerously close we are still to the forest primeval. . . .

BRACKET-CREEP BY THE STATE

Just as the family continuity can fragment into bits, Church and state can be divorced. They can be forcibly separated and bracketed into distinct and then non-communicating and competing and then alienated domains. But hostile takeovers have always been in style. Overreach by either the Church of the state (or Empire) are hallmarks of early European history. Most recently and on the heels of the Enlightenment, Otto von Bismarck, the first chancellor of the very newly united German nation-state, was one of many who sought to re-tangle this knot. In 1871 (the same date as Darwin's *Descent of Man*) the new Germany was intent on domesticating the Church as a department of state. We find in the new Germany the origin of our modern term "culture war" (*Kulturkampf*); again, nothing is new here. And to the south, losing control over the historic Papal States in Italy, the pope is holed up as a "prisoner of the Vatican" within the ancient and suddenly secularized city of Rome and the new Italy. Between 1870 and 1929 he refused to subordinate the small acreage of the Vatican (one hundred and nine acres) of the Church in Rome by accepting any state salary from Rome. Independence for the Church was finally negotiated with fascist Italy in one of several such concordats between Church and domains of the emergent nation-state landscape.

In Germany, one residue of Bismarck's experiment is the requirement that sacramental marriage must be paralleled by a second civil marriage under the secular state. This redundancy continues a trend of nation-state ascendancy dating back to the sixteenth century. Nearly a century before Bismarck, during the French Revolution, the Reign of Terror began to impose marriage on celibate priests as a required sign of loyalty to the new secular regime. In the early twentieth century the same was true in Mexico, at least in the state of Tabasco. Such priests were given a government pension and had no duties. Those who refused were shot. Taking the long view, the Reformation erased the sacramental nature of marriage even as it removed the scandalous "sale of indulgences." As part of the real arc of history, after a short five centuries and with the fully born new religion of Secular Humanism, we now openly market the full range of self-indulgences in a world where rights are stretched and responsibilities are forgotten. Instead of a coin in the cup, an aborted child in the bedpan.

In Revolutionary France, the dominant nation-state at the time, one petition to the National Assembly (dated July 19, 1793, and from the jurisdiction of Condom!) even declared celibacy a capital crime. The total priestly vocation was to be subject to the death penalty. Napoleon's later Concordat with the Church (1801) is silent on priestly celibacy, in effect retaining the internal governance of the Church to itself.[13] To hope today for a similar reprieve from compulsory public conformity from a seemingly less autocratic regime, as in the matter of gay "marriage," should not be too much to expect. But more likely is the threatened removal of tax exemptions from religious institutions as a reprisal for affirming natural marriage against the Zeitgeist of "gay marriage." In Washington State the gay "marriage" law has required all non-complying gay liaisons to be registered as "married." Only by such compulsory uniformity can the fiction of historical inevitability be upheld.

Several centuries before Bismarck the worldly powers controlled the Church's selection of its own bishops (the eleventh-century Investiture crisis). By this device local princes often elevated landowners into their own political orbits. Luther populated his new church with the secular powerful when Catholic bishops refused to comply. And only a few generations after Bismarck, today a devolved understanding of what once was fully human marriage features a spectrum of state-sponsored mutations. As a prelude to gay marriage, the state enabled trial marriages, no-fault divorce and remarriage (sequential bigamy), and high-tech infanticide (late-term abortions), all of this floating atop a "whatever" subculture of ho-hum cohabitation and one-night hookups. What we have here is not a new future, but a disinterred past, the false logic of bracket creep and of renewed and contagious societal chaos.

After six centuries the printing press gadget and civil paperwork have undermined the marriage as the foundational institution of society itself. In the place of the depth of real marriage, a certificate or tattoo. (And now, up-to-date artistry promises tattoos that disappear after a year or two.) The raw power of the state itself becomes a cosmetic atop societal randomness as we drift ever farther toward husbandless wives, fatherless and motherless children, and a very long-armed cradle-to-grave public "safety net" for a social collective in free fall. What is free fall? Free fall is slipping in only a few decades from the decriminalization of sodomy to the prosecution of anyone who might publicly defend traditional marriage.

Other than the crumbled cornerstone of monogamy and exclusive marriage, the only lingering restraint on sexual musical chairs and promiscuity is the primal sense of self-preservation. Prior to the outbreak of the AIDS virus (Auto-Immunodeficiency Syndrome) promiscuity among homosexuals was widespread. In 1978 the Kinsey Institute reported that nearly thirty percent of homosexual males had had sexual encounters with one thousand or more partners. Nearly four out of five said that half of their sex partners where strangers. Only one percent had had fewer than five lifetime partners. "Almost half of the white homosexual males . . . said that they had had at least five hundred different sexual partners during the course of their homosexual careers."[14] This extreme pattern has not continued. And yet today, over eighty percent of male syphilis cases are among gays, barely a few percent of the total population.[15] In addition to sexually transmitted diseases (STD) and especially the fatal AIDS, also reported is a twenty-fold increase in the risk of colon cancer for active male homosexuals.

In its early years and in the United States (1976-81) AIDS was still largely confined (94 percent) to the homosexual and bisexual demographic ("community"). Before being mainstreamed into the general population and politically relabeled, AIDs was known as GRID, meaning Gay Related Immunodeficiency syndrome.[16] Even in 2012 the Center for Disease Control reported that sixty-one percent of all new cases of AIDS-causing infection in 2009 were male homosexuals. The technical fix for all victims is a weak reaction to what Pope St. John Paul II termed "a kind of immune deficiency at the level of essential values." Technocracy offers the one-dimensional marketing of a series of necessary pharmaceutical products to contain the AIDS-causing HIV (the Human Immunodeficiency Virus). Worldwide, one million people in the general population each year still die from AIDS, an incomprehensible tragedy. Each victim has a name.

To teach the foundational underpinning of morality for any sustainable society—including abstinence prior to real and permanent marriage—is almost forbidden in government schools. Meanwhile a parody presents itself in the shift, in barely one generation, from the anonymous bathhouse culture to a more or less monogamous pairing under legalized gay "marriage."[17] All of the natural law realities—a society of marriage, family, and children—are as flexible to re-engineering as are transformer toys and the transformative and elusive HIV virus itself! In the parlance of political correctness, to speak of moral responsibility and fulfillment would infringe individual "rights." More accurately what we have is the "rites" of individualism.

And yet, to its credit, in 2015 the federal Center for Disease Control and Prevention (CDC) has revised its Sexually Transmitted Diseases Treatment Guidelines to report that "abstinence and monogamy are "the most reliable way to avoid transmission of sexually transmitted diseases (STDs)." Were it within the purview of the CDC we might expect a follow-up news flash that the world is round and, with Galileo that the earth revolves around the sun, and someday perhaps that the unborn child is in fact an unborn child.

GOVERNANCE OF THE SELF

All of the permanent reference points of moral society seem now to be movable goal posts that finally disappear altogether. The last reality left standing is a gut-level sense of the self as personal property. Self-governance and self-possession become a sense of absolute control and ownership over the self as personal property. This attitude echoes the mindset of the economic market and the corporate manager over his dehumanized and interchangeable employees as hired "human resources."

Of being a thing barely hired, St. Teresa of Calcutta told us that "the greatest poverty is to be unwanted." Often unwanted motherhood decides that her answer is to un-want and to abandon her pre-born child. Quite often treated by a boyfriend as a unwanted and disposable property, the unwed mother also opts into a world of moral freefall defined in terms of power. "Since even I am now only property," the young lady might say, "at least I still belong exclusively to me. I am more than a human resource and I can still do what I want with my body (bodies?)." Hence the abortion clinic, readily supplied by a spreading welfare state that eventually might undermine even the existence of any kind of private property. But, today the mother must be no more than property, otherwise thrown into question is the assumption that the pre-born child is only property, and just one thing too many in our real-time hassle with life.

Offered here is a reasoned position, not necessarily a religious one. If we were to turn to religion we might listen to St. Paul who, when he visited the morally lax cesspool of Corinth had this to say about property: "Do you not know that your body is a temple of the Holy Spirit who is in you, whom you have from God, . . . and that God's Spirit dwells in you?" (Corinthians 6:3).

On the property principle, the Scottish minister and fantasy writer, George MacDonald had this to say: "The one principle of hell is—'I am my own'."

Today is again a time that understands neither property, nor rights nor obligations. We are instructed by both the courts and Western pop culture that trees have "rights" every bit as inalienable as the sacred rights of human beings. An imaginary Mother Nature is now the sacred womb, and the real wombs of real mothers are imagined away as the bearers of "non-viable tissue," disposable property at most. The archaic Mother-Goddess returns in secular garb to accept the sacrifice of "parasitic" real children. The throwback of the self and the child to the status of property also finds a parallel in a past slave culture. In Rome slavery was widespread and the children of slaves could be bought and sold as the property of the slave owner. This was partly because the slave parents themselves were property and like so often today, were not married (in those days because not allowed to marry).

To the entire ancient world St. Paul offers a different vision entirely: "Do you not know that your members are the temple of the Holy Spirit . . . that you are not your own?" (1 Corinthians 6:19-20). But another more modern throwback other than slavery is the more recent sex deviant and pornographer Marquis de Sade—after whom the spectrum of perversions known as "sadism." He too preached the "equality" of human beings with the animal kingdom and the plant kingdom. De Sade was one of the only seven so-called political prisoners freed in the much-celebrated storming of the Bastille in revolutionary France. (Of the others, four were forgers and two were insane and under observation.)[18] Is the focus on the body as mere property equal to animals and plants a corruption of suffragette Susan B. Anthony's broader and higher vision? Her vision of self-possession and sex equality was not of any kind of property, but (as biographer Rheta Childe put it) that women "might own and possess their own *souls*." Thirteen years after her death the "Susan B. Anthony" Amendment—the right for women to vote—was added to the Constitution.

And in the common event of the disappearing boyfriend the young lady on the street in search of a clinic might well agree about her own soul. When she says "property," is the panicked mother in crisis also overwhelmed with our deepest core of self-worth, now betrayed? In our limited post-Christian vocabulary is she expressing what we too quickly stereotype as selfishness? The body-and-soul mother and sanctuary for an unborn child decides that she must defend (to the death) a "right" over not only her own body as property, but for her very self beyond words. It is a strange culture that in the realm of economics and income champions the plight of the ninety-nine percent, but then in the realm of life and death uses cases of rape—the one percent—as leverage to supply abortion on demand against the other ninety-nine. "Oh what a tangled web we weave, when first we practice to deceive!" (Sir Walter Scott, *Marmion*). And of the one hundred percent, what of the name-

less, dispossessed and "unwanted" pre-born infant? Can we do this math—
are there *two* involved? The modern world of selective outrage steers our
already-mother to amputate herself from her own maternity. Sometimes even
in a sex-selective abortion which is a most telling backslide into our primitive past of female infanticide.

Our mutant notion of property rights then moves on to conjure the "right"
of homosexual households to acquire as accessories the children of others.
The alleged right as a surrogate "parent" to adopt a child eclipses the real
right of the child to a mother and father united in marriage in a morally
grounded—that is to say, less contrived—universe. On the street, family-
oriented adoption services are branded as "homophobic" and boarded up by
the courts. In the socialist state why shouldn't adoption agencies be licensed
more broadly as entrepreneurs linking the supply of unfortunate or unwanted
children to the legally created supply of "married" partners with double
incomes?—the brave new world of legalized human trafficking or whatever.

Popular culture rationalizes this unraveled mindset. Self-exalted as "progressive," it has obsolesced even itself. What comes after "modern?" Absent
the natural law as the real common ground, what comes next? What is meant
by the twilight "postmodern" times? Sweden has been secular for a century,
and now is said to be beyond even the postmodern. By this it is meant that
some of the young are curious again about religion while others are not only
indifferent but identify religion as the source of hatred.

In the twilight environment of the post-modern the authentic definition
and reality of marriage is tolerated legally by nothing more than inertia. We
now live on the vapors of the past. With the dismantling of marriage as
between one man and one woman oriented toward children, waiting in the
wings are multi-party communes as "marriages." Marriage is not so much
broadened as tossed into the dustbins of history. In his critique of political
power and its misuse, the French philosopher Bertrand de Jouvenel gives us
something to think about, whatever our place in the flow of history:

> We humans are not . . . equal to the task of evolving a bubbling stream of ever
> new verities. Ideas are, truly, like infrequent oases in the barren wastes of
> human thought; once discovered, they are for ever precious, even though they
> are left to be silted up by the sands of stupidity and ignorance.[19]

THE DISPLACED RELIGION

With all of its history and, therefore, its insights into the future, how is it that
the Church is again shouted aside as being on "on the wrong side of history"
even when it comes to affirming the family? The Church is dismissed for
proclaiming "in season and out of season" the uncomfortable values by
which even the Church's imperfect members are to be judged.[20] How can

firm foundations stand against the winds of modern secularism and the intolerant tolerance of mandatory indifference? At the end of the First World War, as Western post-Christian culture began to deal the next hand, even the secular sociologist Max Weber saw the future of a mechanical political order: "Not summer's bloom lies ahead of us, but rather a polar night of icy darkness and hardness. . . ."[21]

The self-understanding of the Church of imperfect members still points, most humbly, to its unique and divine origin in recorded history, bowing to the constant indwelling of the Holy Spirit rather than to the world. Such politically incorrect extravagance! Is there no longer a place in society for personal and institutional freedom to reason and freedom of religion—especially for a faith that traces its origin historically to the words and person of Jesus Christ? All the Church really asks is to be what it is. Many centuries before nation-states were even a twinkle in anyone's eye, it was Christ who said:

> Go, therefore, and make disciples of all nations, baptizing them in the name of the Father, and of the Son, and of the Holy Spirit, teaching them to observe all that I have commanded you. And behold, I am with you always, until the end of the age (Matthew 28:19-20).

The Church will always be more than an artifact spun off by the churning wheel of history. It's commission—humanizing because divine—is to teach and baptize, and will always be different from scientific, secularist or even Islamic projects of conquest. The mission is to propose, not impose.

And yet the Church is persecuted now as other religions are not. It is more than an association like the Rotary, or the American Association of University Professors, or any number of well-paid lobbying groups. Religion in general is more than a civil privilege doled out by the Johnny-come-lately nation-state. With all of us as personally bearing the inborn natural law, a universal and real "orientation" that is defended by the Church almost alone, we are always part of the real past and responsible to a future yet to be, always flawed and graced.

From Chapter 1 we recall that the core of the Church's social teaching is the transcendent dignity of every person, without exception. Interpersonal marriage between a man and a woman is part of this permanent universe of nature and of grace. Secularist modernity, to its self-destruction, attacks not only religion but *any* fixed reference points for genuine human flourishing. It claims to be the source and dispenser of human rights when in fact these rights are inborn and discovered, not invented and conferred. The Western state has become the established counter-religion of Secular Humanism. In Nigeria the virginity of young girls is valued, but too often ravaged by terrorist abductors, while in Western cities such dignity is often squandered with barely a second thought, in parked cars and motels and affluent upstairs bedrooms.

Demographically, of the 1.2 billion Catholics in the world, some two-thirds do not live in the modern and declining West. This ratio is expected to grow to three-fourths by the end of the twenty-first century. They will live in the "South" which includes some regions north of the equator such as most of India and all of North Africa. By 2050 there likely will be as many African Christians as Latin America and European Christians combined.[22] Demographics are the future. Under Pope Francis the re-centering of the Church more toward the peripheries like pre-modern Africa really is forward looking, a cause for hope. The fullness of such a "future full of hope" (Jeremiah 29:11) is part of us even today, under the transcendent "Father who art in heaven" as He is addressed in the Lord's Prayer which He gave us.

While corrupt politics can license parodies of the family as advancing marriage "parity," the Church and natural marriages between one man and one woman continue to breathe the indestructible "tiny whispering sound." The whole idea of a resilient family hearth is grounded in openness to the divine within ourselves and in one another—and, therefore, in even the tiny heartbeat in the womb. The natural family is prior to the formation of politicized identities, whether monarchies or dynasties, or modern nation-states, or a new world order vulnerable to backstage puppet masters. The natural family and traditional marriage are a substance that will last beyond the shelf life of any such passing human constructions in history.

THE STONE AGE MEETS THE ATOMIC AGE

Collapsed in time, the historic collision between primitive clan culture and technological modernity actually took place on a single sunny day on the desert of eastern Washington. It starts with a snapshot of frontier Native Americans versus the early twentieth-century American melting pot. As part of the background, my widowed mother at the age of ninety-three had spoken of herself and of the Indians she knew in her childhood in Midwestern Wisconsin:

> I'll probably be the matriarch of the family, but with no wisdom to impart. Nothing. . . . In our town (Ashland, Wisconsin) we liked the nearby Indians. They came to town from the reservation to go to school even through high school. Some went to college. One mother in town was full Indian and rented a room to me so I had a place to stay while attending the local Northland College. Others were one-fourth or one-eighth Indian. They were Chippewa or also called Ojibway, and I learned they were offspring from the Adirondacks in New York. People are so different. You just can't judge them as a lump. . . .
> [The Ojibway chief, Kahge-gagah-bowh, was one of Longfellow's sources in composing his epic, *Hiawatha* in 1855.]

My mother went on, "Wordsworth, he was my favorite English poet... New babies come to us 'trailing clouds of glory' (from *Intimations of Immortality*). Following his voyage on the Beagle, it was Wordsworth (and Coleridge) who replaced Lord Byron as Charles Darwin's favorite poet (his *Autobiography*). I am happy to discover in my mother a very small bit of Darwin's zest for details in nature, his fascination with the past, and his emotional relief found in the English Romantics. And for those so desensitized by evolutionary and material evidence—those who no longer see even pantheistic "clouds of glory," might we consider that the generosity of God is so self-effacing as to be anonymous, like a personal and free gift on our doorstep with no identifying return address? Perhaps this seeming absence of divine fingerprints is the greatest evidence of true glory.

This zest for details in nature was apparent every day as my mother walked the nature trail along the west bank of the Columbia River in arid eastern Washington. On one occasion, exactly in front of the bench that bears her name plate, she identified such a detail, a singular flower that is not supposed to be found west of the Mississippi tributaries (Purple Loosestrife, or *Lythrum*). In a former chapter we already discovered a soft mushroom breaking through the city pavement and blades of grass in a prison camp, and now in this desert an inexplicable blossom. Darwin's favorite writing, he said, had to do with a single flower (Chapter 9).

A few decades before the above events, not long after my parents' storybook years at Northland College, they found themselves in the desolate desert expanses of eastern Washington. Eastern Washington was one key site of the Manhattan Project formed to construct the first atomic bomb. The Project was masterminded by Dr. J. Robert Oppenheimer and engineered by General Leslie Groves (both of whom we will visit in Chapter 10). The restricted Hanford Nuclear Reservation ("the plant") covered an expanse of over five hundred square miles of federal land bordering the free-flowing Columbia River. A few miles south of the boundary "barricade" the company town of Richland sprang up overnight from sage brush and sand. Like wholesale modernity, the town of an initial twenty thousand permanent residents was lifted from the fabric of former and now far distant family connections. An additional fifty thousand migrants were housed in a tent city on the Reservation.

The past was no longer in touch. Incoming "nuclear families" (pun intended) were all very much the same and fit mostly within a narrow adult age group. Relatives were typically two thousand miles away. Sociologists missed a unique opportunity to research this lab experiment of nuclear families who were committed together to a single Project—the birthing of the world's atomic age. Schooled in the lore of urban and regional planning, your author is reminded of the early twentieth-century "Greenbelt Town" movement. The designed neighborhoods all centered on an elementary school, and as a group were centered on the downtown and the single high school a half mile away. Your author recalls that even then there was yet another version of the spectrum mindset. The Western understanding of the human person as a spiritual being seemed bleached away by a few key lines in the standard high school textbook on United States government. Capitalism in some form and Communism appeared as bookends that were probably capable of blending into a third way somewhere in the middle. The brutal Soviet invasions of Hungary (1956), Czechoslovakia (1968) and Afghanistan (1980) likely had little influence on insider publishing contracts and later textbook editions.

The rapid-construction houses in Richland were standardized cookie-cutter and came in alphabetized designs. The two-story "S" house, for example, dwarfed the one-story "H" house, and a "Q" was larger than a "B" or a "T" which were duplexes. The peripheral greenbelt, instead of being devoted to a supporting farming culture was a ring of desert extending at least fifty miles in most directions. And the central city, like London, existed only in the imagination. The galvanizing community orientation was to produce the first atomic bomb and to make a giant step into a science-based city of the future. No one missed the annual riverside carnival called Atomic Frontier Days. An early newspaper science writer explained the new frontier to the uninitiated:

> Instead of filling the gas tank of your automobile two or three times a week, you will travel for a year on a pellet of atomic energy the size of a vitamin pill . . . Larger pellets will be used to turn the wheels of industry and when they do that, they will turn the era of Atomic Energy into the Age of Plenty. . . . No baseball game will be called off on account of rain in the Era of Atomic Energy. No airplane will bypass an airport because of fog. No city will experience a winter traffic jam because of heavy snow. . . .[23]

All adult residents were the same generation, all had the same kind of education more or less—science, technology, engineering, math (STEM fifty years ahead of its time)— and all were equally on the frontier of something unprecedented. Ahead of its time and ahead of Eisenhower's military-industrial complex, here was the twenty-first century educational-industrial complex.

In this particular linking of nuclear reactors and nuclear families, one of the many bonding social events was the monthly citywide cookie bake for the five thousand technician-soldiers of the United States Army stationed at Camp Hanford a few miles to the north. The military task was to service the Nike surface-to-air interceptor missile shield for "the plant" against any Cold War intercontinental ballistic missile (ICBM) strike. Given this single-generation community, and its isolated and technically educated parentage, here before its time was a scale-model Millennial Generation. To civilize this social experiment a neighbor lady, a graduate of Pasadena Playhouse, was active in forming a local thespian troupe (The Richland Players) where she very credibly resembled and patterned herself after Kathryn Hepburn. At her insistence and following her example, the women always wore hats and gloves whenever they "went out." For a kind of balance, her husband was a six-foot six-inch security guard on swing shift (midnight until eight at the plant.)

In the beginning shall we say, in 1942, the initial Manhattan Project surveyors discovered on the edge of the post-Ice Age Columbia River a very different society, a small encampment of indigenous Indians. This clan was all that remained of the historic Wanapums who had never been in direct conflict with our own westward myth of preordained Manifest Destiny. They had not signed onto the Stevens' treaties of 1855 and never had been assigned to a reservation. So here they were, an open range Stone Age band from time immemorial, at the edge of the ancient Columbia River. Here they were now barely a stone's throw away from construction sites for nine twentieth-century nuclear reactors edging into the atomic secrets of the entire universe, plus a few other related blank-wall concrete structures each the size of an aircraft carrier stranded on the desert. The echo of the James Fenimore Cooper's fictional account in *The Last of the Mohicans* (1826) is found in the real words of Tomalwash, one of the last medicine men of the Wanapums. Instead of "I, the last of the Mohicans," we have "when I die, the tribe dies."

Together with its sister city, the Oak Ridge (Tennessee) uranium facility, this Hanford plutonium facility was the first industrial-scale step into the Atomic Age. The Eastern Washington project was the birthplace of the plutonium core for the atomic bomb dropped on Nagasaki at the end of the Second World War. Could there be a more stark and disjointed collision between the Stone Age and the Atomic Age? Much of history is tossed salad. There is something about the discovery of an unsuspected Indian tribe that has fascinated your author since childhood. Something of the human mystery is found even in the desert, or as Abraham and the Hebrews discovered, especially in the desert. Your writer's tiny place in history is that in the frontier days of 1944, I (and an identical twin) was born on the Manhattan Project nuclear reservation, in the small town of Hanford. Hanford was expropriated and then totally evacuated that same summer.

Thirty miles farther south was the bedroom community of Richland. This was a good place to raise a family, and there was a little bit of Tom Sawyer in all of us lucky enough to live not far from the River. Nearly every day for the quarter century after my father died, my mother continued to explore the bird-watcher riverside trail alongside the Columbia. In time a gathering of regular bird watchers and hikers got to know each other, and each other's transplanted biographies, at this remarkable time and place in local and human history. The catalyst for the gathering of trail trekkers was my mother who came to be known locally as "the bird lady." She reminisced: "I used to come down here for the birds. There was always something, and I could watch them through my binoculars. But now, it's the people. I come down here every day for the people, and sometimes I don't even notice the birds. There are so many good people in the world. This is what gives me hope."

To paraphrase lunar astronaut Armstrong fifty years later (1969): "one small town for man, one giant new world for mankind." Only three decades before the Manhattan Project, Henry Ford installed an automobile assembly line for his 1909 Model T. (The first automobile assembly line was actually built at the competing Oldsmobile plant in 1901.) At the forefront of modern industrial history, Ford is reported to have said, "history is bunk." What he actually told the *Chicago Tribune* in 1916 is this:

> I wouldn't give a nickel for all the history in the world. It means nothing to me. History is more or less bunk. It's tradition. We don't want tradition. We want to live in the present, and the only history that's worth a tinker's damn [*sic* for a silversmith's artful clay "dam" for molding molten silver] is the history we make today.

There we have it. The mid-twentieth century especially is a great divide, and history is something to be discarded. The coinage of any historical tradition is nickels compared to the massive investment we push down the conveyor belt today. Better to live in real time and to make history by just moving things along, like an industrial conveyor belt.

With both eyes open can't we see alternative paths? Without the eyes of memory, and of the heart of the artist and of the poet and family, the reality and unique particularity of the wayside tribe or a wayside flower is lost. What chance do these have compared to the exciting dynamism of manmade quantity and measurements? The management expert Peter Drucker asserts that "what gets measured gets done." Carrying this to its extreme we decide that what can't be measured doesn't exist. On the General Motors Building (at the Century of Progress Exposition in Chicago, 1933) the writer G. K. Chesterton was quoted differently than the assembly-line Henry Ford: "The world will never starve for wonders, but only for want of wonder."

THE WONDER OF THE LIVING PAST

History has been here before us. Modern family disintegration is actually a throwback to fallen forms of "family" in the past. We moderns are, in fact, an all too familiar and recurring "type." The history of the Hebrew prophecies was largely a tuned-in awareness to "types" or patterns, rather than our equally valid but different lens of a ever-changing events through time. These types do not simply recycle as under the pagan understanding of history, but show us permanent human tendencies continually rediscovered and relived. The human being is a mystery of pilgrimage whose permanence keeps popping up in different times and places.

Recalling the Big Lie (Chapter 2) we can consider the timeliness of the long-ago prophet, Isaiah: "Oh my people, your leaders mislead, they destroy the paths you should follow" (3:12). Or this: "Woe to those who call evil good, and good evil" (Isaiah 5:20). We should really wonder anew about this permanence. Does seeing in terms of types like Isaiah actually make as much or sometimes more sense than treating human experience as disposable? C.S. Lewis regarded the trashing of history as "chronological snobbery."

Today with all of our ideas and gadgets aren't we still a bit like pagan Canaan in the time of the Old Testament Hebrew immigrants? Rather than being left behind by a chronology of evolutionary progress, the highest pagan deity confronting the Hebrews, Baal, is actually carried along and in some ways intensified by modern rationality. This dark side of modernity is not likely to be reported in the popular media. Instead, young girls are tutored that Canaanite and modern-day child sacrifice—abortion—is a guaranteed rite of passage into the shiny new life of ever-progressive freedom and modernity. Violence has always been seen as a ticket to the future because it destroys the hated grip of the past. Such was the logic of mob action during the Reign of Terror (1791-93) in revolutionary France, and in the Soviet show trials and purges of the 1930s. The indiscriminate bloodletting of the Chinese Cultural Revolution of the later 60s was meant to initiate a new generation into the iconic and grueling Long March of the communists in the 1920s. For well over a year tens of thousands of communist insurgents trekked into the safety of the sand caves of northwest China, crossing over a dozen mountain ranges and countless rivers, often prodded along by machine gun fire. Most perished along the way, but the survivors remembered this new beginning.

In all such cases the path forward is imagined to be a decisive rejection of the past. The "severance pay" is inflicted on those who still value the part of us that came before. Contrary to the modern narrative, religion has no more monopoly on such violence in human history than does any modern utopian ideology. The Big Lie (Chapter 2) is such a mind game, and even begins to resemble the "brainwashing" documented in village China during the Communist takeover of the 1940s. In the interests of ideology, villagers eventually denounced their friends, their families and finally their very concrete selves, anything that wreaks of continuity and personality.

Your author recalls in a graduate-level course studying the typical rural village of Long Bow in northern China. For the individual to finally break under Communist pressure and to convert, or as we would say today to be radicalized, is to "fanshen." And this is the name of the book. (The account was recorded by a visiting American Marxist, William H. Hinton. *Fanshen,*

1966.) Anyone who thinks that today's deified Diversity is not drifting us into new Stalinist-type show trials is not paying attention. With modern media, the dark side of modernity can be less overbearing than in 1940s China, but the flavor is there. Where amnesia is not yet total, our textbooks promiscuously demonize the Western tradition. The past is read in terms of current political preoccupations and political correctness. And why not? After all, part of the "original sin" is denial and shifting of guilt, as when Adam shifted blame onto Eve, and Eve shifted blame onto whatever she could find—the serpent.

By what reflex do we today shift personal responsibility to government for a solution (?)—and of course there is a "solution." During my career in public service I once presented the office legal counsel with the possibility that perhaps the Great Society of the 1960s overreached. Silence. He responded in the genuine wonder of a cleansing "aha" moment: "What you are saying is that there might be some things that should not be done by government!" A seasoned law school graduate, yet this elementary thought had never before even occurred to him.

By what predisposition do all of us suppose that the mystery of the human person is an equation and a problem to be solved. Surely by the curative elixir of public will and politics mixed with a bit of technology? At some point such an "audacity of hope" (a recent book title slogan) evolves into "hope in audacity." The earlier revolutionaries of 1789 France (1793-1805) imposed a new Revolutionary Calendar and new time line, as if to say that all things began when they or "I" arrived on the scene. The calendar featured ten-day weeks specifically designed to eliminate religious Sundays and the traditional opportunity for family gatherings. And even today, with greater subtlety, all of the past two millennia are branded similarly as the current era C.E. (current era), rather than as A.D. (*anno domini,* the year of Our Lord).

Joseph Stalin, the murderous communist of the twentieth century, gave this secularist mindset a devastating shot (pun intended) in the Soviet Union in 1929. In addition to widespread purges, and to keep the factories on schedule, and finally to plow under the institutions of religion and the family. He replaced the seven-day calendar with a five-day calendar.[24] The five work brigades of the "workers paradise" were first branded with numbers but when this didn't take, each brigade was assigned a color (the original "rainbow coalition"?). The members of individual families were divided into different colors and regimented into different work schedules under the new five-day weeks. Under such state-organized veneer of color-coded diversity, gatherings of community and family were impossible, especially for religious observances. Much to be preferred, surely, is the newer Consumerism with its weekend professional athletic extravaganzas and the gluttonous Black Friday national shopping holiday (following turkey day) versus the last shreds of self-denial on the work-day Good Friday (followed by Easter).

Instead of a synchronized lifting of the social order, the assembly line society suffered slowdowns. Adjustments were made. These included, or course, more re-education, but this fiction would not sell. The seven-day week was finally reinstated in the middle of 1940,[25] such that the Soviet Union could participate in the larger dislocation of World War II in step with the other Allies. Stalin was naively referred to by his wartime allies—Roosevelt (Uncle Sam), Churchill and even Truman—as "Uncle Joe." Wartime horrors and the common enemy of Adolf Hitler simplified the bonding process among otherwise very un-alike parties.

This tidbit of world history supplies a lens for viewing the pace-setting city of Seattle. We find in one neighborhood a twelve-foot statue of Stalin's disciple, Vladimir Lenin, and in another at the center of town a neighborhood subculture display of several rainbow-painted public crosswalks—all funded by the city budget. The self-certified "creative class" was ever careful to not violate the first principle of pre-school—they did not color or even look outside the lines and the narrative. In the interests of in-your-face citywide diversity, yet another Seattle neighborhood a few miles to the north has been treated for years to an annual parade featuring rainbow-painted nude bicyclists. Rainbow politics is here to stay—Lenin, crosswalks, and bike supporters. The painted crosswalks remain year around while Christmas manger scenes are totally expelled from even a seasonal week on public grounds. The white poinsettia fiasco in a public space (related in Chapter 2) stands as a prophecy for later rainbow artistry on the public streets of Seattle.

By subliminal suggestion we are weaned or wrenched away from our own past, away from beauty, and away an open public forum. In his *Critique of Judgment*, Immanuel Kant (1724-1804) shows us the seven colors of the rainbow from red to violet as giving us "the ideas of sublimity, courage, candour, friendliness, modesty, constancy, tenderness."[26] In the corrosive politics of the rainbow coalition, are any of these innocent references even to non-politicized colors still possible?

As with colors, and in the name of "tolerance," all of the reference points of the Christian worldview are also being extinguished. We are severed from the historical encounter with Christ and therefore from ourselves. Even moral character, at odds with the trend line, is silenced as evidence of "extremism" or "bigotry," and is targeted for bullying by an alliance of media mockery and blank-staring courtroom persecution. Language is the first casualty. Ralph Waldo Emerson remarked that "the corruption of man is followed by the corruption of language." The modern experience is the other way around. Corrupt the language and the peoples' heads will fall right into the basket. Once the reference points of stable language and concepts are displaced, fair debate is no longer possible.

Traditional marriage becomes only a subset within a fictional spectrum of options. And then traditional marriage becomes only a random and traditional *form* of marriage. Natural family becomes traditional family, and then traditional family is further sidelined as a traditional *form* of family, just one of many forms on the new court-imposed smorgasbord. Reality is sidelined as a special case and then, with the corruption of language, is no longer remembered or even comprehensible. In universities, liberal arts and humanities core courses are first surrounded by other options, and then dropped and finally replaced, possibly by computer code-writing. With Henry Ford we "live in the present . . . and the only history is the history we make today." Memory becomes at best a bone thrown to the losers, and is replaced just as mineral deposits infill fossil impressions left in ancient rocks. Is reality nothing more than what we make? Surely Shakespeare overcomplicated things by understanding a moral content within the flux of human events. But as a recent occupier of the White House has taunted us, defending his sexual exploits with female interns: "it all depends on what the meaning of *is*, is."

Of course, there is much of the past that really is best forgotten. The fifteenth-century St. Francis of Paola often foretold future historical events, like the fall of Constantinople to Islam in 1453. He was a vegan many centuries before this taste claimed a bit part in "modern" health-conscious society. What Francis of Paola had to say in 1486 about the past is that resentful memories of evil, at least, are unnecessary baggage:

> Memory of an injury is itself wrong. It adds to our anger, nurtures our sin and hates what is good. It is a rusty arrow and poison for the soul. It puts all virtue to flight. It is like a worm in the mind: it *confuses our speech* and tears to shreds our petitions to God. It is foreign to charity: it remains planted in the soul like a nail. It is indeed a daily death (italics added).[27]

Confuses our speech? Is personal resentment the root cause of our manipulation of word meanings and our deceptive mind games? The darkness comes from within. While the conservative political philosopher, Edmund Burke (1790) fails to get the whole picture, he does offer a thought about the French Revolution and its wholesale guillotining of the past: "They who destroy *everything* certainly will remove some grievance." The crisis in all this is not as predictable conservatism would have it, of what is discarded, but "in burning the past, [man also] loses the totality of himself" (Cardinal Ratzinger/emeritus Pope Benedict XVI). The bumper sticker mentality of today says "question authority!" Are we too eager to question everything except our own resentments and assumptions?

In our *Brave New World* we can unlock the elemental heat of the sun in a nuclear explosion. We can evacuate an unborn child in a few minutes so the mother can even pick up some fast food—with calories labeled—even before the lunch hour is spent. We finally imagine that we should erase all of the past which actually is part of ourselves. Without a living past and memory, at least a memory of each other as a sort of "human ecology," are we still capable of reasoning together? Or is it all electronic media, tweets, subliminal messaging and political slogans?

As we enter the twenty-first century with all of our smarts, are we simply rationalizing our spiritually bankruptcy? Is modernity in a state of denial? In the early twentieth century, as we have already noted, G. K. Chesterton already put his pre-computer thumb on the answer: "The madman's explanation of a thing is always complete, and often in a purely rational sense satisfactory. . . . The most unmistakable mark of madness is this combination between a logical completeness and a spiritual contraction."[28] The mark of madness today disinters the same kind of legal madness in late eighteenth-century, revolutionary France during the Reign of Terror. Also at the heart of their madness—a rationalized and spiritual contraction—was the degradation of marriage.

> Intimately connected with these laws affecting religion was that which reduced the union of marriage, the most sacred engagement which human beings can form, and the permanence of which leads most strongly to the consolidation of society, to the state of a mere civil contract of a transitory character, which any two persons might engage in, and cast loose at pleasure, when their taste was changed, or their appetite gratified. If fiends had set themselves to work to discover a mode of most effectually destroying whatever is venerable, graceful, or permanent in domestic life, and of obtaining at the same time an assurance that the mischief which it was their object to create should be perpetrated from one generation to another, they could not have invented a more effectual plan than the degradation of marriage into a state of mere occasional cohabitation, or licensed concubinage.[29]

NOTES

1. William Robertson Smith, *Lectures on the Religion of the Semites* (London: A. and C. Black Ltd., 1889/1927); and De Lacy O'Leary, *Arabia Before Muhammad* (New York: E.P. Dutton and Co., 1927).

2. Joseph McSorley, *An Outline History of the Church by Centuries* (St. Louis: B. Herder Book Co., 1949); Walter Cardinal Brandmuller in Robert Dodaro (ed.) in *Remaining in the Truth of Christ* (San Francisco: Ignatius, 2014); and John Ferguson McLennan, *Studies in Ancient History: the Second Series comprising an Inquiry into the Origin of Exogamy* (London: MacMillan and Co., 1896); including *Studies in Ancient History: Primitive Marriage* (1886).

3. Ibid., 1896, 50-55.

4. Jean Herbert, *An Introduction to Asia* (New York: Oxford University Press, 1965), 215-249, 260-268.

5. Philip Daileander, "The Early Middle Ages," *Lecture 23 on Family Life: How Then Became Now*, The Great Courses by The Teaching Company, 2004.

6. For an extended reflection on marriage including these citations, see Pope Francis, "The Vision of the Wedding Feast," *Open Mind, Faithful Heart*, (New York: Herder and Herder, 2013), 145-66.

7. Fifth column: originally a reference to behind-the-scenes rebel sympathizers in Madrid during the 1936 Spanish Civil War. More recently applied to political infiltration by Hitler and especially Stalinist regimes.

8. Cited in Joseph Cardinal Ratzinger, *On the Way to Jesus Christ*, translated by Michael J. Miller, (San Francisco: Ignatius, 2005), 162.

9. The Council of Chalcedon (A.D. 451) affirmed the human and divine nature of Christ with this wording: "We teach . . . one and the same Christ, Son, Lord, Only begotten, known in two natures, without confusion, without change, without division, without separation."

10. Articulated by Pope St. John Paul II in 2001, cited by Raymond Leo Cardinal Burke, in Robert Dodaro (ed.), *Remaining in the Truth of Christ* (Sand Francisco: Ignatius, 2014), 222.

11. Improvised writing/comment delivered in St. Peter's Square, 1994, quoted in *Almost Biography*, Eternal Word Television Network (EWTN), 1994.

12. For a non-Catholic but detailed historical review and perspective on celibacy in the Catholic Church, see Henry C. Lea, *History of Sacerdotal Celibacy* (London: Watts & Co., 1867/1932).

13. Ibid., 538-42.

14. Alan Bell and Martin Weinberg, *Homosexualities: A Study of Diversity Among Men and Women* (Bloomington, Indiana: University Press/Kinsey Institute, 1978), 82, 85. The study is based on surveys done in the San Francisco area in 1969 and 1970.

15. Centers for Disease Control, "Sexually Transmitted Disease Surveillance 1014," cited in *Catalyst*, 43:1, January/February 2016.

16. Gene Antonio, *The AIDS Cover-up?* (San Francisco: Ignatius, 1986), 3.

17. Ibid., 58-59. The "out of the closet" movement followed on the heels of the Stonewall Riot in New York City, on June 27, 1969. The New York City police department conducted a routine raid on bathhouses, but this time at an after-hours homosexual bar, and the patrons rioted. Stonewall marks the beginning of open militancy for a complex social issue under a politicized and "civil rights" branding. Stonewall is elevated to a national monument while at the same time plaques of the Ten Commandments are removed from view in public spaces.

18. Erik von Kuehnelt-Leddihn, *Leftism* (New Rochelle, NY: Arlington House, 1974), 80-82.

19. Bertrand de Jouvenel, *On Power: Its Nature and the History of its Growth* (Boston: Beacon Press, 1962), 314.

20. Among the nominal members of the Church are groups routinely funded by well-known big money and supported by "Catholic" officials aligned with the government-established religion of Secular Humanism. They resent that the universal natural law is affirmed in the moral teachings of the Church, e.g., the right to life, the meaning of marriage and family. Where the Church was once the scapegoat for the decline of Imperial Rome, today radical secularist and anti-Catholic cells infest the Church, e.g., Call to Action, Dignity USA, Future Church, Voice of the Faithful, and Catholics for Choice. Why settle for the abuse of selling indulgences when you can sell the Church itself?

21. Max Weber, "On Politics" (1918), in H.H. Gerth and C. Wright Mills, *From Max Weber* (New York: Oxford University Press, 1946/1958), 128.

22. *2015 International Bulletin of Missionary Research*.

23. Cited forty years later by Terry McDermott, "Atomic City," Pacific Magazine of the Seattle Times, July 28, 1985.

24. John D. Barrow, *The Artful Universe: The Cosmic Source of Human Creativity* (New York: Little, Brown and Company, 1995), 159-60.

25. Ibid.

26. E. F. Carritt (editor), *Philosophies of Beauty: From Socrates to Robert Bridges* (New York: Oxford University Press, 1931), 109-124.

27. Letter by Saint Francis of Paolo (1486), in *Liturgy of the Hours*, Vol. II, (New York: Catholic Book Publishing Col, 1976), 1758.

28. G. K. Chesterton, *Orthodoxy* (Garden City, New York: 1959), 19-20.

29. 29 Sir Walter Scott, *the Life of Napoleon Bonaparte: Emperor of the French*, Vol. 1 (Exeter: J. & R. Williams, 1832), 173.

Chapter Eight

Toward a Human Ecology

How might we combine logical completeness with spiritual expansion rather than contraction? The challenge to do so is imminent. In the late 1960s the first photographs of planet earth were taken from the Apollo 8 spacecraft in lunar orbit. Imprinted for the first time there was impressed on the human imagination the totality and preciousness of the global natural ecology. Today we are beckoned beyond the disruptions of the 1960s and 70s—the "perfect storm" visited in Chapter 3 (spaceship earth environmental-*ism*, with the revolutionary Big Lie, and with the threat of nuclear Armageddon). We are beckoned toward a greater bonding with future generations and with our common heritage on earth. Together we may now ask: what about a closer look at the community of persons—the much neglected "human ecology"?[1]

FAMILIES AND GENERATIONS

The human ecology differs in both degree and kind from any natural ecology, and yet these are interrelated. As for the natural ecology—are our consumer culture and our quest for (economic) equality eating our seed corn, so to speak, at the expense of future generations? And what do human liberty, respect and responsibility look like when seen as a fabric of connections—as a different kind of ecology? The distinctive thing about a human ecology is not reducible to the churning of evolution. When we muzzle morality the thing left over is not neutral; the thing left standing is toxic. A human ecology is a culture of connections and transforming communion, versus abandonment and what Pope St. John Paul II identified as a "culture of death."

What does a "culture of life" look like, with its connections and communion of family, neighborhood, national solidarity, and the entire family of man? The term is introduced and unpacked by St. John Paul II in *The Gospel of Life* (1995). As part of this culture, and as the historical transmitter of culture and values, we have already touched on the family as the cell or DNA of society and how this culture is now discounted and disrupted. The invasive "species" are elements of the market and the state, both, as well as the so-called sexual revolution. The telltale signs of backsliding are cultural, political, economic and social. The family is demoralized in both morals and morale. Let's summarize the score card, partly with some narratives.

With the aid of television remotes and other digital technologies the cultural and social meltdown seeps into every part of every family home. And the political winds that blow are rocking entire societies. Economically, well, the income tax code is a litmus test—when we adjust for inflation the standard deduction for family dependents has been trivialized since the 1940s. Better to offer an entire catalogue of compensating government supports and their bureaucracies. As the saying goes, "we feed the sparrows through the horses, and the horses don't seem to mind." And the earlier fifty-fifty balance between the total personal income tax and *net* corporate tax burdens as a whole is probably demolished once we fold in corporate deductions and subsidies. Burdens on families as such, over the long term, should be at least part of the conversation of overall tax policies.

Contrary to much Western ideology, it is the transcendent human person in the family that is sacred and to be privileged, not individualism or any kind of collectivity like race, or class, or interest group, or age group or street crowd, or even the state, or the natural ecology. From these mindsets there come such tragedies as late-term abortions. Bedecked in the trappings of high office, the courts rise up to defend the backsliding into the pre-modern "right" (rite!) to destroy unborn infants. "[Our] situation has led to a constant schizophrenia, wherein a technocracy which sees no intrinsic value in lesser beings coexists with the other extreme, which sees no [more] special value in human beings."[2] Writing earlier and even fifteen years before the Church's Second Vatican Council (1962-1965), the existentialist philosopher Gabriel Marcel penned this:

> What it is is to belong to a family, and to be attached to it, is something which it seems to me that neither biology nor sociology is capable of probing right to the core; and on the other hand, speaking rather generally, one might say that the family relationship is not one which up to the present has sufficiently engaged the attention of metaphysics.[3]

Metaphysics is simply that higher part of the truth that is left out by mathematics and physics, the natural sciences, and the so-called social sciences. Metaphysics is partly about the *why* of existence, things as they are rather than simply (or even complexly) how they operate and even evolve.

Metaphysics is about the *is*-ness of things. With this is-ness in mind—what the meaning of is, really is—might we think of the family as a real thing, rather than as a "stereotypical" collage serving individuals who in turn are waiting to be redesigned in a digitized imaginary world?

Under paganism each family revered its own imagined god of the ancestral hearth. Looking around, it seems that pagans might have been closer to the permanent truths about the family than we are today. They held some sense of moral continuity across generations. Today marriage is seen too often as a snapshot bundle of advantages and disadvantages between two individuals, in real time as we say. Marriage is thought of only as a means for ill-defined equilibrium rather than a matter of real commitment "for better or for worse." When the wind changes, we file with the state for no-fault divorce, and maybe get an abortion as an exit strategy or as a dead end event (recalling Michael Edwards in Chapter 5).[4] We are taught this disintegrated worldview by subliminal suggestion and emotional argument, and partly through inane television scripts on at least a hundred optional channels, all with canned laughter.

In antiquity the family retained the memories of the past and of the future at the family hearth, the *polis* or the city, and after that, was led by St. Augustine to stay in tune with the enduring tension between love of the world and love of God. St. Augustine's profoundly insightful book, The *City of God*, was a giant in the world of literature for its first one thousand years and is still of great influence even in secular universities. In his thought the ancestral hearth was very much expanded and even replaced by a clearer view forward and upward. This new Christian reality is the "new life" proclaimed so clearly by St. Paul.

For Augustine the most inclusive family is the family of the Church as it is assembled by the table of the Lord. This ecclesial family and natural families based on sacramental marriage are equally enlightened by a full encounter with one another. There is also an encounter with something that had been awaited and missing for centuries, even from "the beginning." Finally He was missing even from the tomb where he was laid. (See Matthew 28:1-8, Mark 16:1-6, Luke 24:1-7 and John 20:1-10.) Always missing from any narrative of antiquity is the Risen One who now enables us to be more human toward each other rather than less, more attentive and affectionate not less, and more forgiving and fully forgiven not less.

For families, this something more, the Incarnation and not our modern idol of human self-sufficiency, is the only thing new under the sun. The Hebrew understanding of a durable Covenant between unequal parties is not simply retained, but fully transformed. We have an entirely new relationship of shared life within and under the accessible fatherhood of God. This is something more than a social contract between a superior and a subordinate. We are now called friends, not slaves: "I no longer speak of you as slaves, for a slave does not know what his master is about. Instead, I call you friends, since I have made known to you all that I heard from my Father" (John 15:15). The problem with the disciples of modernity is that they "have not read the minutes of the last meeting," the testimony to this Encounter.

Today the family dinner table takes the place of the pagan memorial hearth, at the center of a kind of "domestic church." And the sacramental Church as a whole also "assembles" from the periphery to the center. It is not simply a congregation around a shared totem or text, or any merely human founder, or main course plus dessert, but something categorically more. Biblically, the continuity between the Old Testament and the witnessing of the New Testament lies in this, the Encounter and then the enduring gift of Eucharistic presence. The destruction of the Temple in Jerusalem (A.D. 70) and then the Diaspora into rabbinic Judaism is a parallel event in historical time. Historical time is one thing, and the Encounter is another. The Encounter is a moment that can come to any person at any time or place; the expectation of its coming is even back-drafted as prophecy into the lives and history of the Chosen People. The Old Testament is fulfilled in "the Word made flesh" (1 John 1:14).

The Christian family transcends and departs from the insularity of the earlier Chosen People, and the exclusivity of the Temple, or then the later and more scattered tribalism of the rabbinic Diaspora. The Christian encounter becomes a Eucharistic and therefore universal communion beckoning the Gentiles. In the New Covenant, by sacramental incorporation into the Body of Christ each human person is called and invited with others to become a new temple of the Holy Spirit equally scattered across the world and historical time. How pale by comparison is Bismarck's requirement for civil marriage. From this departure, now marriage even as a natural institution is under assault, by court order.

FAMILIES AND "POLITICAL MAN"

Conventional secular history views the human past falsely as through segmented eyes, like an insect. Prompted by the Renaissance poet, Petrarch (1304-1374), we now routinely divide the past history into bite-size pieces: the periodization of the Ancient period, the in-between Dark Ages, and then the Modern, and now the "postmodern." The problem with modernity is that it too becomes obsolete. What then? We drift quietly into the night of postmodernity, playing with the meaning of words along the way. Surely, there must be some other way of regarding our humanity and our pilgrimage in time.

One alternative way of slicing and dicing is to see human history less in terms of grand social periods and more in terms of nested families that are also intergenerational. Such families have been dissolved by the disruptions of industrialization aided and abetted by the secular state. For its part, academia very much has abdicated its responsibility to living memory. It has very little to say to counter the lowest common denominators of collectivism, political correctness and mind-bending technocracy.

Seen in their best light, the large hereditary dynasties aspired to be patriarchal families extending through time and over large parts of Europe. These extended families were sealed by intermarriage across national boundaries. In far-fetched theory, at least, the hereditary monarch might have served as an outside mediator to the identity politics of insular groups (St. Louis IX in France comes to mind). "Together with a Crown Council [the monarch could] act as an umpire between the people and the experts . . . and bureaucrats . . . [and as] the neutral element in the state."[5]

Might we contrast this dated artifact with the current idiom of inward looking and administrative nation-states? Nation-states are keyed to homogeneous identities of history and language. They can puddle out between features of geographic—mountains and rivers—from other such nation-states. France and Germany are the classic examples and were opposed participants in the two world wars atop the centuries-long displacement of a more universal Christendom. While "good fences make good neighbors" (the poet Robert Frost), both of these particular forms—the earlier monarchies and the modern nation-states—are artifacts of recent history. It was the Treaty of Westphalia (1648) that marked the end of the Thirty Years War and the seemingly permanent rise of the secular state. As a transition into the new politics, this war was already more political than religious. As a broadly European civil war it also involved great cruelty as is so often the case.

Intermarried family monarchies were ended decisively by the First World War. The Austria-Hungarian Empire was dismembered, and Czar Nicholas II of Russia was executed along with his family by the Bolsheviks. The Muslim Ottoman Empire was carved up. Of the three major European monarchs King George V of England was the only one whose domain survived this momentum of modern history (The globe-spanning British Empire continued until after World War II). The German Kaiser Wilhelm escaped into exile in the Netherlands. At the Versailles Treaty of 1918 the right to ethnic "self-determination"—part of President Wilson's Fourteen Point of Peace—morphs into a cookie cutter patchwork of separated and fully autonomous nation-states divided one from another.

Identity politics remains the great strength and the great risk posed by bottom-up democracies and, globally, of nation-state politics. Identity politics can either express either mini-patriotism or self-idolatry in a new political form. And hybrid democracies actually retain something of the earlier stability of monarchies and fatherhood. As the best example, from the late eighteenth century the United States Constitution hints at a constitutional monarchy by retaining an executive, but this is balanced by separate centers of power in the legislative and judicial branches of self-government. (Some see dynastic tendencies as in the Adams, the Roosevelts, the Kennedys, the Bushs, and the Clintons.)

Sustainable human flourishing and families today face a new development, an artifact of our most recent history in a complex world. This is the ever more sovereign and centralized *state* itself, and its tendency to substitute itself for the rest of natural *society* served by intermediate groups, and primarily families. The state violates the prior natural law when it displaces natural and voluntary associations. These also are oriented toward the common good. The state violates natural law when its actions discourage or upstage biological families. It violates families with its circular culture of assistance and then dependence upon itself, first as a presumed collective source of funds, then as the source of human rights, and finally an oracle mandating generic marriage certificates. (Why are we reminded of generic holiday wreaths and generic poinsettias, Chapter 2?)

No one seems to wonder why the American citizen cozies up more to a benefactor and generic uncle, "Uncle Sam," rather than to the historically real George Washington, as the historical "Father" of our Country. Harriet Beecher Stowe's book about an uncle, *Uncle Tom's Cabin* (1842), offers a surprising angle. In this most famous American novel of the nineteenth century, a black family is broken up when Uncle Tom, a slave commodity, is sold. Considering the endangered family unit today, maybe our Uncle Sam and Uncle Tom should get better acquainted. Like Stowe's Uncle Tom, and with a complicit Uncle Sam, our younger generations are also "sold down the river." It's a good bet that this familiar expression actually comes from Stowe's novel. The meaning today is the tissue of lies (Chapter 2) that has come to replace the more fostering world of promise that was still ours before the perfect storm of the 1960s (Chapter 3). The Millennial Generation is betrayed and abandoned when human laws hijack the natural law.

FAMILIES AND "ECONOMIC MAN"

Among all of the social sciences, economics has been called the most dismal science. And as far as families are concerned there is often good reason. The system is not molded for the family, but too often for the reverse. Here's an example. As the sexual revolution got well underway in the 1970s, the federal government also began allowing mortgage lenders to consider both husband and wife incomes in establishing the home buying "credit-worthiness" of families. Theoretically, home ownership would be brought within reach. Your author recalls unsuccessfully challenging federal mouthpieces that the market-driven price of homes would simply jump to a new equilibrium inflated by the new definition (the same economics of "rent-seeking" that we discovered above with student loans and rising costs of college tuition). "Nope," they said, "we've run the equations."

Single income families with stay-at-home moms and children were undermined. The family was undermined. Moms were forced to go to work, even if they did not feel such a vocation, and family chit-chat and meals were nudged farther to the sidelines. Thus market adjustment advanced the new world of three-car garages and driveways instead of lawns, family outlays to surrogate day-care centers, and then the rise of "latchkey children" unlocking their way into empty homes after school. It advanced the split of middle income America between the double incomes and the rest. By what diabolic logic do we liberate womanhood by devaluing motherhood? The option of woman careers is not the point here, rather the lost option for anything else.

In terms of broad ideology, Karl Marx's disciple, Vladimir Lenin, conceived the family as essentially an odd artifact of arbitrary economic relationships. Here is another mindset inspecting goat entrails and tea leaves to fix the disruptions of the Industrial Revolution. Marx would have been right if he had made a case for the economic erosion of families, rather than its economic creation. We might ask, for example, to what extent the slave plantation house has simply been replaced by cradle-to-grave government welfare programs? Has the perpetual economic dependence on the plantation house simply been relocated to the new plantation inside the Beltway? It seems the family unit is endangered on all sides; by the breakup of families under the former slave economy; and by new self-perpetuating dependencies under a Black and White "culture of poverty." And even by the erosive power of economic affluence—a three car garage, and in place of a family dining room a television in every bedroom.

Not long before Marx, it was economically convenient for some to deny that American Indians or the Blacks even qualify as human beings. Were they subhuman by nature rather than only by circumstance? Again, former economic times were much like our own, or more to the point, vice versa. On a global scale, the Age of Discovery raised this question in narrowly cultural terms: were people from outside Europe to benefit from the same understanding of the human person as defined by positive law for Europeans? A fading Christendom still asked whether American Indians and Blacks were also "human beings." Does the universal natural law apply to American Indians? In our own Age of Science we now ask—or by court order are prohibited from asking—whether this law clothes the unborn. The pretense that such stature can be either withheld or conferred by the pretended author-State is a naked deception.

Spanish protection of the Indians from raiders was mostly an economic bargaining chip in exchange for tribute, and easily degenerated into a new form of slavery. The sixteenth-century Bartolome de las Casas protested this *econmienda* plantation system in Spanish held regions. Today, very much in the old mold, the United States in the developed world offers foreign aid in exchange for the imposition of the Western abortion culture on indigenous populations. It is this practice in the Philippines that Pope Francis termed "ideological colonization." A few decades after Bartolome, in 1610 St. Peter Claver began caring for slaves in the Columbia slave markets in Latin America. Farther back but still late in human history, in 1435, Pope Eugene IV had condemned slavery off the coast of Africa in the Canary Islands. And Pope Paul III (1534-1549) condemned slavery in the New World, but slave importation to the American colonies, which began in 1619, continued unperturbed for two more centuries.

The natural law reminds us to wake up to the assault against persons and the families. Keying off of the words of Christ, in 1858 Lincoln wrote that "A house divided against itself cannot stand. I believe the government cannot endure permanently half slave and half free." Barely yesterday, in 1863, a total of four million slaves were technically emancipated in the United States and later actually freed at the end of the Civil War in 1865. For two centuries slave families had been divided and subdivided for sale, and the women routinely reduced to sex slaves to produce greater numbers without the bother of expensive African slave ships.[6] Between the War for Independence and the Civil War, church members from the various denominations had remained generally ambiguous and accepted slavery as "not intrinsically wrong."[7]

Today, it is abortion and suicide assistance for the elderly that are gerrymandered into our legal mindset as "not intrinsically wrong." Plantation slavery meant slave-owner breeding to avoid the shipping cost of the slave market, while today implantation (im-*plantation*!) clinics offer a market-price to cash-strapped female egg donors on our overpriced college campuses. Ads are routine on the back pages of student newspapers. But what better way to be initiated into the broad spectrum of big-ticket globalism versus the miniscule family—surrogate motherhood is an established international industry (with the most competitive prices found in Nepal: only thirty thousand dollars!). In the press we now read of another innovation attached to college debt. This is modern-day student temple prostitutes. They offer themselves to whatever older "sugar daddy" they might select from the menu on the Internet. In a system of college education-lite, why not also prostitution-lite?

So, while "marriage" might remain a personal goal, Lincoln's prognosis of a nation divided against itself applies. It applies to the self-government of individual souls and the false notion that even marriage is at best a calculation of fifty-fifty self-interest rather than mutual self-forgetfulness. Such a house divided against itself cannot stand. To this divide within the family, we discover a similar divide between the family and the encroaching state. What kind of national economics do we buy into? Apart from air brush Socialism we seem stuck with the get-along-go-along code words "enlightened self-interest" and an open door to apparently unlimited "creative destruction." What kind of "stuff" are we cajoled into wanting from the big box store compared to what we need? Who controls what we think we want, and how we get it? How does our perpetual buying and selling of stuff weaken our own everyday thinking on what should be the most engaging moral questions of family and society? Good time management is not enough—good management is not enough—as always, who manages the managers?

The twentieth century was about economics and scientific break-throughs—the tools of modern warfare, atomic power, computer technology, and any number of pharmaceutical products. All of this was mingled with a grand economic experiment elevating the ideas of John Maynard Keynes (*The General Theory of Employment, Interest and Money*, 1936) above the other ideas of his critics. One leading critic was the generally like-minded Joseph Schumpeter (*Capitalism, Socialism and Democracy*, 1942). He was both a champion of business creation (entrepreneurship and, yes, "creative destruction") and predicted a world of giant corporations. Long prior to Keynes or his critics, economic thinking was broadly shaped by the mechanistic laws of physics and the devil-take-the-hindmost. To some extent, we still breathe that air today.

The mental map of economics that we carry around in our heads has been shrunken down into the short-term ups and downs of quarterly business reports, day trading on Wall Street, and keeping up with or surpassing the Joneses with three garages rather than two. Keynes gives us personal and national debt, credit card spending, and deferral of long-term obligations—by individuals and government alike. Under Keynes the special case for broad and sustained government intervention only during economic crisis (the Depression) was falsely painted as a *general* theory to be maintained at all times, so said the critic Joseph Schumpeter.

Another readable and more frontal critique is Henry Hazlitt's *Failure of the "New Economics"*. Hazlitt writes of Keynes: "Here is the *General Theory* in a nutshell, with its *transvaluation* of values [a reference to the philosopher, Nietzsche, and his novelty of radically new "values"]. The great virtue is consumption, extravagance, improvidence. The great vice is saving, thrift and 'financial prudence'."[8] What would Hazlitt have to say, though, about rampant income disparity? When asked, corporate climbers netting millions in salaries and bonuses report that "it's not [even] about the money . . . it's about winning!" The careerism of winning what—a couple bucks more and a corner office with windows? Like the public distraction of professional athletics, "modern" office culture mimics the gladiator culture of the ancient world.

A clear alternative to Keynes is at least hinted in the popular work of E. F. Schumacher: *Small is Beautiful: A Study of Economics as if People Mattered*, 1973) Schumacher was not so much against bigness, but encouraged big firms to be internally structured around people as if people still mattered. Keynes' theory was built around big numbers, like total consumer spending for the nation. It muted too much any more consistent start point for personal and family savings with a view to their own futures. A simplistic contrast, perhaps, the collective "economy" versus the family unit as such, but this contrast finds too little room in the public forum for sustained exploration. Instead, on television the nightly business report.

Keynes, who was childless (a homosexual in his early years, then married in 1925) once famously said, "in the long run we are all dead." "Whatever" is an easy call for mathematicians who are not oriented toward children and grandchildren in the long run. In his *Economic Consequences of Peace* (1919) Keynes did correctly foresee the unnecessary damage done to Europe in the Versailles Peace Treaty following the First World War, but he also "was a proponent of eugenics and served as Director of the British Eugenics Society from 1937 to 1944. As late as 1946, shortly before his death, Keynes declared eugenics to be "the most important, significant and, I would add, genuine branch of sociology which exists."[9]

Born the same year as Keynes, 1883, Margaret Sanger, the founder of Planned Parenthood, began advocating eugenics in the early 1920s. Adolf Hitler then picked up their pioneering ideas about eugenics to be up-scaled for the economic recovery of Fascist Germany, as genocide and no longer an incubator business but instead an entire system of crematoria. Today, some key questions for "the common good" might be whether global trade deals (or their absence) prevent the triaging of economic vulnerable nations, or (instead) whether such deals bundle bad apples (debts) with the good as triggered the global economic meltdown of 2008? Or both? Simplistic answers are not better, but too rarely sought are better ways of framing the questions.

NATURAL FAMILIES AND "LEGAL MAN"

Rather than reducing the family to only economic terms, the new elite of today would render the family itself an altogether arbitrary artifact of obsolete vocabulary. Now that abortion is institutionalized and commonplace, close observers report that same-sex "marriage" did not so much evolve onto the front page as it was imposed by well-planned and executed public relations campaigns. The cover story was that the attitude of the supportive President of the United States had "evolved" between 2008 and 2012. In the 2008 election year President Obama said "I believe marriage is between a man and a woman; I am not in favor of gay marriage." This was a flat out lie according to his political advisor at the time, David Axelrod.[10] The campaign slogan "audacity of hope" is exposed as more a hope in audacity. The very credible charge is that militant activists, the media, the entertainment industry, and most of our colleges and universities long before had coalesced into a fifth column movement.[11] By the myth of social evolution we have progressed from the fictional "divine right of kings" to the equally fictional *defining rite* of the courts.

Until mid 2015 in the United States laws defining marriage in traditional terms clung to survival in fourteen states, including Michigan, Ohio, Tennessee, and Kentucky. For these four states the Sixth Circuit was the only Court of Appeals that sustained the voted will of the people on the meaning of marriage. Appellate federal courts already had forced on the people a redefinition in eighteen other states. Commentators said that if the Supreme Court voided these state laws defining traditional marriage, it would be "the worst example of judicial activism since Roe v. Wade" (1973).

During testimony in early 2015 the swing vote on the Supreme Court, Justice Kennedy, remarked on traditional marriage: "This definition [of marriage] has been with us for millennia, and it's very difficult for the court to say, oh, well, we know better." Critics saw this remark for what it is: evasive conceit. Two months later the 5-4 majority opinion of *Obergefell v. Hodges* bent to less than two percent of the population while affecting all the rest. The court overturned past millennia by mainstreaming as marriage the hybrid oxymoron "gay marriage." Canute (995-1035), King of Denmark, is popularly thought to have commanded the incoming tide to recede. The more likely rendition is that he made this command as a way to rebuke his courtiers for thinking the king had power over the wind and sea. But today, our modern-day Canute, Justice Kennedy, commands marriage to be what it is not. Rather than another Reich of a thousand years, this word game fantasy has the permanence of an overplayed poker hand.

As for the majority of voters who went with the flow, the age-old question applies: If a tree falls in the forest and no one hears it, is there any sound? In this case, if the commuter train of life jumps the tracks, but all the passengers are either asleep or distracted, is there still a train wreck? The front page "occupy Wall Street" economic movement served, in effect, as a decoy for the court's novel assault on all of society. The halls of the Supreme Court were occupied by a slim majority (5-4) that assigned to itself a monopoly of legislative power to advance a scavenger hunt bundle of "civil rights," as if the Constitution were little more than a Rorschach ink blot offered by a quack psychiatrist.

In fact, the court legislation from the bench by judicial supremacists cancelled voted actions on the books in thirty-two states just as *Roe v. Wade* did in 1973—and rather than settling things, they have widened a permanent cultural and political chasm in what once was a national republic based on a moral inheritance. Social history turns on the vote of one man, Justice Anthony Kennedy, who as an interested homosexual could have removed himself from court review of Congress's *Defense of Marriage Act.* Instead, he erased the Act and, further, rendered its moral and cultural underpinnings irrelevant.

Under Kennedy's libertarianism the court settles for footnote consistency, rather than for a truth higher than itself. *Roe v. Wade* literally trashed the lives of the unborn, while *Obergefell* erases the rights of surviving children to legally valued "families" and freedom from a culture of same-sex custodians ("Parent A" and "Parent B"). The court mocks even Galileo; the world revolves not around the sun, but around whatever court is in session—"oh well, we know better." As the judicial fig leaf, the misapplication of the Fourteenth Amendment of 1868 (as dissenting Justice Clarence Thomas explained) plants the fiction that "due process of law" is an entitlement to court-declared government benefits, rather than (as originally intended) whatever "process" is "due" before a person is deprived of "life, liberty, and property." *Roe v. Wade* withheld from the unborn the right to due process; *Obergefell v. Hodges* redefines due process altogether. Instead of a protection against government overreach, the Fourteenth Amendment is now the "nuclear option" for arbitrary state power and social and cultural meltdown. In the name of civil equality, and like the fallout from the Chernobyl nuclear disaster, the ruling did treat everybody the same.

The chain reaction of self-deceit and public manipulation is clear. Where the 1965 *Griswold v. Connecticut* ruling discovered a penumbra unrestricted right to a contraceptive world, and where the 1992 *Casey v. Planned Parenthood* discovered the "right to define one's own concept of existence" (and with the 1973 *Roe v. Wade* the non-personhood of the unborn child), the majority of *Obergefell v Hodges* now discovers that legal fiction is a useful contraceptive against rational debate on the meaning of marriage and family. Within the silent Constitution is found the mandatory right of men and women to "define and express their identity . . . by marrying somebody of the same sex and having their marriage deemed lawful." In a stroke of the pen, millennia of human history and the voted position in thirty-one states (and the universal and inborn natural law itself) are tossed into a slop bucket together with extracted "tissue."

The court system presents itself as a sort of multipurpose restroom dispenser of, first, condoms and now generic marriage certificates. But what more can one expect in a culture of downloaded Internet term papers and mail order college diplomas? It's all about credentials. Under the New Math of equality what counts is the desire of the one or two percent of the population who want gay unions to be gay "marriages," while the real rights of sixty million children aborted since *Roe v. Wade* do not count. The new world of generic "marriage" is annexed into the imagery of Wall Street. As with the

Wall Street stock market—with its diversity (!) of corporate mergers, limited "partnerships," day trader relationships, and leveraged buyouts—at the end of the day all transactions are equal elements of the compendium Gross National Product.

With *Obergefell v. Hodges* the term "bully pulpit" again takes on a whole new and literal meaning, beyond anything even President Theodore Roosevelt ever suspected. The dissenting Chief Justice Roberts summarized: "Do not celebrate the Constitution. It had nothing to do with it." The ruling measures up to the most unflinching standards of political correctness. The end game of past decades is finally and fully "transparent:" the Big Lie is transparently corrupt, self-righteous and manipulative, all finally in plain view for those who have eyes to see and ears to hear.

The dissenting opinion gives us the truth: "It is one thing for the majority to conclude that the Constitution protects a right to same-sex marriage; it is something else to portray everyone who does not share the majority's 'better informed understanding' as bigoted." Why does this remark summon up the vapors of exclusiveness in the past, "It is true that liberty is precious—so precious that it must be rationed" (Lenin).[12] Why are students of history reminded of what another power monger had to say about propaganda:

> The function of propaganda is, for example, not to weigh and ponder the rights of different people, but exclusively to emphasize the one right which it has set out to argue for. Its task is not to make an objective study of the truth, in so far as it favors the enemy. . . . Its task is to serve its own right, always and unflinchingly (Hitler).[13]

The martyred Thomas More also came to know the sharp edge of such political orthodoxy. In 1981 a Chief Judge, Howard T. Markey, gave extended remarks to the Thomas More Society, including this:

> More died of a principle dear to every lover of freedom, every respecter of humanity, every admirer of our Constitution. That principle is that there can be something higher than a king's or a state's written law. It matters not whether we call it "fairness," or "ethics," or "natural law," or "moral law" or "God's law." There are higher considerations to which even the state is subject.

The judge continued, pointing to where the pride of legalistic logic can lead us:

> The alternative, of course, is to hold that the writ of ethics and morality does not run at all to the field of human law—and to authorize judges, in all logic, to accept and enforce laws permitting murder—or to approve and enforce the master-race acts of the Third Reich.[14]

The legal profession that "in all logic" gave us dismemberment abortion now gives us the dismembered biological family. Especially in the latter case the court has rendered illegitimate and demonized all dissenters.

Such courtroom puffery has come straight from the veiled wizard in the Wizard-of-Oz. As for the future, media spin will dwell on the undeniable bullying of the LGBTQ demographic, while the much broader momentum is to persecute those who publicly adhere to the traditional family of past millennia. We can expect radical activists to advance poster-child legal cases to solidify domination for their behavioral "orientation" and lifestyle. Getting technical, but this is critical, will those who affirm traditional marriage be protected by only the "preponderance of evidence"? Or will they have to curtsey before the more rigorous standard of "strict scrutiny" in order to freely exercise threatened freedoms—freedom of personal and institutional religion, freedom of speech and even freedom of thought?

As the current Chief Justice Roberts points out, jargon slipped into the new ruling pertains to freedom of religion speaks but only to the right to "teach" religious principles, not to *exercise* them. This is more of the elastic vocabulary magic show. This time a narrowed freedom of "worship" takes another step to dismantle our constitutional freedom of practicing religion.[15] To believe and teach, yes, but if not to live it, then the long-ago Justice Oliver Wendell Holmes Jr. finally wins. "[it would be] a gain if every word of moral significance could be banished from the law . . ." (see Chapter 2). The broader assertion is not really "sexual orientation." Isn't this slogan more like Churchill's "riddle wrapped in a mystery inside an enigma?" The precondition is the banishment of every word of moral significance, namely the natural law—politically aggressive sexual orientation within the mystery of psychological predispositions, all inside the enigma of Oliver Wendell Holmes' moral and cultural disorientation. The riddle is how long it will be until even the reduced freedom to "teach" is strung up as a "hate crime?"

The final litmus test for the gay lifestyle culture might yet come when a constitutional claim to polygamy works its way up to the top of the federal case load. There is at least one case, in Brazil, of a marriage among three parties which has been given legal recognition. An application in the United States came less than a week after the *Obergefell* ruling. The polygamist petitioner mouthed the hackneyed slogan, "it's about marriage equality." If the United States Supreme Court can admit legal decisions in European courts into its footnotes (and it now does), then why not also the practices under Germanic Law from the second century (Chapter 7), or from Islamic law (Shari'a), or from pre-Western tribal cultures from whenever? Whatever.

An earlier Supreme Court found itself eating crow not long after its overreaching *Dred Scott v. Sanford* ruling in 1857 upholding slavery in the Western territories. In defining Scott as "property" the court swept aside anything that the Congress or the territorial legislatures might say, but also declared that the Missouri Compromise of 1820 had been unconstitutional from the start. How very modern sounding. For those radicalized Catholics who take pride in the fact the majority ruling of *Obergefell* was written by a nominal Catholic, the rest of the story is that the flawed Supreme Court's *Dred Scott* decision was written by one "emaciated" Chief Justice Roger Brook Taney, another misguided Catholic. Taney did not live to see the end of the Civil War that he helped ignite. Can we see that he was misguided about the universal natural law, as above any patchwork "property" law lashed to the backs of anyone other than one's own kind?

The 5-4 majority of *Obergefell v. Hodges* is fastidious or clever enough to still draw a line somewhere. This is the fig leaf model of legislating from the bench. Marriage as it has been known for millennia is cornered, but not crushed. Traditional Christian marriage is merely pushed into a waiting clos-et before being silenced by a slim court majority. The delicately retained right to believe and teach the truth remains—the individual mind is un-touched; there is no inflicted brain damage or head injury. Smiley buttons are furnished to one and all—assailants, the taunting mob in the media, victims and witnesses—and society is invited to move on and to make friends as if nothing has happened. (A rape victim with no realistic legal recourse knows the feeling.) Less lucky than isolated individuals are our social institutions—gagged public schools or religious hospitals, schools, and adoption services. Open discourse for all of us in a Public Square is placed under watchful surveillance in search of "hate speech."

Christianity is unlike another great world religion in that it does *not* propose a legal system based on a claimed revelation such as is claimed by only Islam and the opposite and now established anti-religion of Secular Humanism. Christianity points first and directly to nature and to human reasoning as the source of civil laws and courts.[16] Now, no longer defended by the courts are the foundational nature of man himself and the reality of the universal natural law. Rather than reason, and the affirmation that with some effort the human mind can arrive at truth, the legal guide is naked will. If not will, then an amalgam of bubble worldviews sold as tolerance—either Islam-ic or radical secularist. Peace is either imposed from above or is an evolution-ary, rainbow-coalition collage like the duckbill platypus. In the West the seat of tolerant government literally becomes the toilet seat in the girl's restroom. Consider the micro-aggression litigation that awaits any transgender male visitor who leaves the toilet seat up!

There can be no doubt that in direct violation of the First Amendment the courts have *established* Secular Humanism as our civil religion. How clever-ly sinister is this? The First Amendment innocently provides only that "*Con-gress* shall make no law respecting an establishment of religion, or prohibit-ing the free exercise thereof . . ." The need to rein in a rogue United States Supreme Court never occurred to the Founding Fathers. But not to worry;

equality is served. The public can now hold in equal disdain all three branches of the federal government—executive, legislative, and now judicial. The judicial because it has devolved into a redundant legislative body rather than respecting and maintaining the Constitutional division of powers.

In their confirmation hearings, court nominees usually get away with decapitating the Constitution from the natural law tradition expressed in the Declaration of Independence. In 1987 Robert Bork (author of the later Slouching Toward Gomorrah: Modern Liberalism and American Decline, 1996) was an unsuccessful exception. His nomination was replaced by the now Justice Anthony Kennedy whose hand, again, wrote the Obergefell majority ruling. All the better to frame the marriage question as only a procedural issue—state's rights versus Supreme Court interpretation of penumbras and emanations, or as one dissenting justice remarked, "fortune cookies." And, to paraphrase Galileo who was also manhandled by an overreaching tribunal: Nevertheless, this is not marriage.

THE DEATH OF A THOUSAND CUTS

We the peasants can look forward to further legalistic novelties. At this low point in our national history and character, we are reminded of Lincoln's uplifting words in the Gettysburg Address : "Four score and seven years ago, our fathers brought forth on this continent. . . ." Not only was Lincoln unembarrassed to use the politically incorrect term "father" ("our fathers brought forth...") but also notice the historical reference. In 1863 he is pointing back to the Declaration of Independence (1776), not the allegedly freestanding and disconnected Constitution of 1787). The Declaration recognizes "our Creator," a word and a fact expunged from the vocabulary and thinking of our self-supreme/Supreme Court.

Today, not only is abortion legal, it is becoming a mandatory "reproductive health service" for all hospitals and already with universal participation through the tax code (the half-billion dollar per year federal subsidy to Planned Parenthood). Regarding any remaining opposition to abortion "rites", how dare anyone appeal to freedom of conscience or to any higher "law" like the medical profession's duty to "first do no harm"? And now, so as not to even offend anyone, everyone is required to buy into the homosexual lifestyle as well, or at least bake the gay "marriage" wedding cake. We have here the radicalization of an entire society. First, in the military, it was "Don't Ask, Don't Tell." This policy was rescinded by a second Executive Order opening the military to homosexuals. Fine and well, but marketed as an expansion of freedom, the new policy was the thin edge of the wedge that would require all of society to either salute to the Left or else be sued. In barely the winking of an eye the entire society is regimented into a military marching band. Do not step to the tune of a different drummer, least of all a small-town carpenter's Son.

Even the "free speech" protection of internet pornography—probably the greatest destroyer of youth and family in history—does not require all citizens to participate. By the new judicial logic, instead of simply legalizing tavern liquor sales, the end of Prohibition also should have criminalized every outlet—as places of "public assembly" (a civil right)—that happened to include any kind of drinks on the menu, for not being fully stocked with alcohol-on-demand for a rights-conscious public. This would mean every restaurant and burger joint, without exception. Under the "right to privacy," court-ordered public access to contraceptives does not require all citizens to participate . . . except through mandatory universal provisions of health insurance coverage (Affordable Care Act, 2012). As an aside, the penalty for opting out of insurance coverage was cast by the Supreme Court as only a "tax" and, therefore, permitted. Why wasn't this "tax" seen as a non-uniform "head tax," something that is prohibited by the Constitution (Article I, Section 9)? The parallel here is the equally unconvincing Dred Scott ruling that for awhile got away with defining an itinerant slave as "property" to be returned to his owner.

Let's get back now to consider the tune of a different drummer. Certainly reasonable people can respect a typical case of a florist—a florist!—from small-town America in Eastern Washington, Richland, on the banks of the Columbia River (of which more in Chapter 10). A long-time artist, for a decade she has given friendly service to the suddenly aggrieved. Because she declined to bake a cake for a gay "marriage" she finds herself likely headed to the United States Supreme Court. At issue is whether the First Amendment protecting personal freedom of religion (not simply freedom of worship) takes priority over the "legality" of gay marriage (and in this case a state Consumer Protection Act). An inventory of precedents for modern-day wedding cake persecution might include the third- and early fourth-century edicts of Diocletian and Gelarius—either sacrifice to the establishment deities or face the consequences.

In response to a newspaper's attacking guest editorial, the baker (a baker!) is allowed space to respond: "I just couldn't see a way clear in my heart to honor God with the talents He has given me by going against the word He has given us." [17] For the prosecution to propose that not participating in gay "marriage" is equivalent to hypothetical religious discrimination against interracial marriage fails the red face test. The accurate analogy is not with interracial marriage, but rather a point made by St. Thomas More: If the world is really round, a royal decree to the contrary will not flatten it. Would all citizens then be required to join the flat earth society?

Within the West the moral trajectory of court activism after Roe v. Wade continues unabated after half a century. Now the end game is undeniable, to ensure (with Rousseau and his "General Will") that everyone is "forced to be free." With the court's cavalier *Obergefell v. Hodges* ruling the Fourteenth Amendment is no longer about "equal protection;" now an unlimited reading is that this Amendment is the supreme idolatry. How quickly equal protection is inverted into equal un-protection. Whatever. The end game is the fantasy that future generations will look back and notice that the U.S. Supreme Court invented civilization, such as it is.

The Western thing continues its self-hating decline into pagan times. Such is the "logic" exhibited in the court ruling. While fourteen states had not formally recognized gay "marriage," twenty-five others had this recognition imposed by federal or state court order. Of the latter group, only three initially presumed to confer such stature by popular vote. At least ten federally recognized Indian tribes explicitly affirm traditional marriage, and since they are not parties to the United States Constitution, they remain exempt from this ruling by the United States Supreme Court.

In 2015 Ireland became the first nation to approve gay "marriage" by popular vote. But unlike the Irish vote, and caught between the corrupt west and the post-Soviet Union, many other countries are taking constitutional action to ban same-sex "marriages." These include Belarus, Bulgaria, Finland, Hungary, Latvia, Lithuania, Moldavia, Montenegro, Poland, Serbia, Slovakia, and Ukraine (with pending action in Macedonia).[18] As with the vast majority of countries, these are in tune with the 1948 Universal Declaration of Human Rights, in which Article 16 declares that "men and women of full age . . . have the right to marry and found a family" and that "the family is the natural and fundamental group unit of society and entitled to protection by society and the state." In mid 2015, "Family Day" drew hundreds of thousands into the piazza fronting St. John Lateran in Italy (Rome), the last Western European country (at that time) to not join the clique imposing either civil unions or gay "marriage."

What would we think, say, of a bird that recoiled from its own nature by refusing to fly from a tree branch or to sing at sunrise? What if flowers refused their nature to flourish, reproduce and bloom? The natural law is to us what buoyancy is to a fish in water. The difference is that we sink—we regress—if we fall asleep and let it go. Or what of green grass or mushrooms if they decided to never break ground? What then of a people who remain asleep while a courtroom bench presumes to legislate(!) their very nature? As for the future of the "family," social media celebrities do not directly immolate their own children as did the Canaanites. And as did the early Israelites whenever they went native. But our modern day opinion makers are willing enough to indirectly undermine normal family life on which normal childhood depends. In crowd-crazing television scripts the normal family is routinely mocked and ridiculed, and the depiction of normal sexual morality is long gone.

THE CENSUS AND AN ANECDOTE

From the most recent census results, what is actually happening to the family? Here's a look at one geographic area but it should be informative to others as well. The most recent results published in 2013 warranted a local article (in *The Seattle Times*).[19] Surprisingly, of the roughly one hundred thousand children living in Seattle (a city of six hundred thousand), some seventy percent live with two married parents. This percentage is slightly and surprisingly up from fifteen years ago. On the other hand, only fourteen percent of all households have children. Said differently, this is an evasive reporting that an overwhelming eighty-six percent of households do *not* include children. But Seattle is one of only three of the fifty surveyed cities where so-called nuclear families increased marginally as a share of total households. (The others were Washington D. C. and Atlanta.)

Overall, though, the real story is that the number of nuclear families has fallen from twenty-four percent of all households in the nation in year 2000 to nineteen percent today. In 1970 forty percent of American households included children. The quirky Seattle story is attributed to gentrification—the influx of well-paid and educated professionals. Such families tend to stick together. Poverty rates, on the other hand, are highest in the households with a single parent or with two unmarried parents. The reporter might better have said that children of parents less successful or committed in their marriages are likely to end up in poverty and as clients of government programs. Such programs are ever on hand to help a few while they perpetuate the government-dependent "culture of poverty" first spotlighted as early as the 1970s.

But even in Seattle we are consoled by the media gurus that Seattle has not "turned back the clock to the 1950s." Heaven forbid! The local up-tick toward normalcy "doesn't mean we've become an improbable bastion for modern-day Ozzies and Harriets."[20] From on high we are given the predictable spin, between the lines, that the traditional family is passé. But now what have we noticed in these pages? Over the longer time scale the trend line is one of regression and devolution of the "modern" family toward history's most primitive "marriage" patterns. Modernity is another word for backsliding.

Alongside this local article we can view the national work of the Allan Gutmacher Institute, a pro-abortion think tank. The Institute reports that eighty percent of all abortions are sought by single women. Is it no wonder that abortion has become a front end and culture-shaping mindset as it generates nearly as many abortions as live births? The numbers simply confirm that where permanent commitment is lacking, families of mothers and fathers with children are also missing. As for personal "freedom," is there any greater, more significant, freedom than to make such a commitment permanently? Such a commitment creates an ongoing freedom greater than the self.

But if sex is essentially a built-in entertainment center for the uncommitted, special interests inevitably will want to justify their unnatural lives by pressuring the redefinition of society. Why not hear from a writer celebrated by the homosexual "community" itself? In his works the novelist Andre Gide wrote vicariously about his struggles in a bisexual double life up until the very end. What does he actually say? Gide was opposed to sexual license and favored self control and "sublimating sexual energy into desirable moral and artistic qualities." Nevertheless, his biographer concludes that Gide,

> emphatically protests that he has not a word to say against marriage and reproduction (but then) suggests that it would be of benefit to an adolescent, before his desires are fixed, to have a love affair with an older man, instead of with a woman . . . *the general principle admitted by Gide, elsewhere in his treatise, that sexual practice tends to stabilize in the direction where it has first found satisfaction; to inoculate a youth with homosexual tastes seems an odd way to prepare him for matrimony* (italics added)[21] [better to simply redefine marriage!]

Nature or nurture? Is it early tipping points, or worse, that solidify mere tendencies into a more fixed orientation? As in so much else, is the problem is such things absentee fathers as role models? Gide exposes an early personal tipping point as more of a situation than an innate condition—nurture rather than nature—and then he goes on to license such fateful adolescent trial and error. He recommends the now well-established cult of experimentation and readiness. Gide recommends a behavior of indiscriminately fostering unhappy situations. Is Gide's anecdotal history a window on how we should correctly understand the fifth letter in the slogan LGBTQ? Not as a mythical "sexual orientation gene" or even as a "questioning (Q)," but more as a recruiting and "queuing (Q)" of the next generation?

Recent science indicates that the rise in autism (now estimated at one birth in sixty-eight), for example, can be traced to excessive maternal doses of vitamin B12/vitamin B9. Or even to the mercury additive used in the United States, but not Europe (to prolong the shelf life and favorable economics of childhood vaccines). In this age of science some youth predispositions like autism yield to scientific investigation and explanation, while others like sexual tendencies are much more complex. Whatever the situation, a higher consideration is the moral distinction between a predisposition, whatever its source(s), and human actions or even political pressures (to ratify and mainstream the homosexual lifestyle). One recent study in the mix is a review of two hundred peer-reviewed studies on sexual orientation and gender identity. This review concludes that the scientific evidence does *not* support the popular notion that "gender identity is an innate, fixed property of human beings that is independent of biological sex."[22]

The unhappy story is that nationwide, LGBT youth are four times as likely to have been raped as others between ages fourteen and seventeen, and use of heroin is nearly five times as high as for others in the same age group.[23] In addition to bullying by others, failure to resolve confusion over self-identity might foster self hatred and suicidal tendencies. Added to terrorism, this motive was raised in the press as a possible factor for the man pledging allegiance to the Islamic state (a culture that severely persecutes homosexuals) and who massacred forty-nine in an Orlando gay nightclub in 2016. Before burying this thread, the media initially reported that two former same-sex partners came forward to identify themselves.

Unable to judge motives (embedded terrorism) or possibly compound motives, the peddlers of public opinion decided it best to pull a cliché from the drawer—surely it's only about gun control. No less reasonable, in complex cases when might earlier interventions from family and sympathetic and competent psychologists help avert suicidal and homicidal tendencies? Overall, isn't there a personal right to not be profiled into a permanent psychological identity, and instead to possibly achieve a deeper self-understanding, and instead a path onto day-to-day growth in broader social circles? In four or five states the profile sticks and any such restorative therapy (for lack of a better term) is legally prohibited and subject to prosecution.

THE MODERN DEFAULT POSITION: BOREDOM

Plutarch in the early second century said this: "The mind is not a vessel to be filled, but a fire to be kindled." Rather than kindling the mind, however, today's world of organized noise—and yes trivializing sexual experimentation—expands the boredom that refuses to be kindled. Very early in the game young children complain of boredom much more than in earlier decades. Are we listening? Even the later multiplication of sexual excesses of all kinds can be read as a very fleeting attempt to escape the demon of boredom. A far cry, this, from the unity and openness to life of the complete human person, as depicted in the Garden of Genesis.

Though Scriptural guidance may be dismissed, of course, it undeniably does clearly hold that immoral sexual activity, especially between men or between women, is mutual degradation. References can be found in both the Old and New Testament (Genesis 19:1-11 and Leviticus 18:22 and 20:13; Romans 1:18-32; 1 Timothy 1:10; 1 Corinthians 6:9). Is such legalization today just a trendy version of the biblical fig leaf? The critical distinction is between dormant sexual tendencies and reinforcing behavior or actions actually reaffirms a deep respect for all persons at their core. The Church insists that "It is deplorable that homosexual persons have been and are the object of violent malice in speech or in action. Such treatment deserves condemnation from the Church's pastors wherever it occurs . . . The intrinsic dignity of each *person* [as such] must always be respected in word, in action and in law" (italics added).[24]

Today abortion and mass marketed contraception even to youth—like earlier forms of slavery—is held to be "not intrinsically wrong." Such accommodation to popular culture spawns and accelerates a host of family problems. Marriage, again, by its nature, is between one man and one woman and involves a truly permanent decision up front, but marriage is discounted. Either spouse can zone out later. Either spouse or both can walk away in search of fresh pastures. Anything more restrictive—anything more fulfilling—and any kind of absolute is only a "guideline" as from the fantasy Pirates' Code (*Pirates of the Caribbean*).

We are no longer challenged with the greatest freedom to make the kind of permanent commitment—*any* commitment—that moves our entire personal world to a new place. We lose access to a mystery always greater than ourselves. The absence of personal mystery and the mystery of one another, and ultimately the divine mystery, is the sure formula for flat-earth secular boredom and then worse, despair. Once human sexuality is made instrumental—mechanized and randomized—it can be reduced like any other addiction to an anesthetic against the painful and void that it generates and then keeps in play.

One step toward such boredom is the ten-minute children's attention span induced by the spacing between advertisements on television shows. Another is the immediate gratification from video games for which therapists are often quick to prescribe corrective drugs. Once arrested into boredom, childhood often extends into the adult years. It is simply boredom: *acedia*. Acedia translated from the Greek *akedeo* means "I do not care"—here there is nothing new or modern in our cult of "whatever." Acedia is the failure to choose anything at all. It is a spiritual disease as well as a lost appetite for or curiosity about life. But why don't I care? With our new technologies we are programming computers, but in reality these devices are more likely programming us. We can no longer tell the difference between thoughtful broad mindedness and broad band Internet access.

Acedia, then, becomes a strategy of pain avoidance, our modern default position, but we don't have to go this way. Things can be better than that. Archimedes boasted that he could move the weight of the entire world if given a long enough lever. We have the power to move our personal world with the lever of a few words, but too often we select the wrong words. "I do not care," instead of "I do" as in a real marriage. The erased boundary between "friendship" and "sex" today undermines the definition and meaning of marriage and family. A boundary-free world is a bored world, and a bored world turns all of us into gadgets that are too easily either exploited, or unplugged—as through abortion or euthanasia.

The world seems to be dying of boredom yet vainly seeking some kind of relief. The imagination gives way to faster computers and better management theories. Acedia is as much indifferent tiredness of the good as it is despair over evil. The writer G. K. Chesterton gives us a clue:

> Pessimism is not in being tired of evil but in being tired of good. Despair does not lie in being weary of suffering, but in being weary of joy. It is when for some reason or other the good things in society no longer work that the society begins to decline; when its food does not feed, when its cures do not cure, when its blessings refuse to bless.[25]

And we could add that society begins to decline ". . . when sex is no longer a spiritual romance." Ultimately, even the fleeting distractions of the fast lane fail to satisfy; the reward of human effort and good work fails to satisfy; and we feel cheated and think about lottery tickets, casinos and motel rooms. We never learned or else forgot how to get really hooked on lasting desire and the romance of life.

Your author offers a revealing recollection that first drove home the malignant power of boredom. We recall the first Apollo mission to circle the moon and that sent back to earth an iconic photograph of "earthrise" over the bleak lunar surface. This Apollo 8 picture solidified in the human imagination the uniqueness of our bluish green globe in deep space, and the preciousness of our global ecologies. Now, following the sequence of earlier Apollo missions, imagine yourself with me a few months later in the middle of the Pacific Ocean on an aircraft carrier, the USS Hornet of World War II vintage. The crew searches the early morning sky for the first distant sight of a gold medallion bearing three of earth's visitors returning from the moon. On July 24, 1969, this was the returning space capsule from the first lunar landing in all of human history, Apollo XI.

Landing too far from the recovery ship to be seen (about thirteen miles) the capsule safely returned three astronauts from spaceship Apollo to spaceship earth. Apollo XI fulfilled a dream of the ancient Greek poets as well as anyone today still willing to dream. It was the stuff of myths handed on from the ancient world, from generation to generation, to our age of science and technology. The lunar landing site was on the Sea of Tranquility, a region named by the seventeenth-century Jesuit astronomer Riccioli. In the mid-twentieth century human footprints left our mark on the moon for the first time in the history of the world and the solar system and the entire universe. Because there is no atmosphere these traces might remain undisturbed for a million years. Footprints on the moon! A sign of conscious and purposive life finds its place against a backdrop of consuming silence and multitudes of totally deaf and sightless and unconscious stars and galaxies. Six hundred million people viewed all this on television, and yet today with the delivery back home of forty-three pounds of moon rocks, there are still deniers—as with ultrasound imagery—who insist it's not real.

A few months later in November this incredible "Aha" moment of science and human poetry would come a second time. So now let's picture ourselves in the Pacific again at nearly the same recovery spot, on the same ship and with the same crew, and at the same time of early morning. The second lunar landing mission was Apollo XII. And already the muttered comments of boredom could be heard from some of the crew of the recovery ship: "Why do we have to do the same old thing all over again?" *The same old thing?*

This time the conical five-ton Apollo return craft, surfaced with gold-like foil (kapok), was near enough to be seen. Suspended beneath a broken layer of pink cotton clouds and an early morning turquoise sky, and as it trailed a trio of fully billowed orange and white striped parachutes, the spacecraft floated into a vast sea of emerald green. Its slow motion impact drove a vertical geyser of snow white water skyward. Utter silence and wonder through it all.

But even here, there comes the descent of man into gnawing boredom, another bite out of the same old apple from "the beginning." But, then, was the entire lunar landing program itself largely a servant to boredom? At the time in a *Life Magazine* interview, the cultural critic Saul Bellow said as much. He called the Apollo program "the Protestant Ethic with nowhere else left to go." By itself the activism of striving for worldly merit, at the loss of the contemplative side of the human mystery, can eventually become a nose-to-the-grindstone cult of boredom.

Smaller events, but in reality much larger than Apollo, can be made to look like "the same old thing." But seeing not only with the eyes, but through the eyes we know that the totality of even one human birth or death is never "the same old thing." The sad message from Genesis is that the trivialization of all of creation, especially marital and sexual union, makes even the Giver of all gifts routine and boring. Facing homeland earth from deep space, astronauts from an earlier mission chose to read aloud from Genesis. To see *through* the eyes, like this, is to see like a poet or an artist. It is a choice to maintain eye contact with the Other. The early twentieth-century painter, Robert Henri, urges all of us to be artists in our daily lives, if only in our gestures or words from one to another:

> Art appears in many forms. To some degree every human being is an artist, dependent on the quality of his growth. Art need not be intended. It comes as inevitably as the tree from its roots, the branch from the trunk, the blossom from the twig. . . . The whole value of art rests in the artist's ability to see well into what is before him. . . . Those who have lived and grown at least to some degree in the spirit of freedom are our creative artists. They have a wonderful

time. They keep the world going. They must leave their trace in some way, paint, stone, machinery, whatever.[26]

The freedom of questioning "well into what is before [us]" makes all of us artists. To some degree each of us is capable of thinking scientifically but we can also respond artfully, and then spiritually and perhaps even religiously. To buy into this progression toward the sacred otherness of things, and even toward of the Other, is to escape the gravitational pull of bored materialism. It is to escape the possessive mindset that so easily possesses us.

BOREDOM AND THE RELEVANT QUESTIONS

In C. S. Lewis's *Screwtape Letters* the devil, Screwtape, gives special attention to boredom in mentoring his understudy, Wormwood:

> But the greatest triumph of all is to elevate this horror of the Same Old Thing into a philosophy so that nonsense in the intellect may reinforce corruption in the will. It is here that the general Evolutionary or Historical character of modern European thought comes in so useful. The Enemy [God] loves platitudes. Of a proposed course of action He wants men, so far as I can see, to ask very simple questions; is it righteous? is it prudent? is it possible? Now if we can keep men asking 'Is it in accordance with the general movement or our time? Is it progressive or reactionary? Is it the way that History is going?' they will neglect the relevant questions.[27]

We are outraged over specific "hate crimes" while remaining indifferent to our expansive "culture of death" and the well-tutored ordinariness of abortion and euthanasia. Is our outrage largely a feeble cry against our bored indifference? Boredom deadens us to all of the relevant questions. The relevant questions are made into an unwelcome cure for boredom. "Nonsense in the intellect may reinforce corruption in the will" . . . let's think about that. Let's think about the demand for "safe spaces" and pop up "trigger warnings" on college campuses, and about the logic of some Supreme Court rulings.

Self-induced infantilism and boredom robs us of reality and that missing piece—serenity—which eluded for so long Michael Edwards amidst all of his distractions, the stage lights and the trophy partner, Priscilla Presley (Chapter 5). In the race to the bottom for safe spaces—and violating all presumed outcomes of progressive social evolution—Brown University sets the standard for recover from campus ideas felt to be "damaging." The safe space is a room offering "cookies, coloring books, bubbles, Play-Doh [not Plato], calming music, pillows, blankets, and a video of frolicking puppies" (*New York Times* (2016). With all these accessories in the capital budget, no wonder college tuitions are up!

What then of C. S. Lewis's "relevant questions"? The human family is among the questions indicated by C. S. Lewis. With our intergenerational neglect of natural ecologies, the self-enlarging human ecology—rather than quarantined safe spaces—is another relevant question. The term "ecology" comes from a Greek word for study of the house. The connections within natural systems are a special kind of household. But not to be confused with the physical laws of nature, the "human ecology" is rooted in the more deeply human natural law. We maintain contact with our very selves—the universal natural law— when we are attentive to the "tiny whispering sound" and to each other through a well-formed conscience. Human solidarity and our human ecology celebrate the family table of today's society, of our history and ancestors, and of our descendents. When G. K. Chesterton speaks of a "democracy of the dead" he means that institutional memory should not be sacrificed to deliberate institutional amnesia. Our ancestors should not be denied a vote, nor should we be so denied in the future. More than any slippery slope or arc of history, the human ecology is an enduring and present "arc of relations."

So, in our interconnected and compact world, what is the sustainable fit between the natural ecology and this arc of human relations? The universal truth is that disregard for ecological sinkholes *and* the disregard for unborn children are cut from the same cloth. Even the wisdom of indigenous peoples reminds us that we do not own the world; we borrow it from our children. A proper human ecology is respect for each person and for all persons without exception, and for the common good. The human ecology—the natural law as an arc of relations—invites and demands that we protect not only our own children but also their world. Suspended in space, the globe of brilliant blue and green is our shared amniotic sac.

A spokesperson for human flourishing sketches a broadly accepted picture of the common good. Servais Pinckaers[28] tells us that the natural law is the path to true happiness, or better, to real joy—not simply satisfaction—even in the present moment. True joy is found in knowing and doing good rather than languishing in ethical neutrality and the infantile indifference of "whatever." It is found in the affirmation and protection of the real self, in anticipating and self-donation in service to the reality of others and their needs.

Said differently, the heartbeat picks up when we see clearly. In that "aha" moment we see through daily repetitions of systematic lies (the Packrat Factor, Chapter 2). "Then you will know the truth, and the truth will set you free" (John 8:32). Which is to say, human freedom is not really freedom if it is free wheeling; freedom exists only in partnership with the intellect, only if it is conformed to the truth. Libertinism is a fraud. Finally it's about the freedom to love the truth, and in this way to find the joy of being complete persons again. The start point for this kind of belonging is families celebrating the permanent marriage of differences, between one man and one woman. Such belonging is both natural and biblical, very much in this world but also partly above history: "a man leaves his father and mother, and clings to his wife, and the two become one flesh" (Genesis 2:26).The promise that gives us to the oneness of marriage is permanent and exclusive—or else it is not marriage. The young of every new generation must come to know that real personal fulfillment comes with self-mastery and anticipation rather than momentary dissipation.

In a *single word*, all of the bookshelves of the world that seem so exhausted under the weight of natural law writings are about just one thing. The one thing that matters, again, is true belonging. To not belong truly is not simply to be neutral; it is to be betrayed and abandoned. Fourteen-year old girls willingly experiment with sex and then announce to their grandmothers that "things are new and different now." But this non-conformance is not new and not different. This is primitive. It is a *regression* and conformance to such aboriginal folkways as consensual abduction.

We truly *progress* only when we as fully human persons remain receptive to an informed conscience and to real belonging. If we must be "aboriginal" let us be always in step with our true interior echo, what has been called our *"aboriginal* vicar of Christ."[29] It's not that complicated. In the end, it's not really about any information that might be lacking. Lacking more is the day-to-day formation, initially within the give and take of family life. However imperfect, our freedom from the Big Lie and for real belonging and respect is what enables a real sense of place in our little corner of the world, our human ecology. By respect for self and for others we blossom and bloom where we are planted. Each of us has a special vocation tailored to our special day-to-day gifts however ordinary these might seem. In the thicket of daily details we are to discover love, happiness, joy, purpose, and real engagement in the art of living and doing. We can even become "engaged" to another person like ourselves, and commit to a marriage that is permanent and exclusive. It's about belonging or abandonment, honesty or dishonesty, and the true self or the false self.

We need not dwell long here on how we then might even treasure one another in a way that is graced—the "sacramental" nature of marriage. Our focus here is on marriage more as the cornerstone for an outreaching and resilient human and therefore personal ecology. The interested reader can dip into biblical passages (Mark 10:5-9, Matthew 19:4-9, and Luke 16:18), well-selected essays,[30] and more formal teachings. But as a minimum, "sacramental" confirms that each marriage is a solid fact rather than any lesser and more tentative "ideal." The husband and wife cross the one bridge together, and they do this once by promising to each other and to the God within that never again will all of the chips be forced onto the table. Of course there is routine maintenance, but in their very words together they create a new and permanent reality by personally affirming "I do."

PRINCIPLES FOR A HUMAN ECOLOGY

At the interreligious Humanum Conference of November 17, 2014, Pope Francis identified a parallel between unfaithful erosion of marriage and the family and the broad human ecology, and endangerment of the global natural ecology:

> Evidence is mounting that the decline of the marriage culture is associated with increased poverty and a host of other social ills, disproportionately affecting women, children and the elderly. It is always they who suffer the most in this crisis. The crisis in the family has produced an ecological crisis, for social environments, like natural environments, need protection.

Pope Francis then goes on to defend the human ecology. While "the human race has come to understand the need to address conditions that menace our natural environments, we have been slower to recognize that our fragile social environments are under threat as well, slower in our culture, and also in our Catholic Church." His renewed call for a human ecology sounds technical, but the meaning is transparent and common sense. The descent of man (to freely borrow Darwin's term) into the shallows of the pleasure principle spawns social disorders. It has the depth of a spreading ink spot on wet paper. Thomas Dubay, S.M., links faithfulness as in marriage to a durable human ecology in this way: "[under the pleasure principle] commitments to honesty in speech, to justice in work and wages and to sacrifice for the good of others are all slowly debilitated. It is not accidental that permissive sexual morality is accompanied by a rising crime rate."[31]

We can be encouraged that Gallup polls surprisingly offer a glimmer of hope for the human ecology. Well over half of all Americans (58 percent) now are opposed to all or most abortions. From the increasingly defensive pro-abortion faction, President Nancy Keegan of NARAL (the renamed National Abortion and Reproductive Rights Action League) laments what she calls an "intensity gap" among young people at least on the subject of abortion. It seems that the fostered culture of "readiness," and whatever, has gone slack. Half of pro-life young people see abortion as an election issue, while only one-fifth of pro-choice young people see it as an election issue. In 2010 the Gallup firm also declared that "pro-life is the new normal." Only the elitist media has failed to notice. Pro-life demonstrations continue to go underreported by the bored and scripted media.

Even before we entered the new millennium, St. John Paul II began the 1994 Year of the Family by reminded us that, "the family, as a community of persons, is (thus) the first human society . . . in a certain sense (a) sovereign society [and that] every act of begetting finds its primordial model in the fatherhood of God." More recently, in 2007 Pope Benedict XVI met with

Saudi Arabia's King Abdullah, not as a head of state but instead to advance interreligious and intercultural dialogue among Christians, Muslims, and Jews. His purpose was "the promotion of peace, justice and spiritual and moral values, especially in support of the family." In Cameroon in 2009 he repeated the message: "The difficulties arising from the impact of modernity and secularization on traditional society inspire you to defend vigorously the essential values of the African family. . . ." In 2014 Pope Francis in his Christmas Address gave us his countercultural message supporting the traditional family and children:

> The Child Jesus. My thoughts turn to all those children today who are killed and ill-treated, be they infants killed in the womb, deprived of that generous love of their parents and then buried in the egoism of a culture that does not love life; be they children displaced due to war and persecution, abused and taken advantage of before our very eyes and our complicit silence.[32]

On the conflicts between natural law and positive law and a regard for both the rights of the unborn and the meaning of marriage, a layman and martyr to the general cause of marriage is once again our St. Thomas More. What is an unborn child? What is a marriage? What is a family? The meanings are self-evident We appeal to his lucid reasoning:

> Some men think the Earth is round, others think it flat; it is a matter capable of question. But if it is flat, will the King's command make it round? And if it is round, will the King's command flatten it? No, I will not sign.[33]

Substituting the United States Supreme Court for the King's command—on the nature of marriage—More's response cannot be dismissed as either religious or religious bigotry. At another point More then asks Master Richard Rich:

> Suppose the Parliament would make a law that God should not be God. Would you then, Master Rich, say that God were not God? No sir (quothe he), that I would not, since no Parliament may have any such law.[34]

Nor can the Supreme Court declare itself to be God. A bit of comic relief might help here. In this age of science the astronauts of Apollo 8, prior to the lunar landing missions, transmitted to earth a creation passage read from Genesis. Not to be outdone by earlier Russian cosmonauts, who triumphantly reported seeing no angels in space, the American atheist Madalyn Murray O'Hair rose to this new occasion. Her predictable lawsuit, to the United States Supreme Court, protested this cosmic violation of the separation of church and state. How high does that wall of separation really reach? From the wisdom of its lofty bench, the Court declined to rule. It found that outer space is not part of the United States.

The Court "lacks jurisdiction" to impose its legalisms onto a universe that pre-
dates it by almost fourteen billion years.

Does the Court or even the Congress have jurisdiction to legislate against
the natural moral law? The Big Lie today is the pretension that a civilization
of human flourishing and real personal happiness can have any foundation
alien to nature and other than the natural family, or marriage, or that violates
the unborn child. In Chapter 1 we hinted toward a perspective called Catholic
Social Teaching (CST) and early in this chapter we paused at the notion of
"the common good." Working outward from the core principle of the human
person and his/her transcendent dignity, the CST galaxy of the common good
embraces other orbits, we might say.

The *first* such orbit, inseparable from the human person, is the family.
Then, respectful of the family is the *second* orbiting principle, that of "subsidiarity" or the caution against shifting personal or community decisions
away or even to the state and the rich and powerful, especially in politics but
also in economics. I recall a chat with another public service employee, a
well-qualified attorney . . . he went silent and then blurted: "what you're
saying is that there are some things that government should *not* be doing?"
After all those years in law school, the light finally went on. Despite his
cultural obtuseness, Henry Ford got this partly right when he paid his assembly line workers a family wage (five dollars a day was good pay in 1910). He
also offered profit sharing, a tilt toward family ownership of their own futures even in the new world of government largesse and corporate bigness.

A *third* orbit is the combined respect for "rights and responsibilities,"
neither without the other. We have rights because we have duties, not simply
self-interests. The role of "informed conscience" is easy to see—what we
ought to do over what we *can* do.

As the *fourth* orbit, in the political world we have the mutual obligation
for "faithful citizenship" toward the overall common good—maintaining
those conditions necessary for human flourishing. Respect for human labor,
the contribution made by each of us at the family and global work bench, is
one of those conditions and is a *fifth* orbit. We are to put something of
ourselves into our work, and therefore the management of "human resources" demands respect for the human person.

A *sixth* orbit is attentiveness to those marginalized "poor" who really do
need a helping hand. How this is achieved—whether through the state or
privately—is a matter of prudential judgment. And no less than poverty of
economic means there is also spiritual and moral poverty. St. John Paul II
defined broadly *the preferential option for the poor* as "not limited to material poverty, since it is well known that there are many other forms of poverty,
especially in modern society—not only economic, but cultural and spiritual
poverty as well."[35]

The *seventh* orbit, solidarity is not a call for government centralization, and is never to be advanced at the cost of subsidiarity (or vice versa). Solidarity includes an intergenerational touch that rises to the level of the *eighth* orbit, namely, "care for God's Creation." This too is a principle of the human ecology (rather than an ideology), because it remains centered on the transcendent dignity of the human person as well as the world as gifts from the Giver. We are challenged to overcome the disconnect between the natural and human ecologies (plural) to either get what we want or destroy the human persons that are deemed "unwanted."

In 1961 and still in advance of the Second Vatican Council, Pope John XXIII wrote this of finite natural resources and their management: "But *whatever be the situation,* we clearly affirm these problems should be posed and resolved in such a way that man does not have recourse to methods and means *contrary to his dignity. . . .*" (italics added).[36] It was with an eye on our escalating per capita resource footprint, but also giving ample space for human creativity and ingenuity, that Pope St. John Paul II still counseled the need "above all (for) a change in lifestyle (and) models of production and consumption . . . (and) structures of power. . . ."[37] The corporate triple-bottom line is a refreshing step in the right direction: people, planet, profits.

What the writer T. S. Eliot said of society in the 1940s has only gained in meaning over the past half century and more: "When I speak of the family, I have in mind a bond which embraces a longer period of time than this [a single generation]: a piety towards the dead, however obscure, and a solicitude for the unborn, however remote."[38]

The natural law and the biblical riddle are forever up to date: "If the *foundations* be destroyed, what can the righteous do" (italics added, Psalm 11:3)? The right to life is not a defense of a right attached to a disputable whatever. It defends a person who then has a right to live. And the definition of "marriage" is not about the word that has a pliable meaning; it's about the meaning of a reality that has a word. In both cases the difference between words and facts is akin to the difference between statistics and genocide. What, then, is the effect in the West of the descent of man and woman into the violation of facts, into the culture of death and now into gender theory? What is the effect on the family and our broader human ecology?

Sometimes it takes a neighbor to see clearly what's going wrong in a family household. Out of the darkness of Africa at the end of the second millennium came the HIV. But now at the start of the third millennium, also from within our global-village and Africa, comes this prognosis from the clear-sighted Robert Cardinal Sarah: "Gender ideology . . . is about sowing discord over the legitimacy of social norms and introducing a suspicion over the model of heterosexuality . . . [for proponents of gender theory] it is necessary to abolish Christian civilization and construct a new world. . . . The battle to preserve the roots of mankind is perhaps the greatest challenge that our world has faced since its origins."[39]

NOTES

1. This concept is introduced by Pope St. John Paul II, *Centesimus Annus (One Hundred Years)*, 1991, 38.
2. Pope Francis, *Laudato Si (Praise be to him: On Care for our Common Home)*, 2015, n. 118. As moral teaching, many critics detect another kind of disconnect when the papal exhortation on ecology refers to sin, while there is so little such mention in the earlier exhortation regarding human sexuality and the erosion of marriage (*Amoris Laetitia*, 2014).
3. Gabriel Marcel, *The Mystery of Being*, Vol. 1 (Chicago: Gateway, 1950), 241.
4. A blurred mentality sometimes holds that the absolute evil of abortion can be overlooked when combined and averaged together with other actions serving the common good. To this bad-apple approach the American bishops responded: "Indeed, the failure to protect and defend life in its most vulnerable stages renders suspect any claims to the 'rightness' of positions in other matters affecting the poorest and least powerful of the human community" (United States Conference of Catholic Bishops, *Living the Gospel of Life*, 1998). We might be reminded of the analogous national and international financial crisis of 2008, precipitated by the combining of bogus home loans into much larger and diverse investment packages ("derivatives").
5. Erik von Kuehnelt-Leddihn, *Liberty or Equality* (Caldwell, ID: The Caxton Press, Ltd., 1952), passim and 275.
6. By comparison, almost one million are victims of international trafficking each year, and three times this amount are trafficked within national boundaries.
7. McGreevy, *Catholicism and American Freedom*, 2003, 52.
8. Henry Hazlitt, *Failure of the "New Economics "* (Princeton: D. Van Nostrand, 1959), 127.
9. John Maynard Keynes, (1946). "Opening remarks: The Galton Lecture" *Eugenics Review* 38 (1): 39–40.
10. Recounted by Thomas McArdle, "Is Al Smith Dinner Still Worthwhile," *National Catholic Register*, October 30, 2016.
11. The first massively documented exposure came as far back as 1982 in Enrique Rueda's *The Homosexual Network: Private Lives and Public Policy* (Old Greenwich, Connecticut: The Devin Adair Company, 1982). Nearly four decades ago Rueda indicated and documented the threat of embedded shadow organizations advocating normalization of the homosexual lifestyle.
12. Attributed by Sidney and Beatrice Webb in *Soviet Communism* (1936), 1036.
13. Adolf Hitler, *Mein Kampf* (Boston: Houghton Mifflin, 1943), 182.
14. "Thomas More—A Man for All Seasons," entered into *the Congressional Record—Senate*, by Senator Durenberger, June 22, 1982, S 7275.
15. Notice that the 1981 *United Nations Declaration on Human Rights* affirms freedom of religion, while *The Universal Islamic Declaration of Human Rights* (September 19, 1981)—with "Islam" as the first word in its Foreword—contains only one sentence (Section XIII) on religious freedom. As in the new *Obergefell v. Hodges* ruling, this freedom is narrowed to "worship": "Every person has the right to *freedom of worship* in accordance with his religious beliefs" (italics added). St. John Paul II indicated that freedom of religion is "the right to *live in the truth* of one's faith and in conformity with one's transcendent dignity as a person" (*Centesimus Annus* [*The One Hundred Years*, 1991], n. 47, italics added).
16. This theme was developed by Pope Benedict XVI in his "Address to the National Parliament of the Federal Republic of Germany," September 22, 2011 (English translation: *L'Osservatore Romano*, September 28, 2011).
17. Baronelle Stutzman, "Why a good friend is suing me: the Arlene's Flowers story, special to the *Seattle Times*, November 10, 2015. Other similar cases are predictably in Oregon and Colorado. As of this writing it appears that all could end up before the United States Supreme

Court which, following the 2016 Presidential election, will be more balanced and less complicit with the Secular Humanist agenda.

18. Alessandra Nucci, "Europe's War on Christian Ethics," *Catholic World Report* (Ignatius Press, May 2015).

19. Gene Balk, "Married—with Children," *Seattle Times*, Dec. 29, 2014.

20. Ibid.

21. Harold March, *Gide and the Hound of Heaven* (Philadelphia: University of Pennsylvania Press, 1952), 178. Another modern addiction, overindulgence in digital and virtual reality games, is found to produce corresponding neuro-chemical and possibly cellular changes in the brain itself (e.g., dopamine which is responsible for reward-driven behavior). A recent study completed at University College London and using MRI technology (magnetic resonance imagery) strongly implies that a habit of lying tends to suppress the part of the brain (the amygdala) that responds emotionally to a "slippery slope" pattern of small and then larger lies (Neil Garrett, Dan Ariely and Stephanie Laxxaro, *Nature Neuroscience Journal*, October 24, 2016; reported by Erica Goode, *New York Times*, October 25, 2016).

22. Lawrence Mayer and Paul McHugh, "Sexuality and Gender," *The New Atlantis: A Journal of Technology and Society*, (Ethics and Public Policy Center, No. 50, Fall 2016).

23. Centers for Disease Control, *2016 Youth at Risk Behavior Study* (summarized by Jan Hoffman, *New York Times*, August 12, 2016). In a survey of 15,600 students between the ages of fourteen to seventeen one in five gay, lesbian and bisexual students report having been raped, and 1.3 percent use heroin compared to 6 percent of the broad population. One in four have attempted suicide in the past year compared to one is sixteen for others. Forty percent had considered suicide.

24. Congregation for the Doctrine of the Faith, "Letter to the Bishops of the Catholic Church on the Pastoral Care of Homosexual Persons [1986]," (San Francisco: Ignatius Press, 1987), n. 10.

25. G. K. Chesterton, *The Everlasting Man* (Garden City, MI: Image Books, 1955), 154.

26. Robert Henri, *The Art Spirit*. (New York: J. B. Lippincott Co., 1960), 67, 87, 177.

27. C. S. Lewis, *The Screwtape Letters* (New York: The Macmillan Co., 1953), 129-30.

28. Servais Pinckaers, *Morality: The Catholic View* (South Bend, Indiana: St. Augustine's Press, 2001), 67-9, 71, and 97-109.

29. The expression is Cardinal Newman's. Ibid., 56.

30. One excellent and timely collection of short essays is Winfried Aymans (editor), *Eleven Cardinals Speak on Marriage and the Family* (San Francisco: Ignatius Press, 2015). The Ignatius collection also includes Robert Dodaro (ed.), *Remaining in the Truth of Christ* (2014); and Gerhard Cardinal Muller, *The Hope of the Family* (2014).

31. Thomas Dubay, S.M., *Authenticity: A Biblical Theology of Discernment* (San Francisco: Ignatius, 1997), 238.

32. Pope Francis, "Christmas Message," *Urbi et Orbi*, St. Peter's Square, Dec. 25, 2014. Included is religious "persecution." The PEW Center and other research organizations show that three-fourths of governments restrict religious freedom, that eighty percent of those persecuted for their religion are Christians, and that in the states identified as the most serious ("egregious") violators, the Christian religion is the only one persecuted in all sixteen of them.

33. Robert Bolt, *A Man for All Seasons* (New York: Vintage, 1962), 77.

34. E.E. Reynolds, *St. Thomas More* (Garden City: Image, 1958), 269.

35. St. John Paul II, *Centesimus Annus* (*The One Hundred Years*), 1991, n. 57. This encyclical was timed to mark the 100th anniversary of *Rerum Novarum* (*New Things*), the encyclical of Pope Leo XIII asserting the rights and obligations of human beings even in the context of industrialization, capitalism and of atheistic communism (the Communist Revolution came sixteen years later in 1917). Pope St. John Paul II's release date also marked the abrupt demise of the atheistic Soviet Union.

36. Pope John XXIII, *Mater et Magistra*, (*Mother and Teacher*) 1961, n. 191.

37. St. John Paul II, *Centesimus Annus*, n. 58.

38. T. S. Eliot, "The Class and the Elite," in *Christianity and Culture* (New York: Harcourt, Brace Jovanovich, 1940/1968), 116-17.

39. Robert Cardinal Sarah, *God or Nothing* (San Francisco: Ignatius, 2016), 131, 166.

Chapter Nine

Darwin or Darwin-ism

Just how did we get into our current predicament, the modern-day paving over of the real world with the Big Lie? Somewhere in the recent past a packrat got over the fence to trade the deep truth of things with something else. Today the Millennial Generation often seems absorbed in real-time at the expense of both past history and the future. In 1940 Winston Churchill posed this to the House of Commons: "If we open a quarrel between the past and the present, we shall find that we have lost the future." So, what is to be the future of the present if we deny the past? Abandoned? Let's move on to the difference between the richness of Darwin's biological evolution and that hollowness of mutant, atheistic and broad brush Darwin-ism which today is so much part of the air we breathe.

A GREAT MIND TURNS FORTY

Charles Darwin (1809-82) figured out a lot about how biology works. From his writings his devotees have spread a mechanistic explanation across the globe including the notion that even families, in varied forms, are basically evolutionary adaptations to the problem of survival—nothing more. Of religion, Darwin writes: "Belief in God—Religion—There is no evidence that man was aboriginally endowed with the ennobling belief in the existence of an Omnipotent God." There have been many savages and races, he said, "who have no idea of one or more gods, and who have no words in their languages to express such an idea." Only an idea? He never quite puts the last nail in the coffin:

> The question [of belief] is of course wholly distinct from that higher one, whether there exists a Creator and Ruler of the universe; and this has been

answered in the affirmative by some of the highest intellects that have ever
existed (*Descent of Man*, 1871).

More than a matter of intellect, might it be a matter of grace? By our
created human nature perhaps we are meant to participate in the divine? But
do we find ourselves so much on the outside looking in that we no longer
suspect such a future possibility? Instead, we extrapolate and interpolate
from our past bone piles and artifacts, relying finally on statistics and oracles
of ever-modern "social science."

Darwin seemed curious enough to work both sides of the intellectual
street, but he still saw belief in God as completely cultural and learned rather
than even partly innate. He did not speak to the innate thirst for God that
comes even before formal belief. The normal understanding of natural religion is not so much that it is either innate or cultural, but that our inkling
toward God comes from observations of nature, and that with this comes the
notion that perhaps we should pay attention. Knowledge of the natural law,
however mutilated, grows from questioning *what* and *why* and even the *Who*
of things. The whole of natural law is not cultural and learned *into* a person,
but in irrational eras can be cultured and learned *out of* a person. And this is
the point—that today, as with the most aberrant populations—the natural law
is increasingly scorned and abandoned.

In his imprecision, shall we say, Darwin set the table for later materialists
who would upend everything others might say about the natural law as an
inborn capacity or thirst for explanations of what we suspect as God. At the
age of forty Darwin specifically rejected Christianity as a revelation, but in a
letter three years before his death he wrote, "As for a future life, every man
must judge for himself between conflicting vague probabilities."[1] Only
months before, he still had reconsidered "feelings of wonder, admiration, and
devotion" but then concluded against the immortality of the soul: ". . . [N]ow
the grandest scenes would not cause any such convictions and feelings to rise
in my mind."[2]

But, born in 1882, two years before Darwin died, Helen Keller later had
something to say about what is seen and what is not. Blind and deaf from the
age of nineteen months, Keller was introduced by her therapist, Anne Sulli-
van, to Phillips Brooks who then introduced Keller for the first time to Christ
and Christianity. Now at the age of nineteen years, and in a dark silence
deprived of perceptible external and cultural props and visual scenes, Keller
responded from something innate within: "I always knew He was there, but I
didn't know His name!"

Contrast this joy with the plight of those who see only physically with the
eyes, but not through the eyes. Reared in a totally secular fog, they are
brought to suspect that there is more to the stupendous mystery of existence—that there is a universe rather than nothing—more than "whatever."

The surprised and sad response is often: "but I didn't know . . . no one ever told me."

Darwin once had been a believer in natural religion, where faith was understood as another word for "feelings," interior emotion, or intuition. As many say today: "I am spiritual but not religious." But throughout his life Darwin often seemed to withhold final judgments. Would he part company with most of his followers today? A Cornell University survey of leading evolutionary scientists finds that eighty-seven percent do deny the existence of God. Darwin once wrote that "people often talk about the wonderful event of intellectual Man appearing [but that] the appearance of insects with other senses is more wonderful." But then, two years before his death, he also explained, "in my most extreme fluctuations I have never been an atheist in the sense of denying the existence of a God."[3] He could not affirm, but did not deny. Writing to his friend, Rev. Brodie Innes, he said, "You are a theologian, I am a naturalist, the lines are separate. I endeavor to discover facts without considering what is said in the Book of Genesis. I do not attack Moses, and I think Moses can take care of himself. . . . I cannot remember that I ever published a word directly against religion or the clergy."[4]

Did he suspect that for us to attribute religion to emotion or intuition alone is in itself a primitive and potentially savage idea? Without attentiveness to what is behind the existence of what we call the world, emotion and intuition in the world can easily become world-shaking ideology, not authentic religion. Related to our earlier theme of cultural regression and today into perversion and the "culture of death," Darwin also wrote, "Our early semi-human progenitors would not have practiced infanticide . . . for the instincts of the lower animals are never so perverted as to lead them regularly to destroy their own offspring."[5]

DARWIN COLLECTS THE WORLD

Darwin worked with an incredible fascination and ability to grasp an enormous amount of concrete detail. His delight was in sorting and sifting an endless collection of information and in organizing these bits to wherever this led him. Almost everything about him was that of a gifted and energized collector and organizer of small things and facts. All his professional life his theories rested on a vast base of filed writings—his own and those of others—beginning with rocks and insects.[6]

Of his three years at Cambridge, Darwin confides that no pursuit "gave me so much pleasure as collecting"—more pleasure than his attraction to fine engravings and music, and even several evenings of drink and card playing with a few "dissipated and low-minded young men." Of all of his writings, Darwin late in life reflects on a relatively obscure paper of his in the *Journal of the Linnean Society* on something so simple as a particular kind of flower: "I do not think anything in my scientific life has given me so much satisfaction as making out the meaning of the structure of those plants."[7]

The British poet Alfred Lord Tennyson (1809-1892) was as drawn to flowers as much as was the British Darwin, but rather than feeling distanced from God, he felt the opposite. The "flower in the crannied wall" led him to think that if he knew all about it "root and all," then he would also be able to search the mysteries of God and of man. For Wordsworth, too (my own mother's favorite poet): "to me the meanest flower that blows can give thoughts that do often lie too deep for tears" (*Ode: Intimations of Immortality*). And *through* the eyes of Francis of Assisi, the patron saint of ecology, we have a hymn: ". . . He paints the wayside flower, He lights the evening star. . . ."

Darwin's gift was to feel spontaneous empathy for living things. For fishing, Darwin resorted to dispatching his worms before hooking them, because he was "told that I could kill the worms with salt and water, and from that day I never spitted a living worm, though at the expense probably of some loss of success." When he was ten years old, and after consulting with his older sister, he concluded that "it was not right to kill insects for the sake of making a collection."[8] Such sensitivity to even bugs actually helps explain Darwin's unfortunate distancing from religion into a zone of final agnosticism. He was scandalized that some wasps, for example, trapped and paralyzed caterpillars as live food supplies for their eggs.

Darwin could not see an all-powerful deity standing silently apart from so much suffering and pain in the world of insects, and in ours. But instead of stopping in this way at instinct and sentimentality, human empathy can also be the subsoil of a total spiritual conversion. Perhaps Darwin judges too quickly that sympathy in animals and in man differ only in degree and not in kind (*Descent of Man*, 1871). Regarding human society, he speculates that even morality is only a special case of habit solidified into instinct.

But, take the case of a one-time committed atheist, only a generation later in the early twentieth century, the Jewish-born Edith Stein. Her doctrinal dissertation deals with empathy between persons (*On the Problem of Empathy*, 1917). How is it that we actually feel what others feel? At the end she wonders about "religious consciousness," more than a feeling, and then concludes with this final sentence: "I leave the answering of this question to further investigation and satisfy myself here with a '*non liquet*,' 'It is not clear.'" Stein does not allow empathy to be explained away as diluted sympathy or gregariousness or habit solidified into instinct—the view of Darwin and others. She detects a spiritual dimension and then follows it through into conversion to Catholicism. A few years later under the Hitler regime she was incinerated at Auschwitz in 1942. Darwin's questions about morality and evil and about a benevolent God do not go away. Once we move from the insect world and wasps to mankind these questions not only get bigger but quite different. In the afflictions of history some imagine long-term social evolution on the move, but others suffer evil more profoundly as a desecration of what is, and the truly real in the mystery of the human person alone and in society.

Darwin can be accurately located midway between two other great thinkers well before his time. St. Augustine (who was tuned in to a God who transcends the substances of nature) in the late fourth century wrote that when he saw a spider trap a fly in its web he found himself praising the "wondrous creator and orderer of all things."[9] At the other end of the shelf and less squeamish than Darwin, the seventeenth-century philosopher Spinoza (who held that God and nature are a single substance—that there is no distinct God) sometimes simply amused himself by prodding spiders to fight one another. Science tells us of one kind of spider where the egg hatchlings on the back of the mother begin to grow by consuming their mother one bite at a time. We recoil at this, but why then do some eggheads consider it evolutionary progress for the younger generation to destroy both past and future generations one silent scream at a time?

THE MODEL FATHER

Darwin's original acceptance of religion did not take a decisive turn for the worse until his early forties. This rejection of Christianity might well have been guided less by science than hardened by the loss of his young daughter only a few years later. The early and randomly meaningless death to Scarlet Fever of Darwin's beloved young Annie might speak volumes about his recurring ambivalence on questions of religious belief, the seeming alternative of scientific demonstration, and our common and meaningless mortality.

Perhaps an all-encompassing evolutionism is a "projection" from the human mind. Do we project this rather than what we take to be the inscrutable but all-loving God? Far different is evolution-ism from the response of Louis Pasteur (1822-1895), discoverer of the role germs play in human illness and mortality. In 1859 and at the age of thirty-seven he lost his eldest daughter (Jeanne) to typhoid fever, and six year later two other daughters (Camille and Cecile) were taken, one by a fever and the other again by typhoid. Yet Pasteur's life was open to faith throughout: "The more I contemplate the mysteries of Nature, the more my faith becomes that of a Breton peasant. Perhaps, when I learn more, I shall have the faith of a Breton peasant's wife."

Of Darwin, his biographers write of the tension he felt between religious belief, science, and his Annie's passing: "This was the end of the road, crucifixion of his hopes . . . there was no straw to clutch, no promised resurrection. Christian faith was futile. Annie's cruel death destroyed

Charles' tatters of belief in a moral, just universe."[10] In editing his father's autobiography, Sir Francis Darwin adds part of an essay that his father wrote only a few days after Annie's death (dated April 30, 1851). He wrote this of his daughter Annie:

> Even when playing with her cousins, when her joyousness almost passed into boisterousness, a single glance of my eye, not of displeasure (for I thank God I hardly ever cast one on her), but of want of sympathy, would for some minutes alter her whole countenance. . . . We have lost the joy of the household, and the solace of our old age. She must have known that we loved her. Oh, that she could now know how deeply, how tenderly, we do still and shall ever love her dear joyous face! Blessings on her![11]

Thank God? Blessings? Years later, in a letter of 1860, Darwin consoled his long-time defender, Thomas Huxley, on the loss of his own son: "My wife and self deeply sympathize with Mrs. Huxley and yourself. Reflect that your poor little fellow cannot have had much suffering. God [again] bless you."[12] With the vocabulary of God and blessings, are Darwin's animal reflexes simply gnawing on the debris of the past, or is something deeper still going on here?

Darwin describes his focused "love of natural science" as steady, ardent and open: "I have steadily endeavored to keep my mind free so as to give up any hypothesis, however much beloved (and I cannot resist forming one on every subject), as soon as facts are shown to be opposed to it."[13] Perhaps he has not given up on God as a hypothesis, at least. One larger fact that does seem to escape his focused attention is the difference between physical pain within predator food chains in nature, and that whole other category the human pain—moral evil. Random food-chain survival in the natural ecology tells us nothing about purposive human nature and the distinctly different human ecology.

Deeper than the cannibalism of many insects is the meaning of the entire insect world as a whole within yet larger and higher wholes. The Talmud asks the question, "Why was man created on the last day?" And then supplies the answer, "so that he [man] could be told when pride takes hold of him: God created the gnat before thee." Even modern poetry is as revealing here as the microscope. As Coleridge encourages us, "He prayeth best who loveth best/All things both great and small/For the dear God who loveth us/He made and loveth all" (*The Rime of the Ancient Mariner*, 1878). This love for a creature of nature is said about an albatross—symbol of hope—shot dead from a ship becalmed in a stifling arctic sea.

Like Darwin, St. Augustine also had something to say directly about the pain suffered by worms, "We must needs acknowledge that a man in tears is better than a worm full of joy."[14] Is the mystery of pain *and* of insinuated evil really overlooked by an all-powerful deity who is thought by Darwin to remain too silent? Or, in Christ does He finally take on our kind of pain ultimately by allowing himself to be pinned like one of Darwin's insects to two planks of wood supplied by the hands of men? The Resurrection, yes, but first the portal and scandal of a crucified Christ: "to the Jews a stumbling block and to the Gentiles foolishness" (1 Corinthians 1:23-4). Does the wisdom of God truly "get it" after all? If so, then instead of demanding that God justify himself to us, how exactly should we respond to Him?

Darwin's friend, Thomas Huxley (1825-95), a famed English botanist, was not antireligious. He is the one who introduced into the English language the term agnostic or "not to know" (originally a-Gnostic as being counter to the Gnostics of the late Roman times who believed in secret truth gained by private illumination). He was grandfather to the better known agnostic Julian Huxley, and offers a most interesting comment on his own faith in science, a comment bearing on Darwin's passion for facts:

> Science seems to me to teach in the highest and strongest manner the great truth which is embodied in the Christian conception of entire surrender to the will of God. Sit down before fact as a little child, prepared to give up every preconceived notion, follow humbly wherever and to whatever abysses nature leads, or you shall learn nothing. I have only begun to learn content and peace of mind since I have resolved at all risks to do this. [15]

THE WORM TURNS A BIT

Grandpa Thomas Huxley (almost like Christ) counsels humility "before all fact as a little child." And the most singular fact recorded in all of human history is testified by witnesses to their encounter with this Christ. The theologian John Henry Newman vented a bit in 1874 (three years after Darwin's *Descent of Man*) when he wrote, "Doubtless theologians have meddled with science, and now scientific men are paying them off by meddling with theology." He preferred the leavening notion of "development" over the omnivorous term "evolution." He rejected Darwin-ism as a sweeping ideology, and rankled at the assumption that authentic religion and science are contradictory and the bias "that there is no truth in religion." [16]

How much space should we yield in indiscriminate deference to the scientific method as it lures us now into the modern-day ethics of applied Technocracy? Yes to Silicon Valley innovation, but is this all there is? In a California suburb the children of Google, Apple and Hewlett-Packard leaders attend a school where literacy, arithmetic and critical thinking are valued above the overvaluation of computer literacy. Isn't the latter becoming so user-friendly that it can be learned later and soon enough? These kids will not be left behind. As quoted in 2014 an associate professor at Furman University calls technology a distraction from real learning. [17] As we will see below, Charles Darwin himself reflected on what became his own scientific track done narrowly at the expense of other languages of discovery.

Should STEM (science, technology, engineering, mathematics) education go so far as to replace the depths of history and the breadth of non-technical memory? Our cultural and institutional memory is lost in the marginalized liberal arts and humanities core requirements. President Eisenhower warned against the military-industrial complex. We now have pilot-less military air-craft steered without joy sticks, and educators warn against a brainstem (STEM) educational-industrial complex steered by memory sticks.

Friedrich Nietzsche (1844-1900) the godfather of atheistic pessimism and who said "God is dead" (*The Will to Power, The Anti-Christ*) had something to say about science as a sort of safe zone: "Science is a hiding place for every kind of cowardice, disbelief, remorse . . . bad conscience—it is the very anxiety that springs from having no ideal, the suffering from the lack of a great love." A bit too despondent, that; science itself is a great love and a genuine "aha" moment for those who have the aptitude. But might it be that radical Darwin-ism finds in Darwin a useful scientific veneer to Nietzsche's abolition of values? Or at least a veneer for centuries of ungrounded histo-rians who dream that human history is a beast moving on its own legs but with no stable compass points—especially the Italian Vico and the Germans Herder and Hegel?

The educational-industrial complex of today and the evolving dominance of STEM curricula add nothing new to this mindset. It offers too much of a flattened "common core" beneath a very low ceiling, not much more than another recycling of the go-with-the-flow empiricism of John Dewey with an electronic keyboard attached. By itself STEM is another evolutionary adjust-ment, this time to economics and technology rather than race and national-ism. Absent the liberal arts and humanities it's a one room school house with only one shelf of books, if there are books.

In high schools even the pivotal turning points of real human history—and the role of personal character, leadership and finally courage—can be airbrushed as inevitable trend lines in various "social studies." Unbeknown to himself, Darwin is commandeered today as a sort of patron saint of this kind of secular modernity on the move as the highest stage of non-biological evolution. Given a second chance would Darwin confine himself so rigorous-ly to a STEM-dominated educational model? Let's ask him. Late in life here's what Darwin had to say of himself as a premiere case study:

> This curious and lamentable loss of the higher aesthetic tastes is all the odder, as books on history, biographies, and travels (independently of any scientific facts which they may contain), and essays on all sorts of subjects interest me as much as ever they did. My mind seems to have become a kind of *machine for grinding general laws* out of large collections of facts, but why this should

have caused the atrophy of that part of the brain alone, on which the higher tastes depend, I cannot conceive.

Wondering what others might think about things in general, Darwin has some second thoughts:

> A man with a mind more highly organized or better constituted than mine, would not, I suppose, have thus suffered. . . . The loss of these tastes is a loss of happiness, *and may possibly be injurious to the intellect, and more probably to the moral character*, by enfeebling the emotional part of our nature. . . . My power to follow a long and purely abstract train of thought is very limited; and therefore *I could never have succeeded with metaphysics* or mathematics [italics added].[18]

"Injurious to the intellect . . . could never have succeeded with metaphysics. . . ." Today metaphysics is not even regarded as a legitimate perspective. Within the natural sciences, nine years after publication of his *Origin of Species* (1859) Darwin of course rejected the notion of a close colleague that "variation has been led along certain beneficial lines." (This was the American Professor and friend, Asa Gray, to whom Darwin dedicated his two-volume *Different Forms of Flowers*.) The idea of being "led" has enormous implications, and is perhaps a consideration calling for a better word. For Darwin, the single key to food chains was natural selection. The key is not that of being led or guided in any way, or as some scientists today might say: DNA-informed, and in this way channeled or limited within bounds. Some so-called "creationists" also inquire today whether there simply—or even complexly—are too many pivotal coincidences for the randomness of cosmic evolution to work out mathematically all by itself.

At this "asymptotic" gap between science and metaphysics (curves that converge and become parallel, but never actually touch or erase one or the other), Darwin revealed a personal and scientific humility. This humility is less prevalent in his less reflecting imitators today. In words well-deserved by our incoherent point in history, Darwin admitted, "The habit of looking for one kind of meaning I suppose deadens the perception of another."[19] Of the full range of human inquiries, he once acknowledged that

> On the other hand, an omnipotent and omniscient Creator ordains everything and foresees everything. Thus we are brought face to face with a difficulty as insoluble as is that of free will and predestination.[20]

The latter view of predestination, prevalent in his partly Presbyterian setting (as well as in Islam), merited Darwin's disdain as a "damnable doctrine." But, what about other damnable replacement doctrines which are in circulation today? What about those imposed by modernity's self-satisfied view of the world? Should we at least wonder whether STEM advocates overreach when the "perceptions" of other core courses are exiled? How is education to even function when—instead of the natural law of real mutual respect among *persons*—students are taught that "to challenge *ideas* is an attack of the person who holds them"? Is this over-sensitivity thing the real end-state of so-called social evolution and value-neutral indoctrination? Are we witnessing the witless colonization of university campuses by—whatever? Is the purpose of higher education the manufacture of interchangeable bearers of skill-sets all equally attuned to ethics-free Technocracy?

HARD FACTS AND ELASTIC WORDS

Reporting on one of his less convincing works, Darwin recalls how he explained a particular set of geographic formations as due to sea action. He dismissed the workings of an ancient glacial lake as proposed by another natural scientist of the time, Louis Agassiz, an opponent of Darwinism. Of his own erroneous deduction Darwin offers excellent advice that extends far beyond any single science or school of thought: ". . . my error has been a good lesson to me never to trust in science to the principle of exclusion."[21] Does this principle of reasoning also apply to the barrier cobbled in place by Darwinists, between the world of science and the life of faith? Even Charles Darwin's theory of evolution was considerably amended in the early twentieth century, based in part on the work on hybrid plants and biological heredity by Gregor Mendel, an Augustinian monk(!) schooled in mathematics and physics.

In other words, for something to be outside of our own thinking or even one's discipline, as either scientists or metaphysicians, does not mean that it does not exist in fact. Nearly a century after Darwin, Albert Einstein still cautioned against such fragmentation of human thought. Like Darwin, he tended to equate religion with emotion, but he also allowed that "all religions, arts and sciences are branches of the same tree." Looking back before the First World War and the newly gathering storm clouds, he then expressed remorse over the loss of this tree: "the injunctions of the Bible concerning human conduct were then accepted by believer and infidel alike as *self-evident* demands for individuals and society" (italics added).[22]

Even Darwin's expression for how the natural world operates (natural selection) is not quite the blunt instrument bandied about so thoughtlessly: "survival of the fittest." This latter term abbreviates too much the real science, and was coined by an English philosopher, Herbert Spencer. This simplistic slogan was then promiscuously applied by others to the human ecology as *laissez faire* economics and finally totalitarian politics. Darwin himself concedes at least some influence from Thomas Malthus' *An Essay on Popu-*

lation (1798, initially anonymous). In the hands of such Darwin-ists, evolution is imagined to be at the top of some sort of intellectual food chain—and the first principle of human thought. Finally, even the living God is made into only an evolving idea in some peoples' cerebral cortexes, and a mere symbol absorbed into an otherwise evolving and relentless physical universe.

Spencer, more than anyone else in his time, was the one who proposed that because the cosmos is big, (subjective) man is deluded if he thinks that he also has a higher and spiritual nature. The modern-day cosmologist and atheist, Richard Dawkins, is a Johnny-come-lately in this game. His particular mental block, again, is the notion that mindless biological evolution *explains* everything. Economics, culture, history—all of these are only the products of cosmic churning and the sifting and sorting and random survival of the fittest. As an apparent devotee to "whatever," in his *The God Delusion* (2006, an echo of Sigmund Freud's *The Future of an Illusion*) he counsels fundamentalist atheism, radical individualism and moral indifference: "Enjoy your sex life (so long as it damages nobody else) and leave others to enjoy theirs in private whatever their inclinations, which is none of your business." Dawkins announces that all beliefs (or religions) other than his own are no more than an accident of random evolutionary give and take, that spreads to others like any other "virus" or transmittable "meme."

Of this general mindset the earlier G. K. Chesterton (1874-1936) already had asked, "Why should a man surrender his dignity to the solar system any more than to a whale?" We are reminded here of what our second president, John Adams, said about today's moral indifference and our nation's Constitution: "We have no government, armed with power, capable of contending with human passions, unbridled by morality and religion. Avarice, ambition, revenge and licentiousness would break the strongest cords of our Constitution, as a whale goes through a net. . . . Our Constitution was made only for a moral and religious people. It is wholly inadequate to the government of any other."[23]

On the largeness and moral indifference of what has become the Dawkins universe, the English essayist and critic, John Ruskin (1819-1900), was both analytical and richly humble and reverent. Paying his dues to our spatial imagination, he accurately observed that "the soul is larger than the material creation." And about the same time as Galileo, St. Lawrence of Brindisi (d. 1619) wrote that "there are many more ideas and mental images in our memory than there are stars in the sky or drops of water in the ocean, and yet they are all contained in such a small space. The mind [too] is truly a voice and work of God!"[24] Some still pray that the diabolical in the world will not seduce such expansive souls.

A parallel presents itself here between the biologist Darwin and the novelist Mark Twain (Samuel Langhorn Clemens, 1835-1910). From roughly the same century and nearly the same generation and intellectual bubble, Twain also was a materialist and is counted among the historical determinists. What is historical determinism? In one of Twain's most famous novels, *Tom Sawyer*, the vagrant, Injun Joe, is trapped in a cave and is found dead only one day after he expires from dehydration on the wrong side of the sealed cave door. His only source of water was a small hollow in a rock underneath a cave dripping. Had the hollow been even slightly larger he would have had exactly enough water to live another day until being rescued, but the size had been set by geologic action beginning tens of thousands of years before. His tiny fate in the grand scheme of things was determined.

As for Charles Darwin, if microbes had been distributed differently in a purposeless universe, maybe his Annie would not have died of Scarlet Fever. But twenty years after he lost Annie, Darwin the scientist and Darwin the husband and father did still wonder at *purpose* in the universe compared to, say, Dawkins' universe of "blind pitiless indifference:"

> The birth both of the species and of the individual are equally parts of that grand sequence of events, which our minds refuse to accept as the result of blind chance. The understanding revolts at such a conclusion, whether or not we are able to believe that every slight variation of structure—the union of each pair in marriage—the dissemination of each seed—and other such events, have all been ordained for some special purpose (*Descent of Man*, 1871).

TWAIN'S AND DARWIN'S SECOND THOUGHTS

Twain also cuts in a direction opposite to blind chance and historical determinism. In a singular instance, his *Personal Recollections of Joan of Arc* (written from the perspective of a fictional third party, and serialized in 1895), Twain found in a real person all of the lofty human qualities that he sprinkled through the better known characters of his fiction novels. To Twain, Joan was at least one undeniable anomaly within all of our otherwise materially and historically determined human history. Joan was totally detached from self-interest, and it is in this that freedom was undetermined. He discovered her to be totally free and responsive to what we have identified as the tiny whispering sound, the echo of truth from within.

Joan is an undeniable exception that would seem to disprove the absolute, totalitarian and boring rule of historical determinism. Twain behaves in a very scientific way, not unlike Galileo who opened up the skies by noticing through his telescope the anomaly of moons circling around Jupiter. There is even a bit of Darwin's better side here, a thinker who "steadily endeavored to keep [his] mind free." Twain understood the earth-shaking implication of even one person like Joan of Arc. With even one solitary exception determinism is doomed. Though his least known novel, this was the one Twain best loved. We find him "regarding the *Joan of Arc* as worth all his other books together."[25]

Experts in the history of science can and do disregard what might be only random lines in Darwin's abundant writings. In these lines he seems at times to doubt his doubts. This is something our modern day radical skeptics seem incapable or are unwilling to do. In any event, Darwin's tone in his *Autobiography*, and according to his son in all of his works, is one of empathy and friendship with his readers as well as with his specimens. The *Autobiography* softens comments found in his early notebooks for 1837-39 that reek of undisguised materialism. Darwin had asked in one notebook, "Why is thought, being a secretion of the brain, more wonderful than gravity, a property of matter?"[26] This doubt can be read both ways. Overall, he is not a "fanatic," writes Francis Darwin later, and has no wish to force his readers into agreement. Convinced of his findings, he is not yet an ideological specialist driven to impose his point.

Francis describes his father as a "naturalist in the old sense of the word." He worked in many branches of science, rather than only one or two. "The reader feels like a friend who is being talked to by a courteous gentleman, not like a pupil being lectured by an opinionated professor."[27] During the final preparation for publication of his *Origin of Species*, Darwin continues his life-long correspondence. In one to J. D. Hooker (May 11, 1859) he writes: "I fear that my book will not deserve at all the pleasant things you say about it; and Good Lord, how I do long to have done with it!"[28] Good Lord? Four months later he writes, "I corrected the last proof yesterday. . . . So that the neck of my work, thank God, is broken."[29] God is on his lips at least as a social convention, if not in his heart as either a premise or conclusion, or possibly as a silent and sustaining presence. Late in life he writes:

> [Reason tells me of the] extreme difficulty or rather impossibility of conceiving this immense and wonderful universe, including man with his capability of looking far backwards and far into the future, as the result of blind chance or necessity. When thus reflecting I feel compelled to look to a First Cause having an intelligent mind in some degree analogous to that of man; and I deserve to be called a Theist" (*Autobiography*).

As a well-positioned transitional figure into the modern world, Darwin seems to have taken for granted the style or tone that still figures well into humane conversation. The tone mattered as much as the content. Unlike the Darwin-ists of today, Charles Darwin came early enough in the game to not be a one-string violin preaching absolutely the be-all and end-all doctrine of absolutely blind chance. He did dismiss Christianity as being based too much on arguments by analogy, but he was not a total victim to the solvent logic of atheism.[30] It is true that as a researcher Darwin wrote *The Origin of Species* partly to discredit a theological position that species are separately created, but as a human being he also had reservations about reaching for atheistic conclusions. He called himself a Theist.[31]

In his scientific work Darwin was sensitive to the disquieting side of the natural world, even the painful plight of bugs to their tiny predators, but in his more speculative opinions Darwin was governed by a yet higher kind of devotion, as to his family. The year before he died he wrote,

> It has, therefore, been always my object to avoid writing on religion and I have confined myself to science. I may, however, have been unduly biased by the pain which it would give some members of my family, if I aided in any way direct attacks on religion.[32]

Was his term "bias" really the most accurate word? The detail that seems to have eluded Charles Darwin's microscope is that pain and suffering—especially among people—might be the missing key to an ever mysterious, unclassifiable and living and ever present God.

We return for a moment to this theme (from Chapter 6). Might it be that the nature of God is *not* to be absent and silent as the Theist Darwin feared, but to actually suffer with and for his creation in some freely willed and real way? By definition God is "above" our finite world of change and suffering, but if there is a compassionate God, the meaning of com-*passion* is precisely "to suffer with." More than this, it is—more than compassion—intentional and sacrificial love clear through, nothing less. Thinking spiritually—about things that do not fossilize—may it be that the mystery of human suffering can be accepted as a sort of missing link to higher things above—to a God who is total self-donation? Again, we find St. Paul drawing a line in the sand by "describing spiritual realities in spiritual terms" (1 Corinthians 2:13).

Could it have never occurred to Darwin that the compassion he himself felt for probably all living things, and especially for his family, was itself a direct reflection of the compassionate (and always more) deity that slipped between his fingers? Is the inquiring Darwin himself the one specimen he overlooked? Was this "bias" actually a significant anomaly within the grand scheme of things as they really are? Was it empathy? Was it the natural and yet mysterious ability to feel what others also feel, although separated from us by time and space? Was it this more-than-mere-bias that made Darwin both the admirable scientist and family man that he was? Was it empathy that made Darwin?

Empathy is the ground floor for real humanism, a peep hole into a universe with a higher purpose than random outcomes, and even for authentic Christian self-donation. The tiny whispering sound points toward "the other" and ultimately toward one's conversion in the Other.[33] Where Darwin noticed that early man was not capable of committing systematic infanticide, Jacob Burckhardt (whom we met in Chapter 6) had this to say about the universal and permanent human condition: "If, even in bygone times, men gave their lives for each other, we have not progressed since." Another discovery of the innate, permanent and universal natural law. The development of learning and the evolution of science are rendered speechless.

Might Darwin have concluded too quickly that the universal inner voice—more than just the "feeling"—was totally absent from savages and ancient races? Or even if latent, was the natural law at least marginally active? Was it present but mutilated by a mysterious and added fault, human rather than divine? The scandal of Darwin's science is not the science, but that it has become a weapon in the hands of others. The mutability of species—the record that species can change radically—is too readily attached to other intangible things uniquely human.

ISLAND ENGLAND

Several years before Darwin's more final reflections, he wrote against any human inward convictions about the divinity. He stuck with this position, but let's take a close look.

> At the present day [1872] the most usual argument for the existence of an intelligent God is drawn from the deep inward conviction and feelings which are experienced by most people. But it cannot be doubted that Hindoos, Mahomadans and others might argue in the same manner and with equal force in favor of the existence of one God, or of many Gods, or as with the Buddhists of no God. . . . This argument would be a valid one if all men of all races had the same inward conviction of the existence of one God; but we know that this is very far from being the case. Therefore I cannot see that such inward convictions and feelings are of any weight as evidence of what really exists.[34]

A good summary: "feelings" and "I cannot see." Inward convictions are both the most available and potentially most eluding link to what exists outside of our minds. That such convictions might most likely vary is a theme we at least touched upon throughout our examination of "The Family Hearth" (Chapter 7). At about the same time that the naturalist Darwin penned the above, the Russian novelist Dostoevsky had this to say about religious feelings and atheism:

> [T]he essence of religious feeling eludes all arguments; no misdeeds, no crime, no form of atheism can touch it. In this feeling there is and always will be something that cannot be grasped, something beyond the reach of atheist reasoning" (Muishkin in *The Idiot*, serialized in 1868-90).

Solid arguments for an intelligent God stand apart from the solitary and variable inner feelings assumed by Darwin and even Dostoevsky. These feelings are not even the argument of design (always presented as more of a demonstration than a proof) which Darwin challenges with his "mutability of species" (the fluidity of categories), nor a yet more intelligent inquiry. One such inquiry is the most elementary question of "contingency" that we found forbidden by Karl Marx to his anthill of socialist man. Marx simply disallows this question—"Why does anything exist at all, rather than nothing?" Not how does it work, but how is it that it *exists* at all, rather than not, and *why*?

Typically the possibility of blank "nothing" is met by most of us with an equally blank stare. We just take all of this stuff around us, even the universe, for granted. But that's precisely the point. Existence is something to be literally "taken for granted" as much as the non-demonstrable first principle of reasoning. (This is the principle of non-contradiction: a thing cannot both be and not be.) And then as C. S. Lewis finally noticed, where there's a gift, there's a Giver (*Surprised by Joy*). There is a Giver behind Marx's forbidden question about our contingency; and there subsists of His own essence a willful Giver rather than a blind accident in an unending sequence.

Theologically, did Darwin simply find himself in a nineteenth-century niche— merry ol' England with its British imperial pomp and wooded country parsonages, its fashionable palm readings and séances that so repulsed him, and its polite utilitarianism? Was the picture clouded by the entry of short-lived high society and a culture of niceness? Like the Galapagos Islands in natural history, is this cultural setting a mutation from a much richer expanse of human reasoning, religious and Christian history, and possible divine self-disclosure? Did Darwin drift away together with the weak brew of "religious" sentimentalism that in the late twentieth century clearly eroded all of the declining mainline Protestant churches? In this, was Darwin again ahead of his time?

Historians say Darwin's thinking on species might have been partly influenced by the Scottish atheist and "nominalist," David Hume, for whom all naming of "things" and groupings is only an arbitrary convenience of language. Is there a correspondence between the morphing of species and the asserted nominalism and mutability of language? Is the cosmic flux to be sliced and diced into whatever graffiti labels we imagine? One wonders whether what Darwin rejected at the age of forty (1849) was really the core of Christianity, or was it polite neighborhood sentimentalism wearing a collar? In 1845 John Henry Cardinal Newman finally split from such Anglicanism largely because of its indifference as to what doctrines it might retain (or not) in an ecumenical bishopric proposed for Jerusalem.[35]

Just as England is an island, private feeling or intuition (Darwin: "the most usual argument for the existence of an intelligent God") is also a sort of theological Galapagos Island isolated from the faith in its entirety. Should it have occurred to Darwin that human suffering and pain, so much of it self-inflicted, might even be the missing demonstration of what is in fact profoundly spiritual? Nature is violent and painful as Darwin convincingly observed, but nature is *not* perverted as by the spiritual darkness of moral evil. Darker things are afoot than can be handled with only an advanced degree in business technology or system management.

Even Joseph Conrad's *Heart of Darkness* (1899) is about the moral loneliness and descent of a superficially civilized European missionary and would-be reformer in the Congo. It is not about any lesser level of more natural darkness identified with the metaphorical Dark Continent. Some writers see in Hitler's murder of millions a repressed childhood of beatings and a self-loathing for the few drops of inherited Jewish blood in his own veins. Spiritual evil often presents itself as a quest for purity, whether ethnic cleansing, or genetic denial as with Hitler, or the mathematical elegance of a cosmos free of God, or even modern therapeutic release from any more original defect.

And it is precisely such a clever and metastasized moral evil that the Christian God consents to "suffer with." Christ is witnessed to say, ". . . I lay down my life to take it up again. No one takes it from me. I have the power to lay it down, and I have the power to take it up again. This command I received from my Father" (John 10:17-18). So, at least this: the Christian doctrine is of a God who chooses to suffer with us and even within us—this is the only religion that makes some sense of human suffering. This is a clear alternative to atheism and Darwin's lingering ambivalence. Such doctrine exists not as a mind-closing trap, but as an opening of mind and heart and soul to the ultimate "aha" moment, a revelation from beyond ourselves. Such a possible divine self-disclosure is not to be classified by us as a merely intuitional (natural) religion, as Darwin and countless of his followers assume.

In his biological *Descent of Man* (1871 edition) Darwin points to the moral indifference and the "greatest intemperance" that he found among some primitive societies, and to the practice "to an astonishing degree, of utter licentiousness and unnatural crime."[36] He flags crime that is not natural, but "unnatural," and this is the point here! Is it just possible that only a cataclysmic disfigurement of a spiritual kind, from "the beginning" as we say, best accounts for man's descent far beneath the merely violent animal world of natural food chains? In the following century Darwin the thinker would have had decades of total war to help him consider violations that are spiritual and even diabolical—not simply evolutionary—and to consider a distinctly human ecology with spiritual and moral roots, not his facile "secretions of the brain."

Does Darwin's skill in distinguishing and classifying natural species and genera finally distract him? And does he confuse possibly revealed religion with his array of man-made natural religions of varied stripes? Did something escape Darwin's microscope when he despaired of there ever being an "intelligent God"? Each of us in our own mysterious and short mortal life-span has to face this riddle, and is invited to "love the Lord your God with your whole heart, and with your whole soul, and with your whole mind" (Matthew 22:37). In this list of Matthew, the mind does not come before the heart and soul; the mind is not listed first.

So what then is deleted from a transcendent God when we confine Him as only a possibly "intelligent God"? Might it be that the God of intelligence is more a God of love, and a God of will and a God of justice, and always more than we finite beings might think? Within the limitations of language, to say that "God is love" (1 John 4:8, 17) cannot mean that (only) love is God. Again, to say that God is infinitely merciful (forgiveness "seventy times seven") is not to say that God is (only) mercy. To say that God is intelligent is likewise not the same as saying that even supreme intelligence *is* God.

Might it be that God is not reducible to any of *our* own images and likenesses? Might it be that He is not reducible to the learned scratching of innovative researchers in recent centuries? The problem with Darwin-ism, is its imposed single-mindedness as he said of himself. What if God is both the Divine Intellect *and* the merciful and Sacred Heart of Jesus,[37] a poet and artist as well as a scientist, perhaps even a divine playwright? What if marriage participates in his generosity to share his copyright with mutually and permanently committed parents, as co-creators of new and unique selves more in His image and likeness than in ours—children of God each with an eternal destiny? The family has been called "the supporting pillar of creation, the truth of the relationship between man and woman, between the generations."

Children of God? Do we see each child first as a body-and-soul unity, rather than as, say, Descartes' machine with a separable and only hypothetical ghost-soul floating within? Do we accept in the truth our own ensouled bodies, or do we dismiss the natural moral law as an imposed infringement external to ourselves? Is the moral law possibly only an option listed in law school catalogues but, irrelevant to "whatever" we want or decide or do in the new world of constant adjustment? The problem with the mindset of Darwin-ism writ large is not that it disproves Christian ideas, but that it steers the mind from even thinking in Christian categories. These concepts range from the very natural values of modesty, fidelity and permanence to the mystery of personal existence. These realities matter because they are more than matter.

It was Darwin himself who wrote, "I feel most deeply that this whole question of Creation is too profound for human intellect. A dog might as well speculate on the mind of Newton! Let each man hope and believe what he can."[38] Let's chew on that. Should God be awarded at least a temporary school hall pass by the thought police? Without deducting anything from the actual science of evolution, Pope Benedict XVI spoke to the overreach of Darwin-ists at his Papal Inauguration Mass on April 24, 2005: "We are not some casual and meaningless product of evolution. Each of us is the fruit of a thought of God. Each of us is willed, each of us is loved, each of us is necessary." Benedict was not an athlete, but he was a good professor and by his own account he was a great walker. The scientific method plus faith or wisdom: let us hope that in the halls of academia we might some day walk and chew gum at the same time.

The clue to Darwin's real tolerance—not the intolerant tolerance of today's social and political Darwin-ists—is his lament that in his professionalism he discarded the wider interests and reading of his youth. What if this natural universe is *both* naturally complex and an open book transparent to its sacred and transcendent origin—the (Catholic) principle of both and, not either or (How similar, this, to Darwin's "good lesson to me never to trust in science to the principle of exclusion"!) What if nature is to be both understood and respected—such that it is never violated as in abortion, or euthanasia, or any form of short-sighted and self-centered power or economics? The biblical awarding to man of "dominion" over creation (Genesis 1:28) becomes a call for deepening rather than only power or dominion over each other. The integration of such reverence with action unfolds into the Ten Commandments (Exodus 20:1-17) combined with an epiphany recorded as the Sermon on the Mount (Matthew 5:3-12).

Rogue Darwin-*ism* is totalitarian in that it would erase God and even our lofty human "personhood" from the equation. This, by first redefining the unborn child, then marriage, and then our (Constitutional) First Amendment protection of freedom of religion toward what is real. The nineteenth-century Cardinal Newman, whom we met above with regard to questions of conscience, saw nothing new in the radical Darwin-ism of his day. Rather, he saw "the old idea of Fate or Destiny which we find in Homer. It is no new and untried idea, but it is the old antagonist of the idea of Providence" (*Memorandum*, 1861). Our most recent myths about the human mystery replace fate with the technology of a "pendulum" that surely corrects itself automatically, or a clock that must not be turned "back," or the trajectory of "social evolution" that simply cannot backslide. These images rise to the rank of idolatries—the fashionable descendents of Prometheus and Aphrodite, or whatever.

While Charles Darwin does not affirm a religious universe, unlike the Darwin-ism of his later and lesser followers he does not exactly deny it. Again, "let each man hope and believe what he can." This permission came even after he had stood man upright on his hind feet. We are permitted to read between the lines layered records of human and geologic history. Perhaps there is more in the mix than biped structures of highly evolved swamp scum. Are we open to thinking more with the right side of the brain as well as the left? Where is the balance between the rational and the emotional, the material and the spiritual? Can we think more like a poet or an artist, or even a theologian? Born the same year as Darwin, Alfred Lord Tennyson in his

Morte D'Arthur raises our downcast eyes: "More things are wrought by prayer than this world dreams of . . . for so the whole round earth is every way bound by gold chains about the feet of God."

NOTES

1. Letter, June 5, 1879, to N. A. von Mengden: "Science has nothing to do with Christ."

2. Sir Francis Darwin (ed.), *The Life and Letters of Charles Darwin, including an Autobiographical Chapter* (London: John Murray, 1887).

3. Letter to John Fordyce, May 1879.

4. Francis Darwin, *Life and Letters of Charles Darwin* (New York: Appleton, 1888), 2:82-83; cited in William E. Phipps, *Darwin's Religious Odyssey* (Harrisburg, PA: Trinity International Press, 2002), 46.

5. *Descent*, ibid., 122.

6. Charles Darwin, Sir Francis Darwin, ed., *Charles Darwin's Autobiography: With His Notes and Letters Depicting the Growth of the Origin of Species* (New York: Henry Schuman, 1950).

7. Ibid., 59. The flower is described in "On the Two Forms, or Dimorphic Condition of Primula." Darwin shows that the existence of two forms of cowslip, with different lengths of pistils and stamens, is not due to mere variation as was commonly believed (*The Different Forms of Flowers*, New York: D. Appleton and Co., 1877, 14-54).

8. Ibid. 15, 18.

9. St Augustine, *The Confessions*, Book 10, Chapter 35.

10. Adrian Desmond and James Moore, *Darwin* (Warner Books, 1991), 387.

11. Charles Darwin, op. cit., Ibid., 94-5.

12. Frederick Burkhardt and Sydney Smith, *The Correspondence of Charles Darwin*, 7:102 (Cambridge University Press, 1985), cited in William E. Phipps, 93.

13. Cited in Hugh Pope, *St. Augustine of Hippo* (Garden City, New York: Image, 1961), 231.

14. Ibid.

15. L. Huxley, *The Life and Letters of Thomas Henry Huxley* (London: Macmillan, 1900), vol. 1, p. 219; cited in Stanley L. Jaki, *Miracles and Physics*, (Front Royal, VA: Christendom Press, 1989), 104-5555.

16. Letter to Rev. David Brown, quoted in Stanley Jaki, *Newman's Challenge* (Grand Rapids, Michigan: William Eerdmans, 2000), 285.

17. Citation from the *Washington Post*, March 23, 2014, in Johann Christoph Arnold, *Their Name is Today: Reclaiming Childhood in a Hostile World* (Walden, New York: Plough Publishing House, 2014), 54-55.

18. Charles Darwin, Sir Francis Darwin, ed., *Charles Darwin's Autobiography*, op. cit., 66-67.

19. Quoted in Ronald Clark, *The Survival of Charles Darwin* (New York: Random House, 1984), 195; cited in Phipps, 151.

20. Charles Darwin, *Variation of Animals and Plants under Domestication*, Vol. II (New York: D. Appleton and Co., 1883/1868), 428. Regarding religious "doctrine" and the origin of separate species, the Church encyclical *Humani generis* (August 12, 1950), referred this scientific question to the competence of research in the natural sciences but then clarified that man cannot be explained solely in terms of biology, that we have souls directly created by God and that each of us is a new beginning. See a 1986 symposium report partly recounted in *Creation and Evolution: A Conference with Pope Benedict XVI* (San Francisco: Ignatius, 2007), 8-11.

21. Charles Darwin, Sir Francis Darwin (ed.), op. cit, , 43.

22. Albert Einstein, "Moral Decay" (1937), *Out of My Later Years* (New York: Philosophical Library, 1950), 9.

23. From "John Adams to Massachusetts Militia," 11 October 1798, Founders Online, *National Archives*, last modified October 5, 2016.

24. Vernon Wagner, *Seasonal Sermons* (2007), cited in *Magnificat* (New York: July 2016).

25. His words, in Edward Wagenknecht, *Mark Twain, The Man and His Works* (Norman: University of Oklahoma Press, 1935, 1967), 60; cited in the Introduction by Andrew Tadie, Mark Twain, *Personal Recollections of Joan of Arc* (San Francisco: Ignatius Press, 1989), 15. Joan of Arc's view of the Church is in harmony with our text regarding the Eucharistic assembly: "About Jesus Christ and the Church, I simply know they're just one thing, and we shouldn't complicate the matter" (*Acts of the Trial of Joan of Arc*).

26. Cited by Stanley Jaki, *Newman's Challenge* (Grand Rapids, Michigan: William B. Eerdmans, 2000), 267.

27. Charles Darwin, Sir Francis Darwin (ed.), op. cit., 144.

28. Ibid. 238.

29. Ibid. 245.

30. At Cambridge Darwin included in his broad reading the two most influential works of William Paley: *Evidences of Christianity* and his *Natural Theology*. Richard Dawkins opts for blind chance in his *Blind Watchmaker*, but also gives due credit to Paley's clarity of presentation even today. In his later rejection of Christian revelation, Darwin might be overly influenced by the role of "metaphors and allegories" (sic for the disposition to find God behind the wonders of nature) in the apologetics of Paley.

31. Regarding the alleged Christian notion of the separate creation of species, the Thomistic theologian, the twentieth century Blessed Bishop Fulton J. Sheen, offers a little-notice proposition. ". . . each thing is its nature. If the nature remains, as in accidental transformation, it is still identical with itself. If the nature is completely lost, it ceases to be *that thing* and it becomes *that other thing* [species], in which case the intellect knows it as such" (*God and Intelligence in Modern Philosophy* [Garden City, New York: Image, 1958/1925], 160). The intellect is capable of knowing reality, the thing-in-itself, more than simply subjective ideas about things. In the extraordinary case of the human person, Christianity holds that by his very nature wo/man is a pilgrim in time such that neither the material nor the spiritual aspect of this nature as a person-in-itself is to be discounted (neither evolution-ism nor utopian-ism, but rather Genesis and Redemption). How much this overarching insight is like Darwin's "never to trust in science to the principle of exclusion" (Chapter 9)!

32. Letter to E. B. Aveling, October 13, 1880.

33. Edith Stein (Sister Benedicta of the Cross), the Jewish-born convert to Catholicism began her journey as rising intellectual (and atheist) and in 1942 was killed at Auschwitz. Converted in one night by reading the works of St. Teresa of Avila (as Mark Twain was at least fascinated by the life of Joan of Arc), she completed her doctoral dissertation on the mystery of how one person can actually feel empathy for another.

34. Nora Barlow, ed., granddaughter of Darwin, *The Autobiography of Charles Darwin 1809-1882*; with the original omissions restored (London: Collins, 1958), 91.

35. John Henry Newman, *Apologia Pro Vita Sua, being a History of Religious Opinions*, (Garden City, NY: Image, 1956), 240-243. In 1851 a Government survey found that 42 percent of the nation was no longer attending church, and of the remainder nearly half were Dissenters or Nonconformists (cited in the Introduction by Philip Hughes, 19).

36. Cited by Stanley Jaki, 305.

37. The single-hearted receptivity of Mary to the Incarnation invites the insight that Mary's free-will surrender to God (Luke 1:34-37) may be destined to convert some "*followers*" of Islam," the *religion* where "submission" is a translation of "Islam" (but too often misconstrued to license chauvinist and global mandates and even psychiatric and radical terrorism). The modern-day encounter between pre-modern Islam and post-Christian secularism is well beyond the scope of this book. The interested reader is invited to consider one recommended resource, however inadequate: Peter D. Beaulieu, *Beyond Secularism and Jihad? A Triangular Inquiry into the Mosque, the Manger & Modernity* (Lanham Maryland: Rowman and Littlefield/University Press of America, 2012).

38. Cited in *Elbert Hubbard's Scrapbook* (New York: Wm. H. Wise and Co., 1923), 211.

Chapter Ten

Oppenheimer and the Fireball

Have Charles Darwin's empathy for cannibal insects and his expansive theory of natural selection muffled our concern for one-at-a-time, pre-born infants? If so, then the bulk of our technological twentieth and twenty-first centuries will be even more deadening to the spirit. Following the nineteenth-century Darwin, we now turn J. Robert Oppenheimer, part of a premier team of nuclear physicists probing the most elementary secrets of the entire universe. Darwin unfolded the world through his classification systems, and Oppenheimer opened a new world with advanced mathematics. Oppenheimer was the lead inventor of the first atomic bomb—the ultimate fireball now known in many fields of conflict resolution as the "nuclear option."

FROM FOOD CHAINS TO CHAIN REACTIONS

Oppenheimer was not simply a collector and organizer of biological details into the theory and history of evolution. He was drawn to another science and masterminded the ultimate demonstration of another scientific theory with nearly immeasurable consequences. No microscopes needed this time. Instead, dark glasses and a protected observation bunker. In May 1945 at the successful detonation of the first experimental atomic bomb, at Alamogordo, New Mexico, Oppenheimer blurted a possibly rehearsed line from the Hindu Scripture, the *Bhagavad Gita*: "Now I have become death, the destroyer of worlds." His colleague, Kenneth Bainbridge, the physicist in charge of the actual test, spoke in a more common verbiage. Realizing the nearly boundless power of atomic energy for evil as well as good, and the collective nature of the enterprise, he turned back to Oppenheimer and said: "Well, Oppie, now we're all sons of bitches!"[1]

In his own reflections on earlier literary paganism, C.S. Lewis discovered that "[t]here are really only two answers possible: either in Hinduism or in Christianity." But one unavoidable disqualification of Hinduism, he writes, is that "it appeared to be not so much a moralizing and philosophical maturity of Paganism as a mere oil-and-water coexistence of philosophy side by side with Paganism unpurged; the Brahmin [Oppenheimer?] meditating in the forest, and, in the village a few miles away, temple prostitution, *sati* [the widow mounting the funeral pyre of her husband], cruelty, monstrosity."[2] Did Oppenheimer's famously wide-open eyes behold in his bomb the pagan contradiction of "*sati,* cruelty and monstrosity" at a scale unimaginable until the modern age?

During the Second World War the ultimate weapon, the atomic bomb, was researched and developed by the United States in a race against the Adolf Hitler's own atomic program in wartime Nazi Germany. The fantasy of Hitler's Third Reich was to dominate the world for one thousand years. The Third Reich or empire fits in line behind the mostly German Holy Roman Empire (A.D. 962–1806), and the Second Reich of a consolidated Imperial Germany (1871-1918) following the Franco-Prussian War. Along with many other scholars, writers and researchers, Oppenheimer was a refugee from the Nazi European scene of the 1930s and into the safety of America.

At the wartime Potsdam Conference in 1945 with the English Prime Minister Winston Churchill and the Russian dictator Joseph Stalin (1945), the American President Harry Truman alluded only obliquely to "the nameless thing" as "a new weapon of unusual destructive force."[3] The nameless thing could not be contained in a mere name; the bomb at first remained nameless (later: "Fat Man"). Recall here that in Genesis finite man was given the authority to name everything on earth, but not to name the mystery of the divinity. To name something is in a sense to control it, although the thing named is always greater than the nametag, not less.

And even more than the energy inside the atom, the unnamed God is infinite. Even the universe is more than the ancient atomic dust clouds proposed by Lucretius (c. 99 to 55 B.C.), or by our modern calibration in the mathematics of Quantum Mechanics. Everything is more than the sum of its parts. Note that the simplicity of God has no parts. But as for the cosmos, it is still more than the sum of accidental dust. The mind is more than a brain; a person more than an individual; and the unnamed and unborn child more than "nonviable tissue."

After Genesis and only later in the biblical Exodus, in his encounter with Moses, does the absolute simplicity of God as the master of the universe give his own name, as "Yahweh" meaning "I AM" (Exodus 3:14). This name is so awesome that it is almost never to be spoken. It would be an insult to try to put human words to such a living God. Possibly reading too much into

Oppenheimer's above remark, we see that he identifies himself or the bomb with a Hindu name, "I am death." Not life, but death. Again, Oppenheimer speaks of the actual development of a theoretical atomic bomb that unlocks the primal power of the physical universe, the universe that cosmic evolutionists sometimes identity as God himself.

WHAT A DIFFERENCE A CENTURY MAKES

Where Galileo placed the sun at the center of the solar system and where Darwin studied solar-fed earthly food chains, Oppenheimer brought the 6,000 degrees Centigrade surface temperature of the sun directly down to the surface of the earth. The atomic explosion splits the nucleus of radioactive material elements (either uranium or enriched plutonium) in an instantaneous and massively expanding chain reaction. If contained and controlled, the reaction becomes the core to a nuclear reactor and nuclear energy then becomes a brand new and virtually unlimited energy source for the world. If not, then possibly "the destroyer of worlds."

In one century Nature has been removed as a context for human existence to a domesticated tool within the context of the human imagination and within our will to power and intervention. This breakthrough does not replace, but gives new urgency to the human natural law which asks what we *ought* to do, not what we can do.

At such a threshold, and in his own mind, what did Oppenheimer love most of all? Let's ask him. "My two great loves," Oppenheimer once said, are physics and desert country. It's a pity they can't be combined." Enter Los Alamos in the New Mexico desert! Between 1942 and 1945 Oppenheimer ran the nuclear laboratory at Los Alamos (near the Alamogordo test site) that supported the much more widespread total Manhattan Project for bomb production. One of the two major sites, for the concentration of uranium from its ore, was at Oak Ridge, Tennessee. The other, for producing weapon grade plutonium, engulfed the rural town sites of White Bluffs and Hanford in arid and unpopulated Eastern Washington (Chapter 7). The overall workforce for the four-year Manhattan Project topped one-hundred fifty thousand (the same level as the equally innovative ten-year Apollo lunar landing program in all of the 1960s).

The Hanford area is a small part of the Northwest's so-called "channeled scablands." This region is the water-gouged lava country carved by enormous floods following the collapse of enormous Ice Age glacial dams and lakes left over in what is now Montana. Many times up until ten thousand years ago, for dramatically short periods of two or three weeks each, the entire region was deluged with rushing water almost a thousand feet deep. (In the 1930s the largest channel or coulee was spanned by construction of the

Grand Coulee Dam, one mile long with the height of a fifty storey building.) These prehistoric episodes were not gradual or evolutionary but catastrophic.

Now, in his earlier work on evolution Darwin had been unduly influenced by the geologist Charles Lyell and therefore adhered to the school of gradualism or "uniformitarianism" without any added school of abrupt changes or "catastrophism." Is it possible to even think in terms of *both* continuities and abruptness? And philosophically, is it possible to think in terms of both flux and of one-at-a-time integers—the deep-calling-upon-deep reality of real and distinct things as they truly are? In the 1960s recognition of the ancient scabland events in Eastern Washington ended the suppressed debate within a science community. Until then there was admitted only a geology of gradual changes (or flux) to the earth's surface. Anything that smacked of sudden floods sounded too mythical or biblical. But now such catastrophic events were part of a more interesting and bigger picture. Soon after was added the deeper-down movements of entire continental tectonic plates (Continental Drift) covering the entire surface of the earth. We might at least wonder if the human saga involves some version of natural and progressive development and, deeper down, a cataclysmic rupture and then divine redemption?

Returning to nuclear physics and its specialized scientists, J. Robert Oppenheimer was a very extraordinary and slightly strange personality. Very moody and sickly in his youth, Oppenheimer moved on to become fluent in French and German. He graduated from Harvard in three years with high honors, and then finished in physics in England and Germany. Like Darwin, he read more widely than many or most of those who specialize in any of the demanding natural sciences. His interests extended to the classics, novels and plays and poetry. The usual picture is that students pursue either the humanities or the sciences, but not both. Oppenheimer learned Sanskrit, he said, just for fun.

In a brief autobiographical sketch Oppenheimer admits to living for a while in a kind of isolated parallel universe of extraordinary narrowness. He writes, "I never read a newspaper or a current magazine like *Time* or *Harper's*; I had no radio, no telephone; I learned of the stock-market crash in the fall of 1929 only long after the event. . . ."[4] Oppenheimer writes in his sketch that after 1936 and while he was deeply interested in his science, he "had no understanding of the relations of man to his society."[5] A century earlier in his *Autobiography*, the more sociable Charles Darwin likewise credited his concentration partly on his isolation: "Even ill health, though it has annihilated several years of my life, has saved me from the distractions of society and amusement." And in our day the cosmologist Stephen Hawking comments that without the crippling effect of Lou Gehrig's disease, he would not have achieved what he has done in cosmology.

How interesting it is that Oppenheimer chooses to mention *Harper's* magazine by name, because immediately after the Second World War (1846-

7) it is this journal that marketed the cover story that dropping the atomic bomb was possibly the only alternative to a theoretically very costly land invasion of the Japanese homeland. Among others, former President Herbert Hoover had urged an alternative to the bomb and a negotiated end to the war in order to save the "five hundred thousand to maybe one million American lives" that might be lost in the Pacific in a hypothetical long-term invasion of Japan. This large and unquestioned estimate is not documented in any war planning documents or any records of the Joint Chiefs of Staff debates. Better documented estimates are a small fraction of this figure.[6]

At Los Alamos beginning in 1942 Oppenheimer came to appreciate the power of any total conviction when shared with others. If it remained on schedule (he writes) the project "might be successfully accomplished in time to affect the outcome of the war" with a role in the country's future, and it "would be a part of history."[7] Such an attitude toward comradeship in a huge and historic effort serves as an icon for our age of modernity and nearly boundless technology. Words sometimes create later reality. Titanic collective effort sometimes replaces all less contrived and more natural forms of society. Modernity—"the project" (the atheist Jean Paul Sartre's "les projets" as a hedge against despair)—too often stifles other thoughts about, say, the family. Pushed aside, the tiny whispering sound has trouble keeping up with the times.

THE POLITICAL PUZZLE

The jury of popular opinion will always be out on wartime probabilities and possible casualty figures in the final weeks and days of the war. But today a significant minority is persuaded by the much lesser need for or casualties of a possible boots-on-the-ground invasion of Japan. It also is clear that the United States earlier had secretly agreed that the Soviet Union could take part in the initial assault on Japan's Kyushu Island (scheduled for August 15, 1945). Such a role for Russia would have condemned Japan to the same system of police states behind the Iron Curtain as was already occurring in Yugoslavia and Poland and would spread shortly afterward across all of Eastern Europe. This political trajectory was conceded to Russia by the United States, Great Britain and France two years earlier at the Teheran Conference (1943) and later at Yalta (early 1945). In the momentum of events the West was outmaneuvered by the words (about open post-war elections) that flowed from the mouth of Uncle Joe.[8]

Compounding possible missteps in early wartime diplomacy, there was also the inability to communicate between unprecedented and novel scientific facts of an unimaginable scale (the bomb: the "nameless thing"), the rapidly moving battle situation (possible invasion of the main islands), and very long-term global outcomes (the "nuclear arms race" warned about by a few voices in the wilderness.)

The point here is that in only a few years, advances in technology have created a compact world—equally connected and disconnected—where technology seems to generate a freestanding and volatile worldview accountable largely to itself—a cult of getting things done and betting on research toward the next set of inventions: Technocracy. As with the abortion culture, here again the communication gap *between* science, politics and morality remains a troubling and ever-expanding challenge as we enter the twenty-first century. More than a challenge, *esprit de corps* within the specialties can mean a nearly complete rupture between what society as a whole *can* do and what we *ought* to do. This drift is particularly threatening in the fields of basic medical ethics and immoral kinds of genetic alteration. To question the overall momentum is to arouse the self-identity of researchers and their technical competencies within their intricate professional domains. Much easier to "just get on with it." Recall from Chapter 4 that it was Einstein himself who warned against deferring to the scientific method as the source of values and goals.

In the science fiction movie *2001* (1968), the tattered leash of technology was the message in the malfunction of the rogue mega-computer HAL. In the real world the message is a more serious warning coming even from researchers of complex and segmented organizations. We hear the voice of competency within narrow boundaries while, as often as not, the overall mechanism drifts toward rogue and unexamined outcomes that are judged mostly on their effectiveness. As an example, David A. Bella examines in detail the production of biological weapons in the Soviet Union. Narrow competencies conspired unwittingly to support evil outcomes *not* actually supported or even questioned by the pigeon-holed scientists involved.[9] In another example, unreported is the fact that in mid 1945 the one-hundred fifty Manhattan Project scientists stationed in Chicago were surveyed on the approaching military use of the atomic bomb. In that instance, and of the five different options offered, only fifteen percent of the hundred respondents supported the militarily "most effective" choice that was later used.[10]

In recent decades we are more awash than ever before in the confusion attached to ever more momentous decisions. This is true whether it is to possibly deploy atomic bombs against entire urban populations we cannot see from our control panels, or whether to actually abort a single living child we choose not to see. With the bomb, the expected number of deaths at Nagasaki on August 9, 1945, was twenty thousand, because it was *assumed* that the target population would take cover. Beginning the day after the first ever Hiroshima drop on August 6, some six million leaflets were to be dropped on forty-seven Japanese cities warning of destruction, but the shipment scheduled for Nagasaki arrived on August 10, one day after the bomb.[11]

Lost in our Google information world of today are details such as this. The real fatality figure was at least three times as great as was calculated and judged acceptable. In the age of technology, human error or false judgment can carry an enormous mathematical multiplier.

In the baptismal case of the atomic bombs, the case is made that peace appeals of some sort were underway from Japan and that President Truman was aware.[12] However one might decide right from wrong in a fast-moving world, can we not see close up that every momentum consists of decisions and indecisions for which there is responsibility? The difference between the decision to drop the two atomic bombs in 1945 killing nearly a quarter of a million men, women and children, and the Supreme Court's *Roe v. Wade* decision in 1973 affecting sixty million unborn and their mothers, is this: unlike President Truman, the court has had over forty years to reconsider its own "nuclear option." This is its reversible decision in light of scientific facts and the permanent culture war that their fateful decision (in 1973 their refusal to "speculate") has inflicted on human sensibilities and the nation.

Scientists and politicians have often behaved like some irresponsible journalists and headline writers who are bent on spinning their story around sound bites. Bumper sticker education does not serve us well. Apart from the art of self-justification in their work by politicians and scientists alike, the consulted research is so specialized that movers and shakers in both camps are free to cherry-pick their useful facts. Scientists often offer policy opinions (impressions) without weighing options as to highly varied implications and costs. Politicians decorate their rhetoric with one random fact or another. In the numbers and budget game it at least matters where the decimal point is located and where the tight slogans unravel.

PANDORA'S BOX

In Roman times the army was divided into tens, and hundreds and thousands. Even then a decimal system of a sort was in charge. Still, the Christians refused to toss a pinch of ashes on a pagan altar stone. Today, and short of options, we have routinely bombed entire cities all at once. And, we drench countless unborn children one-at-a-time with fatal saline solution. This abortion industry is only the tip of the iceberg in such new worlds as medical technology and their moral dilemmas.

Looking now at microscopic genes, rather than Oppenheimer's even tinier atoms, we see the potential for altering future generations through a method called genome-editing. Where Marx was set on guiding presumed economic evolution, the elites of today fancy themselves guiding presumed human evolution. In 2012 a technique was discovered for altering sperm, eggs or embryos to cure genetic diseases in individuals, but which is *also* capable of altering beauty and even the intelligence in ways that would be hereditary on future generations. As with atomic bombs, another risk is that of disastrously mis-targeting such intervention, in this case the manipulation of DNA (deoxyribonucleic acid), the complex key to heredity and each physical life.

The new research has already caused the moral squint to blink. Some researchers want restrictions defined by basic rightness and wrongness—what we *ought* to do rather than what we can do. Others, including the inventor who will have patent benefits and royalties, want only a moratorium until the routine arithmetic of benefits and costs can be figured out. After all, we already edit society's moral compass through the Big Lie, with good intentions as the guide, why not "just get on with it?"

Like the atomic bomb, genetic technology is not being invented to not be used. Does anyone really think that designer-babies will never make it to the market? Like the bomb, the theoretical and the imagined will become thinkable and then will become history. Current sex-selective abortions are mere child's play in our brave new world of the possible. If the unborn child and his/her sonogram image are no different from a hologram or a Lego toy or an etch-a-sketch, even the diabolic can become routine.

The writer J. R. R. Tolkien, author of *Lord of the Rings*, was opposed to both the atomic bomb over Japan and the indistinguishable alternative of dispersed saturation bombing of targets with conventional weapons. Yet, the latter had been the tactic throughout much of the war. Of conventional bombing in Europe, Tolkien wrote in 1945 to his son Christopher, "the destruction of Germany, be it one hundred times merited, is one of the most appalling world-catastrophes." And this catastrophe was triggered by the neurons inside the single cranium of a democratically elected German lunatic with a moustache and a Swastika armband.

The 1945 fire-bomb raid over Tokyo with incendiary devices killed one-hundred and five thousand in one pass, and all incendiary bombing of Japan killed a total of seven hundred and fifty thousand. This alone was more than either of the later atomic bombs over Hiroshima (one hundred forty thousand from the blast, fires and radiation) and Nagasaki (at least sixty thousand). The total number of casualties, dead and injured, from both bombs was at least six hundred and thirty thousand (a statistic sometimes compared to four hundred and six thousand Americans killed fighting both Germany and Japan in all of the Second World War.)

Yes, from the long perspective of history, the entire twentieth century is a tale of nearly incomprehensible moral dilemmas, decisions and catastrophes made on the run. And our judgments have been saturated and compromised throughout by a circus of cut-and-paste ideologies meant to cauterize the bleeding of amputated Christianity. It is not surprising that part of today's Big Lie is to replace history with current events. We can't walk it back, so just walk away. User-friendly amnesia is offered to the millennials as they are propelled toward an uncharted future. Is it any wonder that many feel abandoned?

After the actual use of the atomic bombs, and in President Truman's presence, the physicist J. Robert Oppenheimer stepped back from the current event and lamented that he had "blood on my hands." In a flash he understood the piecemeal steps into disaster and gained the missing "understanding of the relations of man to his society." To which the political decision maker and Commander-in-Chief, the President, told his Secretary of State (Dean Acheson) "Don't bring that fellow around here again. After all, all he did was make the bomb. I'm the guy who fired it off."[13]

The novelist J.R.R.Tolkien made no distinctions; he felt contempt for both "these lunatic physicists" and the "Babel builders." But maybe Oppenheimer, at least, also had more on his mind. Was his vision more sweeping than that of Truman who by the untimely death of President Franklin D. Roosevelt was elevated into the White House? Was he announcing a pending and possibly avoidable determinism of history, this time a nuclear arms race? In history, blood is the folkway rite of passage into each new world. We are severed from our own past: the symbolic descent of the guillotine on the necks royalty in revolutionary Paris; Czar Nicholas and his wife and children targeted for extermination in revolutionary Russia; and the fate handed to anyone wearing Western eye glasses in late twentieth-century Cambodia (two million tortured and executed by the upcoming generation). Initiation into street gangs works the same way. And even isolated young girls are fed the deceit that their tragic abortion is really an initiation and rite of passage into the brave new world of "modernity." The destructive political strategy of Saul Alinsky works at all levels: pick a target and confront it, attack and isolate, and then destroy it.

MOMENTUM OR DECISION-MAKING

Who, really, is the accurate historian of such complex and horrendous events? Who really is the revisionist historian? Should we just stand back and appeal to, what, the hindsight fiction of long-term social evolution? And how do such global things play out on a more personal scale in our bit-part private lives? For our purposes here, it is enough to notice that the schooled nuclear physicist was as stunned and unprepared to deal with the reality of the top secret "nameless thing" as is our teenage girl headed for the school counselor with the top secret news of an unnamed pregnancy.

In both cases, though at different scales, we face a tangled moment and the total mystery of life and death. In both cases, moral decision making mixes with the scrambling for calculated outcomes and possibly a simplifying exit strategy. With the single abortion is the label "nonviable tissue" more a cover story than reality? Many think that it was largely momentum that led to the Hiroshima decision. And to the decision to target Nagasaki where actual military fatalities numbered only one hundred fifty compared to civilian fatalities in the many tens of thousands.[14] By what momentum or sequence of discrete decisions did a bombing policy against military targets end up this way on the ground? Years later and like Truman himself, a historian marvels at the abstractness of the mushroom cloud as a concealing symbol, and at the "inevitable ordinariness" of the target cities: "Here a uniformed schoolgirl, perhaps nine years old, walks past hand in hand with a friend. There two older women, perhaps sisters, return from shopping."[15] We can recall here (from Chapter 1) survey results that reveal beneath the surface the "ordinariness" of abortion today. By refusing to "speculate" on such realities, the United States Supreme Court in *Roe v. Wade* legislated a culture of ordinariness from the bench.

Only a few years after the theoretical atomic bomb was actually used on urban targets, becoming a practical tool in the arsenal, the Cold War escalated into the inevitable (?) nuclear arms race and the reciprocal targeting of urban areas under deterrent and balanced threats of Mutual Assured Destruction (MAD). Many voices had counseled President Truman against using the weapon and falling into this trajectory. As Oppenheimer had warned, in 1950 a new hydrogen bomb offered one thousand times the destructive power as the earlier products used on Japan. On the new field of play, just move the decimal point over a few notches. Truman approved construction of the hydrogen bomb against the advice of the Atomic Energy Commission General Advisory Committee (AEC-GA), and against three of the five AEC commissioners including the politically independent chairman, David Lilientha who then resigned.[16]

Oppenheimer had shown his misgivings, and now lost his stature as a consultant to the AEC because, in the view of a well-placed colleague, he showed "insufficient" enthusiasm for the hydrogen bomb. The evil of Soviet expansionism cannot be overstated. As part of the bigger picture, the postwar Truman is credited with the countering Truman Doctrine and the Marshall Plan for rebuilding Europe, and the innovative Berlin Airlift (1947-48). But even today, a quarter century after the Cold War ended (1991), the major nuclear powers sit atop touchy stockpiles totaling many thousands of nuclear warheads. Historians seem to disagree on whether Stalin was on pace to produce an atomic bomb within one year or five of the decision to use the bomb, or whether he made his decision only after actually seeing footage of the fearful destruction of Hiroshima.

Reflecting on the long and unique history of the West, the historian W.H. McNeill stresses "a defect of historical essays . . . that the unique individual career and the strategic moment of personal thought or action can easily be obliterated by the weight of inexact generalizations. . . . We, and all the world of the twentieth century, are peculiarly the creatures and heirs of a *handful of geniuses* of early modern Europe, for it was they who defined the peculiar and distinctive modern bent of European, presently the Western, and now to a very substantial degree, or world civilization" (italics added).[17]

The point for us, here, is that the momentum of human history and social evolution are always open ended, consisting as they do of moments bent one way or the other by geniuses or more broadly *by others on the same stage.* Their decisions and acts of freedom or un-freedom are the pivot points that we read after the fact as momentum. When we individually discard our particular inner core of universal and human natural law, settling for half-answers and half-questions, it is then that we become pygmies in the evolving machinery or arc of history. The scientific analogy is Quantum Mechanics—light is both a wave and a particle; the human record is both pivot points and whatever arc of history we choose to see.

During my short career in the United States Navy (1967-70) I found myself touring a Japanese beach near Sasebo on the west coast of Kyushu Island, less than fifty miles from Nagasaki. With a meeting of the eyes I fell into a curious conversation with a particular and older park supervisor. His team of blue-uniformed women was tasked to clean the beach of debris and even seaweed during each low tide. There's something symbolic here, resisting the incoming tide with nothing but a traditional garden rake. Maybe King Canute is smiling. They're not winning, but here they're not losing either; they keep coming back. The weathered supervisor was named Yabe (yah-bay). I say "conversation". . . . I spoke no Japanese and he spoke no English, and yet in our forty-five minutes we made some headway with gestures and single words. He pointed up to the backdrop of cliffs and, after all these years and nearly obscured by mature trees, I could still detect some of the cave openings. As a young man Yabe had hidden there with thousands of other civilians of all ages. His gestured fear was of bombs.

Part of the Second World War story in the Pacific is also the same kind of failure to communicate clearly at very infrequent openings. More word games and mind traps. . . . The Western term "unconditional surrender" has more than one meaning, as does the Japanese "mokusatsu" uttered in response to this 1945 ultimatum in the Potsdam Declaration. The latter term can mean either a tentative "no response" or a final and "total rejection." The meaning of some words omitted, or even of some key words used, matters as much as the placement of arithmetic decimal points and plus and minus signs. Worse than that, the message was intercepted from a radio broadcast intended for only the Japanese military press, not the Allied powers. Today we would see this overflow from communication channels as a prelude to all the hazards of open social media and Twitter.

Mounting concern even in the West over the obscure meaning of "unconditional surrender" had already been expressed in a *New York Times* article reporting that ". . . demands from members of Congress and publicists now [are] coming almost daily, that the President make clearer to the Japanese people what unconditional surrender does *not* mean, as well as what it does mean."[18] In the bubble of Japanese cultural experience, did the term suggest to them mass executions and genocide? President Roosevelt had lifted the expression from our own Civil War history, but in this global context it applied to a very different culture and not the fate of only one embattled fort in the South (Fort Donelson, 1862).

We are all invited to do our own reading, but all can notice here that momentum and calculated technical efficiency can easily step in as an over-simplifying pseudo-morality. Oppenheimer saw the urgency of giving personally his last-minute instructions to a military officer heading for the Hiroshima raid. As paraphrased in the media his message was for precision: "Don't let them bomb through clouds or through overcast. Got to see the target. No radar bombing; it must be dropped visually. . . ."[19] What would *we* have done if we were the bombardier? And what of the second plane that lifted off only three days after Hiroshima? Bad weather diverted this mission from the primary target to Nagasaki, and the gauge indicated only enough remaining fuel for one pass over the target.

Can any such apparent momentum of events be avoided at clear decision points farther back up the line? Back up the line and working with Oppenheimer was General Leslie Groves, the head engineer for the Manhattan Project since his appointment in late 1942. On the manufacturing side of things, Groves succeeded in producing the initial two atomic bombs barely before the war's end. Again, the debate continues whether the drop ended the war, or whether it only punctuated a war already ended by a strangling naval blockade and massive conventional bombing. Critics point to how the mushroom cloud at the Alamogordo test site was altered by the wind as it reached thousands of feet into the atmosphere—forming an enormous question mark.

Politically on the home front, successful use of the new "nameless thing" probably averted Congressional scrutiny of the recent four years of secret and steep backchannel funding for the Project (two billion dollars, a hefty sum in the currency of 1942-5). After all, you do not build such a gadget and then not use it. The devastation sank in during the weeks following the detonation, especially as a future tally of tens of thousands of unexpected radiation poisoning cases and deaths began to mount up. And the trajectory had been set for the competitive production of weapons each with a thousand times the destructive power as that demonstrated at Hiroshima and again at Nagasaki three days later.

What had only been imagined a few years before was now history. The insurmountable irony is that imagination had now become fact, and facts have a way of becoming routine. This connection seems to have escaped the commission investigating the failure to prevent the attack on the twin towers in 2001. One of their recommendations (we recall from Chapter 5) was that "imagination is not a gift usually associated with bureaucracies .... It is therefore crucial to find a way of *routinizing*, even *bureaucratizing* the exercise of imagination." Did the Manhattan Project, in fact, routinize and bureaucratize what until then was only imagined? Once the unimaginable is imagined and then built and actually used, thereafter it is more routine than unimaginable. We render the nuclear arms threat and race routine. We also render abortions routine. All such momentums are like eating peanuts; after the first one, the rest is history.

MIND, MATTER AND THE "ULTIMATE UNKNOWABLE"

What role *must* human freedom and responsibility really play, together, above the momentum of half-understood events and routines? Kafka paused at the point of detached freedom: "I am free and that is why I am lost!" Where above the world of complex modernity does that tiny whispering sound still get a hearing? In all things both large and small, reining in the promiscuous half of imagination is the first protection of all that is real. Is it possible that the priority of wonder over eventual momentum and routine is the heart of the natural law? Are we capable of looking up from the conveyor belt in our lives? Who is it who warns us even today about the slippery slope from vagrant imaginings into action and deadening routine? "But I say to you that whoever looks at a woman to lust for her has already committed adultery" (Matthew 5:27-28).

How are we to un-invent Hitler and, most certainly, but also every false arc of history, personal and collective? How to remain above the historical determinism that captured the mind of Mark Twain? How to remain above the "survival of the fittest" as applied to the social order? Darwin once wrote this about the riddle of God: "a dog might as well speculate on the mind of Newton." How strangely similar this sounds to a comment of his contemporary, Herbert Spencer:

> I think it quite a defensible proposition that humility is better shown by a confession of incompetence to grasp in thought the Cause of all things; and that the religious sentiment may find its highest sphere in the belief that the Ultimate Power is no more representable in terms of human consciousness than human consciousness is representable in terms of a plant's functions. [20]

In a preceding sentence, Spencer refutes the pious but confused remark of a theologian (a journal article by a Mr. Martineau). Spencer argues that instead of mind developing seamlessly from matter under the guidance of Divine Actor, that [he does not see] "how piety is especially exemplified in the assertion that the Universe contains no mode of existence higher in Nature than that which is present to us in consciousness." So, is there a higher mode of existence—that we call God?

Overall Spencer maintains that in Evolution itself there is no "higher" or "lower" and no "possibility of better or worse" as is implied in a purposive "world prearranged for progress," or in "a directing Will intent upon the good." He sharpens Darwin's "law of natural selection" into "the law of the survival of the *fittest*." Late-stage parasites, for example, are often the fittest. Rather than Evolution and Materialism, Spencer writes: "Involution would much more truly express that nature of the process. . . . [By involution he means ever more complex entanglements, but no overall direction] The Doctrine of Evolution, *under its purely scientific form*, does not involve Materialism, though its opponents [as well as modern-day Darwin-ists!] persistently represent it as doing so" (italics added).[21]

Spencer defends science against a churchman who commingles Mind and human consciousness with the evolution [or involution] of Matter. That consciousness is a secretion of matter is also the view of Karl Marx. Spencer's rejoinder inadvertently can serve as an entry point for the divine *into* the human being and thus into "human consciousness." He assumes that there is "no mode of existence higher *in* Nature, while theologians more clear than Mr. Martineau proclaim the Divine as sovereignly *above* Nature. Spencer sees contemplation of the "Ultimate Unknowable" as the final stage in evolution, but other minds propose—do not impose—that the living and more original God, subsists in His unique "nature" as the Other, and chooses in freedom and divine charity (neither our concept of mind or matter) to reveal Himself to receptive souls.

Such a revelation would be an Encounter with an *intimate* Other who also lies infinitely beyond *any* of our concepts—and yet, *this* concept about our limited concepts is true! Such a self-disclosure by the otherwise Ultimate Unknowable puts into clear relief the proposition that the fully human "natural law" is above any lesser physical laws of measurement and classification as confine and define the doctrine of Evolution. This divine self-disclosure also confirms that the natural law—which also can be known in part by human reasoning—is our protection against some of Spencer's "involution" or what we have identified as moral regression, backsliding and devolution in human relationships.

THE MIRROR OF HISTORY

Modern history remains content to follow the evolutionary/involutionary mindset, with the self-appointed enlightened ones culling the herd. But, how open-minded and well prepared is the new generation of millennials to pause, in true freedom, to fully engage the human mystery and our human ecology in the twenty-first century? Is this new generation better disposed than the most recent two generations to soberly weigh the fit between technology, political power and real morality? Is this fateful intersection even on our radar screen?

The atomic bomb story above was triggered by the aggressions of Nazi Germany across Europe. How do we compare? A comparison table, the "Third Reich and Contemporary Society,"[22] connects that Fascist era to our own drift—similar and different—into another kind of culture of death. Here are some side-by-side snapshots with the first years, at least, of the abortion revolution: "I know of not a single case where anyone came out of the chambers alive" (Auschwitz commandant Rudolf Hoess on the destructive capacity of Zyklon B gas, 1947) and "It never ever results in live births" (an experienced abortionist on the merits of dissection and extraction, 1981); "the subjects were forced to undergo death-dealing experiments 'without receiving anesthetics'" (Dachau freezing experiments, 1942) and "the fetuses are fully alive when we cut their heads off, but anesthetics are definitely unnecessary" (Fetal researcher Dr. Martti Kekomaki, 1980); "no criticism was raised" (conference of German physicians to the Ravenbrueck death camp sulfanilamide experiments, Berlin, May 1943) and "no one ever raised an eyebrow" (meeting of American pediatricians to an experiment involving beheading of aborted babies, San Francisco, 1973); and "what should we do with this garbage"(Treblinka, 1942) and "an aborted baby is just garbage" (fetal researcher Dr. Martti Kekomaki, 1980). In *Mein Kampf* (1925) Adolf Hitler referred to Jews as "a parasite in the body of other peoples"; fifty years later, the year of *Roe v. Wade*, a radical feminist group branded the unborn as "a parasite within the mother's body" (an early edition of *Our Bodies, Ourselves: A Book By and For Women*). In recent years the abortion culture has dolled-up itself with euphemisms, but even in 2016 those opposed were still labeled in Presidential campaign rhetoric as "deplorables."

Cruelty has become routine, part of the bland wallpaper of life. Under the Hitler regime human skins were stretched and fabricated into fashionable lamp shades for the high command, a detail reported by Albert Speer in his *Inside the Third Reich* (1971). Today, in important moral situations are we equally incoherent and routine—neutral as we say—and content to stay with "whatever"? Abortion, premature organ harvesting to where dying organ donors are treated as elements of a nation-wide organ farm, embryonic stem cell harvesting and destruction of "extras," gene splicing of future generations, human egg marketing, trafficking of fetal body parts, euthanasia which in parts of Europe now includes some unwilling patients, the numbed and mindless cult of "whatever," and the scamming of young adults with the clichés of "freedom of choice" and sexual "readiness."

Let's get better introduced to the twentieth century writer C. S. Lewis. All of his works are a good read, but an especially clever little piece is his *The*

Screwtape Letters. Again, Screwtape is a satanic functionary who advises an understudy nephew on how to worm his way into the moral life of a selected and targeted human being. "The safest road to Hell is the gradual one—the gentle slope, soft underfoot, without sudden turnings, without milestones, without signposts." In short—euphemisms and word games.

Screwtape much prefers corrupting the vulnerable patients in hospitals to dealing with the more difficult task of capturing men in the edge of being killed in wartime. Such men on the edge are likely to be more alert and inclined to give more serious thought to serious questions, what Screwtape calls the "relevant questions" (and the communist Marx's "forbidden" question). Precisely because there are no atheists in foxholes,

> . . . how much better for us [says Screwtape] if all humans died in costly nursing homes amid doctors who lie, nurses who lie, friends who lie, as we have trained them, promising life to the dying, encouraging the belief that sickness excuses every indulgence, and even, if our workers know their job, withholding all suggestion of a priest lest it should betray to the sick man his true condition.[23]

Why should we take time to notice Screwtape and the demonic in the writings of C. S. Lewis? Perhaps to wake up to the fact that in mid-century he did not yet have a clue of the diabolical practices that now have been annexed into parts of the medical profession.

Using a wartime image, St. John Paul II spotlights a close fit between unquestioned applications of modern technology and demographics. Western foreign aid is linked to the requirement that the Western abortion culture also be accepted. This blackmail, he wrote, is "poisoning the lives of millions of defenseless human beings, as if in a form of 'chemical warfare'."[24] Barely heard in the turbulent 1960s, the earlier Pope Paul VI had already sounded the warning in his *Humanae Vitae* (*Of Human Life*, 1968), on the future of a morally unhinged world and contraceptive mentality. Dismissed at the time as an alarmist, he asked,

> Who will stop rulers from favoring, from even imposing upon their peoples, if they were to consider it necessary, the method of contraception which they judge to be most efficacious?[25]

Technical efficiency is God, far removed from the intimate personalism of sexual encounter as unfolded later by St. Pope John Paul II in his *Theology of the Body*. Pope Paul VI's controverted encyclical (a letter) serves as an introduction by affirming that spousal unity and openness to procreation cannot be morally disconnected, either purpose from the other, as by anti-conceptive interventions. This consistent teaching across the centuries contrasts with the earlier and trend-setting (Anglican) Lambeth Conference decision. When in 1928 at Lambeth the majority of Anglican bishops opened the door to direct separation of human intercourse from even the possibility of procreation. At the same time the widely influential philosopher, Bertrand Russell, himself a champion of trial marriages and who eventually married four times, muddied the waters further. He publicly advised pre-marital sexual relations and, even for life-long marriages, the side plate of extra-marital relations. Given this history, in *Humanae Vitae* Paul VI was still a few years ahead of his time and our recent culture wars:

> . . . It is also to be feared that the man, growing used to the employment of anti-conceptive practices, may *finally lose respect for the woman* and, no longer caring for her physical and psychological equilibrium, may come to the point of considering her as a mere instrument of selfish enjoyment, and no longer as his respected and beloved companion (italics added).

In the following decades Hugh Heffner and then the Hollywood sit-com writers have filled the airwaves with the warned-against disrespect. The only women receiving respect are those in high action sequences and who excel in karate, that is, unisex male females.

Not to be outdone by the entertainment complex, Washington state was the first to approve by ballot abortion (1971), and gay "marriage" (2012), and most recently the first to approve recreational marijuana (2013). The marijuana licensing and sales taxes are every bit as reasonable as taxing the very similar and free-wheeling opium trade that so victimized all of China in the nineteenth century. And in 2014 when the City of Seattle voted for a local minimum wage of fifteen dollars an hour, we began to hear proposals that, as yet another "civil right," prostitutes should be allowed to unionize as we already find in, say, tolerant Amsterdam.

On the international scene, Amnesty International also seeks to decriminalize sexual exploitation, mouthing the "human rights of sex workers."[26] Under the Big Lie one thing leads to another. Apparently even male fornication and adultery are to be indirectly admitted into the big tent of "civil rights." In our lonely and disrupted society, freed again and again from the universally human natural law, is it too fanciful to wonder whether rape and incest will someday be defended within the spectrum of options as, what, "unilateral outreach"?

GENERALS AND GENERALITIES

Real historical events can be made too conceptual and abstract, too statistical, and too much through the lens of current biases. History used to be understood as a fabric of concrete decisions and events, biographies and particulars, all ultimately on the human scale. Real history is more an artifact of human ideas and actions and inactions than it is of inevitable evolution as explained by economic mathematics and real-time opinion surveys. The mindset of social evolution and the right side of history is not only boring, but a dictation of lazy research.

At the terminal point for this kind of thinking we have already met the dictator Joseph Stalin. He stood on the shoulders Vladimir Lenin who schemed to accelerate the trajectory of dialectical materialism invented by Marx. Joseph Stalin did so by standing on the graves of tens of millions. He put into words what a growing number are conditioned today to tolerate: "a single death is a tragedy, a million deaths is a statistic." Was the fourteenth-century Asian conqueror, Tamerlane, actually an early modern? Is our modernity a throwback? His monument was a landscape punctuated with pyramids of human skulls said to number in the thousands. Our widely dispersed abortion numbers dwarf these pyramids.

The parroted commonplace is that violence is a product not of ideology and adrenaline, but mostly of religion! Does this bumper-sticker slogan really hold up? Playing the numbers game, the Inquisition, widespread threat that it was, accounts for probably a couple of thousand deaths across all of Europe and spread over two centuries. Yes, horrendous religious wars have extended over many decades and centuries, but even these are heavily alloyed with politics. And these pale in comparison to our modern non-religious ideological wars. Following the Reformation and the birth to nation-states, the Thirty Years War was actually more about politics than religion. It was for political reasons that Catholic France, steered by the Catholic chief minister of state, Cardinal Richelieu under King Louis XIII, sided with the Protestant countries to the north. By this alliance, and even with the Turks (Moslems), France upstaged the Catholic Austro-Spanish Empire of the Hapsburgs for supremacy on the European political game board.

Given today's agnosticism, does any motive of war matter if, in reality, humanity is really only an accident within the sightless extent of a dust cloud universe? Under the evolutionary-technological mindset, genocide becomes applied mathematics like economics or quantum mechanics. And what could be more impolitic in cocktail company or on prime time news than to mention anything like modern Christian martyrs? Their story begins in the first century with St. Stephen and then Sts. Peter and Paul, and erupts afresh into our own times especially in North Africa and the Middle East, and in more subtle forms in the post-Christian West. To give suitable air time to such anti-Christian persecution would surely muddy the fading smiley-button secularist narrative. Among the tens of thousands of Syrian refugees into the United States all but one or two dozen are Muslims. Christians don't make the cut, so to speak.

Look at the beheadings in North Africa and the Middle East today. And what is the remotely informed observer to make of recent history in antireligious communist China, the earlier state-sponsored atheism of the Soviet Union, and National Socialism of Nazi Germany? From just these three pseudo-religious movements—religions without God—we can number an estimated one hundred thirty million victim Christians and others in less than one century. Nevertheless, religious fault lines are deeply entangled in, and useful to, economic and political strife:

> At the turn of the third millennium, religious loyalties [again] are at the root of many of the world's ongoing civil wars and political violence, and in most cases, the critical division is the age-old battle between Christianity and Islam. However much this would have surprised political analysts a generation or two ago, the critical political frontiers around the world are not decided by attitudes toward class or dialectical materialism, but by rival concepts of God. . . . But whatever the reasons, inter-religious violence in recent years tends to be initiated by Muslims against Christians, and that trend is unlikely to change."[27]

Playing into this tension is the feeble worldview of Secular Humanism—a *non-concept* of non-God—that cannot even begin to understand the human person and the deeper currents of human history. In a fully human universe radical secularism is like an inchworm on the lens of the Hubble telescope imposing its impressions of the constellation Hercules.

A twentieth-century writer explains that the easy dismissal of mass murders within the statistics of human history comes from the "habit of abstract thinking." Among the "liberal" mindset, he discovers, is the lost "faculty to [even] imagine what they know."[28] In a 1978 "Commencement Address at Harvard University," Aleksandr Solzhenitsyn (an eight-year survivor of the Soviet Gulag) issued a still-relevant alert to the West:

> The fight for our planet, physical and spiritual, a fight of cosmic proportions, is not a vague matter of the future; it has already started. The forces of Evil have begun their decisive offensive. You can feel the pressure, yet your screens and publications are full of prescribed smiles and raised glasses. What is the joy about? . . . All the celebrated technological achievements of progress, including the conquest of space, do not redeem the twentieth century's moral poverty, which no one could have imagined even as late as the nineteenth century."[29]

The denial of reality comes with the refusal or incapacity to see or to imagine what we really do know. All of us must pinch ourselves to stay awake spiritually in this day and age. This pinching is the natural law. In its place and camouflaged as modernity, are we to believe that abuses done falsely in the name of religion are improved upon by much more catastrophic and compulsory non-religious belief?

President Gerald Ford declined to even meet with Solzhenitsyn when he was invited to the United States to deliver the Commencement Address at

Harvard University. This was the presidential candidate who near the same time on national television insisted that Poland in the 1970s was a free country and not under (Soviet) tyranny. The elected president (Ronald Reagan) cut through the smoke when he named the Soviet Union the "Evil Empire." With Margaret Thatcher and Pope St. John Paul II in 1991 he tilted the presumed arc of history to finally dismantle the Soviet Union "web of mendacity," with barely a few dozen shots being fired.[30] Two decades later such an historic reversal, equivalent to the centuries-long fall of the Roman Empire, barely merits a spot in the short-term memory of the distracted West. Instead, a future defined by computer career tracks, ticker-tape politics and turbulence over international trade deals.

Does the "whatever" generation of today even hear any of this, as if it matters? What is missing today is that too many students are not challenged to even identify something so recent as the Manhattan Project, or the Cold War, or the meaning of a real human heartbeat revealed by ultrasound. History does not exist in real time. In a 2015 radio show the talking heads were unable to agree whether Galileo's moon circling the earth was—a sun or a planet! For at least a few, the Manhattan Project is probably nothing more than a mixed drink.

GROUND ZERO AND SACRED GROUND

Idolizing science into theology, J. Robert Oppenheimer gave the atomic bomb project the code name "Trinity." This branding is possibly based on reading of the English poet, John Donne: "Batter my heart, three person'd God, for you as yet but knock, breathe, shine, and seek to mend." The Trinity: until now this referred to the Christian witness as to whether God actually makes himself known to us both in human history and as Father. To Moses God names himself as "I AM", but at Ground Zero the modern era Oppenheimer labels a fireball as the Christian Trinity. Something like this "Trinity," in his early years Nietzsche—an early influence on Adolph Hitler—often signed his letters "Anti-Christ" and "The Crucified One." Nietzsche referred to contraception as "mutual masturbation." The cause of his early death is widely debated, but has been attributed to syphilis contracted early-on in a Cologne brothel or even to a male brothel in Genoa.

Brilliant physicist that he was and master of word selection, Oppenheimer was outdone by a later and well-placed political animal. In the summer of 2013 the Speaker of the House opposed any limits on late-term abortions. As a feminist antipope and a high priestess of the Big Lie, she pronounced, "As a practicing and respectful Catholic, this [late-term abortion] is *sacred ground* to me when we talk about this. . . ." This is an astounding claim, even biblical—with a blinded self-will so confused about the sacred as to "be like

God" (Genesis 3:5). In Exodus Moses removed his sandals before even approaching truly "sacred ground" (Exodus 3:5). After four millennia of social evolution, modern politics puts its foot in its mouth.

The Speaker continued: "This shouldn't have anything to do with politics." The naked truth comes out. In a reasonable world the most basic right to life would never be politicized. Like the moons of Galileo, late-term abortion would be seen for what we know it is. But since we refuse to imagine what we know, grisley dismemberment needs to be accurately defined for all to see:

> . . . with the purpose of causing the death of an unborn child, purposely to dismember a living unborn child and extract him or her one piece at a time from the uterus through the use of clamps, grasping forceps, tongs, scissors, or similar instruments that, through the convergence of two rigid levers, slice, crush, or grasp a portion of the unborn child's body to cut or rip it off (proposed House Bill 920 in Missouri, 2015).

How is it that we have replaced morality with politics, politics with ideology, and ideology with the "forceps, tongs, or scissors" and a "culture of death"? Where Herod and the Roman soldiers punctured the two-year old children of Bethlehem with lances (Matthew 2:16-18) from the nearest iron foundry, we dispatch near-birth children with chrome-steel scissors from the lowest-bid pharmaceutical supplier. Who is it that has redefined the unborn child and the meaning of such other terms as suicide, marriage, and family? We hear from a nurse who discovered a late-term abortion found to be still alive, but then abandoned to helplessly cooperate by dying alone. In this case the child was undamaged, alive, and trembling on the operating table. What are we to make of the federal goal for "no child left behind?" "Why," asks the passer-by nurse, "did I not just grab this baby and run for a taxi to another hospital?"

Perhaps our coarse confusion and descent into regimentation began with Napoleon who fully organized the novelty of universal military conscription (earlier the emergency measure of 1793). Or, was the West desensitized by the First World War which tore asunder any remaining boundaries between combatants and civilians? Normal distinctions today qualify as discrimination and are shrink-wrapped as "civil rights" violations and then outlawed and penalized. Why shouldn't young women enjoy an equal place in compulsory registration for Selective Service (the military draft)? This agenda is proposed as the "next logical step in gender equality." Exercising predictable double-speak, the sitting President supported the proposal while also insisting that the voluntary service should remain in place barring a declaration of war. Why shouldn't women enjoy an equal and compulsory right to have both legs blown off by roadside bombs? Until now the doctrine that modernity was all about removing limits rather than legs. But surely modern society can match the equality found in ancient Rome where men, women, and children alike were equally martyred in the Coliseum. How discriminatory when it was only men who performed as military gladiators in the afternoon.

Albert Einstein records a remarkable conversation on our new mentality. Still at the front edge of a colossal nuclear arms race he spoke with "an intelligent and well-disposed man." He explained the real danger of an unrestrained arms race built atop soon-to-be enormous stockpiles of atomic bombs. But the visitor in his own mind had already advanced across this bridge: "Why are you so deeply opposed to the disappearance of the human race?" What!? Writing about this moral abyss Einstein reflects from his twentieth century back to Darwin's nineteenth: "I am sure that as little as a century ago no one would have so lightly made a statement of this kind."[31]

Today the gladiator Coliseum is new and improved. It has been electrified. The ancient entertainment is still very much with us on the big screen and on countless smaller screens saturated into the market segment of family billing addresses and every bedroom entertainment center. St. Augustine recounts the universal human weakness of his best friend. Alypius was drawn to the ancient gladiator spectacles. Like us, Alypius could have chosen not to go to the Coliseum, but there was the allure, and there were his friends. Then he would have averted his eyes, but there was the roar of the crowd and step-by-step he became part of the "madness."[32] Not the needed yes *or* no, but more of a common-ground muddle of indecision (as with Michael Edwards who became "confused," Chapter 5).

In modern times, the greatest mind behind the physics of atomic power (and the bomb) was, of course, Einstein. Einstein regretted deeply that human morality did not develop apace with development of atomic physics. He speculated, however, that "there is nothing divine about morality; it is a purely human affair" (1954). Is this true; is there nothing divine and is morality only a calculating and evolving layer—a purely human affair? Are we to settle for—and be saddled with—a morality that in the end is just another idea or maybe politeness—a fluid and less than "sacred ground"? Is morality essentially enlightened frosting atop Herbert Spencer's earthier survival of the fittest, or much worse, a superstructure as Marx would have it, above his "dialectical materialism"? A keen observer of the twentieth century concludes other than with Einstein, that morality is more than a purely human affair: "Indeed, there is no 'compelling argument' not to slit anybody's throat except for the Commandments given on Mount Sinai."[33]

NOTES

1. Michael B. Stoff, Jonathan F. Fanton, R. Hal Williams, *The Manhattan Project: A Documentary Introduction to the Atomic Age* (New York: McGraw-Hill, Inc., 1991), 5.
2. C.S. Lewis, *Surprised by Joy* (New York: Harvest/HBJ Book, 1955), 235-36.

3. Ibid. 11.

4. Ibid. 29 (Document 7).

5. The non-social period in Oppenheimer's life hints at what is seen today in web junkies. Their actual brain development is physically retarded by the combination of computer game addiction and social withdrawal. For them, finely-honed virtual reality skills first cause and then anesthetize intense loneliness.

6. Oppenheimer, Compton, Lawrence, Fermi, "Recommendations on the Immediate use of Nuclear Weapons," June 16, 1945, Document 51 in Michael Stoff, op. cit., 149-53. For example, Admiral King argued that the total casualties (killed, wounded, missing) of the initial Kyushu invasion would be less than catastrophic (between 31,000 and 41,700). Reports after the war place the number of averted deaths at less than 20,000 and, based on planning reports for a full scale invasion, 46,000. See Gar Alperovitz, *The Decision to Use the Atomic Bomb* (London: HarperCollins, 1995), 466-68 and 743: citing Rufus Miles, Jr. in *International Security*, Fall 1985, and independently by Barton Bernstein in the *Bulletin of the Atomic Scientists*, June 1986).

7. Ibid. 31-2.

8. Details on the "appeasement" of Stalin at Yalta by an exhausted President Roosevelt, and Congress' cover-story portrayal as an outstanding achievement are noted in a first-hand volume by Arthur Bliss Lane: *I Saw Poland Betrayed: An American Ambassador to the American People* (The Bobbs-Merrill Co., New York: 1948).

9. David A. Bella (Oregon State University), "Emergence of Evil," E:CO (Emergence: Complexity and Organization), Vol. 8, No. 2, 2006, 102-115.

10. "Poll on the Use of Weapons" (July 13, 1945), Document 61 in Stoff, Fanton and Williams, 173.

11. Jon Krakauer, "The Fall of 'Fat Man': Why Nagasaki?", Universal Press Syndicate, *The Seattle Times*, March 5, 1995.

12. In the peace feelers addressed through Russia, one of Japanese Foreign Minister Togo's cables reads in part: "so long as England and the United States insist upon unconditional surrender the Japanese Empire has no alternative but to fight on with all its strength for the honor and existence of the Motherland," which is to say that (due to an off-putting catch phrase) a more direct appeal to the U.S. seemed to him out of the question. Truman, onboard ship in the middle Atlantic, was informed about these intercepts (i.e., what did he know, and when did he know it?) . . . based on Truman's handwritten journal this entry (July 18, 1945) was discovered in 1979: "...telegram from Jap Emperor asking for peace" (Gar Alperovitz, 238).

13. Peter Pringle and James Spigelman, *The Nuclear Barons* (New York: Avon Books, 1982), 95. Truman's later decision making became more institutionalized; he relied upon consensus advice from a three-man committee composed on the Secretaries of State and Defense and the chairman of the Atomic Energy Commission (ibid.). In 1953 letter to a member of the Atomic Energy Commission, Truman wrote: "I rather think you have put a wrong construction on my approach to the use of the Atomic bomb. It is far worse than gas and biological warfare because it affects the civilian population and murders them by the wholesale" (Gar Alperovitz, 567).

14. Gar Alperovitz, 534; citing the *Strategic Bombing Survey*, 1946. Part of this momentum was the apparent understanding that use of the bomb would serve well as a bargaining chip after the war in dealing with Russia. Alperovitz discounts the momentum theory and gives greater weight to Truman's specific *decisions* supported by his Secretary of State and opposed by many other advisors, e.g., unconditional surrender and rejection of any post-war role for the Emperor.

15. Ibid., 636-7.

16. Ibid., 88-89.

17. William H. McNeill, *The Rise of the West: A History of the Human Community* (New York: Mentor, 1963). 652.

18. Ibid., 310.

19. Thomas Powers, *Atlantic Monthly*, July 1995.

20. Herbert Spencer, "Mr. Martineau on Evolution," in *Recent Discussion in Science, Philosophy, and Morals* (New York: D. Appleton And Co., 1873), 349

21. Ibid. 339, 341, 347.

22. William Brennan, *The Abortion Holocaust: Today's Final Solution* (St. Louis: Landmark Press, 1983), Chart 6, and 100-102.

23. C. S. Lewis, *The Screwtape Letters* (New York: The MacMillan Co., 1953), 32.

24. St John Paul II, *Centesimus Annus* (*The One Hundred Years*, 1991), n. 39.

25. Based on respect for women, the encyclical also call for better scientific understanding of the female fertility cycle (natural family planning or NFP). As we might add today, global attention to the climate-change cycles of Mother Earth invites equal scientific attention to the personal fertility cycles or natural patterns of real mothers.

26. Darren Geist, "Amnesty International Betrays Women," *First Things* (New York: Institute on Religion and Public Life, August/September 2016).

27. Philip Jenkings, *The Next Christendom: The Coming of Global Christianity* (New York: Oxford University Press, 2002), 163.171.

28. Max Eastman, "Freedom and the Planned Economy" (1955), citation in William F. Buckley, Jr. (ed.) *American Conservative Thought in the Twentieth Century* (New York: Bobbs-Merrill Co., 1970), 203.

29. Aleksandr Solzhenitsyn, "Commencement Address delivered at Harvard University," June 8, 1978, in Edward E. Ericson, Jr. and Daniel J. Mahoney, *The Solzhenitsyn Reader* (Wilmington, DE: Intercollegiate Studies Institute Press, 2008), 561-576.

30. The term is applied by George Weigel, *The Final Revolution: The Resistance Church and the Collapse of Communism* (New York: Oxford University Press, 1992).

31. Albert Einstein, "Why Socialism" (1949), *Out of My Later Years* (New York: Philosophical Library, 1950), 124-25.

32. St. Augustine, *The Confessions*, Book 6, Chapter 8:13.

33. Erik von Kuehnelt-Leddhin, *Liberty or Equality* (Caldwell, Idaho: The Caxton Printers, 1952), 85. Similar insight is found in Dostoevsky.

Chapter Eleven

The Light of Fifty Thousand Suns

In these pages we have discovered that in the very air we breathe something is profoundly missing. We wink and pretend moral neutrality but this is evasion, is it not? The loss and replacement of truth with the Big Lie (Chapter 2) anesthetizes us. The tiny whispering sound of conscience no longer beckons. The mystery of good and evil no longer excites. Instead, "whatever is, is right." We just "get on with it," and justify it as the arc of evolving history. So, here we are, finally, hijacked into what we list as the "Chapter Eleven" of (moral) bankruptcy.

What is our answer? As an odyssey with a direction, the field trip offered in the preceding chapters can be summarized in a few Big Questions. First, is there an overlooked natural law which is really the beautiful transparency of everything—including each and all of us—orienting toward the goodness of an uncreated Source? Second, does this goodness beckon us further into a direct encounter—an encounter with the face and the words and deeds of a totally self-donating Other? And third, and if so, can we modern folks still walk and chew gum at the same time? Can we think of the world and of God in the same mind? Is each of us more than we have dared ti imagine? Is it true that, "Christ the Lord, Christ, the final Adam, by the revelation of the mystery of the Father and His love, [also] *fully reveals man to man himself* and makes his supreme calling clear."[1] If we are not alone, but can receive the divine indwelling within ourselves, then *we ourselves* can become reason enough "why whatever is not enough." Self respect is a strong argument.

It is self respect to reject the Big Lie. We cannot help but notice that Cardinal Bellarmine and Galileo, both, would be astonished today with how scientific evidence of the pre-born child—an inner universe—is shunted aside in the Scientific Age. The ultrasound and fiber optics technology are made into as much of a negligible curiosity today as was the telescope back in the less scientific (?) seventeenth century. We also find that rather than something new, the wholesale redefinition of sexual morals is really a throwback to earlier tribal cults. Abandoned in such a meaningless cosmos the human person and our human ecology do not develop; instead we rationalize and self-destruct.

POETRY BETWEEN THE NUMBERS

Even the ancients conceived stories of mysterious beginnings and of purpose in the cosmos. They connected the dots of apparent chaos into a cosmos of eighty-eight star constellations that we can still trace out today. And the biblical psalmist also sees not only with the eyes, but *through* the eyes, the eyes of the heart: "When I behold your heavens, the work of your fingers, the moon and the stars which you set in place—What is man that you should be mindful of him, or the son of man that you should care for him?" (Psalm 8:4-5). This is the same wonder, is it not, that gives us poetry and music and theology, and then even the telescope and microscope, and today an ultrasound picture of each new and trusting child-universe stirring at home within?

For some the distance to the stars and nearness of the inner universe erases the kind of wonder that, for others, opens beyond ourselves into beauty, and toward belief in the Other. While probably ninety percent of the world populations today are still religious believers, less than two percent claim the presumed superiority of atheism. The followers of atheist Richard Dawkins (*The God Delusion*) ridicule the supposed cumulative stupidity of the rest of mankind today and of all human history. The like-minded and late Christopher Hitchens echoed the master with, "God is not great. Religion poisons everything" (*God is Not Great*, 2007). Hitchens was justifiably scandalized, at least in part, by the silence and complicity between the churches and the secular ideologies of the world. He could no longer see the difference. The worst case, as he saw things, was silence and accommodation with fascism and National Socialism,[2] whose massive cruelties we have noticed in previous pages.

Hitchens, also a practicing bisexual, preached yet another new Enlightenment under the belief that all earlier beliefs other than his own were frauds. Judging from his final chapter this enlightenment is defined less by conceptual positions than it is by total sexual liberation for human "mammals." We are mammals and nothing more distinctive. Even mainstream perversity has us suppose that we do our real thinking below the belt rather than above the brainstem. This is the cult of readiness foisted onto the Millennial Generation. In Old Testament times the Hebrew infidelities to the One God were intermingled with such sexual perversion and with adultery. Having surrendered to the Freud and the subconscious, Secular Humanism would have us linger again in such contradictions. We do opinion surveys. We use reason to prove the futility of using reason (and natural law) to deal with moral questions.[3] Ours is the religion of external circumstances and technical fixes. Surely sanitized chrome steel is a vast improvement over the Aztec obsidian axe.

Hitchens painted Mother Teresa of Calcutta (canonized June 4, 2016) as nothing more than a product of the queen-makers in the mass media. And yet where Dostoyevsky said that "[b]eauty will save the world!", Teresa added that "the purpose of life is to make ourselves beautiful for God." The atheist will have none of such transparency. And when is the last time Hitchens' media queen-makers valued or even understood this vocabulary? Twain's approach to the fact of Joan of Arc was at least scientific. For historical determinists she will always be an inconvenient fact in history. As with any other fact Twain (like Darwin) knew that open minds could not ignore the phenomenon called Joan. Likewise, even in an age reduced to the physical sciences, any unborn child cannot be simply left out of sight and out of mind. Through our abortion culture, a full third of all millennials have been totally abandoned in this way, even before birth.

In these pages we have discovered that a God who really is God is One who by his very nature cannot change and therefore cannot suffer. But by divine choice, He "suffers with" and even within each of us. He is closer to us than we are to ourselves. We have discovered that this is the meaning of compassion (com-*passion*). Despite the modern agnostic mindset, even and especially in our distress we are not alone. This is also the central point rejected equally by atheists and radical secularists *and* by the *Qur'an* of Islam. And today resurgent Islam is knocking at the door of a very demoralized West. We moderns are actually living once again in the seventh century.

While the Qur'anic "dictation" begins every chapter or surrah with the expression that Allah is "the compassionate, the merciful," nevertheless, Allah keeps his distance, very much like the Enlightenment God of Descartes and Enlightenment Deism in the West. God is compassion, but not love. Deism is the notion that our brainy human race has been abandoned by a God who is infinitely less interested in his universe than is a small child about his sand castle on an ocean beach.

The distant Allah of Islam (and of Secular Humanism) is most unlike the Trinitarian God of Christian witness and the "passion" of Christ, and his death, and resurrection for each of us. Of the Passion, we must ask, just what is it about the obviously fallen human nature that attracts total self-donation by the Supreme Being and master and Father of all that is? Better to ask, what does this availability tell us about the nature of God? Far from the bland neutrality of modernity or the alternative dictates of a remote Allah, the Christian hears that "the man who cleanses his [own] heart of every created thing and every evil desire will see the image of the divine nature in *the beauty of his own soul*" (homily by St. Gregory of Nyssa, italics added). Again, with St. Teresa of Calcutta: "the purpose of life is to make ourselves beautiful for God."

How much more ennobling of mankind is it to notice the fact that we are truly fallen *and* beautifully redeemed, rather than only an ever evolving work-in-progress? What does it actually mean to proclaim a God of such glory *and* of such delicacy toward His creations? A point for quiet meditation in all times—that the mystery of divine com-*passion* pitches its tent in each of us. God with us: Emmanuel. Might this be the most real "common core" of human education, as it is witnessed and testified in the New Testament by the four evangelists (Matthew 26:36-27:61; Mark 14:32-15:47; Luke 22:39-56; and John 18:1-19:42)?

This missing piece, this buried treasure at the center of our very selves, is our real orientation toward a Truth finally not of our own imagination or of self-sufficient evolution. This Truth can only be revealed and *discovered*, not constructed. The inborn and universal natural law is, finally, part of the divine law. This center of ourselves is finally a thirst for something outside of ourselves. This thirst for the Other must be guarded against habits of neglect, the settling dust of boredom, and any patterns of deceit like any Big Lie of the passing moment.

In the words of St. Paul, we are to guard against the always present "perverse generation" (Acts 2:40). Good management is not enough. Thinking real-time about our simultaneous destiny in eternity, emeritus Pope Benedict XVI put it this way:

> . . . [T]here will never be a situation where the charity of each individual Christian is unnecessary, *because in addition to justice, man needs, and will always need, love*. . . . One does not make the world more human by refusing to act humanely *here and now*. We contribute to a better world only by personally doing good *now*, with full commitment and wherever we have the opportunity, independently of partisan strategies and programs. . . . My deep personal sharing in the needs *and* sufferings of others becomes a sharing of my very self with them: if my gift is not to prove a source of humiliation, I must give to others not only something that is my own, but my very self; I must be *personally present* in my gift (italics added).[4]

In such a world of real encounter, where even God himself is personally present as the Encounter, we are never alone. Speaking scientifically, social evolution doesn't have a clue. This is to say, isn't each of us is more than congealed star dust barely scratching out markings on space rock earth as it spins meaningless around the sun? Isn't it the truth that "before I formed you in the womb I knew you, before you were born" (Jeremiah 1:15)?

THE PRESENT MOMENT: ONLY A PASSING PHASE?

In its early centuries Christianity bonded itself to the pagan and agrarian culture of the ancient world. The pagans, too, in their better moments were looking for God. Today, for all of its material benefits, Technocracy has displaced the agrarian world but also has disrupted the "new life" of self-donation to which we are called. Our most common entry point for the new life is the natural law as seen, for example, in marriage and the family. But in the toxic world of individualism, self indulgence and the marketing of confusion—in a matter of only a few decades—the institution of the family is literally being dismantled. At one end we have the reset button called "freedom of choice," in the middle the cavalier redefinition of "marriage," and at the far end the "compassion" of physician assisted suicide. In such a disenchanted universe, can there be any wonder that millennials feel cast adrift, and then search in all the wrong places for relief from boredom?

At risk and shunned is the Christian vision of the human person as always something more than a social digit, or a biological complexity, or a "nonviable tissue" deprived of even a name. St. Thomas More was less inclined than Darwinists to see human nature as part of a tangled trap of ever readjusting food chains. Instead, a symphony for the soaring human spirit:

> God made the angels to show him splendor—as he made animals for innocence and plants for their simplicity. But man he made to serve him wittily in the tangle of his mind! . . . And no doubt it *delights* God to see splendor where He only looked for complexity . . . (italics added). [5]

Delight rather than Darwin's mere complexity! We are invited also by a saint of long ago (Iranaeus I think) to "allow God to take delight in us." The emeritus Pope Benedict XVI contrasts narcissist self-improvement with actual conversion toward an Other, toward a God who would delight in us:

> This means, in turn, that man does not find salvation in a reflective finding of himself but in the being-taken-out-of-himself that goes beyond reflection—not in continuing to be himself, but in going out from himself. . . . Man finds his *center of gravity*, not inside, but outside himself (italics added). [6]

Center of gravity . . . the transcendent human person and his fulfillment in the human ecology. We can almost speak of a special science of the human soul. Pope St. John Paul II recognized that,

> "Youth is the time *for new contacts, new companionships and friendships,* in a circle wider than the family alone [and then, from the Second Vatican Council, he added] Man, who is the only creature on earth *which God willed for itself,* cannot fully find himself except through a sincere gift of himself" (italics in the original). [7]

Pause at this, the fact that each of us is willed for his/her own sake, not as part of anything else and least of all as a speck in some process called social evolution. God loves the particular into existence and into his vast and intimate presence. From the very beginning, we are not alone; we are not abandoned. The possible maturation of history depends on this light.

And yet, as a backsliding toward pre-Christian times, today we permit and even promote with state power, the destruction of the young. The birth of a child—especially a most singular child in a manger—is no longer an encounter with another, no longer a mystery and an epiphany. Mark Twain had at least something to say about our almost totally lost presence to the sacred in each other. He remarks that "among the three or four million cradles now rocking in the land are some which this nation would preserve for ages as sacred things, if we could know which ones they are."[8] By Pope Benedict's "sincere gift of self," if not simple justice, might we suspect that *all* of these cradles are sacred? This—not late-term abortion!—is the "sacred ground."

It seems that God's work is discovered in such small, delicate and sacred details. In the first reading of the book of Exodus we find that the Egyptian midwives were unwilling to kill newborn Hebrew boys, and then that Pharaoh's own daughter overlooked his royal decree to drown the males (Exodus 2:5-10). Lifted from the waters, the single and insignificant slave-child Moses becomes a pivot point in all of human history. How very different are the mysterious workings of God from the routines of today's many technicians and statisticians and pretended managers of "change."

Each of us is the sum total of an interwoven history of what are in fact details, and yet always something more and indefinable. Each of us is a body-soul unity, and in this way we always have an open future ultimately linked to the Beatific Vision of seeing and therefore becoming like God, face to face as we say and anticipate. The respect due to each of us is as an irreplaceable link in the "human ecology" especially including the family. The nineteenth-century John Henry Cardinal Newman described each of us as "a link in a chain, a bond of connection between persons," members of an arc of relations.

We find that authentic freedom is not invertebrate; it is not an opting out, but an opting in. It is an opting in to the good, the true and the beautiful, and to the moral categories of right and wrong.[9] By comparison, late modernity's identity politics and competing narratives of victimhood are the death rattle of box-canyon liberal education, and of real personal and democratic self-governance. As New York's Cardinal Timothy (Dolan reminds us, young people will give their lives for a mystery but not for a question mark. Dolan is actually paraphrasing Newman: "Many a man will live and die upon a dogma: no man will be a martyr for a conclusion.")

It might be a novelist who gives us even more of a clue. In his *Diary of a Country Priest* (1937), George Bernanos proposes this:

Purity is not imposed upon us as though it were a kind of punishment, it is one of those mysterious but obvious conditions of that *supernatural knowledge of ourselves* in the Divine, which we speak of as faith. Impurity does not destroy this knowledge, it slays our need for it. I no longer believe, because I have not wished to believe. You no longer wish to know yourself (italics added).[10]

We have slain our need for supernatural knowledge. Is this the virus that now infects even many Catholic institutions of higher learning? What if by our nature and the built-in need for the independence of asceticism, we can be part of an Ultimate Reality that actually does transcend "the world"? What if Ultimate Reality is a personal God of infinite justice and availability, and mad-boundless love and delicacy toward each human and personal biography? What if God is not an absentee landlord or an absentee father or a salaried social worker? What if it's a lie to reduce the human mystery to a manageable version of the natural sciences? What if we need truth even more than therapy?

In the Christian cosmos and the "new life"—unlike the animal kingdom—we are called to sometimes resist our natural and evolutionary instincts. The persecuted Christian sees through the curious postmodern mindset that claims absolutely that absolute values do not exist. As in pre-modern times, in our postmodern present and across the globe, peoples of "the Way" are again thrust into martyrdom. A mid-twentieth century Chinese Communist executioner of Christians paused long enough to remark to a Christian pastor: "I've seen many of you die. The Christians die differently. What is their secret?"[11]

Their secret? Yes, what is the missing piece hijacked today by the Big Lie in all of its forms large and small? Read again the previous few paragraphs. . . . Today much of post-Christian Europe is a picture of the future of the entire West in decline. There are now more active Catholics and more active Muslims in Great Britain, the birthplace of Anglicanism, than there are Anglicans in their nearly deserted churches. Of the modern world, the Englishman G.K. Chesterton said that "a person who ceases to believe in God does not cease to believe; he believes in everything." To believe in everything is the theology of "whatever." Chesterton's timely hint is that the vacuum of supposed neutrality of values—our radicalized secularism and new religion of Secular Humanism—is the incubator for our social malaise and boiling-over violence.

Our personal task is at least to question this drift and even the underlying boredom and monotony of our times (under-*lying*: an apt term). Maybe we should even reconsider the convert Chesterton's discovery that in history "[T]he Catholic Church is the only thing that frees a man from the degrading slavery of being a child of his age." On this point, Chesterton actually gets ahead of himself. Before any church, it is our universal human nature that lifts all of us above the possible limitations of any particular human culture. Defensive identity politics has its place, but it also sells all of us short.

To this truth about the human person, Chesterton then adds the fact that in all times and places the Church members assemble (not merely congregate) around what is believed to be the unchanging and abiding presence of Ultimate Reality—the Eucharistic real presence of the Lord: "Do this in remembrance of me."[12] This gifted supernatural unity, especially, is more than sociological, more than a quaint artifact, more than any community or political identity, and instead is a spiritual unity shared across the ages. It is shared with all those of faith from "the beginning" and especially since the "descent of the Holy Spirit" on the Apostles at Pentecost. As a descent narrative, Darwin's "descent of man" is not the whole story. (The whole point of the Resurrection is that matter and spirit are not as divided as we so conveniently imagine.)

Why do we moderns settle backwards into an infantile spectrum of "whatever," instead of growing forward and upward such that our real selves are centered in Him? Academics locate us here or there on the conveyor belt of progressive history, pointed toward such a lowered horizon. Why, at this late hour, are we so docile to this humiliation? Is it the ease of living a double life? Are we post-Christian moderns to be counted among the barbarians who earlier nearly absorbed a declining civilization? Is it possible that our life in a whole world that is fallen is meant to be more than one of evolved stuff, and even a divine adventure? As in the psalms, again, does the living God long to take "delight" in us? Can we listen to the tiny whispering sound: "Do not be conformed to this world, but be reformed in the newness of your mind" (Romans 12:2)?

Today it is we who shield ourselves from this forever newness of mind. We miss the splendor and glory of God (*kabod*) apart from ourselves and his abiding presence (*shakina*) given and found at first in the Old Testament. We moderns see only with the eyes and no longer through the eyes. And finally seeing beyond even these words of the poet Blake, there is always something more—[real faith is] "the assurance of things hoped for, the conviction of things not seen" (Hebrews 11:1).

In St. Augustine's words, "Let us rejoice then and give thanks that we have become not only Christians, but Christ himself." By this encounter in person with the personhood of Ultimate Reality, the entire created universe—including each of us—can be elevated into St. Teresa of Calcutta's thing of delightful beauty. Is each of us, then and without exception, worthy of reverence from one another *and* no less from ourselves? Instead of "whatever," are we something that God finds to be not only good but "very good" from the very beginning (Genesis 1:31)?[13] We are no longer alone, no longer abandoned from one another and from ourselves.

How can we be so easily bored and seduced into the gray twilight of the Big Lie? Drudgery might be one thing, but all-out boredom is another. In our new appreciation for all the stuff around us, St. Francis of Assisi—now the patron saint of ecology—spoke with birds and held the sun to be his brother and the moon his sister—one big family with one Father. A universal family precisely because He is forever above as the radically Other, in heaven and even far above what we feebly imagine as the heavens (e.g., Psalms 57:6, 108:6). In the world but not of the world, He pervades all this stuff in every detail, even more closely than the finest mathematical constructions.

Having finally been rinsed clean of the lingering pagan stumbling blocks of the Roman Empire, the reality of a distinctly human ecology was open to the unbounded beauty of nature as a book in its own right. It beckons almost as deeply as the personal Encounter witnessed partly through another "good book." The very last act of the pagans was to accept baptism, but today the first act of the backsliding neo-pagans is to renounce or reject baptism into the new life. St. Francis seems doomed to revert back to just another cryptic and moss covered lawn ornament alongside ancient Rome's Saturn and Apollo. We drift back into the Coliseum which has become the electronic centerpiece of every home.

In our stranded civilization we are challenged—forever invited—to find a radically better answer to our alienation deeper than any politics or economics. In the mid twentieth century, Cardinal Danielou suggested that current "atheism is no more than a transitional phase, a momentary crisis, located as it is between the paganism of the rural civilizations of yesterday and [our] paganism of the industrial civilization of tomorrow."[14] The cult of whatever is an empty holding pattern with no future. We each must ask ourselves, are we living in a momentary and flickering interlude between the jaws of two dark Ice Ages? Or is each of us capable of acting in true freedom because it is the Truth that has set us free (John 8:32)?

FROM GALILEO TO STEPHEN HAWKING

The icon for a fully human ecology and authentic modernity of tomorrow—on both the personal and global scales—is found in sidewalk prayer groups gathered in front of neighborhood abortuaries. Countering our electronic fictions, these groups of witnesses are a kind of virtual cathedral, a cathedral without walls. Mark Twain asks the question—which of millions of cradles should we "preserve for ages as sacred things?" Were the minds of Darwin and Oppenheimer sacred? Are you and I? What about another earthling in the genius class who early in life was physically reduced to a lifetime of debilitating paralysis? Yes, what about the more recent cosmologist Stephen Hawking? Are we to count this one among the sacred? Who does the counting?

Even confined to his wheelchair, Hawking rises atop the shoulders of other former giants including Galileo and Newton. More than his predecessors Hawking is equipped to ask the biggest questions of all. . . . The Hubble telescope is like an ultrasound held up not inwardly to the womb of a mother but outwardly to the center of the entire interstellar cosmos. And unlike Darwin, the scientist Hawking never stopped listening to music (in this case Richard Wagner). He asks, when and how did this cosmos begin, if ever? Hawking seeks to show mathematically that the "beginning" of an evolving universe of near infinite power possibly does not require a transcendent God at "the beginning" or anywhere else, for that matter. The question can be approached mathematically, and in this way fully exhausted with possibly no loose ends—no possibility of "nothing"—for theologians to grab onto. Unlike Darwin, in 2014 Hawking declared himself an atheist.

In layman's terms Hawking would have it that a "God" above is an imaginary projection of the human mind rather than that the universe, instead, is a projection—a creation *ex nihilo* (from nothing)—from God's infinite power and creative love. Hawking theorizes that there is no "nothing" before the front end of stuff, no need for a physical beginning. He points to collapsing stars ("black holes") that are so dense and heavy that even light waves do not escape. He proposes that some of these black holes do still spin off stray particles which then eventually form new stars and each new galaxy, even today. As an all-encompassing black hole, and when viewed in reverse (as collapsing), the "original" Big Bang of nearly fourteen billion earth-years ago seems to suggest an endless series of such new endings and beginnings. By these mathematics Hawking intends a "fundamental logic that does not allow for 'nothing'."

One need no longer ask the ground-floor philosophical question, "*why* anything rather than nothing." Philosophy is replaced by mathematics, and God is replaced by self-sufficient change. "Forbidden" by the social radical, Karl Marx, the question of contingency is now rendered irrelevant by science. Like the self-centered individual, existence itself is self-sufficient (!), born of the most recent of endless Big Bang "singularities" that in volume are infinitely smaller than a nutshell, smaller even than a proton, but in this case containing the seeds for one hundred billion galaxies, each galaxy unfolding an average of one hundred billion stars, more or less.

Where science once proved that maggots do not spontaneously appear in rotten meat, does it now propose that the emergence of the entire universe is, what, spontaneous? One can imagine an interdisciplinary panel, a century or two from now, discoursing the parallel between a self-sufficient universe mathematically rinsed of God and Wagner's engulfing music of Teutonic nationalism. For its part, Christian faith is not vulnerable to the science of whether or not there is a chronological beginning to the universe. The tie to a Creator is more relational, a matter of total existence rather than only the existence of matter. Still, a harmony beckons, between the things of science and the things of faith: the Gospel of John speaks of a "beginning" as generally understood to be both relational and a thing of time (John 1:1-3).

On the problem of what it all means, all of these wonderful stars are as sightless as a grain of sand a thousand feet beneath the shifting sands of the Sahara Desert. Not a single one is capable of wondering "why?" In the deep space that it generates, Hawking's cosmic expansion was more silent than even one "silent scream" of a single pre-born child. The silent Big Bang began infinitely smaller than a fertilized human egg. From the vantage point of a more infinite Divinity, however, this universe is barely a twinkling of an eye. The ancients said it well enough: "For a thousand years in your sight are as yesterday, now that it is past, or as a watch in the night" (Psalm 90:4); and "before You the whole universe is as a grain from a balance" (Wisdom 11:22).

Where the poet William Blake would have you "Hold Infinity in the palm of your hand/And Eternity in an hour" (*Auguries of Innocence*), the Christian would simply have us stop squinting long enough to see each hour of time held up by Eternity. Are we finally lifted above even poetry by a Source and a Presence above any chronology or measurement? Are we hard-wired from the beginning to seek the "cause of causes" outside of physics and mathematics and even poetry? Such a Source wills and accounts for the original *existence* of a mathematically coherent universe, each and every grain held in the hand. This Source in some way also shares its permanence as we see in the *sustained* fruition of changing things—rather than suddenly nothing at all.

And the incomprehensible radiance of the Big Bang and billions of billions of suns doesn't really hold a candle to our Encounter with the gifted presence in time and history of the Source "in person", as "the Word made flesh." The Spirit made visible, beyond anything we find in the physical universe: "Heaven and earth shall pass away, but my words shall not pass away" (Matt 24:35).

But Hawking proposes that knowing *how* things change is "to know the [very] mind of God." There is no longer any mystery. Reality is a math problem and the mind of man is the mind of God! He suggests that a Creator God above all this stuff does not *ex*ist, or rather *sub*sist by its very nature and on its own power. Other scientists might vigorously review and possibly refute the math equations and then this remarkable conclusion. As for non-scientists, the lens and mind of Shakespeare, for example, still counts as much as the Hubble telescope: "To be or not to be, *that* is the question" (*Hamlet*).

For his part, Hawking still opens his earlier and reader-friendly *Brief History of Time* (1988) with this: "Where did the universe come from, and where is it going? Did the universe have a beginning, and if so, what happened before then?"[15] Fifteen centuries earlier, the theologian St. Augustine looked at the same stars and in not so different words already wondered: "My mind is on fire to understand this most intricate riddle. . . . In what space, then, do we measure passing time?. . . . [T]here can be no time without creation."[16] Modern science adds decimal places and fills the blackboard, but does it fully put to rest this insight? Does science explain why the work of modern-day computer code writers is regarded as "intelligent" while the 3.2 billion bit information system in each human genome is not?

It might be that Isaac Asimov, the science fiction writer, understood better than many scientists what we are really dealing with: "I believe that scientific knowledge has fractal properties; that no matter how much we learn, whatever is left, however small it may seem, is just as infinitely complex as the whole was to start with. That, I think, is the secret of the Universe."[17] At the other end of the scale, a particle physicist (William Oerter) concludes his work with this quotation from a colleague: "[I think] that as we learn many additional facts, we will also come to comprehend more clearly how much we don't know—and, let us hope, learn an appropriate *humility* (italics added)."[18] Oerter adds: "There is a possibility, then that the origin of the universe could be explained as a transition from a state with no spacetime to a state with a spacetime like ours: a real creation *ex nihilo* [from nothing]."[19] The string theorist Brian Greene suspects that even cosmology may have its outer limits: "Maybe we will have to accept that certain features of the universe are the way they are because of happenstance, accident, *or divine choice*" (italics added).[20]

BETWEEN HUBBLE AND GOD

Within the physical universe, can science and the Hubble telescope render the living God superfluous to our fully human reality? Are our goals and values really only a "purely human affair" as Einstein announced? To really know the mind of God, why not simply ask Him in ways other than the digital Braille of mathematics and physics? Perhaps mathematical order is not his only word and not His only language. C. S. Lewis writes of our flirting with a distant and irrelevant God: "We could talk religiously about the Absolute: but there was no danger of Its doing anything about us. It was 'there'; safely and immovably 'there.' It would never come 'here,' never (to be blunt) make a nuisance of Itself."[21]

What would God say if He ever dropped in and actually gave us a piece of his mind, so to speak? Let's ask him. Prayer is nothing more or less than lifting the heights of the mind *and* depths of the heart to God. Or more accurately, it is the being lifted up by minds and hearts that in some way are more than ourselves. Another experiment or conversation is possible, and listening should be part of this. With Hawking, what is the Mind—but then, in addition we ask, what is the Will—what is the will of God? Openness to the inscrutable divine Will invites renewed wonder at the meaning and purpose of the outer universe and of our bodily and inner selves. When we finally get to the gut-level it is not enough to wink at Screwtape's "relevant" and creative Big Questions like "why anything rather than nothing." The Big Questions are infinitely bigger than the Big Lie.

Even before we finally reach or return to this threshold, is there already given to us the Word of God, namely Christ or the *Logos*, the Mind as creative reason not limited to our mathematics? Of this possible Encounter and this totally new life, he himself says, "I have the power to lay it down, and I have the power to take it up again" (John 10:18)—to pass into the nothing of non-existence and then to exist and live once more (!). We are invited to consider whether the transcendent God has entered into his own transparent creation once and for all, as the Incarnation. Might it be that "His is a single, uninterrupted utterance, because it is continuous and unending"?[22]

In his infinite simplicity God does what he is, and is what he does: "God is love" (1 John 4:8,16). Not an expression of our own making, not a projected idea only, not an extrusion of history, but a living reality of truth and mercy who discloses himself to reasoning and thirsting beings as unconditional love. Might He infinitely exceed the external laws of nature and fulfill the interior and inborn natural moral law. Might he give us the higher math of the Commandments, then adding the Sermon on the Mount (Matthew 5:1-12) as his *self-portrait*, much more revealing, shall we say, than our two-dimensional selfies?

Are we meant to be open to such blessedness, the interior voice of natural law now with the distinctive accent on divine charity and "going beyond oneself?" Instead of disposing of God in the context of a "brief history of time," do we see the brevity of time—a few billion years—in the context of a higher God? Recalling our investigation of history as involving "types" rather than only timeline chronology, the Bible becomes incredibly compact. It is more than a "type" in that the Old Testament prefigures the New, and the New Testament fulfills the Old. We read that "one day within your courts is better than a thousand [or even a billion] elsewhere" (Psalm 84), and then ". . . a single day is like a thousand years with the Lord and a thousand years are like a single day" (2 Peter 3:8).[23]

Are we meant to discover a kind of "fear" as the reverence that is proper to our real freedom to really wonder? Are we still capable of such wonder and such true belonging? This wondering and belonging is the biblical fear of God as the beginning not of knowledge, but of Wisdom. We are free to wonder *who* it is that we even presume to label as the "the Mind of God." At the front edge of such wondering, for the Hebrews, such naming of God was rarely permitted to human lips. To Moses it was revealed: "I am who Am"

(Exodus 3:14), a divine self-disclosure of the Other as later announced of Himself by the incarnate Christ (John's Gospel many times finds Christ saying "I Am").

Even a single sunrise in one speck of one galaxy speaks of this infinitely higher wonder from far above what Scripture speaks of as the (lower) heavens. It is this "dawn from on high [that] shall break upon us" (Luke 1:78), nothing less. Yes, there might be and is a preciousness and purpose to each human life, to my life, to real marriage and family, to the life of the pre-born infant—rather than not. Again, from C. S. Lewis, another convert from atheism, we have this: "To discover Him in the tiniest thing that is [perhaps an unborn child?], and give Him joyous welcome, is far more important for the devout soul than to comprehend the entire Universe."[24]

FIFTY THOUSAND SUNS

In the nineteenth century, Thomas Carlyle (1795-1881) got it just about right in describing modernity, but even he was too optimistic in failing to mention martyrdom. What he said was this: "If Jesus Christ were to come today, people would not even crucify him. They would ask him to dinner, and hear what he had to say, and then make fun of it." Today we would take Him to a fast food joint, order take-out or whatever, leave Him with the bill and never look back. In this there is nothing new under the sun. Even the term Millennial Generation is a disinterment of the distant past. Western history is a dumping ground and wreckage of millennial movements. Norman Cohn in his *Pursuit of the Millennium* (1961) writes this of such movements:

> The old religious idiom has been replaced by a secular one, and this tends to obscure what otherwise would be obvious. . . . It is characteristic of this kind of movement that its aims and promises are boundless. A social struggle is seen not as a struggle for specific, limited objectives, but as an event of unique importance, different in kind from all other struggles known to history, a cataclysm from which the world is to emerge totally transformed and redeemed. This is the essence of the recurrent phenomenon—or, if one will, the persistent tradition [!]—that we have called "revolutionary millenniarianism."[25]

If it could speak, what might the silent and unblinking and unseeing cosmos really have to tell us about our self-conscious present moment in this tradition? During the disrupted 1960s I spent many silent hours on the bridge of a Navy aircraft carrier in the vast Pacific, high-powered binoculars in hand. Under an extravagantly star-rich sky, time stood still. The ocean remained as unchanged for a billion years and more. The arc of the Milky Way stretched across the black void in silent wonder, reaching back many more billions of years. Here "deep is calling upon deep" (Psalm 42:7).

Our scientific moment of the telescope *and* the ultrasound, of big numbers and little numbers, brings us to a father and his son probing upward under the same stars. The one-time atheist Whittaker Chambers had been an operative for the communist fifth column movement of the 1930s (like today's radical "sleeper cells") intent on expanding the malignancy of worldwide Soviet Communism. By his own admission he fell into this camp not because of any attractions to it, but because Western civilization after the First World War was already a catastrophe in freefall. The personal instinct toward some kind of hope led Chambers into the revolutionary mood to "at least smash something."[26]

Years later, after having discovered the greater reality that we call God—greater than history—Chambers lived out his life as a spiritual refugee and Quaker rancher in Maryland. Of our Big Lie and its ilk he once wrote in a letter: "what is this [Socialism] but Communism with the claws retracted?"

As a man of the family, not unlike Charles Darwin in this respect, he guided his son to a hilltop free from any pavement under foot or any dulling haze of city lights. He encouraged his son to simply look up at the real stars—not celebrity stars—and to see not only with the eyes, but *through* the eyes. In his words:

> What little I know of the stars I have passed on to my son over the years....we often stop to watch through the apple trees the great sky triangle tipped by the evening stars: Vega in Lyra, Altair in Aquila and Deneb, burning in the constellation of the Swan.
>
> Sometimes, I draw my son's eye to the constellation Hercules, especially to the great nebula dimly visible about the middle of the group. Now and again, I remind him that what we an just make out as a faint haze is another universe—the radiance of fifty thousand suns whose light had left its source thirty-four thousand years before it brushes the miracle of our straining sight.
>
> Those are the only statistics that I shall ever trouble my son with....I want him to have a standard as simple as stepping into the dark and raising his eyes whereby to measure what he is and what he is not against the order of reality. I want him to see for himself upon the scale of the universes that God, the soul, faith, are not simple matters. . . .
>
> I want him to remember that God Who is a God of Love is also the God of a world that includes the atom bomb and virus, the minds that contrived and use or those that suffer them, and that the problem of good and evil is not more simple than the immensity of worlds.
>
> I want him to understand that evil is not something that can be condescended to, waved aside or smiled away, for it is not merely an uninvited guest, but lies coiled *in foro interno* [that is] at home with good within ourselves. Evil can only be fought. . . . I want him to know that it is his soul, and his soul alone, that makes it possible for him to bear, without dying of his own mortality, the faint light of Hercules' fifty thousand suns.[27]

In *foro interno*: evil "at home" with the good within ourselves. As auda-
cious managers of change we deny human nature. Does the fatal attraction of
Communism (Whittaker Chambers' "statistics") simply come to us repack-
aged? Exaggerated "diversity" seems mostly an engulfing homogeneity, and
one that tolerates even formless gender theory within its fickle embrace.

The early twentieth-century writer G. K. Chesterton, like Charles Darwin,
noticed the indifferent starkness of a disenchanted Nature in the icy cold
silence of galaxies lost in boundless space. But Chesterton concluded differently: "The size of the scientific universe gave one no novelty, no relief. The
cosmos went on for ever, but not in its wildest constellation could there be
anything really interesting; anything, for instance, such as forgiveness or free
will."[28] Another writer, Alexander Dumas, earlier remarked that "not even
genius avails to explain what God is; but the kindness of men is proof that He
is." In answer to our opening chapter, we are not alone.

Today the Hubble telescope tells us that Hercules' galaxy is many more
than Chambers' fifty thousand suns, but rather a hundred billion. We might
still tremble at the ancient question: Am I just a patch of congealed star dust,
an accident, nothing? But like Chambers and his son, another who learned
better from this abyss was one Ernst Psichari, a member of the early twentieth-century French Foreign Legion.

Psichari was in his late twenties, the same age group as our millennials
today. He learned something personal during three years of patrolling the
sands of Western Africa in the last days before Europe collapsed into the
trenches of the First World War. Under the silent and nearly eternal stars he
wrote this to a close friend:

> All that is great and lofty in our morality also comes from this unique and great
> source of Christianity—from the *abandonment* [italics added] of which flows
> false morality, as also does false science. . . . [We] are living at a time when
> the danger of barbarity and impiety is so great that one no longer has leisure to
> stop at theological arguments. . . . What matters before anything is to destroy
> this 'intellectual' gang, and all that clique of mediocre people who dominate
> us—novelists of adultery, worldlings . . . radical socialists who give to our
> time its aspect of anarchical confusion, so striking as soon as one sees it from a
> distance. . . . Grace! That is the mystery of mysteries!"[29]

In 2013 at his first World Youth Day, in Rio de Janeiro, Pope Francis
challenged the current "whatever" younger generation: "Yes, I am asking
you to rebel against this culture that sees everything as temporary and that
ultimately believes you are incapable of responsibility—that believes you are
incapable of true love . . . Have the courage 'to swim against the tide'. And
also have the courage to be happy."

The seventh-century St. Columban explains the source of true joy and
happiness: "It is no God dwelling far off from us that we seek, whom if we

merit it we have within us.[30] St. John proclaims: "We have seen and testify that the Father sent his Son as savior of the world. Whoever acknowledges that Jesus is the Son of God, God remains in him and he in God" (1 John 4:14-15). Even the conflicted and tormented Andre Gide (whom we met in Chapter 8) was not entirely beyond the gentle reach of such grace—this Encounter. From his own darkness Gide wrote this, *"Lord, it is not because I am told You are the Son of God that I listen to Your words; but Your words are more beautiful than all human words, and it is in this that I recognize that You are the Son of God."*[31]

NOTES

1. Second Vatican Council, *Constitution on the Church in the Modern World*, n. 22. See Galatians 1:15-16: St. Paul discovers that the Father "reveal(s) his Son in me."

2. Christopher Hitchers, *God is Not Great* (New York: Hatchett Book Group, 2007), Chapter 7. An even better informed but less breezy treatment of German voting patterns, contrasting the Protestant north with the Catholic south, supports a more detailed thesis, in Erik von Kuehnelt-Leddhin, *Liberty or Equality* (Caldwell, ID: Caxton Printers, 1952), Chapter 7 and Figs. 2, 3.

3. In 1892 the sculptor Louis Laniere carved a headboard, no less, depicting a snake whose contorted body outlines a human face as the snake swallows its own tail. Modernity becomes primitive as we "can no longer trust rationality, but instead make reason feed upon itself by rationally arguing the helplessness of reason" (W.H. Nc Neill, *The Rise of the West* (New York: Mentor, 1963), Fig. 129 and caption).

4. *Deus est Caritas (God is Love)*, 2005.

5. Robert Bolt, *A Man for All Seasons* (New York: Vintage Books, 1960),73.

6. Joseph Ratzinger, *Principles of Catholic Theology* (San Francisco: Ignatius, 1987), 171.

7. St. John Paul II, "Letter to the Youth of the World" (International Youth Day of the United Nations, March 13, 1985), including a citation from the Second Vatican Council, *Pastoral Constitution on the Church in the Modern World*, (*Gaudium et Spes*), nn. 24, 81.

8. Answering a toast "To the babies," at a banquet in honor of General U.S. Grant, November 14, 1879.

9. This paragraph paraphrases interviews given by emeritus Pope Benedict XVI.

10. George Bernanos, *The Diary of a Country Priest* (New York: Carroll and Graf Publishers/Avalon Publishing Group, 2002), 126.

11. Jean Monsterleet, *Martyrs in China* (Chicago: Henry Regnery, 1956), with a Foreword by John C.W. Wu.

12. Matthew 26:26-28, Mark 14:22-24, Luke 22:17-20, 1 Corinthians 10, and the *Catechism of the Catholic Church*, n. 1374.

13. The Catholic is astonished to find that the Lord is truly present in a new and distinctly unique way in the Eucharist. The Catholic goes with the mystery of the Real Presence—a unique transparency within history—for scriptural reasons as well as Tradition (the "living book"). The Eucharist is both a symbol *and* that which it symbolizes—*"This* is my body . . . *this* is my blood". The "I AM" spoken to Moses in the Old Testament, in the New Testament becomes "This is." The modern mind probably objects less to this astounding doctrine than to the irreducible distance that this sacramental presence maintains between ourselves and the Divine Intimacy—we and our ideas are not God even as we are gathered into [the] One by the Holy Spirit. See the *Catechism of the Catholic Church* (n. 1374).

14. Jean Danielou, *Prayer as a Political Problem* (New York: Sheed and Ward, 1965), 100.

15. Stephen Hawking, *A Brief History of Time* (New York: Bantam Books, 1988), 1.

16. St. Augustine, *Confessions*, Book 11, Chapters 21, 22, 30.

17. Attributed to Isaac Asimov in book reviews by Stratford Caldicott (ed.), *Second Spring*, XIII, (Merimack, N.N.: Thomas More College of Liberal Arts, 2011), 77.

18. Robert Oerter, *The Theory of Almost Everything* (New York: Pi Press, 2006), 278; citing Frank Wilczek from a CERN talk (European Organization for Nuclear Research), October 11, 2000. CERN is the world's largest particle accelerator facility, in Geneva, Switzerland.

19. Ibid., 271.

20. Brian Green, *The Elegant Universe: Superstrings, Hidden Dimensions and the Quest for the Ultimate Theory* (New York: Random House, 1999), 385.

21. C.S. Lewis, *Surprised by Joy* (New York: Harvest Books, 1955), 210.

22. Sermon by St. Bernard, *Liturgy of the Hours*, Vol. IV (Catholic Publishing Co., 1975), 231.

23. The glory of the Gospel (and a possible start point for the Church's New Evangelization) is in (1) the revealed mercy of God, (2) the encounter and intensified motive to obey Christ, (3) a spiritual obedience deeper than the letter of the law, (4) fellowship with the Father, and (5) the assurance of immortality. (Abbreviated from Canon T. R. Birks' editorial footnote to William Paley, *A View of the Evidences of Christianity* (London: The Religious Tract Society, 1850/1794), 206.

24. St. Augustine, cited in Hugh Pope, OP, *St Augustine of Hippo* (Garden City: Image, 1961) 231; *De Genesi ad Litteram*, v. 34, c. AD 401-415.

25. Norman Cohn, *The Pursuit of the Millennium* (New York: Oxford University Press, 1970/revised and expanded edition), 281, 286.

26. Whittaker Chambers, "Morningside," *Cold Friday* (New York: Random House, 1964), 91-144.

27. Whittaker Chambers, *Witness* (New York: Random House, 1952), 797-8.

28. G.K. Chesterton, *Orthodoxy* (Garden City, New York: Image, 1959), 62.

29. Raissa Maritain, *Adventures in Grace* (Garden City: Image Books, 1961, originally Longmans, Green and Co., Inc. 1945), 276-77; citation from a letter to Jacques Maritain, a prominent convert and Catholic theologian of the twentieth century (June 15, 1912).

30. From Sermons of Columbanus, Sermon 1, Corpus of Electronic Texts Edition compiled by Beatrix Farber (Cork, Ireland: University College, 2004; www.ucc.ie/celt/published).

31. Andre Gide, quoted in his *Journal* (1916-19) and cited by Raissa Maritain, ibid., 319.

Bibliography

Abbott, Walter M., S.J., *The Documents of Vatican II*. New York: Guild Press, 1966.

Arnold, Johann Christoph, *Their Name is Today: Reclaiming Childhood in a Hostile World*. New York: Plough Publishing House, 2014.

Antonio, Gene, *The AIDS Cover-up?* San Francisco: Ignatius, 1986.

Augustine, *The City of God*. Garden City, New York: Image, 1958.

————. *The Confessions of St. Augustine*. Garden City, New York: Image, 1960.

Aymans, Winfried (editor), *Eleven Cardinals Speak on Marriage and the Family*. San Francisco: Ignatius, 2015.

Balthasar, hans Urs von, *Bernanos: An Ecclesial Existence*. San Francisco: Ignatius, 1996.

Barlow, Nora (editor, and granddaughter of Darwin), *The Autobiography of Charles Darwin 1809-1888*. London: Collins, 1958.

Barrow, John D., *The Artful Universe: The Cosmic Source of Human Creativity*. New York: Little, Brown and Company, 1995.

Barrows, Marjorie, *One Thousand Beautify Things*. Chicago: Peoples' Book Club, Inc., 1947.

Bella, David A., "Emergence of Evil." *E:CO (Emergence: Complexity and Organization)*, Vol. 8, No. 2, 2006.

Benedict XVI (Pope), *Deus Caritas Est (God is Love)*, 2005.

Bernanos, Georges, *The Diary of a Country Priest*. New York: Carroll and Graf Publishers/ Avon Publishing Group, 2002.

Blehl, Vincent Ferrer (editor), *The Essential Newman*. New York: Mentor-Omega, 1963.

Brandmuller, Walter Cardinal. "Europe, in its Crisis, Needs a Catholic Revolution," *Inside the Vatican*. Rome: December 2014.

Bolt, Robert, *A Man for All Seasons*. New York: Vintage Books, 1960.

Brennan, William, "The Abortion Holocaust: Today's Final Solution." St. Louis: Landmark Press, 1983.

Brown, Calavin (general editor), *The Reader's Companion to World Literature*. New York: Mentor, 1956.

Brown, Peter, *Augustine of Hippo*. Berkeley: University of California, 1969.

Buckley, William F. Jr. (editor), *American Conservative Thought in the Twentieth Century*. New York: Bobbs-Merrill Co., 1970.

Carlson, Allan, "As Goes Sweden: Neo-Pagan Family Policies Doom Any Recovery." *Touchstone*. Chicago: The Fellowship of St. James, March/April 2015.

Carroll, Warren H., *A History of Christendom: The Cleaving of Christendom*. Front Royal, VA: Christendom Press, 2000.

Chambers, Whittaker, *Witness*. New York: Random House, 1952.

————. *Cold Friday*. New York: Random House, 1964.

Chesterton, G. K., *The Everlasting Man*. Garden City, NY: Image Books, 1925/1955.

———. *Orthodoxy*, Garden City, NY: Image, 1959.

Clark, Ronald, *The Survival of Charles Darwin*. New York: Random House, 1984.

Cohn, Norman, *The Pursuit of the Millennium*. New York: Oxford University Press, 1970.

Congregation for the Doctrine of the Faith, "Letter to the Bishops of the Catholic Church on the Pastoral Care of Homosexual Persons (1986)." San Francisco: Ignatius, 1987.

Daileander, Philip, "The Early Middle Ages," *Lecture 23 on Family Life: How Then Became Now*. The Great Courses by the Teaching Company, 2004.

Danielou, Jean, *Prayer as a Political Problem*. New York: Sheed and Ward, 1965.

Darwin, Charles, in Sir Francis Darwin (editor), *Charles Darwin's Autobiography with his Notes and Letters Depicting the Growth of the Origin of Species*. New York: Henry Schuman, 1950.

———. *Variations of Animals and Plants under Domestication*. Vol. II. New York: D. Appleton and Co., 1883, 1868.

———. "On the Two Forms, or Dimorphic Condition of Primula," *The Different Forms of Flowers*. New York: D. Appleton and Co., 1887.

Darwin, Sir Francis (editor), *The Life and letters of Charles Darwin, including an Autobiographical Chapter*. London: John Murray, 1887.

Dawson, Christopher, "The Patriarcal Family in History," *The Dynamics of World History*. New York: Mentor Omega Books, 1962.

De Maistre, Joseph, *On God and Society*. Chicago: Henry Regnery Co., 1959.

De Marco, Donald, "How the U.S. Supreme Court is Waging War on Marriage." *National Catholic Register*, EWTN, April 18, 2004.

De Smet, Pierre-Jean, "Origins, Progress, and Prospects of the Catholic Mission to the Rocky Mountains." Fairfield, WA: Ye Galleon Press, 1967.

———. *Life, Letters and Travels of Father Pierre-Jean De Smet, S.J., 1801-1873*. Vol. 3, Washington State University, n.d.

Desmond, Adrian and James Moore, *Darwin*. Warner Books, 1991.

De Wolfe, Mark (editor), *The Pollock-Holmes Letters 1874-1932*. Cambridge, England: Cambridge University Press, 1942.

Dodaro, Robert, O.S.A. (ed.), *Remaining in the Truth of Christ*. San Francisco: Ignatius, 2014.

Donohue, William, "The Secularist Assault on America's Moral Consensus." *Catalyst*. Catholic League, May 2016.

Dubay, Thomas, S. M., *Authenticity: A Biblical Theology of Discernment*. San Francisco: Ignatius, 1997.

Durenberger (Senator), "Thomas More—A Man for All Seasons." *Congressional Record— Senate*. June 22, 1982.

Edwards, Michael, *Priscilla, Elvis and Me: In the Shadow of the King*. New York: St. Martin's Press, 1988.

Einstein, Albert, *Out of My Later Years*. New York: Philosophical Library, 1950.

Eliade, Mircea, *The Sacred and the Profane: The Nature of Religion*. Orlando, FL: Harcourt, Brace and Jovanovich, 1959.

Eliot, T. S., "The Class and the Elite," *Christianity and Culture*. New York: Harcourt, Brace Jovanovich, 1940/1968.

Ericson, Edward, and Daniel Mahoney (editors), *The Solzhenitsyn Reader*. Wilmington, DE: Intercollegiate Studies Institute, 2008.

Esolen, Anthony, "Suffer the Children," *Touchstone*. Chicago: Fellowship of St. James, March/ April 2015.

Facts and Documents, *The Persecution of the Catholic Church in the Third Reich: Facts and Documents* (1941). Fort Collins, CO: Robert A. McCaffrey Publishing, n.d.

Francis I, Pope, "Address," 2013 World Youth Day, Rio de Janeiro.

———. "The Vision of the Wedding Feast," *Open Mind, Faithful Heart*. New York: Herder and Herder, 2013.

———. "Christmas Message," *Urbi et Orbi*. St. Peter's Square, Dec. 25, 2014.

———. *Laudato Si* (*Praise be to Him: On Care for our Common Home*). 2015.

Geist, Darren, "Amnesty International Betrays Women," *First Things*. New York: Institute on Religion and Public Life, August/September 2016.

Gilson, Etienne, *The Unity of Philosophical Experience*. New York: Charles Scribner's Sons, 1965.

Giussani, Luigi, *The Religious Sense*. San Francisco: Ignatius, 1990.

Hawking, Stephen, *A Brief History of Time*. New York: Bantam Books, 1988.

Hazlitt, Henry, *Failures of the "New Economics."* Princeton: D. Van Nostrand, 1959.

Hegel, George Wilhelm Friedrich, *A Philosophy of History* (lectures of 1830-31). New York: The Colonial Press, 1900.

Herbert, Jean, *An Introduction to Asia*. (New York: Oxford University Press, 1965.

Hitchers, Chrstopher, *God is Not Great*. New York: Hatchett Book Group, 2007.

Hitler, Adolph, *Mein Kampf*. Boston: Houghton Mifflin, 1943.

Hubbard, Elbert, *Scrapbook*. New York: Wm. H. Wise and Co., 1923.

Jaki, Stanley L., *Miracles and Physics*. Front Royal, VA: Christendom Press, 1989.

———. *Newman's Challenge*. Grand Rapids, MI: William B. Eerdmans, 2000.

Jastrow, Robert, *God and the Astronomers*. New York: W. W. Norton and Co., 1978.

Jenkins, Philip, The *Next Christendom: The Coming of Global Christianity*. New York: Oxford University Press, 2002.

Johnson, Abby, *Unplanned*. Tyndale House Publishers, 2010.

Johnson, Abby and Kristin Detrow, *The Walls are Talking*. San Francisco: Ignatius, 2016.

Jouvenal, Bertrand de, *On Power: Its Nature and the History of its Growth*. Boston: Beacon Press, 1962.

Kaler, Patrick, C.S.S.R., *The Silent Screams: Abortion and Fetal Pain*. Liguori Publications, 1984.

Kuehnelt-Leddihn, Eric von, *Liberty or Equality*. Caldwell, ID: The Caxton Press, Ltd., 1952.

———. *Leftism* (New Rochelle, NY: Arlington House, 1974).

Kanzelberger, Kirk, *The Mystical Daydream: Fictive Being and the Motive of Evil* (doctoral dissertation). Fordham University, 2011.

Lea, Henry C., *History of Sacerdotal Celibacy*. London: Watts & Co., 1867/1932.

Lewis, C. S., *The Screwtape Letters*. New York: The MacMillan Co., 1953.

———. *Surprised by Joy*. New York: Harvest Books, 1955.

Marcel, Gabriel, *The Mystery of Being*. Vol. I. Chicago: Gateway, 1950.

March, Harold, *Gide and the Hound of Heaven*. Philadelphia: University of Pennsylvania Press, 1952.

Maritain, Raissa, *Adventures in Grace*. Garden City, NY: Image Books, 1961.

Mayer, Lawrence and Paul McHugh, "Sexuality and Gender," *The New Atlantis: A Journal of Technology and Society* (No. 50). Washington, D. C.: Ethics and Public Policy Center, Fall 2016.

McLennan, John Ferguson, *Studies in Ancient History*: the Second Series comprising an *Inquiry into the Origin of Exogamy*, and *Studies in Ancient History: Primitive Marriage*. London: MacMillan and Co., 1886 and 1896.

McNamarra, Sylvester J., *American Democracy and Catholic Doctrine*. Brooklyn: International Catholic Truth Society, n.d., c. 1920.

McNeill, William H., *The Rise of the West: A History of the Human Community*. New York: Mentor, 1963.

Mc Sorley, Joseph, *An Outline History of the Church by Centuries*. St. Louis: B. Herder Book Co., 1945.

Melville, Herman, W., Somerset Maugham (editor and introduction), *Moby Dick of the White Whale*. Philadelphia: John C. Winston Co., 1949.

Michael Jones, E., *Living Machines: Bauhaus Architecture as Sexual Ideology*. San Francisco: Ignatius, 1995.

Monsterleet, Jean, *Martyrs in China*. Chicago: Henry Regnery, 1956.

Muggeridge, Malcolm, *The End of Christendom*. Grand Rapids, MI: William B. Eerdmans, 1980.

Muller, Gerhard Cardinal, *The Hope of the Family*. San Francisco: Ignatius, 2014.

Nathanson, Bernard, *The Abortion Papers: Inside the Abortion Mentality*. New York: Frederick Fell Publishers, 1983.

National Commission on Terrorist Attacks, *The 9/11 Commission Report*. New York: W.W. Norton and Co., 2004.

Nehru, Jawaharlal, *Glimpses of World History*. New York: John Day Co., 1942.

Newman, John Henry Cardinal, *Apologia Pro Vita Sua*. Garden City, NY: Image, 1956.

Nucci, Alessandra, "Europe's War on Christian Ethics," *Catholic World Report*. Ignatius, May 2015.

O'Leary, de Lacy, *Arabia Before Mohammad*. New York: E. P. Dutton and Co., 1927.

Olson, Carl, *Did Jesus Really Rise from the Dead?* San Francisco, and Greenwood Village CO: Ignatius and Augustine Institute, 2016.

———. "More Sex Scandals," *Catholic World Report*. Ignatius, July 10, 2016.

Osborn, Henry Fairfield, *From Greeks to Darwin*. New York: Charles Scribner's Sons, 1894/1929.

Paley, William, *A View of the Evidences of Christianity*. London: The Religious Tract Society, 1850/1794.

Pinckaers, Servias, *Morality: The Catholic View*. South Bend, IN: St. Augustine's Press, 2001.

Phipps, William E., *Darwin's Religious Odyssey*. Harrisburg, PA: Trinity International Press, 2002.

Pope, Hugh O.P., *St. Augustine of Hippo*. Garden City, NY: Image, 1961.

Pringle, Peter and James Spigelman, *The Nuclear Barons*. New York: Avon Books, 1982.

Ratzinger, Joseph Cardinal (later Pope Benedict XVI), *Principles of Catholic Theology*. San Francisco: Ignatius, 1987.

———. *Truth and Tolerance: Christian Belief and World Religions*. San Francisco: Ignatius, 2003.

———. *On the Way to Jesus Christ*. San Francisco: Ignatius, 2005.

———. *Values in a Time of Upheaval*. New York: Crossroads Publishing, 2006.

Reisman, Judith and Edward Eichel, *Kinsey, Sex and Fraud: the Indoctrination of People*. Huntington House Publishers, 1990.

Reynolds, E. E., *St. Thomas More*. Garden City, NY: Image Books, 1958.

Rowland, Tracey, *Ratzinger's Faith: The Theology of Pope Benedict XVI*. New York: Oxford University Press, 2008.

Rommen, Heinrich A., *The Natural Law: A Study in Legal and Social History and Philosophy*. Indianapolis, IN: Liberty Fund, 1936/1998.

Rueda, Enrique, *The Homosexual Network: Private Lives and Public Policy*. Old Greenwich, CN: The Devin Adair Company, 1982.

Ruskin, John, *The Seven Lamps of Architecture*. 1849.

St. Augustine, *The Confessions of St. Augustine*. Garden City, NY: Image, 1960.

———. "Advice and Reproof for a Military Commander," in Henry Paolucci, The *Political Writings of St. Augustine*. Chicago: Henry Regnery Co., 1962.

St. Francis de Sales, *Introduction to the Devout Life*. Garden City, NY: Image, 1955.

St. John XXIII, *Mater et Magistra* (*Mother and Teacher*), 1961.

———. In John P. Donnelly (editor), *Prayers and Devotions from Pope John XXIII*. Garden City, NY: Image 1969.

St. John Paul II (translated by Jerzy Peterkiewicz), *The Place Within*. New York: Random House, 1982.

———. "Letter to the Youth of the World," *International Youth Day of the United Nations*. March 13, 1985.

———. *Centesimus Annus* (*The One Hundredth Year*). 1991.

———. *Evangelium Vitae* (*The Gospel of Life*). 1995.

———. "Message on Evolution to the Pontifical Academy of Sciences." Oct. 1996.

Santillana, Giorgio de, *The Crime of Galileo*. Chicago: University of Chicago Press, 1955.

Sarah, Robert Cardinal, *God or Nothing*. San Francisco: Ignatius, 2016.

Schoenborn, Christoph Cardinal (Foreword), *Creation and Evolution: A 1986 Conference with Pope Benedict XVI*. San Francisco: Ignatius, 2007.

Schuschts, Bob, *Be Healed: A Guide to Encountering the Powerful Love of Jesus in Your Life.* Notre Dame, IN: Ave Maria Press, 2014.

Second Vatican Council, *Constitution on the Church in the Modern World.* 1965.

Solzhenitsyn, Aleksander, *Warning to the West.* New York: Farrar, Straus and Giroux, 1976.

———. "Men have forgotten God," *National Review.* July 22, 1983.

Smith, Janet, "Pope Paul as Prophet." *Catholic World Report,* July 1993.

Smith, William Robertson, *Lectures on the Religion of the Semites.* London: A and C Black Ltd., 1889/1927.

Spencer, Herbert, *Recent Discussion in Science, Philosophy, and Morals.* New York: D. Appleton And Co., 1873.

Stoff, Michael B., Jonathan F. Fanton, R. Hal Williams, *The Manhattan Project: A Documentary Introduction to the Atomic Age.* New York: McGraw-Hill, Inc., 1991.

Tocqueville, Alexis de, *Democracy in America.* New York: Vintage Books, 1961.

Twain, Mark, (Foreword by Andrew Tadie), *Personal Recollections of Joan of Arc.* San Francisco: Ignatius, 1989.

Vitz, Paul, *Faith of our Fathers.* San Francisco: Ignatius, 1999.

Weber, Max, in H. H. Gerth and C. Wright Mills, *From Max Weber.* New York: Oxford University Press, 1946/1958.

Wilhelmson, Frederick D., *Citizen of Rome.* La Salle, IL: Sherwood Sugden & Co., 1980.

Weigel, George, *The Final Revolution: The Resistance Church and the Collapse of Communism.* New York: Oxford University Press, 1992.

Wolfe, Thomas, *From Bauhaus to Our House.* New York: Farrar Straus Giroux, 1981.

Weaver, Richard M., *Ideas Have Consequences.* Chicago: University of Chicago Press, 1948.

Wiker, Ben, "Anthropology Afoul of Facts." *National Catholic Register,* May 19, 2002.

Wright, John Cardinal, "Reflections on the Third Anniversary of a Controverted Encyclical," St. Louis, MO: Central Bureau Press, 1971.